Frank

Forgotten Frontier

Christmas 1997

To Dad
Happy reading
and Merry Christmas!
Love Ya!
Franki Jane

Forgotten Frontier

THE STORY OF SOUTHEASTERN NEW MEXICO

Carole Larson

Published in cooperation with
the Historical Society of New Mexico

UNIVERSITY OF NEW MEXICO PRESS: ALBUQUERQUE

For Bob

Library of Congress Cataloging-in-Publication Data

Larson, Carole.
Forgotten frontier: the story of southeastern New Mexico / Carole Larson ; [map by Bill Nelson].—1st ed.
  p.   cm.
"Published in cooperation with the Historical Society of New Mexico."
Includes bibliographical references (p.) and index.
ISBN 0–8263–1439–2 (cl.)—ISBN 0–8263–1440–6 (pa)
1. Frontier and pioneer life—New Mexico.
2. New Mexico—History.
I. Title.
F796.L27   1993
97—dc20
93–3631
   CIP

Design by Susan Gutnik.
Map by Bill Nelson.

© 1993 by the University of New Mexico Press. All rights reserved.
First edition

Contents

Illustrations vii

Foreword ix

Preface xi

PART I THE TIDE OF EVENTS

1 *The Timeless Land* 3

2 *The Imprint of Conquest* 17

3 *Native People and the Land* 37

4 *Power and Populism* 67

PART II THE IMPACT OF INDIVIDUALS

5 *John Chisum, L. G. Murphy, James Dolan, John Riley* 101

6 *Alexander McSween and John Tunstall* 131

7 *Billy the Kid and Pat Garrett* 153

8 *Joseph C. Lea, Martin Corn, John Poe* 195

9 *J. P. White and J. J. Hagerman* 231

10 *The Land Endures* 279

CONTENTS

Notes 289

Bibliography 303

Index 309

Wednesday

Wherever you may be, it is your friends who make your world.

New Moon

January 8

Frank I thought of you
when I saw this picture
Love
Eva

Illustrations

MAP
Southeastern New Mexico (c. 1900). ... 2

FIGURES
1. Quanah Parker, last great Comanche chief. ... 91
2. Kit Carson in his Army Colonel's uniform during the Civil War. ... 92
3. Cattleman John Simpson Chisum as a young man in Texas. ... 93
4. John Chisum in New Mexico in the early 1870s. ... 93
5. James J. Dolan and Lawrence G. Murphy in 1873. ... 94
6. Patrick F. Garrett in his twenties, c. 1875. ... 94
7. Billy the Kid in Fort Sumner in 1879. ... 95
8. Sallie Chisum Robert, niece of John Chisum, c. 1880s. ... 96
9. Captain Joseph C. Lea in the early 1890s. ... 96
10. Lea family and friends in front of the Lea house in 1879. ... 97
11. Lea family portrait in the early 1890s. ... 98
12. Mescalero Apache schoolchildren with their teacher in 1892. ... 187
13. John and Sophie Poe on their wedding day, May 5, 1883. ... 188
14. John W. Poe in the early 1900s. ... 189
15. A roundup crew around the campfire on the Pecos range, 1892. ... 190
16. Cowboy chuckwagon and crew at roundup time, Eddy County 1893. ... 190
17. James J. Hagerman on the grounds of the South Spring Ranch, 1905. ... 191
18. Ella Lea in 1899. ... 191
19. Captain Joseph C. Lea and a new artesian well in Roswell, 1893. ... 192
20. J. Phelps White, c. mid-1920s. ... 193
21. The first train to enter Roswell, 1894. ... 193
22. Main Street in frontier Artesia. ... 194

Foreword

Forgotten Frontier: The Story of Southeastern New Mexico is a history of that section of the state as well as a general history of New Mexico. This book is another in the continuing co-publication series between the Historical Society of New Mexico and the University of New Mexico Press. The Society is proud to co-sponsor such well-researched and well-written studies as this one.

Carole Larson's scholarship is superior. Her work is just the kind to appeal to the general and serious reader of New Mexico history. This book also may prove useful to the public schools as a textbook. It will be especially attractive for use in junior and senior high schools.

Larson has concentrated on the southeast part of the state, the area encompassing the lower Pecos valley and the people and events there. There are other books of a general nature on the history of New Mexico, but none address the southeast side of the state in any detail.

The Historical Society of New Mexico is delighted to co-sponsor the work. The current members of the board of directors of the Society are: Robert R. White, president; John W. Grassham, first vice president; Darlis A. Miller, second vice president; Andres J. Segura, secretary; Spencer Wilson, treasurer. The other members are: John Baxter, Susan Berry, Maurice M. Bloom, Jr., Thomas E. Chavez, John P. Conron, Richard N. Ellis, Elvis E. Fleming, Austin Hoover,

FOREWORD

Myra Ellen Jenkins, Margaret Espinosa McDonald, Riley Parker, Agnesa Reeve, Carl D. Sheppard, Robert J. Torrez, David Townsend, and John P. Wilson.

> SPENCER WILSON, Chairman
> Publications Committee
> Historical Society of New Mexico
> *March 1993*

Preface

SOUTHEASTERN NEW MEXICO, ENCOMPASSING FIFTY THOUSAND square miles, remains one of the least-known areas of the state despite its stunning and varied landscape and its rich and exciting history. The purpose of this book is to provide an overview of the region's historical evolution, from the time of Paleo-Indian pottery makers to Plains Indian buffalo hunters, from early Spanish explorers to American pioneers, with particular emphasis on the period of frontier settlement from the 1850s until the turn of the century.

The first four chapters of the book provide a narrative account highlighting a number of important historical events. The next five chapters are devoted to profiles of people whose actions significantly affected events in the region; interwoven in their stories are accounts of events in which they participated. An attempt to give equal weight to narrative and to particular individuals seemed appropriate in a context where the impact of personality and character was heightened by a frontier environment in which pioneering figures were often taking the first steps toward permanent settlement of a new land. And as it happened, southeastern New Mexico attracted a wide range of character types, including extreme opposites in terms of greed and selflessness and in terms of attitude toward the use of violence. A final brief chapter summarizes major themes and highlights the important effects that both national trends and individual efforts had on the history of southeastern New Mexico.

A number of eminent historians, including William Keleher, Maurice G. Fulton, Eve Ball, Marc Simmons, Robert W. Larson, Robert

Utley, and John P. Wilson, have done groundbreaking research and written compelling books and monographs dealing with various phases and aspects of southeastern New Mexico history, particularly the fascinatingly complex episode known as the Lincoln County War (1878–81). This book draws upon the work of these and other historians to present in a single volume a synthesis of an extended period of time, with the aim of relating parts to the whole and identifying themes that bind together the history of the area.

While making no claim to have made use of every available published source, and still less claim to have based this work on primary research, the author nonetheless hopes that the reader will come away from reading this book with a deep feeling for the land, for its ancient lineage as a place of pre-European human habitation, and for the truly breathtaking rapidity with which American settlement came to the region that had long been known as 'the empty quarter.' And it is the author's hope that this book will enable the reader to place the region within the broader contexts of New Mexico and American history.

After moving to Roswell in 1978, I discovered a very different New Mexico than the one I had encountered while living at various times in Albuquerque, Santa Fe, and Taos; different in tone, feel of land, culture, accent, historical traditions. And I discovered that the uniquely American experience of the 'Old West' was a reality, not a myth. As a staff writer for the *Roswell Daily Record,* I had a rich variety of opportunities to talk with, interview, and write about people from all walks of life who are part of the dynamic social interaction of contemporary southeastern New Mexico. Among them were ranchers and farmers, oilmen and roustabouts, politicians and judges, teachers, oldtimers, young people, business people, leaders of the Hispanic community.

A number of people had a profound influence upon me as a result of their personal links with the region's history, their commitment to their community, and their individual integrity. This book might be said to have grown from seeds planted by some of these special people. Walt Wiggins, part of a pioneering family and the author of numerous art books in addition to his other accomplishments as photojournalist, publisher, and gallery owner, was a generous mentor who shared his knowledge and library, encouraging me as I moved in new directions in my research and writing, away from my previous studies in the field of African history. Art McQuiddy, retired senior executive of a multinational corporation, is married to Alene Hinkle, granddaughter of New Mexico governor James F. Hinkle (1923–24). A man of broad interests,

PREFACE

McQuiddy is deeply in tune with the region's history and its potential. From him I gained insight into a tradition of responsible leadership that has been one strand of southeastern New Mexico development. I especially value a copy of Hinkle's "Early Days of a Cowboy on the Pecos," given to me by McQuiddy.

I also wish to acknowledge some of those who extended their help to me during the writing of this book. Elvis Fleming, professor of history at Eastern New Mexico University–Roswell, guided me to research materials at the Chaves County Historical Museum Archives, of which he is director. Raymond Burrola, historian and teacher, formerly a research fellow at the Hispanic Studies Research Institute at the University of New Mexico, provided me with several sources and gave me the confirmation I sought for several of my assessments concerning Hispanic settlers in southeastern New Mexico.

Tom Hall, Roswell publisher, and Frank O. Papen, Las Cruces banker, each guided me to a valuable published source. David Orr, director of the Chaves County Historical Museum, and Lillian McDonald, the former director, were unfailingly kind in extending the facilities of the museum and its archives. J. P. White III, president of White Industries of Roswell, gave me hours of his time and shared with me some of his knowledge of his grandfather, pioneer cattleman J. Phelps White, and his general knowledge of regional history. Clarence Corn, the last living of pioneer Martin Van Buren Corn's nineteen children, granted me an interview at his home, lent me valuable documents, and provided insights into the life of his father.

My work was made easier by the cooperation of the staff of the Roswell Public Library, which has an outstanding Southwest collection. I am particularly grateful to reference librarians Loretta Clark, Rosemarie Klopfer, and Barbara Harris. Lee Dixon, a friend and fellow writer with a master's degree in language, stood by with the comforting assurance that I could call upon her for advice in matters of language use.

And finally, I especially wish to acknowledge the moral support given to me by my former husband, Robert W. Larson, retired professor of history at the University of Northern Colorado in Greeley and author of books and monographs on New Mexico history and western populism.

CAROLE LARSON
Roswell, New Mexico

PART I

THE TIDE OF EVENTS

SOUTHEASTERN NEW MEXICO (c. 1900)

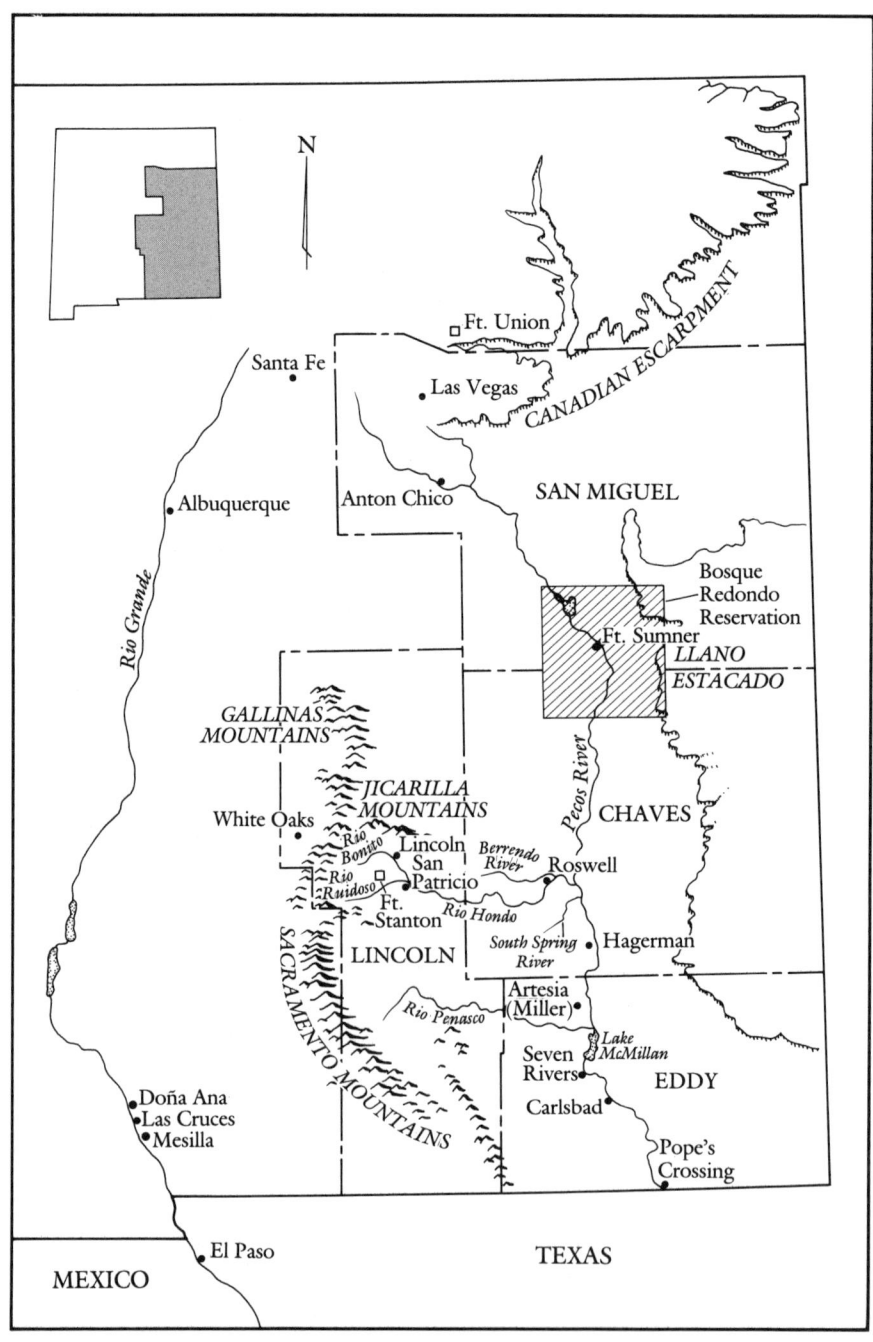

I

The Timeless Land

NEW MEXICO SEEMS ALMOST A COUNTRY UNTO ITSELF SO UNIQUE among the states is its historical experience as cradle of Indian cultures, outpost of imperial Spain, province of Mexico, and American territory from 1850 until 1912, when statehood was granted. It is separate, too, as a result of its complex variety of land features: mountain chains, river valleys, plains, and deserts, woven into a landscape of universality as though by a creator who willed upon one large canvas a masterwork. And as in any place notable for its distinctive formative history and encompassing a range of ecological environments, this land has its identifiable regions, each with different nuances of custom, language, and thought pattern.

Southeastern New Mexico, a compelling blend of pure frontier West and the dynamic cultural eclecticism characteristic of the state as a whole, is the region settled latest and yet the one whose name became synonymous with the dangers and opportunities to be found 'west of the Pecos.'

The area comprises some 50,000 square miles of the state's total of 121,666 square miles. Dauntingly vast and sparsely populated, southeastern New Mexico is bordered on the east and south by Texas, on the north by the Canadian Escarpment in northeastern New Mexico, and on the west by a southern offshoot of the Rocky Mountains, which divides the eastern part of the state from the western part. Its dominant land features are the Llano Estacado, a high plain of extreme flatness extending from West Texas into the eastern third of southeastern New Mexico; the Pecos River, which runs the length of the region through its central portion; and the series of mountains including the Guadalupe, White, Capitan, and Sacramento ranges, which rise to snow-capped summits all along the region's western section.

From a vantage point anywhere along the broad Pecos Valley, the eye encompasses an undulating flow of subtly shifting colors and delicately delineated landforms, moving from the pale greens of rangeland in the near distance, to the darker blue-greens of low hills in the middle distance, and finally to deeply colored lavender-toned mountains hugging the western horizon and topped by a crystalline blue sky. It is a vista of hundreds of miles and yet one in which distant objects appear closer than they actually are, due to the clarity of the air, the intensity of the light. The land abounds with white-blossomed yucca, yellowish mesquite, russet-tinged salt cedar, and purple sage, all of which flourish in the semiarid environment. Southeastern New Mexico is, in fact, one of the dryest regions in the entire United States; rainfall averages less than twelve inches a year, and the Pecos River is the only perennial source of surface water in an area of sixty thousand square miles stretching from the Sacramento Mountains in the west to Lubbock, Texas, in the east.

Southeastern New Mexico as it exists today began to take shape about ten thousand years ago, when the last of four successive Ice Ages affecting most of North America ended. The ice sheet that covered much of New Mexico during the Pleistocene epoch, from sixty-five thousand years ago until ten thousand years ago, began to melt and recede. In succeeding periods, vast amounts of sedimentary material were washed eastward from the mountains by rainfall in amounts up to four hundred inches per year. As the mountains wore down under this torrent of water, the annual rainfall gradually decreased, because air masses were no longer forced high into the cooler levels of the upper atmosphere, where rainclouds form easily. The sediment distributed over eastern New Mexico solidified into the dry plains known today, a plateau region crisscrossed by the remains of ancient riverbeds that once channeled rainwater rushing from the mountains. Even so the mountains continue to be a life source. It is from the ranges lying east of the Tularosa Basin—the Gallinas, the Jicarilla, the Capitan, the White and the Sacramento—that the only tributary sources of the Pecos River flow, including the Rio Hondo, the Rio Feliz, and the Rio Peñasco.

Worn down over eons by the action of rain and wind, the plains of southeastern New Mexico are not only remarkably flat but are also different in elevation from the remainder of New Mexico. While 85 percent of New Mexico lies at an elevation of over four thousand feet, southeastern New Mexico is about three thousand feet above sea level, rising gradually toward the western portion, where the mountains break the flatness with heights ranging from eight thousand feet to over twelve thousand feet.

The headwaters of the legendary Pecos River are found in other, yet higher, mountains. It is at levels of thirteen thousand feet and more in the Sangre de Cristo Mountains northeast of Santa Fe that streams cascading down from snowy peaks come together to form the river that winds in a south-southeasterly direction for 755 miles to its meeting place with the Rio Grande in south Texas. The Pecos River valley varies in width from twenty to forty miles and is at its widest in the stretch from just north of Roswell to just south of Artesia. A singular feature of the broad river valley is the line of craggy gypsum bluffs lying along the east side of the river for many hundreds of miles.

From plateau plain to river valley to mountain foothills, the contours of the land are writ large against the dome of sky. The land-space of southeastern New Mexico is whole and integrated, meant to be felt in its entirety, a truth driven home by the relentless, seamless roof of sky bright with sun fire that covers it in splendid unity. One is given all of the land, never part; the ochres, browns, silvery greens, and sages, the purples, burnt umbers, and golds are interwoven ceaselessly across the landscape from one end of the land to its farthest horizon. And just as it integrates space and claims wholeness, so too does this land demand recognition that time is eternal and circular, not to be conceived in the short gulps of human breath in the marked-off centuries.

It is not an easily accessible land, not a land immediately assimilated into human emotions. It overwhelms; it is subtle, vast, even savage in its stark forms and endless horizons. Its very largeness can conceal forever the intricate beauties of the small-scale natural phenomena found within it. It presents the individual with a continual choice between watching its larger outlines or pausing to absorb the valley places, canyon places, mesa or desert places within it. It will not be tamed. It will be windswept, self-determining, dynamic under a sun that seems to hold the land as laboratory to test its own powers of intensity. The air itself takes on visible shimmerings under the sun's relentless penetration.

It is a landscape one either grasps and feels imprinted on one's soul or else finds vaguely unsettling, taunting, even repugnant and antithetical to the civilizing ways of people. There are on the wide stretches of the plateau plain no deep green grass carpets, no lush forests, no shaded tumbling streams, no craggy peaks over misted valleys. There are, in

CHAPTER ONE

short, no places to hide, to be caressed by nature, no places to believe in abstract beauty; there is no surcease from reality, no real smallness within which to shield oneself from the largeness, no aids from nature encouraging belief in one's uniqueness or protected status. And yet, ultimately, there is something in the landscape that enfolds, uplifts, strengthens, and places people firmly in a tapestry being woven into geological, anthropological, cultural history.

The people of southeastern New Mexico are, in fact, bound together as much by their history as by the feel of the land they occupy. For what the entire Llano Estacado and the trans-Pecos region have in common is that it was their destiny to be among the last frontiers of the American West to be tamed and permanently settled. In the year 1876, when the United States was celebrating its first centennial with all the hoopla and optimistic faith in the new machine age displayed at the Philadelphia Exhibition, the entire area from the Texas Panhandle through eastern and southeastern New Mexico was caught up in another kind of fervor—not one of celebrating past accomplishments but of clearing the plains of Indians, stocking the public domain with cattle, homesteading, establishing mail routes, building new towns, and creating county governments and courts of law.

But if Americans of European ancestry, whether Spanish, English, Irish, French or German, discovered southeastern New Mexico in a serious way only in the last quarter of the nineteenth century, Native Americans knew the entire area from plain to mountain as an ancestral homeland going back as far as the tail end of that last Pleistocene-era Ice Age some ten thousand years ago.

The story of the prehistoric peopling of New Mexico is one of evolutionary, ages-long progression from Paleo-Indian hunter group to nineteenth-century Indian of plain and pueblo. It begins with the nomadic bands of big-game hunters who roamed New Mexico during the last centuries of the last Ice Age. These clan-based groups were part of a broadly similar ancient Native American culture that prevailed over much of the North American continent for thousands of years after people first began crossing a fifty-mile land bridge that existed between Siberia and Alaska for tens of thousands of years. Well before the low-lying Bering Straits land bridge disappeared back into the depths of a rising ocean about ten thousand years ago, an untold number of migrations had brought human settlement to all parts of North and South America. Anthropologists now believe that the Indians of the Southwest, including those of New Mexico, stem from a major migration that brought peoples who eventually became the Eskimos, the Aleuts, and the Athabaskans, although it was many centuries before organizational and linguistic variations evolved into the differentiated tribes encountered by the first Europeans to enter the continent.

There is no evidence that any other primate in the direct line of human evolution ever crossed the Bering Straits before *Homo sapiens* did so. While the exact time of the first crossing is not known, and the earliest accepted evidence of people in North America is dated to thirteen or fourteen thousand years ago, "analysis of the aboriginal languages of North America has led to the conclusion that the numerous tongues spoken at the time of the European discovery required at least fifteen to twenty thousand years to diverge" from the common tongue spoken by the earliest Asian migrants upon entering North America.[1] And it is known from evidence that by eleven thousand years ago the migrants from Asia had moved all the way to the tip of South America, indicating that the first crossings may have been thousands of years earlier, for the process of spreading southward was probably slow and sporadic.

The Asian migrants who crossed the Bering Straits belonged to a stock of people who evolved about twenty thousand years ago in adaptation to a cold climate. In China on the Eurasian continent this physical type was eventually absorbed into the classic Mongoloid type after a process of invasions and intermarriage. The older, pre-Mongoloid race survives only because of the migrations to North and South America, where the newcomers developed their societies in an atmosphere of total isolation from humans of other racial groups.

The oldest known Paleo-Indian habitats in all of North America are located in New Mexico. They provide archaeological evidence indicating human presence as far back as twelve to fourteen thousand years ago, with some estimates that the sites were occupied as far back as twenty thousand years ago. More than thirty thousand archaeological sites have been found in New Mexico over the past fifty years, and many more remain to be discovered, for only some two million of the state's eighty million acres have been surveyed.

The people called Sandia Man, named for the mountain slopes east of Albuquerque where their remains were found, were a hunting people who used flint knives and scrapers and made spear points of flint to use in killing the mammoths, tapirs, ground sloths, wolves, and saber-toothed tigers found in abundant numbers in the Ice Age environment of New Mexico. The time period for these people has been variously estimated at between twelve and twenty thousand years ago.

CHAPTER ONE

Artifacts and remains of the Clovis complex were first found near the town of Clovis in southeastern New Mexico. The Clovis complex was part of a hunting culture found throughout much of continental North America east of the Rocky Mountains in the period between twelve and fourteen thousand years ago. At nearly every Clovis complex site, mammoth bones are found piled up in large quantities, clear evidence that hunts were cooperative ventures.[2] The hunts for the woolly mammoth, a relative of the modern elephant, were carefully planned and often involved a skilled ambushing of prey by Clovis hunter groups, who would drive mammoth herds over the edges of ravines or arroyos.

Remains of the Folsom complex were first found at a site thirty miles east of Raton in northeastern New Mexico, the artifacts indicating a hunting culture more recent than the Clovis complex and dating to a period of nine to eleven thousand years ago. Using skillfully fashioned flint spear points, Folsom people also hunted for the giant big-horned bison, which provided food for the small, family-based hunter groups. Excavated in 1927, the Folsom site provided anthropologists with the first clear evidence that the earliest Bering Strait crossings took place more than five thousand years ago, the estimate previously accepted as most likely to be the time of the first migration.

The Folsom complex was part of a hunting culture that was changing in response to dramatic climatic changes. As the Ice Age ended, the climate grew warmer and drier. The herds of bison moved closer to the rich grasslands of the Rio Grande and Pecos River valleys, while other species, including the tapir, sloth, tiger, and even the camels once native to the continent, became extinct. As the remaining bison sought out forage and water in more narrowly confined areas, hunting for them became an all-too-easy enterprise. Hunter groups may have killed more of the animals than were actually needed for survival; by 7000 B.C. the giant bison had vanished, to be replaced by a smaller type, able to survive on the grasslands of eastern New Mexico.

By about 6500 B.C., buffalo hunters, armed with dagger-like stone blades longer and thinner than those used previously, had become adept at coordinating group kills of a hundred or more of the new, smaller bison. But the disappearance of many other species of animals, combined with the appearance of new vegetation in the warmer climate, resulted in increasing reliance upon collection of wild plants, seeds, and insects as a means of survival. Corn already was being cultivated in Mexico far to the south, the development of agriculture having evolved in Central America independently and several thousand years after the cultivation of wheat, barley, and rye began in the Old World, some eleven thousand years ago. Maize (corn) was first cultivated in central Mexico seven thousand years ago, although reliance upon agriculture as the principal source of food supplies there did not occur until about fifty-four hundred years ago.

In New Mexico, however, foraging for small game and use of wild plant food remained prevalent between 5000 B.C. and 1000 B.C. During this period lanceheads often were made of glassy black basalt, a material seldom used in earlier periods. Migratory patterns changed, with groups returning regularly to the same base camps and remaining there longer. Cooking of rabbits, birds, fox, or antelope was done in scooped-out earthen hearths. Wild rice, yucca plants, and other vegetal foods supplemented the diet.[3] Under conditions of low population densities and uncertain weather, hunting and gathering were logical, as these methods provided better yield with less work than cultivation of plants through domesticated agriculture.[4] New Mexico had become hotter and drier at some point after 6000 B.C., and this caused the herds of bison to retreat from the plains of eastern New Mexico to grassier plains far to the north.

By about 3000 B.C., however, the climate of New Mexico had changed yet again, becoming somewhat cooler and wetter. Under these improved conditions, settlements grew in size, new groups entered New Mexico from the west, and the cultivation of such plant foods as corn, squash, and beans began. Agriculture developed slowly and unevenly. Nevertheless crop cultivation began to play an increasingly important role in the life of village people, providing a larger share of total food intake and serving as the impetus for new forms of social organization. The earliest evidence of corn cultivation in New Mexico dates to about 2000 B.C., the time period for the primitive, small-cobbed corn found at Bat Cave in west-central New Mexico in 1948. Other evidence indicates that cultivated plots of corn and squash gradually became a common feature of village life during the period between 1800 B.C. and 500 B.C.

Just as it has in every human society, agriculture brought with it new opportunities for population growth, for assurance of survival, and for the differentiation of labor into new efforts at building, crafting, and ritualizing. In New Mexico the result was the rather sudden and dramatic rise of several distinctive regional cultures that not only provided stable environments for their own people but whose influence spread through trade and expansion to other areas of the state. The Anasazi culture was centered in west-central New Mexico, and the Mogollon culture took root in the southwest part of the state; but each of these societies had some degree of influence upon people living in scattered settlements along the valleys and byways of southeastern New Mexico.

The Anasazi ("ancient ones") were a farming people who lived in small villages and farmsteads in what is now the four-corners area. Anthropologists refer to them in the period before their development into the Anasazi culture as the Basketmakers. Between A.D. 500 and A.D. 900, their pit-house villages grew larger, and the population spread out to new villages. During the A.D. 900s, pit houses were abandoned and the Anasazi built large villages (pueblos) with long room blocks of aboveground masonry. The architecture of the Anasazi took on new symmetry, size, and grandeur in design, as the political center of Anasazi culture strengthened and consolidated in the austere mesa-and-butte environment of Chaco Canyon, located in the heart of central-west New Mexico.

During this Chaco building period, crop harvests grew larger, larger grinding stones for corn began to be used, and the striking Red Mesa black-on-white pottery unique to the Chaco people began to be made. By A.D. 1050 Chacoan-style pueblo farming villages were in existence as far from Chaco Canyon as the upper Pecos River valley, several hundred miles to the east.[5] And in Chaco Canyon itself, located 140 miles northwest of present-day Albuquerque, a viable polity existed in an atmosphere of organized agriculture and other types of work. By the end of the first millennium, the Anasazi had built Pueblo Bonito, which housed more than twelve hundred people, and had built a system of roads leading from the Chacoan political center in all directions to other towns. The great building period of the Chacoan culture lasted from about A.D. 1050 to A.D. 1120.

There is some evidence that it was the influence of another culture, the Mogollon, or Mimbres, culture, developed to the south of the Anasazi, that first motivated the Anasazi innovations in building, making pottery, and trading over wide areas. The Mogollon culture, which eventually extended over a forty-thousand-square-mile trading area in New Mexico and Arizona, saw its beginnings as early as 100 B.C., when pit-house villages, ceremonial lodges, farming, and decorated pottery began to characterize the life of a people living in southwest New Mexico's Mogollon Mountains. The early development of the Mogollon may have been influenced by cultural contacts with Mexico, resulting in the introduction of squash, beans, gourds, and pottery, passed along in turn by the Mogollon to their neighbors to the north in the four-corners area.

By the A.D. 800s the Mogollon were a growing influence in southern New Mexico, although their greatest period of accomplishment did not occur until after A.D. 1000, when they began to build cobble and dried-mud pueblo villages and to produce their finely decorated Mimbres black-on-white pottery, a contrast with their previous brown ware. Mimbres pottery was highly prized as a trade item as far north as Chaco Canyon and as far east as the Pecos River valley. Before the Mogollon heartland was abandoned in roughly A.D. 1450, Mogollon-type villages had been built as far east as the Sierra Blanca and Sacramento ranges of southeastern New Mexico. The classic Mimbres pottery period ended about A.D. 1150.

For both the Anasazi of Chaco Canyon and their Mogollon neighbors to the south, the eleventh and early twelfth centuries were a golden age of peace, security, trade, growth, and expanding influence. For reasons not known by modern-day archaeologists, both polities saw a period of decline beginning in the 1100s. Whether it was drought, disease, or internal strife that caused the Anasazi to leave their golden-brown canyon communities by 1150 is not known. But during the last half of the twelfth century, Anasazi villages were abandoned, and the people moved eastward in family groups to settle in the forested highlands west of present-day Santa Fe. Mogollon decline took longer and culminated later, but as in the case of the Anasazi, the reasons for this disintegration can only be surmised. By the mid 1400s Mogollon culture no longer was a cohesive force, and the heartland villages in the Mimbres River valley were no longer inhabited, their people scattered elsewhere.

Following the decline of the Anasazi and Mogollon cultures, there was a return to earlier pit-house methods of construction. The latter part of the 1100s seems to have been a time of upheaval, violence, and uncertainty. Archaeological remains reveal that pit-house villages constructed in colder, higher country to the east of the earlier homeland often were vacated suddenly; skeletons, often decapitated, show that fighting had occurred, and there is ample evidence that homes had been looted and burned shortly before remaining villagers fled. There is no way of knowing whether the fighting was between rival groups of Anasazi or came from outside raiders.

By the mid-1200s peace had been restored to the degree that aboveground pueblos were once again being built. But the high country was not to remain home for long for the troubled inheritors of the Anasazi tradition; a searing dry period, known as the Great Drought, began in 1276 and continued to the close of the century, its effects felt all the way from Colorado to central Mexico, where the Aztecs were beginning to build their empire. In New Mexico, conditions in the high reaches of mountain country where new pueblos rose like small fortresses became too dry and harsh for successful farming. Once again villages were abandoned.

This time the people chose wisely, building their puddled-mud pueblos along the Rio Grande and its tributaries, such as the Rio Chama and the Rio Puerco, and also along the upper Pecos River. These new pueblos built during the late 1200s and early 1300s proved to be permanent settlements. Francisco Vásquez de Coronado and his conquistadors encountered the pueblo peoples in their stable, autonomous communities along the Rio Grande when they entered New Mexico in 1540; the Pueblo Indians remain there today.

To the east of the pueblo people, out on the flat plains and particularly along the reaches of the broad Pecos Basin, patterns of Indian settlement and development varied in significant ways from those of either Anasazi or Mogollon peoples. The nomadic hunting-and-gathering lifestyle remained prevalent on the eastern plains for quite some time after the rise of regional cultures in other parts of the state had led to pueblo building. Population sizes remained smaller among the groups scattered over the eastern plains and in the mountain foothills. And there is no evidence of the kind of political cohesion that marked the ascendant periods of the northwest and southwest culture centers. Nor was there as much wealth in grain, pottery, and other forms of expansionary success.

Nevertheless settled villages as opposed to movable camps were being built in the Pecos Valley by the late 900s A.D. and it appears that by A.D. 1050, villages were increasing in size and were more densely populated.[6] Corn was being grown, but harvests were not large, and collection of wild plant foods continued to supplement the diet. Traces of early farming settlements have been discovered along the Pecos River south of Fort Sumner, located on terraced slopes. Along with dart points and other tool artifacts made locally, Anasazi pottery also has been found at these sites, proving the far-flung nature of a trade and barter system that fostered cultural interaction among New Mexico's Native peoples.

The decline of the Anasazi and their abandonment of Chaco Canyon, however, was accompanied by a diminishing of trade in terms of volume and geographic area. As the 1100s progressed, local peoples, among them those of the Pecos region, compensated for the loss of imports by stepping up their own production of utilitarian items such as pottery for use in cooking over open fires. A type of locally made pottery dating to the period after 1100 has been found at several sites in the Fort Sumner area. Because it was the women who made pottery and there is evidence that Fort Sumner men obtained their wives from groups living south of them near present-day Roswell, archaeologists refer to the plain, durable pottery ware found in large quantities near Fort Sumner as "Roswell brown."

At some point in the 1200s, another type of local pottery became ubiquitous to the area, and variations of this type of ware, known as Chupadero black-on-white, continued to be made for several centuries. Chupadero pottery was made in villages as far west as the White Sands area and as far east as the Fort Sumner area on south to the Carlsbad area. It is believed that an Indian village in the Hondo Valley west of Roswell "was probably the geographic center of the vast Chupadero pottery country."[7]

Agriculture as a way of life and means of survival hardly had time to take root among Pecos Valley dwellers before it was supplanted by the enticements of buffalo hunting. Well before the onset of the Great Drought in the 1270s, Pecos peoples were putting more effort into the hunt than into corn crops, which became relatively rare. Buffalo had returned to the grassy plains, and while their numbers were kept down during the dry spell, the return of taller grasses at the beginning of the 1300s brought with it large herds of buffalo. At excavated sites dating to the 1200s, located between Fort Sumner and Roswell, bison bones have been found in abundance.

This renewed dependence upon buffalo—for meat, hides, grease, bone material, and sinew—began a trend that was to continue right up to the time of westward expansion by the United States in the 1840s. From A.D. 1350 onward, Plains Indians from the north and east entered New Mexico, sometimes only for yearly hunts but more often to establish new territories within which they moved from one camp to another. During the eighteenth and nineteenth centuries, their entire way of life came to revolve around the horse, the bow and arrow, the gun, and the buffalo. The buffalo-hunting tribes, including the Apache and the Comanche, dominated southeastern New Mexico. The small number of older village groups still carrying on the tradition of corn cultivation had long since moved west to the Sacramento Mountain highlands.

For the Plains tribes, including those inhabiting southeastern New Mexico, the 1700s and early 1800s were a time of dynamic dominance of their environment, a time of unprecedented opportunity for acquisi-

CHAPTER ONE

tion of trade goods and strengthening of tribal ties, and a time destined to end in disaster, a time never to be repeated. Ironically enough, this golden age of the Plains Indians, with its integral links with the American bison, was made possible by the penetration of the Spanish into New Mexico in the sixteenth century and their subsequent attempt to develop the area as the northern border province of a regime based first in Madrid and later in Mexico City.

For it was the Spanish who introduced the horse to North America. Without the horse the Plains Indian culture could not have taken on its mobile, warriorlike aspects. It was the Spanish, too, who brought guns into America north of the Rio Grande, and it was the Indians of the plains who were quick to see the gun's value both as a fighting weapon and a means of carrying off successful raids for additional horses. Indeed before the coming of the Spaniards with their tough mustang cow pony, buffalo hunting, though a regular feature of tribal life, was a risky affair, still tied to the old methods of stampeding herds over bluffs and finishing off trapped animals with well-placed arrows or lances.

When the first permanent settlements were established in New Mexico by the Spanish starting in 1598, a number of tribes occupied fairly specific areas of the large territory. Of the nomadic Athabaskans then in New Mexico, the Navajo tribal grouping occupied the northwest, while several distinct Apache groups occupied the other three sectors.

In the early 1700s, the Comanche entered the Llano Estacado and for a time controlled the buffalo-filled plains, driving many Apache groups southward into Texas and Mexico. The Comanche made good use of the wild mustangs roaming the plains. But eventually the Mescalero Apaches made the Sacramento and Guadalupe mountains their homeland and fortresslike sanctuary while moving freely over the remainder of the area. Their name derives from their use of the mescal plant, a small, spineless cactus with rounded stems, whose buttonlike tops were traditionally chewed during religious ceremonies for their hallucinogenic effects. It was the women of the tribe who went forth each spring to gather the mescal that abounded in the mountain foothills.[8] In far southeast New Mexico lived the Jumanos Apaches, whose economy was based on the buffalo.

Under both Spanish and Mexican rule of New Mexico, firearms were available by official decree only to the small numbers of soldiers assigned to guard the local citizenry. Not only did it prove difficult to totally enforce this policy, but by the late 1600s Plains tribes were obtaining guns from other Europeans to the east. As for horses, the Spaniards maintained an outright prohibition on the sale of horses to Indians.

The first major breach came when the Pueblo peoples along the Rio Grande rose in revolt in 1680, driving the Spanish colonists south until their return in 1693, following the retaking of Santa Fe by Diego de Vargas in 1692. When the Spanish fled in 1680, many horses came into Indian hands. From then on horses were traded and stolen by Indians. "By the first half of the 1700s, horses had spread as far north as the Shoshoni of Wyoming. The entire way of life of the Plains Indians changed. New groups came in from east and west. Buffalo hunting replaced agriculture as a mainstay for many tribes."[9] Eventually more than thirty different peoples belonging to at least five different language stocks comprised the Plains Indian culture.

Thus by the early nineteenth century the very shape and tenor of American Indian life had been deeply influenced by the presence of Europeans of both Spanish and Anglo ancestry. But as the American nation expanded westward, the stage was set for a quickening of the historical tempo with a new, non-Indian population poised and prepared to do far more than merely interact on a relatively equal footing with the Native Americans. The new peopling of the western half of the continent, this time by citizens of a nation whose numbers were being annually swollen by immigrants from abroad and which possessed a superior technology, a functioning bureaucracy, a strong military, and a written language, would soon result in the sweeping aside of the evolved prehistoric order and its replacement with the forces of modern history.

After 1830, the year in which Congress passed the Removal Act giving the president the authority to "extirpate" the rights of all Indians living east of the Mississippi River, between 70,000 and 100,000 Indians were forcibly resettled in the West. Thousands more died of disease and starvation during the thousand-mile forced marches to barren reservations. By 1850 when the Midwest was rapidly filling with new towns and farms and the westward movement out across the remainder of the continent had begun in earnest, the Indian population had fallen to its lowest level, 250,000, representing a sharp decline from the Indian population of the 1600s.

With the end of the Civil War in 1865 came a concerted and ultimately successful drive by the American military to make the land safe for the thousands of pioneers trekking westward each year. It took most of the last three decades of the nineteenth century to accomplish this task, as the Plains Indians employed tactics ranging from bloody raids to ritual to futile rebellions in a doomed effort to stave off the end of their nomadic, hard-riding years of glory on the Great Plains.

2

The Imprint of Conquest

WHILE IT WAS AMERICANS REPRESENTING A BUOYANTLY BRASH young nation who finally extinguished the lingering nomadic life-style of the Plains Indians, it was Spaniards representing an ancient culture and a rigidly authoritarian nation-state who began the process of change 350 years prior to that final erasure, when they first breached the pristine environment of the North American continent, bringing with them a new concept of recorded time, a new image of social order, and a new notion of reward for goodness after death.

For tragic, brutal, and exciting as the last years of Plains Indians cultural conflict were, the fact is their full meaning can be felt only by seeing the fate of the Indians as part of an intense drama of symbiotic interrelationships that began with the Spanish conquests of the 1500s and only ended with the United States taking physical control of the western territories, completing the national unification of middle North America from the Atlantic to the Pacific.

It was the years of Spanish rule, then, that brought to the dusty plains of southeastern New Mexico the region's first overlay of Europeanization. The impact was for long felt primarily in a curiously negative way, for Spain's political control left the area virtually untouched on the ground. No settlements, forts, or administrative centers were established, and Spain's presence in New Mexico manifested itself principally along the reaches of the central Rio Grande corridor. Even so Spain's hegemony over the entirety of the huge land mass extending from Texas westward through New Mexico, Arizona, parts of Colorado, Utah, and all of California was a decisive factor in the historical development of southeastern New Mexico, if only because Spain and its successor as ruler of the area, Mexico, lacked the resources to colonize the region effectively and yet were able by their broad political claims to prevent settlement by other nations.

The Spanish first began to take an active interest in the lands that now comprise the American Southwest in 1536, when Alvar Núñez Cabeza de Vaca arrived in Mexico City with a vivid account of the continental interior. Cabeza de Vaca had set sail from Spain in 1528 as official treasurer for the Narváez expedition. When the ship reached Florida, Spanish soldiers accompanying the expedition marched inland and were defeated in fierce fighting with local Indians. Retreating to their ship, the Spaniards set sail across the Gulf of Mexico for New Spain, which had been established in 1521 by Hernán Cortés upon the ruins of the Aztec Empire.

But the remaining 250 expedition members, including Cabeza de Vaca, were shipwrecked off the coast of Texas. Cabeza de Vaca was among the small number who survived to reach land in Texas. He eventually gathered about him a tiny band of ragged, hungry, barefoot survivors, including the Moorish slave Estevan, and led them on an epic journey through Texas, across the Pecos River, and into northern Mexico, enduring perilous episodes of harrowing Indian encounters and periods of near starvation. The arduous trek finally brought Cabeza de Vaca to the Rio Grande just north of the site where El Paso now stands. After crossing the river, de Vaca turned south and made the long march to New Spain's administrative capital at Mexico City.

During 1536 and 1537, Cabeza de Vaca did more than report to the viceroy, more than tell fascinating tales of adventure. He also wrote a detailed account of his journey, which was published and subsequently read with great interest by many of the young, ambitious Spaniards seeking their fortunes in the New World. They paid particular attention to testimony that the wanderers had seen Indians who possessed precious metals, including gold.

By the late 1530s documents written in New Spain spoke of New Mexico as "la Tierra Nueva" (the new land). It was not until the late 1570s that the name "New Mexico" became the accepted designation for the northern interior region that included present-day Arizona and New Mexico. New Mexico was made a province of New Spain. While there is no accepted origin for the word *mexica*, a number of authorities agree that it probably meant "navel of the moon" in the Nahuatl language spoken by the Uto-Aztecan peoples who dominated Mexico in the period prior to the arrival of Cortes.

Motivated by the prevailing Spanish ethos of seeking gold, glory, and conversion of the Indians to the Christian gospel, Fray Marcos de Niza led a small group into New Mexico in 1539, hoping to confirm the existence of the fabled "seven cities of Cibola." Although he viewed Zuni Pueblo in northwest New Mexico only from a distance of several miles, Fray Marcos was convinced he had located Cibola, and upon returning to Mexico City, reported that it had appeared more "resplendent" than the cities of Mexico encountered by Cortes.

Inspired by the new report that riches lay northward, Francisco Vásquez de Coronado obtained a commission from Viceroy Antonio de Mendoza and in 1540 led the first expedition of conquistadors into the lands that now are California, Arizona, New Mexico, Texas, Oklahoma, and Kansas. Coronado wintered at Tiguez Pueblo near Bernalillo and during his time in New Mexico personally traveled as far east as the Kansas prairies; his party of men were the first official body of Europeans to see the Llano Estacado, the "staked plains" thought to have been given their name by Cabeza de Vaca during his unofficial wanderings. An exploring party sent westward by Coronado reached the Grand Canyon in Arizona. But no gold was found, and no new signs of Indian wealth or great cities were discovered.

In 1581 Fray Augustín Rodrigues and two other missionaries traveled north along the Rio Grande under the protection of a small contingent of soldiers commanded by Francisco Sánchez Chamuscado. After the group visited pueblos found by Coronado forty years before, the soldiers returned to New Spain in 1582. One of the priests had been martyred, and the other two remained in New Mexico to proselytize. The Chamuscado expedition was the first to use the Rio Grande as a route to New Mexico. Prompted by the concern of fellow Franciscans for the fate of the two friars remaining in New Mexico, Antonio de Espejo led thirteen soldiers and one friar up the Rio Grande in 1582. After discovering that both missionaries had been killed, the Espejo party returned to New Spain by way of the Pecos River.

In 1586 instructions were given by the king's council to officials in Mexico City to "carry out the discovery, pacification, and settlement of the said New Mexico." In 1590–91, Gaspar Castaño de Sosa, lieutenant governor and captain general of Nuevo Leon in northeast New Spain, led an expedition into New Mexico in the first attempt to establish a permanent settlement. So eager was Castaño de Sosa to start a colony, that he gathered together the entire village of Almadén in Nuevo Leon and began to move north before receiving the license for colonization for which he had applied.

CHAPTER TWO

Castaño de Sosa and his party of some 170 people including soldiers as well as family groups traveled north along the Pecos River, reaching Pecos Pueblo near the river's headwaters after five months on the march. Along the way the expedition camped just north of present-day Carlsbad on 29 November 1590, and on 4 and 5 December camped near what are now the small communities of Hagerman and Greenfield. On 8 December the group reached the confluence of the Rio Hondo and the Pecos where Roswell now stands, and the day-to-day journal kept by Castaño de Sosa indicates that camp was made in an area of "ravines and groves," where Bitter Lake National Wildlife Refuge now is located.

Imbued with the cultural values of his age, Castaño de Sosa believed simultaneously in his faith, in the right of Spain to colonize, and in the ability of the Spaniards to convert the Indians yet protect their rights within the framework of a universally applicable moral code. With the goal of founding a settlement taking priority, the expedition did not include missionaries, and it was the first to take two-wheeled carts to the northern frontier in New Mexico.

After exploring much of the upper Rio Grande Valley area and making peaceful contact with many of the pueblos, however, Castaño de Sosa suddenly was arrested by soldiers sent from Mexico City because he had failed to obtain the required state approval for his venture before leaving Nuevo Leon. Castaño de Sosa, known as a magnanimous though strong-willed leader, submitted without anger when placed under arrest by fifty soldiers at Santo Domingo Pueblo, where the expedition had established camp. He was led back to Mexico City in irons.[1]

The considerable promise shown by this aborted expedition was, however, a factor in the official sanction given to a new settlement effort. In 1598 Juan de Oñate led the first successful colonizing expedition into New Mexico. The wealthy son of the owner of a silver mine in Zacatecas, Oñate had won a royal mandate from the Spanish crown by agreeing to pay most of the expedition costs out of his own pocket. After recruiting and equipping two hundred soldiers and their families, Oñate led his group northward, having been granted the titles of governor and captain general and having authority to distribute land to his followers. The cost for ten missionaries who accompanied the expedition was borne by the royal treasury.[2]

Oñate selected the pueblo of Yunque-Yunque, on the west side of the Rio Grande across the river from San Juan Pueblo, as the site for the first colony in New Mexico. But political problems and Indian problems both kept the colony, named San Gabriel, in constant turmoil. In

1607 Oñate was removed as governor, and early in 1610 his appointed successor, Pedro de Peralta, arrived to direct construction at a new colonial site named Santa Fe that had been started by the former residents of San Gabriel.

Santa Fe became the administrative capital of the province of New Mexico. By the year 1680, when the Pueblo Revolt occurred and the Spanish settlers fled southward, around twenty-five hundred Spaniards had settled in villages and haciendas along the Rio Grande. Most of the settlements were founded in the area extending from Socorro in the south to Taos in the north, and many were located near pueblos, which served as sources of indentured Indian labor. Even in the years after the return of the Spanish in 1693, the Pecos Valley was settled only in small numbers, near the headwaters of the river in mountainous country southeast of Santa Fe. It was not until the mid-1700s that Spain began to establish military forts and towns in Texas, and even then central New Mexico was viewed by the crown as its most important holding along the northern frontier of New Spain.

New Mexico was considered a defensive buffer state standing between potential intruders on the east, north, and west, and New Spain's rich mineral sources south of the Rio Grande. For by the time of the American Revolution, Spain's outposts in California, Arizona, New Mexico, and Texas all were under varying degrees of threat not only from Indians but from Russians along the Pacific, French fur traders moving south from Canada, and English moving west toward the Mississippi River valley. France had ceded its Louisiana Territory to Spain at the end of the French and Indian War in 1763 to prevent it from coming under British control. But in 1800 Spain, under military threat from Napoleon, returned the territory to France, and in 1803 France sold Louisiana Territory to the United States. American interest in the West was accelerating rapidly; in 1806 the U.S. government commissioned Zebulon Pike to explore Colorado, Texas, and New Mexico, testing the extent and effectiveness of Spanish authority in those lands.

Throughout this period the windswept Llano Estacado was virtually a no-man's-land, crisscrossed continuously by raiding, nomadic bands of buffalo-hunting Indians. The Spanish presence was largely a transitory one, as Spanish trading and buffalo-hunting parties set forth periodically to move eastward from the colonized area along the Rio Grande. While the Spanish settlers obtained most trade goods from Mexico, with many essential supplies moving northward in long trains of pack animals along the Camino Real through the Rio Grande Valley, trade with the Indians was also a source of support for the hard-pressed Spanish settlers of the northern frontier. Wool, live sheep, and animal hides were New Mexico's principal exports back to Mexico. With so little in the way of revenue-earning export production, the settlers astutely exploited the buffalo of the Llano Estacado, recognizing as did both the Pueblo and Plains Indians that the grazing herds were too valuable a resource to be ignored.

The Spanish did not have the military and financial resources needed to subdue the Plains Indians and enable settlement, but they nonetheless felt a natural affinity for the high plains. The land bore a marked resemblance to the high, dry country of Salamanca in Spain from which many settler families had come. Even the Spanish horse, with its mix of Arabian and North African blood, was well suited to the desert Southwest, able to survive on sparse grass and travel long distances between water holes.

Spanish buffalo hunters, known as *ciboleros*, were particularly adept at surviving on the plains. Early fall was their traditional time for heading east in caravans of wagons and horses to search for buffalo. The hunts were carefully prepared for months in advance, and the ciboleros were all highly skilled in specialized aspects of the lucrative venture, which produced hides for tanning, tallow for grease and candles, and beef jerky for use during the winter months. Many of the earliest rough wagon trails in southeastern New Mexico, later to become regular roads, were first cut by the cibolero caravans. The ciboleros had the status of folk heroes as they set forth in their distinctive garb of leather shirts and short leather pants, moccasins and pointed leather hats. When they returned, wagons laden with provisions, they often took on further stature as fighters, telling stories of having successfully defended themselves against the Indian attacks that were inevitable for all who ventured out onto the eastern plains.

Despite the steady growth of New Mexico's population, settlements continued to concentrate along the Rio Grande and the upper Pecos River until the 1840s, when a combination of land pressure and intensified efforts to control the Plains Indians made the eastern plains look increasingly attractive.

In 1800 there were 18,826 Spaniards and 9,732 Pueblo Indians living in New Mexico. By 1821, when Mexico became an independent nation retaining its northern provinces, New Mexico had 30,000 Hispanic residents, far more than lived in either Texas or California. Growth accelerated fairly rapidly during the years of Mexican rule; according to census figures, New Mexico had 43,433 inhabitants in 1827. By 1850, two years after the signing of the Treaty of Guadalupe Hidalgo, which ceded New Mexico to the United States at the close of the Mexican War, the territory had a population of 61,547, not including Indians. By this time the movement of Spanish settler groups to new areas southeast of Albuquerque and Santa Fe was well under way.

But while it is true that Hispanic groups were starting new farming communities in an ever-widening pattern of geographic expansion even before the American conquest of 1846, the establishment of American control lent fresh impetus to population growth in outlying areas, and at the same time improved survival prospects for the tiny communities springing up to the east and southeast of the Rio Grande Valley. Political control by the United States set in motion a number of economic and institutional forces that mitigated the harsh conditions under which new settlement took place, and these same forces ultimately played a decisive role in bringing to an end the isolation and emptiness of southeastern New Mexico.

The new era began when American military forces made New Mexico part of the United States with one unexpectedly sudden strike. On 13 May 1846, Congress approved President James K. Polk's statement that a state of war with Mexico existed, after Mexican troops crossed the Rio Grande and attacked forces led by General Zachary Taylor. On 18 August, after marching his sixteen-hundred-man Army of the West from Kansas over the Santa Fe Trail, General Stephen Watts Kearny entered Santa Fe without facing armed opposition and proclaimed the province of New Mexico to be under American control. Santa Fe was the first foreign capital ever taken in conquest by the United States. The Mexican War ended with the 2 February 1848 signing of the Treaty of Guadalupe Hidalgo, which gave the United States the last third of its continental domain, including New Mexico and California; Arizona and parts of Utah and Colorado were at that time part of New Mexico. The treaty also confirmed American title to Texas.

Not even conferment of territorial status in 1850 and the subsequent bureaucratic control of New Mexico through appointments made in Washington were sufficient, however, to bring rapid progress to a land that for many years after it became American could still be called raw, wild frontier country. Progress was made—in improving roads, expanding commerce, and controlling Indian raiding—but as Jean Baptiste Lamy, bishop of Santa Fe from 1851 to 1875 and archbishop from 1875 to 1885, was to note often during his long tenure, the pace of change was slow and uneven. Progress was often impeded by political feuding, by corruption, and by the simple enormity of the problems facing New Mexico.

Without exception each of the early territorial governors expressed high hopes for rich mining revenues, public education, the establishment of manufacturing, and the granting of statehood. The reality remained one in which New Mexico was viewed by Washington as unique and somewhat suspect among the western territories, because it was the only American acquisition to have a large foreign population at the time of conquest; statehood was not granted immediately, and the other goals proved equally elusive. In addition emigration to New Mexico from the states always fell short of rosy predictions from territorial officials, although by the mid 1860s between twelve and fifteen thousand Anglo-Americans were living in the territory, creating the conditions for a "collision and mingling of cultures."[3]

Nevertheless, the decades of the 1860s through the 1890s brought enormous change, often accompanied by disruptive strife, to New Mexico. The southeastern part of the territory, most of which in 1869 became a single entity named Lincoln County, in honor of the slain president, experienced in particularly intense manner the interplay of frontier violence, partisan politics, and ethnic conflict that characterized the territory as a whole. Yet in these same years, the southeast quadrant developed as an important cattle-producing region, built its first towns, and saw them grow as the Indian threat was removed, roads were built, and rail service reached the area.

A number of catalytic events, some related to the national destiny, others deriving from local factors, worked together in an overlapping, typically unpredictable fashion to bring about the settlement of the southeast quadrant. Foremost among the factors facilitating emigration to the region were the need of Hispanic farmers and sheep ranchers for new land; the post–Civil War movement of southerners into Texas and then New Mexico; the presence of the U.S. military to control Apaches and other nomadic tribes; the discovery of underground artesian water sources in the Pecos Valley; a growing national market for the beef cattle raised in southeast New Mexico; and the building of a railroad linking the region with the rest of the country.

Indicative of the depth and nature of the ecological, social and economic changes occurring in the second half of the nineteenth century in western America are several discrete but nonetheless related facts. In 1850 there were more than twenty-five million buffalo on the western plains; by 1900 there were less than one thousand. In 1852 New Mexico's first appointed territorial governor, William Carr Lane, reached Santa Fe after forty-two days of travel from St. Louis over the Santa Fe Trail; in 1881 territorial governor Lew Wallace left Santa Fe by pullman car on the Atchison, Topeka and Santa Fe Railroad and reached St. Louis two days later. In 1850 not a single town or road existed in southeastern New Mexico; by 1900 the area had five county governments, several sizable towns, growing commerce and agriculture, and a population of over 25,000. (The total population of New Mexico in 1900 was 196,310. The five counties that in 1900 comprised southeastern New Mexico were Eddy, Chaves, Guadalupe, Lincoln, and Otero.)

Pioneering settlement of southeastern New Mexico came principally from two different directions, with Hispanic groups moving southeastward from the Manzano Mountains east of Albuquerque, beginning in the early 1850s, and Anglos moving westward from Texas into the broad Pecos Valley and beyond, up into the foothills of the mountains. It was in this western mountainous border area of the region, ideal for lumbering and sheep and cattle raising, that the two groups with their divergent cultures and economic systems first came into contact. The settlement process throughout New Mexico during this period was being aided by the ongoing work of the government in establishing military forts and surveying land for town sites and major roadways. Between 1848 and 1865, most of the territory was surveyed and mapped, and the U.S. Army made fifteen official exploratory expeditions in New Mexico, providing information on topography, flora, fauna, and the Native inhabitants.

By 1868, when the telegraph reached Santa Fe, migration to the territory from the states was also being sparked by widespread reports of new mineral discoveries. Wherever people gathered in the territory, there was heady talk of the riches to be had from filing claims in the mountains of central and southwest New Mexico, where gold and silver mines were opening at a feverish pace. Within a few years, miners from all parts of the nation were trekking into the territory, creating a new labor group, a new political force, and new kinds of communities, as company towns sprang up almost overnight at such sites as Elizabethtown in northeastern New Mexico and Golden in the mountain foothills southeast of Santa Fe. The air of optimism was heightened by public knowledge that engineers were surveying routes for a number of proposed railroads. Territorial governors William S. Pile (1869–71) and Marsh Giddings (1871–75) repeated with renewed conviction the claims of their predecessors that New Mexico soon would take its place among the states as an industrialized region.

By the mid 1860s, southeastern New Mexico had Hispanic settlements in the mountain foothills and at the site now occupied by Roswell. It also had a few Anglo settlers scattered along the Hondo and Pecos rivers, and at the same time cattlemen were beginning to build a new cattle industry on the southeast rangeland. But the area was notably slower in feeling the ripple effects of the development impacting other parts of the territory. As late as 1880, Lincoln County had but 2,513 residents. Indian troubles, range wars, and ethnic conflict all impeded population growth during the 1870s and early 1880s. It was the period from the mid 1880s to 1910 that brought a faster-paced development to southeastern New Mexico.

It was a broad-based development, involving all aspects of life; much of the impetus for the faster pace can be traced to the inexorable force of the national movement westward. In particular, events in the state of Texas played an important role in the final surge of settlement that brought southeastern New Mexico into the national mainstream.

Americans had started moving into Texas in the 1820s, and after wresting permission from Mexico to remain as settlers, they established towns, farms, and ranches in increasing numbers. Mexico allowed the resident Americans to own slaves under the term "permanent indentured servant," a status not legal in Mexico outside Texas. Growing conflict between the Americans and their Mexican hosts culminated in the defeat of a handful of Texans by Mexican forces at the Alamo in San Antonio in February 1836. The bravery of the doomed Texans stirred Anglo settlers throughout Texas to rally around the cause of freedom from Mexican rule, and independence was declared on 2 March 1836.

The new Republic of Texas adopted a constitution permitting slavery and in August 1837 asked President Martin Van Buren for annexation by the United States. Abolitionists resisted entry of another slave-holding state. Knowing a treaty would not win a two-thirds vote of approval by the Senate, President John Tyler instead sought and won congressional approval of a resolution of annexation, which he signed on 1 March 1845. From the start of its negotiations with the United States, Texas had rejected the notion of federal control of its public lands. Under terms of the 1845 annexation agreement, Texas became the only state to control its own public land, which amounted to 170 million acres. The U.S. government assumed Texas's debts in the amount of $13 million. In 1848, following the signing of the Treaty of Guadalupe Hidalgo, Texas pressed its claim to an additional 79 million acres of land in New Mexico, Kansas, Colorado, and Wyoming. In a final settlement of the case, the United States gave Texas $15 million in compensation for the disputed lands.

Mexico had never been able to colonize Texas effectively or control it militarily. Thus it was inevitable that Texas, which stood directly in the path of the American movement westward then under way, would become part of the American expansion to the Pacific. And indeed, once it became part of the United States, Texas rapidly became the destination of choice for thousands of pioneers each year, and it served as a gateway to the Far West for thousands of others.

After the Civil War, Texas, possessing all the rights and privileges of statehood and the added advantage of a state-controlled public domain, capitalized on its assets by introducing its own homesteading program. In the economic and social upheaval stemming from the war, numerous families from the Old South welcomed the chance to begin anew in Texas; many of the towns started in the 1870s were composed almost entirely of Confederate veterans and their families. The homesteading movement brought farmers to places in Texas that previously had known only cattlemen. And resented though they were by ranchers accustomed to freewheeling use of the public domain, these new cropmen were there to stay. They carved out farms and started towns where the Texas longhorn once roamed free.

Texas cattlemen looked westward; southeastern New Mexico offered a natural extension of the ecological environment they knew and understood. Between 1865 and 1900, many hundreds of Texas cattlemen took their herds across the Pecos and reestablished their operations along the Pecos River, farther west in the mountains, and even beyond, in the Tularosa Basin of south-central New Mexico. The steady emigration from Texas, which intensified after 1880, when even the Big Bend and West Texas regions began to fill with farmers, strongly affected both the development and the culture of southeastern New Mexico: the beef-cattle industry thrived and became a mainstay of the local economy; and the Texas ranching life-style and a southern influence that often accompanied it became part of southeastern New Mexico culture.

Of all the events that had a catalytic effect upon the territory as a whole and southeastern New Mexico in particular, none was as dramatically visual or as eagerly anticipated as the coming of the railroad. The Atchison, Topeka and Santa Fe Railroad was the first to arrive. Having laid track southward from Colorado over the Raton Pass route that began as the Santa Fe Trail, the AT&SF reached Las Vegas on 4 April 1879. By 10 April 1880, track had been laid to Albuquerque, and on 10 March 1881, the Santa Fe line joined with the Southern Pacific Railroad at Deming in southern New Mexico, creating the first all-rail route through New Mexico linking the territory with the rest of the nation. The availability of trains to move people and goods "significantly increased New Mexico's involvement in the affairs of the country."[4]

Close to two hundred railway companies were incorporated in New Mexico during the territorial period, and communities competed eagerly for the laying of track, even as local entrepreneurs sought just as eagerly to profit by acquiring in advance land they believed would be sought by the railroad companies for right-of-way.[5] Attempts to profit from railroad building sometimes backfired; confident that the Atchison, Topeka and Santa Fe had no option but to purchase land they had acquired between Las Vegas and Santa Fe, Santa Fe businessmen placed so high a price on their land parcels along Glorieta Pass that the company decided to bypass Santa Fe altogether and proceed southwest through Lamy to Albuquerque. Only a last-minute fundraising effort by concerned local citizens enabled the capital city to acquire the consolation prize of a spur line from Lamy. Regardless of minor setbacks, however, rail-line construction proceeded at a rapid pace; by 1890 there were 1,284 miles of rail line, and in 1914 eleven companies were operating a total of 3,124 miles of railroad track in New Mexico.

The southeast quadrant initially was ignored by the larger railroads, in the belief "that there was not enough traffic there to make a railroad profitable."[6] But southeastern New Mexico eventually benefited from the construction of two rail lines, one in the eastern part of the region, the other running through the mountainous border area to the west. The Pecos Valley Railroad was built from Pecos, Texas, to Eddy (later renamed Carlsbad) in 1890, extended to Roswell in 1894, and in 1899 reached Amarillo, Texas, where it linked up with a national east-west line. In 1901 the Pecos Valley line was purchased by the Santa Fe Railroad. The region's second line was built in the 1890s from El Paso northeastward through Las Cruces and Carrizozo to Tucumcari in northeast New Mexico, where it joined the Rock Island line built into the territory in 1898.

The impact of a railroad on the community of Roswell, lying west of the Pecos at its confluence with the Rio Hondo, was felt immediately. Although there were by 1885 many ranchers and farmers living within a ten-mile radius of Roswell, the town itself had just nine houses, two stores, and scarcely a hundred residents. Then, in 1890, artesian water was discovered, and there was good reason to spread the word by newspaper and advertising brochures that a rich farming area was opening up, creating opportunities for merchants, doctors, teachers, and laborers. Growth in population and production accelerated but required transportation improvement if it was to proceed much further.

Before the railroad came, wool from Roswell sheep ranches was piled high on wagons, horsemen riding along on each side for protection, and an arduous journey north to Las Vegas was made in order to market the wool. Roswell also received most of its essential outside supplies of foodstuffs, medicine, and machinery from Las Vegas by wagon. Descendants of the pioneering Cobean family recall tales of the children being sent out to watch the road to the north for the first glimpses of wagons raising dust on the long road. Farmers living east of Roswell drilled hundreds of irrigation wells after 1890, turning the middle Pecos Valley into a lush oasis of apple and peach orchards that annually produced a crop so large that it required a bigger market than existed in the immediate area.

The arrival of the railroad in 1894 brought beneficial changes of several kinds. Emigrants could travel into eastern New Mexico by train from Texas. Brick, glass, and other building materials became available. And the produce of the valley—wool, hides, livestock, fruit, and vegetables—was carried to distant markets. In 1891, when Roswell was incorporated as a town, the population was barely 400. But by 1900, six years after the rail line arrived, the combined impact of abundant water and regular rail service was readily apparent: Roswell's population had grown to 2,049.

From the moment the U.S. government took control of New Mexico in 1846 and on to the end of the century, New Mexico was ceaselessly affected by national and even international forces, which took the form of new people, new money, changes in government policies, and new local government entities. These penetrating, irresistable forces were spelled out in a series of landmark events that included the granting of territorial status in 1850; the Confederate invasion of 1861; the arrival of Union troops from California in 1862 and their subsequent use in Indian campaigns; the 1863 separation of Arizona from New Mexico; expansion of mining in the 1860s and 1870s; the arrival of the railroad in 1879; the post–Civil War movement of pioneers; the 1880s surge of foreign investment; New Mexico's involvement in the Spanish-American War of 1898; and intensified efforts during the closing years of the nineteenth century and beginning years of the twentieth century to achieve statehood.

Each of these events, whether economic or political in nature, drew New Mexico more closely into patterns of active realization of the territory's human and natural resources. And yet the day-to-day quality and tenor of life throughout the territory continued during these same decades to be constrained and in part determined by a number of problems that, if not intractable, yielded to improvement only with protracted effort. In fact such social realities as a high rate of infectious disease, widespread illiteracy, and social dislocation stemming from conflicting Spanish and Anglo traditions of land and water use were to remain serious problems to the end of the century and even beyond.

Among the infectious diseases, the two which had the most devastating impact were cholera and smallpox. Epidemics of cholera, an intestinal disease accompanied by high fever and often resulting in death, were recurrent throughout the southern, midwestern, and western portions of the United States during the nineteenth century. From the 1840s on into the 1870s, travelers making the journey across the Great Plains in wagon trains starting from Independence, Missouri, counted themselves fortunate if no more than one or two of their party had to be buried along the way. On his first trip west across the prairie to New Mexico in 1853 (having first entered Santa Fe to take up his duties by way of the Gulf Coast and a journey northward), Bishop Lamy, shepherding a desperately needed group of priests and teaching nuns he had recruited in American and European cities, found himself sorrowfully obliged to bury in a lonely prairie grave the mother superior of the nuns after she died of cholera during the journey.

Smallpox was an even more dreaded scourge of life for those on the frontier. It had been a killer disease in New Mexico as far back as the earliest days of the Spanish colonial period. "Of the several afflictions plaguing New Mexico in colonial times, none was as constant or as fatal as smallpox."[7] An acute, highly contagious viral disease, smallpox frequently resulted in death for its victims. Although the dread disease struck individuals of all ages, "the young, the old, and the undernourished" were most vulnerable.[8] Even those who survived did not escape its clutches, for they were left with permanent deep facial pits and scarring as a result of the skin eruptions that accompanied the disease. Nevertheless, "those surviving an attack of smallpox obtained the gift of life-long immunity, which explains in part why the disease tended to occur in cycles— after a widespread epidemic, a period of years is needed for an unprotected population to grow up."[9]

Records show that major epidemics of smallpox occurred in the Rio

Grande and Pecos River settlements on an average of once a decade during the 1700s and early 1800s. Vaccination against smallpox was discovered in 1796 by an English doctor and promptly utilized by the Russian and French armies. In 1801 smallpox vaccination was introduced in Spain and an expedition was sent to offer it to the Spanish colonies.

In 1804 Don Fernando Chacon, governor of New Mexico, started a vaccination program that eventually was to have a beneficial long-term impact. During the first half of the nineteenth century, the population of New Mexico nearly doubled, and as there was only a trickle of immigration during that period, it is quite probable that a decrease in the number of early deaths due to smallpox played a part in the population increase. But even into the 1880s in such isolated areas as southeastern New Mexico, efforts were hindered by lack of refrigerated transportation for the perishable cowpox material used for the life-saving vaccination.

In attempting to raise the level of education in New Mexico, territorial officials faced a unique problem. Although a public school had been operated for a brief time under Mexican rule, there had been no comprehensive school system during the Mexican period from 1821 to 1846. Illiteracy was widespread by the time American rule was established. The problem was compounded by the fact that English was not the mother tongue of a majority of New Mexicans, and yet would be the language needed to read everything from school textbooks to newspapers. In 1860 an estimated forty-six thousand of a non-Indian population of eighty-two thousand was illiterate. Finally responding to the exhortations of the early territorial governors, the Territorial Legislature passed a law that year, stating that "all persons of school age must attend school."[10] The law, unfortunately, did not address the problem of how to provide the schools the children were supposed to attend.

Seven years later, in 1867, Governor Robert B. Mitchell (1866–69) had to admit to members of the legislature that New Mexico was still "without a single free school to educate a single child."[11] Schools run by the Catholic church and various Protestant denominations offered valuable education, although they could not compensate in quantitative terms for the lack of public education. Two colleges, eight academies, numerous parish schools, and several Indian schools were established by Bishop Lamy.[12] Even so a territorial report of 1880 revealed that "the average school attendance was only a little over 3,000 out of a population of 110,000."[13]

Not until 1898, when Congress passed the Fergusson Act, named for the territorial delegate to Congress who worked hard for its pas-

CHAPTER TWO

sage, was the foundation laid for an adequately funded and comprehensive public-school system. By that time a number of communities, among them Roswell as the most sizable town in the southeast sector, had taken steps to open public schools on their own. By 1895 Roswell had two schools within the town limits and another two schools located in the farming area southeast of the town. These elementary schools served a county population of about four thousand. A high school was started in Roswell in 1899. The town also had what was perhaps the most unusual education institution in the territory, New Mexico Military Institute, founded in 1891 as Goss Military Academy and made a territorial school in 1893.

Between 1850 and 1900, New Mexico changed from Spanish settler region to western frontier society to modernizing territory on the verge of statehood. No better metaphor for the dynamics of this half-century of change can be found than the evolving pattern of landownership and water usage.

Two divergent systems of land and water allocation—one deriving from the traditions of Spain and the other from English custom embedded in American law—coexisted side by side in shifting degrees of relative predominance throughout the period, with final resolution coming by the turn of the century, as Anglo systems of water and land rights took clear precedence over Spanish systems that had been used in New Mexico for 250 years before the American conquest.

In the wake of the 1492 discovery of the Indies, which led to colonization of the Americas, the Spanish crown decided the ownership of all land held by Spain in the New World. The crown provided land for settlers and for towns by giving land grants to individuals and corporate bodies, each grant specifying location, amount of land, and type of land, and bearing with it rights to water use based on whether the land was categorized as cropland, pastureland, grazing land, or community land. The crown owned all land not deeded away through grants, and also continued to own all water rights not made part of grants. A land grant did not, therefore, include full rights over water located on or flowing through the site, but only the rights associated with the particular type of grant and, in most, though not all, cases, specified in the grant document.

Shortly before the retaking of Santa Fe by de Vargas in 1692, a royal decree gave New Mexico governors authority to grant lands. Throughout the Spanish period, "governors in a clearly defined procedure made grants from the royal domain to both individual Spaniards and to groups of family heads who established separate communities."[14]

Spanish law distinguished between two types of water use on these grant lands: first, water used by occupants for economic purposes such as livestock raising, crop production or mills; and second, water used for domestic purposes such as drinking, cooking, bathing, and watering of domestic livestock. Water could be privatized for economic purposes, but it remained public for domestic purposes and could be used for domestic purposes not only by the grant holders but also by individuals not included in the grant ownership. This meant that water, whether on grant lands or land still held by the crown, was "free for use by all of the inhabitants" if intended for domestic purposes.[15]

While Spanish law was the basis of New World legal structure, the laws of Spain often were "modified to meet local conditions and accommodate Indian customs." By 1681, in fact, it became essential to publish a code of law laying out all of the various laws on land and water applicable in Spain's New World colonies. New Mexico, however, remained one of those outlying parts of the empire where Spanish custom rather than the 1681 colonial code "conditioned legal practice."[16]

New Mexico's land-tenure and water-use patterns were characterized by traits that also typified the system predominant in Spain itself. Communities were accorded a distinct legal status in the distribution of both land and water. "In the settlement grants, cultivatable land was divided among the heads of households while the large areas of grazing land were used in common."[17] And in the arid conditions of New Mexico, community control and distribution of water was not only a practical method of insuring the economic viability of agriculture-dependent settlers but "was not in violation of the Spanish tradition."[18] In general, Spanish law that accorded "special privilege" to "municipalities in control over water was carried to America."[19] Also in keeping with Spanish tradition was a system of water usage in New Mexico that gave the highest priority to agricultural needs and therefore centered around the community-owned irrigation ditch (*acequia*) as a means of "fair and agriculturally productive distribution."[20]

Although no land grants were made in southeastern New Mexico, the Hispanic settlers who emigrated southeastward from the Rio Grande Valley in the years following the American conquest of 1846 brought with them a concept of community, agriculture, and land and water distribution that reflected the traditions that had evolved over the course of two centuries in north-central New Mexico. And in fact Hispanic emigrants to the southeast quadrant were under no legal pressure to alter their customary land-tenure and water-allocation customs, for the prevailing system was deliberately embodied in statutory form by the first Territorial Legislature when it convened in 1851. Legislative members, many of them Hispanos, saw no reason to substitute a new system for one that "was already working effectively."[21] Thus southeastern New Mexico Hispanos at such settlements as Rio Bonito (Lincoln), Missouri Plaza, Rio Hondo, and El Berrendo relied upon the customary application of Spanish law, which allowed water needed for domestic purposes to be obtained by conducting it by ditch from a stream located on another person's land when and if that proved necessary.[22]

But in southeastern New Mexico the communal system of commonly grazing livestock, allocating crop water from a community acequia, and retaining the right to domestic use of flowing stream waters was not to have the luxury of undisturbed development that it had enjoyed in north-central New Mexico. For almost simultaneously with Hispanic infiltration of the area there came the infiltration by Anglo cattlemen and settlers, who naturally gravitated toward land where streams, water holes, or running river water made feasible their settlement activities. And these Anglo pioneers did not consider it the right of one settler to cross another's land to obtain water, even when an upstream user was preventing the flow of water to a downstream user. Thus a de facto system created on the ground in the valleys and on the ranges of southeastern New Mexico was anticipating as early as the 1860s and 1870s a major change that for the territory as a whole did not culminate until the early years of the twentieth century.

It was the need to regularize and confirm land titles that gave rise to this change, the result of which was the clear supremacy of Anglo-American law over custom and law derived from Spain. In January 1855 the first surveyor general for New Mexico issued "a notice in both Spanish and English requesting all inhabitants in the territory to file their land claims."[23] But by 1890 a large number of claims, including many for grant lands, were still in a state of confusion and dispute. In response Congress created the Court of Private Land Claims in 1891. Relying upon "common law interpretation which denied to claimants rights which they had enjoyed under Spanish civil law," the court recognized barely three million acres of the thirty million acres of land-grant claims submitted to it.[24]

In addition the doctrine of prior appropriation emerged as the federal and then territorial basis for water-rights claims by the turn of the century. This meant that the first or oldest-in-time user had legal right to continue receiving water in the amount historically used, before downstream users could make any claim to what remained. And while the doctrine "bore some resemblance" to the complex system of water use that previously prevailed in New Mexico, the loss of a large portion of grant lands and therefore their waters inevitably meant that the self-sufficiency that characterized Hispanic settlements early in the territorial period gradually was replaced by a trend toward economic displacement as the numbers of landless Hispanos grew.[25]

Corruption played its part over the years as well. Surveyors general were authorized only to survey "arable" portions of the public domain. But with some office holders linked through private business deals to the big cattle interests, nonarable land was sometimes surveyed and thus made available for private land claims. Pecos cattleman John Chisum was among those who benefited from the willingness of surveyors to facilitate transfer to private ownership of water frontage land in essentially arid range portions of the public domain.[26]

In southeastern New Mexico the Anglo-American system of water rights had especially harsh ramifications for sheep ranchers in the mountain valleys west of Roswell and also within the Pecos Valley, as sheep raisers found themselves cut off from water holes increasingly absorbed into private landholdings.

Clearly the blossoming of activity in every sphere of human endeavor experienced in southeastern New Mexico during the late 1800s laid a firm basis for future development. Yet even as it proceeded, development brought problems. While some of these areas of human need, such as the need to alleviate the spread of communicable disease, were common to many parts of the West, others, such as the higher-than-average illiteracy rate and the simmering conflict over land and water, were unique to New Mexico, a legacy of the territory's former position as an isolated frontier province of Spain and Mexico.

3

Native People and the Land

THE POST–CIVIL WAR IMPETUS TOWARD BORDER-TO-BORDER OPENing up of New Mexico to settlement, agriculture, and mining served to strengthen the consensus among many government officials and territorial residents that such development could be pursued effectively only if the nomadic Indian population was brought under permanent control—either by confinement on reservations or death in battle.

The Indian threat was real enough, a constant of daily life for the thousands of New Mexicans who either lived beyond, or found it necessary to travel beyond, the narrow confines of a string of protected settlements along the central portion of the Rio Grande Valley. Even those traveling in armed convoys of wagons were not immune to harrassment from encircling parties of Indian warriors who might menace a caravan for hours or for days, eerily appearing and then disappearing, before attacking. Priests carrying the sacraments for mass to Indian missions and outlying Hispanic villages were sometimes waylaid, a few even killed. Children were kidnapped from Hispanic villages and sold into servitude south of the border. Cattle being herded to market were always under threat from Indians in search of livestock.

Even so the record shows that the frequent characterization of Indians in newspapers of the day as "savage killers" may well have been a stereotyping not wholly justified, perhaps having more to do with the Indians as a presence that impeded total control of the land by new pioneering elements than with the actual reality of Indian actions. Not only are there recorded instances of Indian cooperation with pioneers caught in difficult circumstances, but a survey done by one historian shows that of the many thousands who moved along trails into the trans-Mississippi West between 1840 and 1860, "perhaps 360 immigrants were killed by the Indians on the northern trails . . ."[1] And while the Indians themselves certainly regarded their tribes as being under threat from the U.S. government and from pioneer movement into their traditional hunting grounds, the literal facts of their warring activity often seem to have had more to do with hunger, frustration, and desperation than with any deliberate scheme to kill indiscriminately.

It is true that the Indians were guilty of murders. One prominent example was the 1849 J. M. White affair, in which the St. Louis merchant and several others were killed by Apaches at Point of Rocks in eastern New Mexico and his wife and child kidnapped, with Mrs. White later killed during a rescue attempt by the military. Yet travelers often dealt with raiding parties by barter; the Indians would ride away satisfied if they received supplies of beans, biscuit, perhaps a slab of bacon, sometimes a bolt of cloth.

In northwestern New Mexico, where Navajo and Ute raiding was a long-standing problem, their propensity to ride forth from local tribal areas and stage raids to capture livestock was sometimes fostered by frustration over the failure of territorial officials to live up to agreements to supply the Indians with corn, beef, and salt needed for the winter months. And increasingly as the years went by, the Indians were asked to comply with ever stricter regulations as to where they could graze their animals, plant crops, and travel. Lacking the agricultural skills and stable settled towns developed over centuries by the Pueblos, the Plains Indians were bewildered and angry as they faced a future that seemingly had no place for them or their traditional way of life.

The underlying causes of Indian despair were of little interest to the majority of New Mexicans, however, as they sought to make the land theirs and productive. What they wanted was for the U.S. government to fulfill the promise made by General Stephen Watts Kearny when he entered Santa Fe in 1846 and proclaimed that the new government would "protect the people from their Indian enemies."[2] The promise proved easier to make than to keep.

But as the nation restored itself to civilian calm following the ravages of civil war, New Mexico stood ready to participate in, and benefit from, the intensified Indian Wars that eventually would make the promise a reality. In striking contrast to the largely defensive strategies of the Spanish and Mexican periods in New Mexico, strategies that had been based on protection of existing settlements and the making of treaties of friendship with a few allies among the Plains tribes, the American strategy was an increasingly offensive one, designed to seek out confrontation with the tribes, destroy their leadership, and plan entirely new ways of life for them.

Southeastern New Mexico, regarded as traditional homeland by the Mescalero Apaches but also used by other Apache and Comanche groups, became a key testing ground for the new offensive strategy and was the scene of some of the most searingly dramatic and poignantly tragic events of the Indian campaigns. And while the intended effect of the military strategy was to protect settlers and their property, its largely unintended but perhaps equally significant effect was to serve in and of itself as a powerful stimulant to the general growth of the area, bringing people with a wide variety of skills into southeastern New Mexico and opening up new markets for local production of cattle, grains, lumber, and other primary goods.

The network of army forts constructed and operated throughout New Mexico at various times from 1846 through the 1890s was an important element in the offensive campaign. Fort Marcy, established at Santa Fe by Kearny in 1846, was the first fort to be built, although it was never garrisoned, and the name eventually came to refer to the military complex in Santa Fe. Fort Union, established in 1851 to the east along the Santa Fe Trail, was the largest and most important of New Mexico's forts. Operated until 1891, Fort Union served as headquarters for the Ninth Military Department, which covered all of New Mexico and the southern portion of Colorado. Other forts included Fort Wingate II in Navajo country, Fort Bayard near Silver City in southwestern Apache country, and forts Craig, Selden, and Fillmore along the Rio Grande between El Paso and Socorro. Of the twenty-three forts operated by the army in the Ninth Department, only two were located in southeastern New Mexico, but without doubt the existence of Fort Stanton and Fort Sumner mitigated the Indian threat even as the presence of these forts sparked new economic enterprise.

It took all of forty years to resolve the Indian problem in New Mexico, from 1846 to 1886, when the Apache leader Geronimo and his followers finally were captured in the wild reaches of southern Arizona near the Mexican border. The Indian campaigns were not always well coordinated, flawed tactical decisions were not uncommon, and setbacks were inevitable in a conflict where the Indians were using a form of guerrilla warfare in a land well suited to unorthodox methods. But the military did, of course, ultimately achieve its objective.

CHAPTER THREE

A sense of just how daunting the challenge was when first confronted by the American government may be acquired by referring to a detailed—and urgent—proposal made to the last Mexican legislative body at Santa Fe in 1846, only weeks before the American invasion of August. The author of the proposal, Donaciano Vigil (1802–77), was a soldier and well-educated government officeholder of considerable accomplishment, who later functioned capably in the American government and served for a time as governor of New Mexico under U.S. administration.

When he presented the proposal he hoped would be implemented by the Congress of Mexico, Vigil, like other officials of Mexico's northern province, was unaware of U.S. President Polk's declaration of a state of war with Mexico. Couched in the language of reasoned analysis and supporting changes in policy designed to alter a situation viewed as no longer tolerable, Vigil's proposal for better defense against Indian raids was in reality a cry of anguished outrage from citizens of an isolated province who felt both threatened and defenseless, abandoned in effect by their mother government in Mexico City.

Vigil argued that the Indians were better armed than the civilian Mexican population. While Mexico forbade free trade in arms and munitions, the Indians had acquired guns, rifles, and munitions from American traders. Settlers, Vigil claimed, fortified themselves as best they could against Indians better armed than they themselves were. He asked that civilians in New Mexico be granted access to weapons, and he made an urgent plea for additional troops to battle the Plains tribes surrounding the Rio Grande Valley.[3]

Just six weeks after Vigil presented his eloquent plea for help to Mexican officials, the Indian problem became an American one and part of the enduring dilemma faced by Americans moving in ever greater numbers into the lands of the West.

From the start of the American government's relationship with the Native American population, there had been divergent philosophies as to how best to deal with the tribes and how to envision their role in American society. New Mexico soon found itself caught up in the web of conflicting views over goals and methods, with an 1849 government decision to remove authority over the Indians from the military and place it in the Department of the Interior symbolizing the division between those hoping to foster a viable but peaceful Indian social structure and those wishing only for a free hand to use military means to bring troublesome Indians under control. There were cases to be made on both sides of the argument. In practical and immediate terms, however, the decision to give responsibility for controlling the Indians to Interior had the effect of "seriously weakening the effectiveness of efforts to pacify the Indians."[4]

But even among territorial officials in New Mexico there was no consensus on how control of the Plains Indians was to be achieved. James S. Calhoun, who served as Indian agent before being appointed governor in 1851, was a proponent of harsh military solutions and favored the use of the civilian militias that had done much to prolong Indian hostility in the past. While a staunch friend of the Pueblo Indians who urged government protection for their lands, Calhoun at the same time recommended that the Apaches, Comanches, and Navajos, known for their fearsome fighting prowess, be immediately placed on reservations, using whatever military means were necessary.

On the other hand, those who sought to resolve specific areas of dispute with particular tribes often found their actions, even when producing peace, undermined by lack of cooperation from other officials or agencies. Governor David Meriwether, who served from 1853 to 1857, found himself facing an angry Navajo delegation and subsequent violence in the northwest, because officials had abrogated a treaty made by the previous governor under which foodstuffs were to be supplied to the Indians in return for their restriction to lands not capable of providing for their needs over the winter months.

Turning his attention to the Mescaleros in the southeast, Meriwether negotiated a treaty with them in 1855, following a military campaign in which the Indians were defeated with heavy losses. The treaty provided for a reservation to be established in the vicinity of Fort Stanton, which had been built and opened that year in the Sacramento Mountains. The fort was named in honor of Captain Henry W. Stanton of the U.S. Cavalry, recently killed in battle with the Mescaleros. Announcement of an impending reservation, however, brought cries of protest from New Mexicans, with Indian Agent Michael Steck reporting complaints that the Mescalero reservation would close off land "in the centre of the most valuable portion of New Mexico."[5]

The Meriwether treaty with the Mescaleros, along with other treaties negotiated by him, was not approved by the U.S. Senate, leaving the Mescalero problem to fester for close to another twenty years.

The Mescalero Apaches continued to roam the southeast plains. Their depredations, as well as those of the Navajos, who made frequent attacks throughout the 1850s, finally brought about the formulation of a bold but tragically flawed plan for crushing once and for all the war-making capacity of both the Navajos and the Mescaleros. The plan was designed and executed by three men in particular, each of whom played a distinctive part in the drama that they jointly set in motion.

Henry Connelly was one of the most respected men in New Mexico when he was appointed governor in 1861 at the age of 61. Born in Virginia and raised in Kentucky, where he earned a medical degree, Connelly had made his living as a trader and store owner in Mexico and New Mexico since the mid-1820s and was living in Santa Fe when the 1846 U.S. invasion took place. By the time of his own inauguration as governor, Connelly was the owner of a large store in Bernalillo County and maintained a hacienda at Peralta, where he lived with his children and his wife, daughter of the influential Don Pedro Perea.[6]

Already an important figure in territorial politics, Connelly had participated in the 1850 Constitutional Convention, where his name was proposed for gubernatorial candidate should statehood be granted. And having served in the Territorial Council from 1853 to 1859, Connelly was on intimate terms with the many problems besetting the young territory, the Indian problem not least among them.

Connelly had deep roots in New Mexico after many decades as a resident, and he also had an understanding of Hispanic culture surpassing that of previous territorial governors, as a result of family ties; his first wife, who died when their three sons were still young, was a native of Chihuahua, while his second was part of the wealthy "rico" class of Hispanic New Mexicans. Perhaps because of these emotional bonds, Connelly's sympathies clearly lay with the Hispanic villagers long troubled by Navajo stealing of livestock. As governor, Connelly made no attempt to halt the numerous unlawful incursions into Navajo lands by New Mexicans, which continually exacerbated the state of hostility between the two groups, and despite policy to the contrary emanating from the Department of the Interior, Connelly called for the formation of civilian militias to enter Navajo country and take retribution for Indian raids.[7]

This hint of underlying attitudes, however, was forgotten in the early months of Connelly's governorship, as the Civil War came to New Mexico in the form of a Confederate invasion, creating an emergency of crisis proportions and, coincidentally, proving to be the event bringing together the men most responsible for what became known as the Long Walk to the Bosque Redondo in southeastern New Mexico.

Connelly, an ardent Unionist, was decisive and effective as a wartime gubernatorial executive. Even as he was being sworn in on 4 September 1861, the Confederate flag was flying over Fort Fillmore near Mesilla in southern New Mexico. Henry Hopkins Sibley had resigned his army post with the Ninth Military Department, joined the Confederates in Texas, and was leading a force of twenty-six hundred troops up the Rio Grande toward Fort Craig, which was under the command of Colonel Edward Canby, Sibley's replacement as commander of forces in New Mexico. Early in 1862 Connelly sought and received Territorial Council repeal of New Mexico's Slave Act of 1859, under which slaves were permitted to be retained as personal property when brought into the territory by their owners.

The Battle of Valverde, the first major conflict between Union and Confederate forces in the Southwest, took place in February 1862. Moving up the west side of the Rio Grande, General Sibley confronted Canby's Union troops at Fort Craig, located about one hundred miles south of Albuquerque. An inconclusive skirmish between the two sides on February 16 prompted the Confederate forces to cross to the east side of the river, where they planned to bombard the fort from a hill. Canby, with a force of just over thirty-eight hundred men, including many who were recently trained militia and volunteers, had declined to be fooled by several Sibley maneuvers designed to draw his troops out into the open and away from the protective defenses of the fort.

But on February 21, when Sibley took his troops to the Valverde Ford, six miles north of Fort Craig, a move indicating he might return to the west bank, Canby immediately countered by ordering his troops out to defend the river crossing. The day-long Battle of Valverde that ensued was fought fiercely in hand-to-hand combat with weapons ranging from Bowie knives to double-barrelled shotguns to artillery batteries. Although some of the raw Union recruits broke ranks before the Confederates, many Union units displayed unshakable courage in defending their positions; militia serving under Colonel Kit Carson from Taos demonstrated their ability to hold firm under close and bloody attack from Texas Confederates who clearly understood the implications of the battle for their campaign. By day's end, with several hundred men from both sides lying dead or wounded on the field, the fighting ended with Canby's men moving back to the fort and the Confederates momentarily jubilant in the belief they had won the day, or at the least had not been defeated.

But while able to regroup and resume their march northward along the Rio Grande, the Confederates had failed to take Fort Craig, and it remained safely in Union hands, occupied by Union forces. As he pro-

CHAPTER THREE

ceeded north, Sibley dispatched a contingent of troops eastward from the Rio Grande to occupy Fort Stanton, whose troops had been evacuated for duty elsewhere at the outbreak of the war. The Texas Confederates held Fort Stanton for about a year, and while occupying the mountain fort built of native stone and adobe were frequently forced into battle with attacking Mescalero Apaches.

The main body of Sibley's men, now numbering close to twenty-five hundred, marched on Albuquerque and then entered Santa Fe, which was occupied for several tense days in early March 1862 before the Confederates moved east to take on Union forces waiting for them in the high, rugged pine country between Santa Fe and Las Vegas. It was here, at the Battle of Glorieta Pass on March 27 and 28, that the Confederates finally were turned back.

The rout was accomplished not only by adroit skirmishing and direct confrontation in heated battle, but also by a daring behind-the-lines attack on the Confederate supply train. Guided over a rocky mountain trail by Colonel Manuel Chaves of the New Mexico Volunteers, Major John M. Chivington led a raid on the Confederate camp that destroyed mules, horses, food, and munitions, ending all possibility that the remaining Texans could continue to feed themselves, travel, and fight in enemy territory. By August 1862 all of the invading troops led by Sibley, including those who had occupied Fort Stanton, had retreated southward down the Rio Grande and were out of New Mexico.

Union leaders at the national level had not been oblivious to the strategic importance of the Confederate attack on New Mexico, knowing that if it succeeded, the way would be open for the South's control of the West from the Rocky Mountains to the Pacific Coast. The Colorado Volunteers had arrived in time to take part in the Battle of Glorieta Pass. But had Union forces not prevailed there, the tide would have been turned in other battles, which as it turned out never needed fighting. For the almost twenty-four hundred men of the California Column under General James M. Carleton arrived on the banks of the Rio Grande on 7 August 1862, with orders to preserve New Mexico for the Union.

The battle-hardened Carleton brought more than cavalry troops with him to New Mexico. He also brought his driving commitment to American expansion, a mid-Victorian Christian piety, an abiding belief in the innate superiority of Anglo-Saxon ways, and a corresponding conviction that the Indians must not only be physically controlled but must also be converted into contented emulators of the American way of life.

Born in Maine and a graduate of West Point, Carleton had fought with General Zachary Taylor in the Mexican War and subsequently participated in numerous Indian campaigns before returning to New Mexico, where he had been previously posted, at the age of forty-eight. His experience did not go unrewarded; following the transfer of Colonel Canby, Carleton assumed command of all military forces in New Mexico on 18 September 1862.

With the Confederate threat removed, Governor Connelly was free to direct his efforts once again to resolving the Indian problem. Well aware that Indian raids had increased with the absence of army troops called to Civil War duty, Connelly increasingly thought in terms of a policy that would produce permanent peace by combining the use of all-out military force with the establishment of clearly defined reservations. And in Carleton, Connelly found a firm and enthusiastic supporter, a man fully prepared to implement a plan that seemed to him to embody all the military and social principles he deemed essential for ultimate success. Connelly and Carleton were in agreement that the nomadic Plains Indians of New Mexico, principally the Navajos of the northwest and the Mescaleros of the southeast, must be "subdued and civilized on reservations or exterminated."[8]

To direct the campaign against the two troublesome tribes, Carleton turned without hesitation to a man who knew the West, the Indians, and the particularities of New Mexico as well as any man alive. That man was Kit Carson, whose national fame rested solidly on close to forty years of adventure and accomplishment as fur trapper, scout, Indian fighter, and government agent in virtually every part of the West, from the Rockies to the High Sierras to the rugged open country of northeast New Mexico, where he had fought the Jicarilla Apaches in 1855 in the company of Carleton. Carleton had forgotten neither the fighting ability nor the leadership qualities of the rough-hewn but always astutely effective Carson, a man quick to see where his duty lay and to act accordingly.

Carson was born in Madison County, Kentucky, in 1809, and moved with his family to a farm at Boon's Lick, Missouri, as a young boy. At the age of sixteen, with little formal education but an unquenchable thirst for adventure, he ran away and joined up with a wagon train loaded with trade goods destined for Santa Fe. By the early 1840s, his success as a trapper and scout enabled him to establish a permanent home at Taos, long the gathering place for some of the most intrepid mountain men of the West. It was there, in 1843, that Carson was married to Josefa

CHAPTER THREE

Jaramillo of Taos, a beautiful, dark-eyed girl eighteen years younger than the thirty-three-year-old Carson. They were married by the parish priest, Padre Antonio José Martínez, and their marriage lasted twenty-five years, until Josefa's death shortly after giving birth to their eighth child.

A devoted family man who often sought to end his traveling days by becoming a full-time rancher, Carson nonetheless continued to periodically heed the call to duty of a more adventuresome kind. He accompanied John Charles Frémont in his arduous second and third western expeditions in the 1840s, and he was serving as Ute Indian Agent based at Taos when the advent of the Civil War caused him to resign his post in June of 1861 and enlist as a lieutenant colonel in the First New Mexico Volunteers, a fighting detachment he headed after September 1861.[9] After participating in the Battle of Valverde near Fort Craig, Carson was ordered to hold the fort as Confederate troops advanced northward after the battle.

Once home in Taos after the invasion had been repelled, Carson had no plans for further military service. But the doughty survivor of Indian and Confederate wars had not reckoned with Carleton, who undoubtedly used the great respect in which Carson held him to convince Carson that it was once again his duty to take up arms and help make the West safe for settlement. By the end of 1862, Carson was stationed at Fort Stanton as commanding officer of five companies, ready to undertake the first phase in the new campaign planned by Connelly and Carleton, which entailed battling the Mescaleros into surrender or death. Even as Carson was establishing himself at Fort Stanton, the two masterminds of the impending campaign were proceeding with plans for the second phase, which aimed at nothing less than total defeat of the far larger Navajo tribe.

Having gained approval of the plan from the commissioner of Indian affairs, who acquiesced to War Department management of the Indians on the grounds of their hostile actions, Carleton became the driving force behind implementation of an Indian campaign more ambitious and sweeping in its implications than any previously undertaken in New Mexico. Even so, Carleton could not have executed the plan as singlemindedly as he did without the active political backing of Connelly in the territory's highest political office and the doggedly tenacious efforts of Carson on the military field of battle.

None of the elements of the campaign and resettlement plan was new; the U.S. government previously had broken treaties made with Indian tribes, endeavored to change Indian culture, waged all-out wars of attrition that included using crop destruction as a tactic to insure surrender, and established Indian reservations. Carleton's unique contribution was to use these elements simultaneously, in a rigidly uncompromising manner, and to apply his policy to a Navajo grouping that comprised, at over ten thousand in number, one of the largest, most cohesive, and culturally distinctive Indian tribes in the nation. Carleton himself saw the plan as genuinely humanitarian in aims, if not in the method of achieving them; he believed wholeheartedly that he was leading the Indians to a higher level of civilization and hence to happier, more satisfying lives.

Without doubt the extreme nature of the plan was in part the consequence of the failure of past attempts to subdue the Navajos as well as the Apaches of southeast New Mexico. But the failure to establish peace was in turn the result of more than a simple Indian refusal to live on peaceable terms with whites; the failure also stemmed from the refusal of whites to take into account any legitimate grievances of the Indians over such matters as land and food, and over past betrayals by whites of treaties and agreements made in good faith by the Indians. Carleton's plan for defeating, resettling, and Christianizing the Indians epitomized, in fact, the assumptions made by whites in mid-nineteenth-century America as they set about finalizing their relations with the original Americans.

These assumptions were that the American nation, through its governing and military agencies, was entitled to make and then break at will treaties with the tribes; that the nation had the right to ask the Indians to change their culture, including economic systems and religion; and that the government had the right to remove Indian groups from ancestral homelands. Indeed if in some cases it chose not to pursue one or any of these policies, it was an American decision, not one made in recognition of the Indians as partners in a negotiating process. Any acts of humanity toward the Indians were considered to be largesse on the part of the American authorities, not something to which the Indians were entitled by virtue of their status either as individuals or as part of a legitimate people, culture, or ethnic group.

The assumptions that underlay Carleton's conviction about the correctness of his Indian policy could be justified by his belief in the doctrine of Manifest Destiny and his belief in Christianity as a civilizing tool. Carleton made other assumptions when it came to practical matters pertaining to the plan, and these proved harder to justify.

Moving rapidly, he decided that largely empty southeastern New

CHAPTER THREE

Mexico offered the best place for a reservation, and he personally selected a forty-square-mile area on the Pecos River known as Bosque Redondo ("Round Grove"). The site was 150 miles south of Fort Union and 165 miles southeast of Santa Fe. On this land, which had seen no previous development and had poor soil, he proposed to locate all of the Navajos then living in what is now northwest New Mexico and northeast Arizona and all of the Mescaleros then scattered through the Davis, White, Sierra Blanca, Sacramento, and Capitan mountains.

The Navajos and the Mescaleros were traditional enemies; Carleton assumed they would live together in peace. He assumed the Indians could be persuaded to change their way of life from seminomadic to agricultural, sedentary, and Christian, writing in one report that only the first generation would remember the old ways, while the children would grow up as members of a new generation with new ideals of virtue and duty, becoming, as he put it, "tamed" and "civilized." Carleton also made the assumption that the new reservation, often referred to as Fair Carletonia in its early days, was large enough and fertile enough to supply the food needs of the Indian population he envisioned living there in perpetuity.

Construction of a new fort, named for Colonel Edwin Sumner, the first commander of the Ninth Military Department, began in 1862 on land immediately adjacent to the Bosque Redondo. Fort Sumner was not completed until several years later, with much of the work done by Indians interred on the reservation. Even as the project got under way, a few voices of protest were heard. Dr. Michael Steck, now serving as superintendent of Indian affairs for the Interior Department, objected to the plan on the grounds that the Bosque Redondo was too small and arid to support both Mescaleros and Navajos, and that it was dangerous to place enemy tribes on the same land. After battling Carleton bureaucratically for two years, Steck resigned his post in 1865.

Connelly and the Territorial Legislature, on the other hand, were amenable to the mass removal of the Navajos to a reservation far from the traditional homeland to which they held title by virtue of several treaties with the government. Connelly informed Congress that valuable minerals could be found in Navajo country but could not be exploited as long as the Indians possessed the lands.

Carson's reoccupation of Fort Stanton in the fall of 1862 brought the army back into the Hondo Valley and surrounding area for the first time since the early days of the Civil War. Prior to that time, the army had induced the Mescaleros to remain in confined areas and cease livestock raiding in exchange for essential foodstuffs given to them on a regular basis at Fort Stanton. In the absence of the army, the Mescaleros had resumed raiding for livestock, and settlers in the area had in turn resumed retaliatory raids against the Indians.

Facing a situation requiring immediate action, Carson had in his hands written orders from Carleton which included instructions to kill all Mescalero Indian men resisting transfer and keep the women and children as prisoners at the fort. Male Indians agreeing to confinement, together with the women and children, were to be transferred to the Bosque Redondo, where they would be guarded by five companies of troops at Fort Sumner. In actuality Carson pursued a policy of subduing and transferring the Mescaleros, but he never carried out the order to kill all male Indians resisting transfer.

Early on in the series of skirmishes between Fort Stanton soldiers and Indians that ensued, however, an important and tragic encounter took place, when troops opened fire on a party of Mescaleros traveling to Santa Fe to meet with Carleton, hoping, they said, to "parley a peace."[10] Among the ten Mescaleros killed were one woman and two leading chiefs, Manuelito and José Largo. Toward the end of 1862, following a battle at Dog Canyon near the Guadalupe Mountains, Carson permitted a group of Indians to go to Carleton in Santa Fe, where the general informed them of the plan to place all of the tribe at Bosque Redondo. Told they would be hunted down and remorselessly killed if they did not submit, the tribal representatives reluctantly agreed to the removal.

By March of 1863, around four hundred Mescaleros had been taken east across the plains from Fort Stanton to Fort Sumner on the Pecos, a distance of about one hundred miles. Although additional removals to the Pecos eventually swelled the numbers of Mescaleros to close to eight hundred, the campaign to bring in the entirety of this mountain-dwelling, nomadic tribe never achieved total success; the Mescaleros continually managed to slip away from the Bosque Redondo in small groups and return to their native lands. And in 1865, a particularly harsh year of deprivation for the interred Indians, virtually all of the five hundred Mescaleros then at the Bosque Redondo fled confinement and filtered back into hidden strongholds in the Sacramento and White mountains.

In early 1863, however, it appeared to Carleton that the Mescaleros were under control. Carson, too, seemed to feel that the fight with the Mescaleros was essentially complete; upon receiving news of the Mescaleros' acquiescence to removal, Carson wrote to Carleton stating his desire to return to his family and asking to resign from the army. But

CHAPTER THREE

Carleton, who had prepared for the coming Navajo campaign by having Lieutenant Colonel J. Francisco Chaves oversee construction of Fort Wingate on the eastern border of Navajo country, was determined that Carson should continue as commander of field forces and declined to accept Carson's resignation.

Carson's desire to return to Taos undoubtedly was genuine, but he also had misgivings about the harshness of the campaign, evidenced by his response to the incident in which the chiefs Manuelito and José Largo had been killed unnecessarily while on a mission of peace; Carson had seen to it that the bodies were returned in honor to the tribe. Despite his misgivings, however, Carson allowed himself to be convinced by Carleton that he must see the campaign through to its end and move on to Navajo country as the next theater of action.

By late spring of 1863, Carson had gathered his officer staff and troops for what was intended to be the last war against the Navajo. A small war in a sparsely populated and remote place, the campaign of attrition and sporadic military battles went all but unnoticed by the nation at large during a year that proved to be the climactic one in the Civil War, as the tide turned against the Confederacy and in favor of the Union in the great battles at Chancellorsville, Vicksburg, and Gettysburg. By the end of the year, the Confederacy no longer had the capacity to win its independence by military means.

A total of about one thousand troops served under Carson in the Navajo campaign, operating out of forts Wingate and Canby. Although many of the officers had come to New Mexico with the California Column, one of Carson's staff officers was Lawrence G. Murphy, later a powerful political and commercial figure in Lincoln County. The army's fighting capacity was augmented by Ute Indians, who were paid as scouts and fighters.

As they headed west from Las Lunas in early July 1863, Carson and his men faced an enemy widely dispersed in isolated settlements and long accustomed to a seminomadic existence in a region of sparse vegetation, stony soil, deep canyons, high mesas, forbidding volcanic outcroppings, and little water either in the form of rain or rivers. An Athabaskan-speaking people, the Navajo had occupied the area since the late 1600s. Beginning as hunters and gatherers, they had incorporated into their economy several elements of Hispanic life. They grew small crops, had adopted the horse, and by the early 1800s were sheep and cattle herders of great skill. Along with the Navajos' increasing use of livestock as a means of survival came increasing dependence upon raiding as a source of sheep, cattle, and horses.

The relationship between the Spanish and the Navajos had been one of enmity and deep distrust from the beginning. A pattern of attack and counterattack, with private citizens permitted by Spanish and Mexican officials to form militias to raid the Indians for personal gain, had steadily heightened hostilities. Thousands of Indians had been captured and sold into servitude; children between five and fifteen years of age brought as much as two hundred dollars on the auction block in Santa Fe during the 1840s and 1850s.[11]

Soon after arriving in 1851 to head the Ninth Military Department, Colonel Edwin Vose Sumner concluded that "unless some change is made the war will be interminable."[12] Until it was undermined in 1853, Sumner's policy of trying to halt raiding by all parties succeeded in diminishing hostilities. After the death of the experienced Indian agent Henry Lafayette Dodge in 1856, hostilities worsened once again.

Fort Defiance in Canyon Bonito was on Navajo land taken by the army without prior consultation with the Indians. By 1858 the best grazing lands had been closed to the Navajos. Chief Manuelito, whose family previously had occupied land near the fort, herded his stock onto the closed-off land; soldiers killed sixty head of his stock. A short time later, apparently in retaliation, a Navajo warrior killed a black slave boy owned by an officer at Fort Defiance. The army refused offers of reparation and sent a punitive force against the Navajos. On Christmas Day of 1858 a treaty was signed at the fort, moving the eastern boundary of Navajo land far to the west, cheating the Navajos of land recognized as theirs by Meriwether in 1855. The Indians probably were not aware of the details of the treaty.[13]

By 1860, with less opportunity for crop farming on their remaining land, the Navajos had risen in united raiding, which caused Governor Abraham Rencher to call for militias and for Ute attacks on the Navajos. The militias proceeded to battle the Navajos even when Rencher retracted his call at the instruction of the secretary of the interior. At this point Canby, newly appointed field commander, initiated a joint military action against the Navajos by Utes, Pueblo Indians, civilian volunteers, and regular army forces.

Canby decided that relentless pursuit should be combined with deliberate burning of Indian hogans, fruit trees, fields, and livestock. By midyear the Navajos were starving in small wandering bands. By early 1861, just before Canby was called away to Civil War action on the Rio Grande, he reached agreement with fifty-four chiefs representing most of the Navajos that food, clothing, and protection would be provided

CHAPTER THREE

in return for complete cessation of hostilities. But when the army withdrew to fight the Confederates, the supplies were not provided, and the Indians grew desperate. Navajo attacks resumed.

It was this situation that Carson faced as he entered the harsh precincts of Navajo country in the summer of 1863. Even as Carleton had been building Fort Wingate, Indian delegations had come to him seeking peace; the general's response was that there would be no peace until the Navajos agreed to go to the Bosque Redondo.

There were no set battles, no large-scale encounters, no great victories when Carson and his troops headed into the trackless country where Navajo bands were camping, moving, hiding, and already suffering from the effects of years of fighting and drought. The soldiers followed up on reports of encampments, or followed such visual pointers as recently abandoned hogans or smoke seen in the distance. Their fighting encounters yielded little in the way of either captured or dead Navajos, despite the fact that the soldiers were the victors in most skirmishes. Nevertheless, with the army's firm intentions being testified to by burned crops wherever the military came across Navajo fields, groups of Navajos under chiefs or family leaders began walking in to surrender at Fort Wingate as the summer wore on.

By late 1863 several hundred Indians had been gathered at the fort and sent under guard to Carleton in Santa Fe. Carleton was not satisfied with the pace of the campaign or its meager results. He also expressed his disapproval of Carson's acquiescence to Ute sales of Navajos captured in battle. The Utes must transmit captured Navajos to the forts, Carleton insisted. He wanted all of the tribe to benefit from the education and opportunity he envisioned being offered at Bosque Redondo.

Carson sought permission to halt the campaign during the winter of 1863–64; Carleton refused the request. He believed a large group of Navajos were hidden in the fortress-like Canyon de Chelly, located in northeast Arizona and to that date never traversed by regular army forces. He ordered Carson to take Canyon de Chelly and force the Indians who had taken refuge there to surrender. Carson prepared his forces, but before his departure submitted an official request for blankets and other supplies for the additional Indians arriving daily at forts Canby and Wingate in rags and displaying signs of severe malnutrition and several infectious diseases.

On 6 January 1864 Carson and his troops left Fort Canby for Canyon de Chelly, reached six days later. The canyon walls were one thousand feet and more in height and nearly perpendicular. Heavy snow was on the ground and it was bitterly cold. Oak and cottonwood trees, as well as scrub oak and peach trees, all grew within the canyon. Entering the canyon's starkly majestic central corridor from the west, the army convoy proceeded with difficulty. Many of the mules stretched out in a long line and heavily laden with supplies slipped and broke down completely under the strain of movement along pathways of solid ice.

Indians were captured along the way; they were naked, freezing, and in starved condition, offering little resistance. Other Indians were high on the walls of the canyon, near the cliff houses of the Anasazi who once had lived there. When Carson refused to hold a peace council with the captured Navajos, those high up on the walls threw rocks down on the troops. Most had only bows and arrows, which did little damage from such a distance. The soldiers fired up at the Indians and their dead bodies fell down into the canyon. The remaining women, children, and old men were afraid to light fires for fear of giving away their places of hiding.

After many days of cold, death, and terrible uncertainty as they had no means of communicating from one group to another, the Indians surrendered. Three Indians went to Carson and spoke for all, saying they agreed to go to the Bosque Redondo. On 21 January 1864 Carson returned to Fort Canby, and the Indians began moving in to the forts to be held until time for their walk to a place known to them only by name.

The Long Walk began at Fort Wingate, proceeded through Albuquerque, then southeastward to Bosque Redondo, a distance of over three hundred miles. The Navajos walked in long lines under army guard. Army reports told of numerous deaths from natural causes along the way. The Indians told of additional deaths by gun at the hands of soldiers when stragglers fell behind or escape attempts were made.

The 1,500 Navajos delivered to Fort Sumner on March 12 joined some 500 Navajos already under internment on the Pecos. Tears flowed in emotional joy among the normally stoic Navajos as families were reunited and friends thought dead were seen to be still alive. An additional group of 2,500 Indians already was gathered at Fort Canby, farther to the west in Navajo country and therefore entailing an even lengthier walk to the new reservation. Of this group, 126 died before the trip could start. Dysentery and malaria were common among those being held for transfer.

Upon arrival at Bosque Redondo, the Navajos were permitted to build family hogans in the dispersed manner that characterized their settlements. All were put to work on irrigation projects and crop cultivation, although equipment and seed were always in short supply. Food shortages became a serious problem even during the first year of operations and steadily worsened as the number of Indians brought to Bosque Redondo grew larger. The Department of the Interior made clear that it regarded the fort and its Indian prisoners as an army project and refused to serve as the provider of food and clothing. The army bought whatever grain and beef provisions were offered by local settlers.

But the local market was unable to produce supplies sufficient to meet the growing demands of a fort and reservation whose population eventually numbered about twelve thousand. Rationing became necessary. Coupons were given to the Indians, redeemable for beef and flour. The coupons quickly became the only meaningful currency at Bosque Redondo. Corruption flourished even as hunger continued to plague the Indian population.

It became common practice for the Indians to dig with their hands through the manure of the soldiers' horses. The horses were fed corn; undigested grains of corn found in the manure were cleaned and cooked with water by the desperate Indians, who also resorted to trying to catch rabbits with their bare hands. Many Indians died of pneumonia, as there was never enough wood for fuel during the winter months. Indian agent Theodore Dodd reported that "during the severe cold weather last winter [1866–67] the Indians suffered a great deal for the want of wood, as they were compelled to go from six to twelve miles to procure mesquite roots and dig them up and pack them on their backs to their homes."[14]

By 1864 there were nine thousand Indians, of whom eighty-two hundred were Navajos, at Bosque Redondo. Carson, who again had been asking to resign from the military, was asked to take over as supervisor of the now clearly troubled reservation experiment. Carson spent three months on the Pecos, futilely struggling to overcome the problems of hunger, disease, supply shortages, fraud, and insect infestation of crops. He then resigned and went home to Taos. In the meantime army troops were still chasing down bands of Navajos who had either escaped and returned to northwest New Mexico or had never surrendered. Chief Manuelito did not surrender until 1866, when he arrived at Fort Wingate, wounded, and with his followers all in deteriorated condition. They were walked to Pecos country, where the famous warrior chief was welcomed with emotion by his people.

Crisis conditions prevailed at Bosque Redondo throughout 1865 and 1866. A succession of flood, severe frost, and drought resulted in total crop failure. Thousands of Indians died of starvation. Disease was rampant among a population weakened by hunger and lacking access to adequate medical care. "Of the 8,200 Navajos ultimately imprisoned at Bosque Redondo, at least 2,321 perished from smallpox, most of them in 1865."[15] A group of thirteen hundred Navajos escaped during the year, along with numerous Mescaleros, each group returning to its respective homeland.

Although the Indians at Bosque Redondo struggled to raise crops and learn the ways of sedentary farming, they did not change the religious beliefs and customs that lay at the heart of their culture. Both Navajos and Mescaleros continued to perform their traditional dances and reenact their mythic beliefs. Despite constant conflict between the two tribes, there was even a certain amount of eclectic borrowing of ritual from one group to another. And neither group ever ceased asking the authorities to be allowed to return to their traditional homeland, with the Navajos telling government officials they had been instructed by their "holy people" to remain within the boundaries of the Rio Grande, the Rio San Juan, and the Rio Colorado.[16]

By 1865 it was no longer possible to defend the Bosque Redondo as a noble experiment holding promise of a satisfying resolution of the Indian problem. The only aspect of Carleton's plan to have succeeded was the Carson campaign to coerce the Mescaleros and Navajos into surrender. In all other respects failure was nearly total. After the Indians were gathered at Bosque Redondo, the land proved too arid for subsistence farming, the bureaucracy failed to provide efficient and honest administration, the Indians did not adjust to a new homeland, and their physical misery was surpassed only by their spiritual misery.

Visiting Bosque Redondo in the summer of 1864 to assess the possibility of establishing a mission school, Bishop Lamy was appalled by what he saw.[17] Abject poverty, degradation and loss of pride, unchecked epidemics of disease, and outright starvation were not what New Mexicans had in mind when they demanded control of the Indians and protection of settlers and their property.

As newspaper reports heightened public awareness of conditions at the reservation, criticism of Carleton among ordinary citizens and government officials began to grow. And because he steadfastly defended Carleton, Connelly also became the target of growing dissatisfaction with the army's project on the Pecos. The public outcry prompted the Territorial Legislature to petition the secretary of war for a court of inquiry into the whole messy matter. On 16 July 1866 Connelly's term in office expired, and he was succeeded by Robert B. Mitchell. On 12

CHAPTER THREE

August following a brief illness, Connelly died in Santa Fe. In September, following the court of inquiry's investigation of Carleton's conduct in office, the strong-minded general was removed from his post as military commander in New Mexico. In April 1867 responsibility for the Indians at Bosque Redondo was transferred to the Department of the Interior.

Food supplies at Fort Sumner and Bosque Redondo improved during 1867, following the opening of a new cattle trail from Texas up the Pecos River. Nevertheless long-term prospects for viability continued bleak in the face of poor farming prospects, Indian intransigence, frequent escapes, and periodic raids on the Bosque Redondo by Comanches.[18] After lengthy negotiations, chiefs Manuelito and Barboncito were permitted in April of 1868 to journey to Washington, where they were taken to see President Andrew Johnson. The president did not immediately acquiesce to their request for permission to return to Navajo country, but he subsequently named a peace commission to consider the request.

Headed by General William T. Sherman, the commission toured the Bosque Redondo. Commission members reported their shock at the poverty and despair they encountered in what they called a desert environment. On 29 May 1868 Sherman met with Navajo chiefs and headmen. He told them they would be returned to their former homeland. Speaking for the tribe, Barboncito said to Sherman, "what you have said to me now I never will forget."[19] On 1 June twenty-nine Navajo leaders signed a treaty with the government, which was ratified by the Senate and proclaimed on 12 August. By mid-June, however, the Navajos had en masse begun the long walk home. The terms of the treaty gave them a reservation of 3.4 million acres, 10 percent of the land they had previously considered theirs.

In the meantime the Mescalero Apaches again were raiding across southeastern New Mexico and even into Texas and Mexico. They had no fixed land to call their own and viewed livestock raiding as a principal means of survival. From 1867 through 1872, their predatory actions had an inhibiting effect on settlement in the mountain valleys of southeastern New Mexico and eastward onto the grassy plains surrounding the Pecos Valley. Under Department of the Interior guidance, action to resolve the problem finally came on 29 May 1873, when a presidential executive order established a Mescalero reservation in the Sacramento Mountains. The reservation contained about forty square miles of which only about six hundred acres were suitable for cultivation.

A final move to make the entire Llano Estacado safe for settlement came in 1874, when a winter campaign launched from forts Union, Bascom, and Sumner defeated the Comanche, who had been raiding eastern New Mexico from bases in the southern plains of Kansas and Colorado.

By the time of statehood, there were approximately twenty thousand Indians living in New Mexico, of whom about half were Navajos.

Kit Carson did not live to see the resolutions that provided reservations for the Indians and a modicum of peace for the rapidly evolving territory he had chosen as his home. After a reunion with his family following his term as Bosque Redondo administrator, Carson had decided to accept the post of commander of Fort Garland in southern Colorado. Carson moved his entire family to the fort, although he retained ownership of the family home in Taos.

An old injury stemming from a horse accident was causing health problems for Carson. His aorta, pressing against the trachea of his upper chest, had ruptured, rendering Carson, then in his mid-fifties, subject to frequent bouts of pain and coughing. His condition worsening, Carson resigned his command of the fort in July 1867. He and his family remained in southern Colorado, spending much of their time with friends who had a ranch at the settlement of Boggsville, near the mouth of Las Animas River. Despite a reputation so widespread and unsullied that prominent political leaders had regularly visited him at Fort Garland, Carson found himself without income and too weakened by illness to engage in ranching following his resignation. The oldest of his six living children was then sixteen, and his wife was expecting their eighth child.

In February of 1868 the old warrior gathered his energies for one last effort; in response to a request from the commissioner of Indian affairs, Carson traveled by stage coach and train to Washington, where he was greeted and acclaimed by the president, congressional leaders, and old comrades in arms. He also sought medical help in Washington and New York, but to no avail. Although he had felt a resurgence of strength at the start of the journey, by its end he was severely weakened from the exertion. Josefa was waiting for her husband at La Junta, Colorado, upon his return in April and was frightened by his pallor and weakness. On 23 April 1868, fifteen days after giving birth to a baby girl who survived, Josefa Carson died at the age of forty-one.

Kit Carson's condition deteriorated rapidly; he was taken to the rough adobe house of the military surgeon at Fort Lyon, five miles east of Boggsville. There, attended by a friend and the doctor, he accepted unflinchingly the telling signs that his time had come. He died at Fort Lyon on 23 May 1868.[20] The bodies of Carson and his wife eventually were brought to Taos for burial in the Taos Cemetery, also the final resting place of Padre Martínez, the famous pastor of Taos who had married them.

Events in southeastern New Mexico, from 1855 when Fort Stanton was built on through the 1880s, were intertwined with the ebb and flow of efforts to control the Indians. It is true that a reputation for Indian troubles deterred many pioneers from choosing the wilds of southeastern New Mexico as a place to settle. But it is equally true that for numbers of hardy, entrepreneurial souls, the ongoing Indian wars presented commercial opportunities too rare to pass up.

Isolated at long distances from urban centers, the two southeastern forts—one on the Pecos River, the other on the Rio Bonito in mountain country—both had need of regular sources of supply for goods and services ranging from lumber to blacksmithing, from wheat flour to vegetables to beef. And whether it was the Bosque Redondo or the Mescalero reservation, the existence of reservations where the government had committed itself to ensuring certain minimal Indian provisions also offered an opportunity for local citizens to contract with the government to supply needed goods.

Among those who carved out personal commercial niches in the military-Indian network was Dr. Joseph C. Blazer. His experience illustrates the possibilities that were opened to the enterprising as a result of the military's activities. Blazer was a dentist from the Midwest who had served in the Union Army during the Civil War. After the war he became a trader, buying up surplus military supplies and taking them to El Paso to sell. He then obtained a government contract to haul supplies to Fort Stanton. Arriving in the Hondo Valley in 1866, Blazer bought an interest in land that included a sawmill. By the mid 1870s Fort Stanton was a four-company post with responsibility for guarding some twelve hundred Mescalero Apaches living on the newly established Mescalero reservation.

Recognizing that the requirements of the fort offered a steady demand for lumber products, Blazer bought out his partners and became sole owner of the sawmill in 1877. For a number of years the mill had furnished lumber to the military and Indian agencies at forts Stanton, Sumner, Selden, Bliss, and Davis. Blazer's Mill was also a principal source of lumber for the growing number of settlers in the Hondo Valley. In the early years of Blazer's operation, the Mescaleros were as wary of him as of other whites, particularly as numerous attempts were being made by ranchers and others to encroach upon reservation lands. But within a few years Blazer had won enduring respect and affection from the Mescaleros as a result of his fair treatment of them.[21]

Although its origins remain shrouded in mystery because its inhabitants left no written records, the once extant Hispanic community of Missouri Plaza offers another example of the galvanizing impact of military activity in the area. What is known of Missouri Plaza comes from the reports of visitors to the small town during its brief existence.

In 1867 J. Francisco Chaves, campaigning as a candidate for delegate to Congress, traveled south along the Pecos River from Las Vegas to Fort Sumner and on to the North Spring junction with the Pecos, where Roswell later would be located. Traveling by coach, he then turned west and following a rough cart road soon found himself in a small but bustling community laid out in typical Spanish fashion with a plaza and surrounding houses, beyond which lay cultivated fields.

The site of the community was fifteen miles southwest of present-day Roswell, on the north bank of the Rio Hondo. Chaves was welcomed, and he stayed overnight in the town, which was home to between thirty and forty families of Hispanic descent. Residents told Chaves they had come from Manzano in Valencia County, and that many of the men had been freighters to Kansas and to St. Joseph, Missouri. They had decided to name their new settlement "La Plaza de Missouri in order to give it distinction."[22] The following day Chaves was escorted by Missouri Plaza residents to La Placita on the Rio Bonito, thirty-five miles west and the nearest settlement to Missouri Plaza; in 1869 La Placita was renamed Lincoln and made the county seat.

In 1868 the first surveyors of the Roswell area recorded the presence of Missouri Plaza, noting in their official report that the town's first houses had been built in 1867. Missouri Plaza residents apparently intended to raise crops to sell as food and forage at Fort Stanton, which lay forty-five miles to their west, and at Fort Sumner, about fifty-five miles to the northeast. The site they selected was an excellent one for agricultural purposes. Water flow in the Rio Hondo was sufficient for several hundred acres of cultivation, and the grazing range was sufficiently covered with grass to sustain sheep and cattle.

Because no records were left, it is not possible to know precisely what caused the abrupt abandonment of Missouri Plaza in 1871–72. But several events had occurred that would have had a devastating impact

CHAPTER THREE

on whatever hopes the townspeople had of earning income as suppliers to the forts. In January of 1868, the settler Robert Casey bought land and a grist mill on the Rio Hondo, six miles below the junction of the Rio Bonito and Rio Ruidoso, where the Hondo is formed. The mill's overshot water wheel was operated with river water. At that time no settlers lay between the Casey land and Missouri Plaza, farther downstream. But within a few years the twenty-five-mile distance was filled in with new people drawing even more water from the Hondo.

Casey later wrote, "when we came here that [Missouri Plaza] was the biggest town in this country . . . we took all of the water away from them and dried them out."[23] And in the summer of 1868, demand for food supplies at Fort Sumner abruptly diminished as the Navajos left Bosque Redondo and returned to their homeland. By the summer of 1869, most of the troops stationed at Fort Sumner also had been transferred elsewhere, as the fort ceased to operate as a regular military post.

There were, as seen in the examples of Joseph Blazer and Missouri Plaza, cases of both success and failure as settlers looked to the military forts for a means of getting a start in a new place. In general, however, the forts may be characterized in an economic sense as focal points that offered the possibility of initial financial security for enterprises that might then prove capable of surviving on their own. A government contract to supply a military fort was the opening wedge for business ventures that might later find wider markets.

The beef-cattle industry of southeastern New Mexico preeminently exemplifies this phenomenon of the military's catalytic impact. In a few short years it rose from nonexistence to the stunning size and soaring profitability of a great cattle boom that was unlike anything seen before or since on the windswept plains of Pecos country. While Texas cattlemen undoubtedly would have eventually spread west into New Mexico, the fact remains that they discovered just how ideally suited to their enterprise the southeast plains were as a direct result of the news that beef supplies were urgently needed at Fort Sumner in the mid-1860s. The military forts thus were a spark lighting a fire that burned on long after they were gone.

It was the early Spanish explorers who first brought cattle to Mexico, and it was there that the longhorn strain developed. In time the mossy-headed, leathery longhorns crossed the Rio Grande into Texas, where they found a natural home. Texas settlers frequently entered the cattle business by rounding up wild longhorns and starting a herd. In the early days, with no developed cattle market, many cattle were slaughtered for the tallow and hide, products that could be shipped without refrigeration. Juan de Oñate brought the first cattle into New Mexico in 1598. But in New Mexico it was sheep rather than cattle that became the economic mainstay of Hispanic agriculturists. And even after Anglo settlers began bringing cattle into the territory after the American conquest, sheep raising remained predominant, and Texas continued to dominate the beef-cattle industry.

In the year 1866 Charles Goodnight and Oliver Loving changed all that with one bold stroke, when they struck west across the lower Pecos and blazed a new cattle trail northward. As a result of their decisive response to the need for beef at Fort Sumner, the grazing lands of New Mexico's public domain were developed by a new industry; such local markets as military forts, Indian reservations, settler towns, and mining areas were supplied from a source within the territory; and New Mexico became the site of several major cattle trails leading to marketing centers in the Midwest and West.

Goodnight and Loving, both experienced Texas trail drivers, joined forces on the upper Brazos River and headed southwest to Horsehead Crossing on the Pecos River, two hundred miles south of Roswell. After crossing the river and trailing their cattle up its west side, they delivered most of their combined herd of twenty-two hundred steers to Fort Sumner in June 1866, before Oliver Loving continued on north to Denver. The route established by Goodnight and Loving became the standard trail for cattle drives from New Mexico and Texas to markets in Colorado and Wyoming.[24]

In December 1866 fellow Texan John Chisum joined Goodnight at Fort Sumner with six hundred steers he had driven up the new trail. By the spring of 1867, so many cattle were moving up the new trail that a cattle rest and campground was started near the confluence of the Rio Hondo and the Pecos, where Roswell now stands. Camped there in the spring were trail drivers for Hubbard and Farrar of San Saba, Texas, with sixteen hundred head of cattle. The Rio Hondo cattle rest was known to have better water and grass than any other site along the Pecos from Fort Sumner to south of Horsehead Crossing. Later in 1867 Loving was wounded by bow and arrow during an Indian attack while on the trail at Loving Bend on the Pecos; he died several days later after reaching Fort Sumner.

In 1868 Goodnight and Chisum formed a partnership. Chisum delivered cattle to a new headquarters established at Bosque Grande, south of Fort Sumner. Chisum received from Goodnight a price equal to the price per head paid in Texas plus one dollar per head in profit.

CHAPTER THREE

The cattlemen of the early boom years were tough and aggressive, waging incessant battle against Indian raiders, cattle rustlers, periodic droughts, and prairie grass fires. And from the beginning they showed no mercy toward sheep ranchers and small farmers wherever they were encountered, but particularly in the mountain foothills where cattle kingdoms rapidly took hold once the initial trails had been blazed and the suitability of the new land to cattle had been favorably assessed.

During the 1870s several national factors, including increasing urbanization, the expansion of the railroad system, and new methods of shipping refrigeration, combined to increase the demand for beef and facilitate the development of the beef-cattle industry. Southeastern New Mexico benefited from the existence of a national cattle-marketing system. Its public domain was used to graze ever-larger herds, and its trails were heavily used by both New Mexico and Texas cattlemen. In 1872 H. M. Beckwith of Seven Rivers, twelve miles north of present-day Carlsbad, reported that 90,000 head of cattle moved up the Goodnight-Loving Trail to market during that one year alone.

By 1880 there were 3,750,000 cattle on the western ranges of the United States. Some 500,000 of them were in the territory of New Mexico, and of that total, 300,000 were grazed in Lincoln County, which at that time comprised almost all of southeastern New Mexico. Governor L. Bradford Prince reported in 1881 that young cows and calves were bringing $25 and high-grade bulls $75.[25]

But nothing remains unchanged forever; southeastern New Mexico's cattle boom was over by the mid 1890s. Like many other parts of the West, the Pecos rangelands became overstocked and overgrazed. When the inevitable happened, in the form of a severe drought, the consequences were devastating for the land, for the cattle, and for the wealthy, colorful cattle barons who had built their fortunes on a now no longer tenable system of freewheeling use of the public domain. The beef-cattle industry survived, but in changed form, as cattlemen cut back on the size of their herds, strove to ensure survivability by drilling waterholes and building windmills, and eventually enclosing their herds on privately owned or leased ranchland.

The drought of 1886–87 was called "the great die-up," and it stretched across cow country from Texas through all of New Mexico east of the Rio Grande and north through Colorado, Wyoming, Montana, and into Canada. A bitterly cold winter was followed by an almost total lack of rainfall during the spring and summer months. The carrying capacity of the land fell precipitously. On the rangeland lying on both sides of the Pecos and stretching west of the river as far as the mountains, thousands of cattle died, as tributaries to the Pecos dried up, and prairie grasses grew sparsely or not at all.

Although the drought of 1886–87 was a sobering experience for the cattlemen of southeastern New Mexico, it had the beneficial effect of forcing them to adopt sounder methods of managing their livestock and the land. Cattle continued to be the mainstay of the region's economy.

James F. Hinkle of Roswell, who joined the CA Bar Ranch in 1885 and was manager until its closeout in 1901, recorded his memories of the last big roundup carried out in the old way as a joint undertaking by all the cattle ranchers grazing cattle on range from fifty miles west of the Pecos to fifty miles east. It took place in 1894. A total of 50,000 head of cattle were driven into the Roswell area by about 175 cowboys, each with a string of 6 to 8 horses, a total of about 1,000 "cow horses." The roundup covered about twelve thousand square miles and took four weeks to complete, with each section covered by cowboys working under an assigned leader.[26]

Patterns of land use underwent several major changes in southeastern New Mexico between the 1860s and the 1890s. At the beginning of the period, Indians were a shifting presence across land they still regarded as their own, while Hispanic sheep ranchers and small farmers were establishing a strong base for future growth in several pockets of settlement. Then came the middle of the period, the 1870s and 1880s, a time during which Anglos in general and cattlemen in particular gained the upper hand, as they saw the Indian threat recede and as they undertook on their own to eliminate competing sheep ranchers by consolidating their control of water sources. And finally came the late 1880s and early 1890s, which, ironically enough, saw cattlemen forced to retrench in the face of overgrazed land and falling cattle prices.

The Indians did not get back any land, of course, and Hispanic settlers who had lost cropland or pasturage were not in general able to capitalize on the fact that cattlemen now operated under more stringent guidelines. But farming and sheep ranching did return to the region, this time in the hands of Anglo agriculturists: unlike their Hispanic predecessors, they were able to survive and sometimes flourish both in the mountain valleys and in the fertile portions of the Pecos Valley.

The amount of cultivated acreage in New Mexico increased throughout the 1880s, and nowhere did it increase more rapidly than in the middle Pecos Valley around Roswell.[27] It was recognized as well that many acres of land in the area were even better suited to sheep than to cattle.

CHAPTER THREE

The first Anglo sheep rancher to bring flocks into the Roswell area was Judge Edmund T. Stone, who arrived in 1878 after traveling from Colorado City with his sons John and Price and fifteen hundred sheep. Stone irrigated his land and also started a fruit orchard. Soon after, James M. Miller bought sheep in the Roswell area, started his own ranch, and became one of the territory's biggest sheep producers. By the 1890s sheep ranching was contributing strongly, along with cattle raising, to the economic viability of Roswell.

The land itself was determining the course of development in the region. In addition to its suitability for cattle, sheep, grains, fruit, and lumber in various locations, the land also yielded up for a brief, glorious period that most desired of all resources—gold. It was found in the Sacramento Mountains in amounts large enough to justify full-scale commercial development and a gold rush that brought in miners, settlers, engineers, and lawyers from many parts of the country. The gold rush resulted in the overnight building of a boldly confident new town called White Oaks. Located twelve miles northeast of present-day Carrizozo at an elevation of sixty-five hundred feet, White Oaks was the largest town in all southeast New Mexico during the early 1890s, with a population of twenty-five hundred.

The first discovery of gold in solid rock veins was made in 1866 by a Billy Gills on the small Jicarilla Indian Reservation that had been established sixteen miles southeast of the later site of White Oaks. A short time later, Congress abolished the reservation and moved the Indians elsewhere.[28] Some years later a major discovery was made by a Missouri prospector named John Baxter. The gold ore was found near a clump of white oak trees and the place instantly became the boom town of White Oaks.

By 1882 production of gold from underground mines was well under way, and the population had reached five hundred, mostly men and many still living in tents while awaiting completion of the boarding houses and hotels that were springing up in a profusion of Victorian-influenced styles. There was no shortage of saloons. Rising in gently rounded conical form just west of the town proper was Baxter Mountain, where the richest of the gold-bearing formations were found. Over the course of twenty years, from 1880 to 1900, the gold mines of White Oaks produced $4.5 million worth of the precious metal.

But White Oaks declined almost as rapidly as it had arisen. In 1893 the owners of two of the three large mines began to think about selling their holdings. Several interested buyers appeared on the scene to negotiate with the mine owners but withdrew after learning that the richest veins were giving out, that the better ores now lay at increased depths, and that the mines required large new expenditures for such surface equipment as hoists and compressors.

Shortly after the turn of the century, with lower grades of ore resulting in lower profits for the mine owners, the last of the major mines was closed down.[29] With most of its population already drifting away, White Oaks then suffered a further blow that ended forever the dream its hustling newspaper once had touted, of becoming a metropolis of the American West. In 1902 a new rail line going north from El Paso toward northeast New Mexico was completed. White Oaks residents had been asked to pay a $50,000 bonus to the railroad company in return for the building of the line through their community; they had refused. The railroad company laid out a new town, Carrizozo, and built the line through the new town instead of through White Oaks. Within a few years White Oaks was a ghost town.

4

Power and Populism

*H*AVING BEGUN AS A TRICKLE DURING THE 1850S AND 1860S, EMIgration to the southeastern New Mexico frontier swelled during the 1880s and 1890s like water rushing through a break in a sea wall. And like the nation's other frontiers, this one, too, was a place where an unmistakably American brand of rugged individualism flourished. In addition the very suddenness of the region's surge in historical momentum tended to attract individuals who were either especially ambitious, or outcasts, wanderers, or outlaws, or simply in need of new beginnings.

Inevitably then, the history of the development decades is a story of bold moves, power grabs, conflicts of interest, and clashing personalities. It is the winners who stand out in the historical record. Yet here as everywhere, history was in fact multilayered, and within it were many swirling eddies where people and whole groups were sometimes losers as a result of either prejudices carried to the new frontier from older places or disparities in the amount of wealth and influence held by the various players in the game of life being played on this new field of action.

For despite the fact that emigrants came as single individuals or in family units, together they formed groups representative of their original cultures and lifestyles. Southeastern New Mexico became a crossroads where incoming groups from a number of distinctive origins converged; out of this confluence of settler groups there emerged a new society with its own social order based on cultural and economic differentiations.

Hispanos moved into the southeast quadrant not only from north-central New Mexico but also from Texas and Mexico. Anglo settlers tended to emigrate principally from Texas, from the Old South, and from previous points of pioneering settlement such as Missouri, Colorado, and sometimes California. It is the Texas cattlemen, the British and other foreign investors, and the railroad builders and land grabbers who made the biggest names for themselves in the heady days of late-nineteenth-century development of the Pecos country and its western rim in the mountains. But beneath this overlay of risk-taking empire building lies the fact that Anglo economic development was superimposed upon an established pattern of small-scale Hispanic settlement in *placitas* (towns) and on sheep ranches and small farms along the valleys of the Rio Hondo, the North Spring, and Berrendo rivers, at Roswell, and the Rio Feliz, south of Roswell.

The Hispanic people of New Mexico continued to speak Spanish and to perpetuate the customs of their Spanish and Mexican heritage, a right guaranteed them under terms of the Treaty of Guadalupe Hidalgo, which made them citizens of the United States. Throughout the territorial period, all official documents and voter ballots were printed both in Spanish and in English, in recognition of the dual language reality.[1]

As Anglo and Hispanic settlers in southeastern New Mexico came into closer proximity, however, Anglo perceptions of Hispanos were colored not only by such discernible reminders of cultural difference as language but also by attitudes carried by Anglos from regions where negative stereotypes of the Mexican people had gained wide currency over preceding decades. In the years immediately following the American conquest, a spate of books, travelers' reports, and letters "from Santa Fe traders, California merchants, and Texas colonists" had all conveyed to Americans living in the East and Midwest, some of whom would themselves be moving westward, that Hispanic people were less moral, less hard-working, less frugal, and less enterprising than were U.S. citizens of Anglo descent. Although later reports were more favorable, and the overt and socially condoned prejudice of the 1850s had largely dissipated by the Civil War period, many emigrants to New Mexico nevertheless arrived with highly distorted perceptions of Hispanos and their culture.[2]

No documents exist to confirm the exact date of the earliest Hispanic settlement in southeastern New Mexico. But by the 1850s settlers were farming in the Hondo Valley and had founded La Placita on the Rio Bonito, later renamed Lincoln. And it is known that by 1850 Hispanic settlers were engaged in placer gold mining in the Jicarilla Mountains near the later site of White Oaks.³ Amelia Bolton Church, an early Roswell resident who had lived in Lincoln as a young girl, said that El Torreon, Lincoln's lookout tower and place of protection from Indian attacks, "was built between 1840 and 1850, according to all of the native people who were here at the time I came to Lincoln to live, which was 1873. Andricus Trujillo, the man who built it, died in 1870."⁴ The construction date for El Torreon was not recorded, however, and the three-story stone tower may have been built as late as 1863, following a series of Indian raids that resulted in the deaths of several farmers and sheepherders on the Rio Ruidoso and the Rio Bonito.

Trujillo claimed to have been the first settler of La Placita, and he, like those who joined him in the narrow, winding valley with its rounded hills and rushing mountain stream, was said to have come from either the Rio Grande valley or the Manzano Mountains, east of Albuquerque. Trujillo also was said by his neighbors and family to have been "a strong penitente," which if true would strengthen the case for a Manzano Mountains origin for the Hondo Valley settlers, as the indigenous Penitente brotherhood, a secretive and stringently ascetic Catholic lay organization never condoned by the church hierarchy, was particularly strong in the mountain villages of north-central New Mexico.⁵

Manzano Mountains emigrants also were the founders of Missouri Plaza, on the Rio Hondo southwest of Roswell, and El Berrendo, in north Roswell, communities that came into existence in the mid-1860s. Developing in the same area at the same time was another small Hispanic settlement, observed in 1867 by a U.S. surveyor, who called it Rio Hondo. (The cattle rest being developed just to the west on the Hondo also was referred to as Rio Hondo.) Located in what is now southeast Roswell, the Hispanic settlement of Rio Hondo survived to become a large barrio within Roswell and in later years became known as Chihuahuita in recognition of the fact that many of its residents came from the Mexican state of Chihuahua.

Even by the turn of the century and the decade that led to statehood in 1912, a difference between the Hispanic settlements in the mountains and the one at Roswell was apparent. Roswell became the county seat of the new Chaves County in 1889; Lincoln lost its county-seat status to Carrizozo and its economic status to Roswell. As a result of these changes, it was Roswell that became the region's agricultural and commercial center, attracting growing numbers of Hispanic workers from Mexico and Texas in the decades following the founding of Rio Hondo (Chihuahuita).

CHAPTER FOUR

Chihuahuita became a multigenerational community with an eclectic Hispanic culture merging the folkways of Mexico, the Mexican traditions of Texas, and the more purely Spanish traditions brought from north-central New Mexico. Descendents of the early Hispanic settlers in the Hondo Valley, on the other hand, retained much of their traditional body of crafts, music, and religious custom, as their communities remained small and somewhat insular despite infusions of migrant workers from Mexico over the years. But even as the social traditions of Hondo Valley Hispanos remained largely intact, their economic position changed; while the earliest valley residents had raised corn and sheep on their own land, which usually had been claimed under the "squatter's rights" system that prevailed until passage of the Homestead Act, many Hispanos in the valley became cowboys, sheepherders and farmworkers for Anglo settlers as the years went by.

It was the construction of Fort Stanton, ten miles west of La Placita in 1855, that marked the beginning of Anglo settlement along the Rio Ruidoso and Rio Bonito, the two small rivers that join to form the Hondo and are considered part of the Hondo Valley. The father of Amelia Bolton Church was one of the young soldiers stationed at Fort Stanton. Bolton's wife and children, including Amelia, who had been born in 1862, came directly from Wexford in Ireland to Lincoln County to join Bolton in 1871. After living first at the fort, the family built a house in Lincoln, where young Amelia observed that despite social separation between Anglos and Hispanos, "at least ninety percent of the American men married Mexican women."[6] Even if this estimate is an exaggeration, it is a fact that Hispanic women were more numerous than Anglo women in frontier Lincoln, and that ethnic intermarriage was one of the means by which a number of Hispanic customs were introduced to Anglo settlers.

Adobe-walled corrals were used throughout southeastern New Mexico, for instance, adopted by Anglo sheep ranchers and cattlemen, who had used only wooden corrals before coming to New Mexico. Wooden beams were referred to as *vigas*, the Spanish word for beams, by Anglos and Hispanos alike. And an original plat for land in Roswell dated 1885 shows three irrigation ditches, listing them not by the English word but rather by the Spanish term, *acequitas*.

The first Anglo known to have settled in what is now Chaves County was Heiskell Jones, who arrived with his family in July of 1866 and lived for some time at a site about six miles above the confluence of the Hondo and the Pecos.[7] But only a handful of Anglos came to this eastern portion of Lincoln County before the late 1870s. Even in 1878, seven years after the first land claims at Roswell, only two Anglo families lived at Roswell, while there were many more Hispanic families at the El Berrendo and Rio Hondo sites north and southeast of Roswell.

Anglo settlement at Roswell and on nearby farms and ranches accelerated during the 1880s; among the few hundred courageous souls who came to pioneer in a remote, treeless place two hundred miles from the nearest rail depot and lacking access to many essential goods, there was a high percentage of emigrants from the South and from Texas. "The southern link with early Roswell was strong."[8] In 1878 town resident Ash Upson, an itinerant newspaperman whose observant eye missed little, wrote to his sister in Connecticut: "Several from here have gone back to Mississippi to harvest their cotton. They come from Satartia, Yazoo County and Warrenton."[9]

The link with the South remained strong even after the initial settlement period. Upson was referring in his letter to the family of Joseph C. Lea, the man whose consistent promotion of Roswell laid the foundation for its emergence as a viable town. But numerous other early settlers also had southern roots.

Jack B. "Billy" Mathews, who came to Roswell in the mid-1870s and gained fame as the deputy who wounded Billy the Kid in 1878, had been discharged from the Confederate Army at Pulaski, Tennessee, in 1865. Martin V. Corn, also a Confederate veteran, arrived from Kerrville, Texas, in 1878, to become a prominent farmer. James Oliver Carper, born in West Virginia in 1880, arrived in Roswell in a wagon train at the age of eight with his family. Lillie Roberts, who later married cattleman-politician-banker James F. Hinkle, came to Roswell at the age of twelve from Gillespie, Texas. Lily James Kellahin arrived in 1893 from Delhi, Louisiana. Georgia B. Redfield, who reached Roswell in 1893, was also from Louisiana.

Granville A. Richardson, who came to Roswell as a young lawyer in 1888 and went on to become Roswell's most prominent judge, came from Kentucky. Charles L. Ballard, born in Texas in 1866, arrived in New Mexico in 1878, making his way from Fort Sumner to Lincoln before settling upon Roswell as his permanent home. John R. Joyce, partner in the early mercantile business Joyce-Pruit Co., was a native of Tennessee. Lucius Dills, early newspaper owner and attorney, was born in Kentucky, moved to Texas, and then moved to New Mexico in the early 1880s. Among those who came to southeastern New Mexico from Missouri was the sheep rancher James M. Miller, who moved west to Colorado before coming to New Mexico in 1878.[10]

Chisum's cattle operation, headquartered after 1875 at South Spring south of Roswell, provides insight into the pattern of hierarchical relationships that came to prevail on the southeastern frontier. The ranch was owned by an extended family of Anglo origin. The family had roots in the Old South, followed by an emigrating period in Texas before the start of the cattle industry in New Mexico. The hundreds of Chisum cowboys who worked the herds and filled foreman jobs included both Anglos and Hispanos, while a few of the cowboys were blacks from the South. Extra cowhands hired during roundups were usually Hispanic, and most had been born of parents who lived in the territory prior to the 1846 conquest.

The case of John Chisum and black cowboy Frank Chisum provides an example of post–Civil War adjustment by at least one white southerner. John Chisum had owned slaves in Texas; during the Civil War he freed them. He took to raise in his home a five-year-old black boy whose name was Frank and to whom he gave his family name. Although free, Frank Chisum chose to go with Chisum as an employee when Chisum moved to New Mexico. While most blacks with cattle outfits were cooks, Frank Chisum was an all-round cowboy, whom Chisum repeatedly placed in positions of responsibility. Frank was a chronic stutterer and was frequently laughed at by fellow cowhands; he was said always to have responded with humor. During the early 1880s, Chisum culled a small herd of fine steers from his stock and gave them, perhaps in lieu of wages due, to Frank Chisum. After John Chisum's death, Frank Chisum ranched on his own, later retiring to Roswell, where he died as an old man with vivid memories of the early cattle empire.

In general a southern view of race relations held sway in the Roswell area during the development decades, and separatism marked the tenor of social relations between Anglos and Hispanos. "The Southern influence predominated in Roswell, so much so that when the word reached here that a traveling show was headed this way with 'Uncle Tom's Cabin' as the piece de resistance, a delegation on horseback met them at the outskirts of town and told them to move on. Without questioning their authority, they kept moving," one early resident recalled.[11] Judge Richardson, naming more than fifty early residents who played a part in the town's development, included only two Hispanos, Juan Chaves and Cosme Sedillo, in his list.[12]

Violence on many levels and in several forms accompanied, and was an outgrowth of, the settlement process from the 1870s to the 1890s.

This new land was untamed, not yet developed, and no one was yet consigned a place within it. The violence was an expression of the struggle for power before the lines were drawn and the social order set. Those who found a lucrative place in the earliest days by monopolizing some niche of economic activity felt entitled to defend it—sometimes violently—against assertive newcomers. Although violence in Lincoln County reached its zenith in the second half of the 1870s, southeastern New Mexico continued to experience "deeply felt social strife," often bursting forth in overt violence, throughout the 1880s and 1890s.[13]

Every conflict was rendered potentially explosive by the ready availability of guns and whiskey. "The over-generous consumption of hard liquor, and the widespread practice of too hastily resorting to the use of improved deadly weapons" were key elements in the violence.[14] The improved guns developed during the Civil War came onto the New Mexico market just as newcomers to wide-open Lincoln County were feeling an increased need to arm themselves against others deemed threatening because they stood on the opposite side of an economic or political or ethnic dividing line. The new guns killed more reliably, prompting men to practice the quick draw and the accurate shot, as failure to be fastest in a shoot-out meant almost certain death.

The incidents of sudden, often unexplained, sometimes unpunished, deaths by gun were many over the years. Former Texan Robert Casey, the respected father of eight who owned a cattle ranch and grist mill on the Rio Hondo, was shot and killed in Lincoln just after denouncing political boss Lawrence G. Murphy at a political convention. The man who killed Casey in August of 1875, William Wilson, was convicted and became the first man to be legally hanged in Lincoln County. Some said Wilson and Casey had a dispute over an eight-dollar debt; others insisted Wilson had been hired by Casey's political enemies.[15]

Paul Dowlin, captain in the New Mexico Volunteers during the Civil War and later a Fort Stanton trader and substantial property owner, was killed without explanation in May of 1877 by Jerry Dillon, a former employee, who escaped into Texas after the shooting and was never caught.[16] These cases are but two among many. And not only was the gun a weapon of offense and defense, but it also was regarded as a normal part of everyday, even joyous, occasions. Well into the 1890s, the main street of Roswell periodically was closed for horse racing by cowboys "shooting off their pistols into the air as they went."[17]

Although the population of the territory as a whole grew by 40,717 between 1880 and 1890, reaching 160,000, 93.8 percent of all New Mexicans lived in rural settings, and the eastern third of the territory was the least populated.[18] For southeastern New Mexico, the result of this demographic situation was a dispersed population lacking the law-and-order constraints associated with long-established towns. The tendency toward violence also may have been related to the low educational level of many of the opportunistic drifters who came into southeastern New Mexico and were ready to use their guns on behalf of any man who would hire them. For it is a fact that while such men as Lincoln attorney Alexander McSween and Roswell cattleman John Chisum made a point of not carrying guns on their persons, men who worked for them or took sides with them in the not infrequent bloody showdowns of the time did carry and use guns in the names of these leading figures.

Yet the gun, though an ever-present element on the southeastern frontier, was only a symbol, an outward sign, of the social conflict and tension rampant within the new society taking shape during the turbulent decades leading to the turn of the century. Not only were there ethnic differences between Anglos and Hispanos, there also were the hostilities pitting big cattlemen against small; cattlemen against farmers and sheepmen; one big cattle company against another; cattle rustlers against all cattlemen; and land grabbers against all who stood in the way of their acquisitions.

Prejudice against Hispanos, not universally present among Anglos but a latent social force nonetheless, could turn viciously harmful when mixed with outlawry, as it was in the case of the Horrell brothers gang, which terrorized the Lincoln area in late 1873 and early 1874. There were, according to court records, five or six Horrell brothers. They were residents of Lampasas County, Texas, where they were known for wild and lawless behavior. Brother Ben went west to Lincoln in New Mexico, got into a fight with a deputy sheriff, and was killed. Not long after, the remaining brothers, along with other men from Lampasas County, moved in on Lincoln, demanding an investigation.

When an investigation was refused on the grounds that Ben had been lawfully killed while resisting arrest, the Horrells took their own retribution.[19] They broke into houses where Mexican dances known as *bailes* were being held; intoxicated and wild, they shot their guns with abandon. At one Horrell invasion during December 1873, two Lincoln lawmen and two of the Horrells lay dead at the end of the shooting melee, and several others were wounded. On Christmas Eve the remaining gang members shot through the windows of another Lincoln house where townfolk were gathered, killing four Hispanic citizens.

With the violence escalating daily, news of the Horrell infestation spread with reports in the *Santa Fe New Mexican*, including an eyewitness account provided by Lincoln County Clerk Juan Patron on 9 January 1874. Over the ensuing weeks, numerous other people were killed, including an Anglo married to a Hispanic woman. It was said that the Horrells were openly vowing to "kill all Mexicans."[20] Local citizens took action. On 3 January a public meeting elected probate judge L. G. Murphy, store owner José Montaño, and former army major William Brady to organize a vigilante committee. The *Santa Fe New Mexican* reported on 27 January that all Lincoln County was armed for "the unfortunate war between the Texans and Mexicans."

In early February Lincoln County officials asked Governor Marsh Giddings for help from federal troops. At about this time, the Horrells seemed finally to understand that their actions would not be tolerated.[21] They took their belongings and retreated toward Roswell, killing several Hispanos in cold blood along the way. But after stealing horses and mules in the Roswell area, the Horrells finally met their match; Aaron and Frank Willburn of Roswell formed a posse that chased the Horrells south to Seven Springs and then westward toward the mountains. Catching the gang members by surprise early one morning, posse members "showed no mercy" toward the men who had murdered so many New Mexicans.[22]

Hispanos were victimized in another outbreak of violence in 1878. Following the failed attempt of a Hispanic group from the Rio Grande valley to irrigate cropland along Roswell's North Spring River, ten of the families joined the Hispanic settlement on the Berrendo River. "About 20 of the outlaws and desperadoes roaming the country descended on the settlement and robbed it of about everything, even the women's shawls. They told the Mexicans to leave the country or they would come back and kill them." Deeply bitter, the Berrendo residents were on the verge of openly attacking Anglos at nearby Roswell, whom they easily outnumbered, "for there were but two families at Roswell proper."[23] It may be that the just behavior of Joseph Lea, now the leading citizen of Roswell, toward all parties was becoming known, for the threatened attack never took place.

Nevertheless attitudes that violated the American principle of equality under the law continued to exist. During 1894, when rail for the Pecos Valley Railroad was being laid from Carlsbad to Roswell, Anglos were paid $1.50 per day, while Hispanic workers were paid $1.25; the Anglo railroad workers were charged $3.00 per week to eat at the company mess, while the Hispanic workers were charged $3.50.[24]

Still there were situations in which ethnic-group competition was not a determining factor. Ethnic conflict cannot, for instance, be construed as the basis of, or even a major element in, the fierce rivalry that led to the Lincoln County War of 1878. Each side in the episode had its Hispanic supporters. The McSween-Tunstall faction had more Hispanic adherents, and it had the general support of the townspeople of Lincoln. But the reason for that was made clear by Hispanos themselves. They had an economic rationale for their actions, claiming they were aligning themselves with the McSween side because the Murphy-Dolan firm had exploited them, along with Anglos, for years by charging high prices and denying them a fair price for their produce.

Southeastern New Mexico began to throb with the hoofbeat of cattle herds just as the nation was entering the Gilded Age, characterized by concentrations of extravagant wealth. In keeping with the spirit of the times, a substantial portion of the region's beef-cattle industry was controlled by big companies rather than small ranchers. Certainly there was during the 1870s and 1880s general acceptance in the public mind of the notion of a man quickly enriching himself even at the cost of his neighbors, or a foreign company eagerly investing in the American West for big returns.

The predominance of big operators over small ones in southeastern New Mexico can also be explained in part by the fact that Gilded Age overachievers who had made good elsewhere were looking for places to invest their excess profits; with growing national demand for beef and numerous new railroads across the country to transport it, southeastern New Mexico inevitably was one of the places to which investor money flowed. In addition the topography of the land helps explain the large-scale nature of much of the development activity on the ranges of Lincoln County. Only near the few rivers where irrigation was possible was the land suitable for crops. The vast majority of it was good only for the grazing of cattle, an enterprise that easily lent itself to aggrandizement during a period when the public domain was there to be used by anyone astute enough to move in and monopolize those parts of it that either included or were adjacent to sources of water.

The first big cattle companies were the Chisum Cattle Company, the Lea Cattle Company, and the Littlefield (LFD) Company. Among the large cattle enterprises organized in the 1880s and 1890s were the El Capitan Cattle Company, the Cass Cattle Company, the Cox and Peacock Cattle Company, the British-incorporated Carrizozo Cattle Company, the Bloom Cattle Company, the Anderson Cattle Company, the

Dolan Fritz Cattle Company, the CA Bar Cattle Company, the Kirby and Cree Cattle Company, and the Milne-Bush Cattle Company. Also important as big cattle ranchers were Charles B. Eddy, who controlled about twenty thousand acres of Lincoln County rangeland, and Pete Maxwell, who controlled sizable acreage in the Fort Sumner area.

The Cass Cattle Company provides one example of the profits to be made by investors. The Cass outfit had good relations with J. J. Cox, of Cox Cattle Company. When Cox died in 1889, his widow sold his operation to Cass Cattle for about $100,000. Cass Cattle was entirely backed by a group of investors in Missouri. The company was in business from 1884 until 1909. During that time, according to W. C. Urton, one of the company founders, Cass Cattle branded 88,336 head of cattle, sold 46,966 head, and paid annual dividends of 20 percent on capital stock for twenty years, despite losses of cattle due to rustling and deaths ranging from 5 to 20 percent per year.[25]

In terms of actual landownership, as opposed to use of the public domain, some of the biggest private landholders were Eddy, Carrizozo Cattle, Cox and Peacock, and the El Capitan Land and Cattle Company. "These large enterprises, not content with the sizable acreage they owned, were continually in search of water rights and exercised great political and economic power in the county."[26]

None of the large cattle companies, even those that owned large amounts of land, depended solely upon privately held lands for cattle range. All made claim on the public domain; but gradually, through the use of purchased land scrip exchangeable with the U.S. Land Office, the large owners extended their privatized holdings to huge areas of Lincoln County. Many of these companies were backed by, or directly owned by, English and Scottish financial interests. The infusion of large amounts of money from foreign sources increased local demand for goods and services, dislocating prices to such a degree that small ranchers found it hard to compete.

Those parts of the public domain that were not claimed or purchased by the large cattle companies often were useless to the small cattlemen, because such areas usually lacked access to water. And the smaller ranchers, along with the larger outfits, were reluctant to dig wells on public land that could be used by anyone coming in with enough men, cattle, and guns.

Governor William T. Thornton went so far as to say in 1895 that "the open cattle range business in New Mexico is a failure, because no man will improve his ground by opening water holes, storing water, or any other way, if his shiftless neighbor has the right to run his herd at will over the same ground."²⁷ In fact the existence of the public domain generally resulted in slower development of the land than would have been the case if small-scale private ownership had prevailed. And, of course, freewheeling use of the public domain without accountability led to overstocking and deterioration of rangeland quality, a result apparent by the early 1880s.

The public domain also was the direct cause of open conflict, as more and more small cattlemen began to challenge the longstanding claims to sole use of vast tracts by such large operators as Chisum and Lea. While gunfights were frequent between the hired men of Chisum and those of small ranchers, Chisum usually managed to reach private agreement with the large cattlemen over use of the range without resorting to guns.

Sheepmen attempting to use the Pecos range were not as fortunate. Cattlemen regularly sent their cowboys out to drive off sheep being grazed legally on the public domain. In 1884 sheep rancher James M. Miller had his flocks grazing in the vicinity of Bottomless Lakes, east of Roswell, when suddenly "Pat Garrett came with some cowboys and small cowmen and told the sheep men that if they did not take their sheep out of the country they would kill every one of them. So both parties got ready to shoot it out in a few days."²⁸ The dispute was mediated by John Poe, the calmly efficient sheriff who had been Garrett's deputy before replacing him in office.

As it happened the new Anglo sheepmen were among the first to dare to remind Chisum that he did not own the public domain but was only using it as others were entitled to do. Chisum himself had taken two of his cowboys out on the range and driven off sheep owned by Judge Edmund Stone, merely because the sheep were crossing public land claimed by Chisum while on the way to a privately owned lambing ground. That was in 1881; challenges to Chisum multiplied and began to succeed from that time onward, as the numbers of small cattlemen grew and as other newcomers arrived with plans to grow crops where land could be irrigated.

Even so crop farms and sheep ranches took up only a relatively small proportion of the total of privately owned land. In fact southeastern New Mexico exemplified in extreme form some of the deficiencies of the Homestead Act and the Timber Culture Act, congressional measures of 1862 and 1873, which allowed a settler to obtain for a small fee 160 acres if occupied and improved for five years and an additional 160 acres if 40 acres of trees were planted. In arid New Mexico, 160 acres was too small for successful grazing or crops. More importantly the land was worth little in a climate giving twelve or less inches of rain a year, unless a spring or source of irrigation was included with the land. In short, successful homesteading in southeastern New Mexico was feasible only along the Pecos and its few tributaries. That fundamental reality, when combined with the aggressive, well-financed acquisitions by large cattle companies, meant that big business controlled much of the land, in the same way that big business controlled major sectors of commerce and industry in the nation as a whole in the years between 1870 and 1890.

New Mexicans who were part of the territory's political and commercial establishment did not fail to see the connection, recognizing that in southeastern New Mexico big land was big business. Thomas B. Catron of Santa Fe, the gruff, bluff Missourian-turned-New Mexican who was a dominant force in territorial politics for decades before he was elected one of New Mexico's first U.S. senators in 1912, fully understood the value of the rich cattleland he saw lying there ripe for the plucking. Not only did he advise an erstwhile professional gambler acquaintance by the name of Van C. Smith to seek his fortune in Pecos country, but he himself invested in several Lincoln County ventures over the years and took a keenly protective interest in the large companies operating in the county. And Governor Thornton, although he later decried the corruption inherent in the use of the public domain, welcomed a chance to become a founding investor in the CA Bar Ranch when it was organized in the early 1880s.

But it must be admitted that the grabbing of huge tracts of land by means both legal and illegal was not unique to Lincoln County; it was common to New Mexico as a whole, and it was in keeping with the contemporary spirit of American capitalism. Land grabbing in New Mexico had been greatly facilitated by congressional legislation that required all claimants of land under Spanish or Mexican grants to pay for their own surveys and to undertake long, expensive litigation to protect their titles. From the 1850s until the end of the century, lawyers in New Mexico, often Anglo, were able to acquire large amounts of grant lands while providing legal services for Hispanic grantees.

The problem of deciding claims to grant lands was complicated by a number of factors. Boundaries were imprecise and not based on accurate surveys. "Familiar landmarks such as mesas, arroyos and trees . . . were used to designate the boundaries of the grants." When surveys were done they often revealed overlapping grant boundaries. In addition many grant documents had been lost over the years, some had been fraudulently manufactured, and "many claimants, often victims of sharp practices, had conveyed their rights to speculators."[29]

The very nature of the titles held by Hispanic grantees posed a problem, for titles to individuals sharing in a community grant originally had been given only for the grantees' stipulated amount of irrigated cropland, while they shared ownership and use of the far more extensive common grazing land with other community owners of the grant. Yet in terms of earning a livelihood, it was the grantees' use of the grazing land that provided a substantial portion of their incomes. The Court of Private Land Claims, which operated from 1891 to 1913, accepted the precedent set by the surveyor general in allowing title to community-grant grazing lands to be given to individuals by dividing the land in portions through specific partition suits brought to court.

But in permitting titles to be given for the land that had been held in common, the court enabled a large amount of land either to be obtained by noncommunity individuals or simply to be taken over by the federal government and incorporated into the public domain.[30] The negative impact of the claims-settlement process upon many occupants of grant lands was compounded by the frequent cheating of their clients by lawyers, many of whom managed to obtain portions of the land in question even when Hispanic land-grant residents lost their cases in court.[31]

When the Territory of New Mexico held a constitutional convention in 1889, a body of seventy-two Republicans and one Democrat was present in Santa Fe to draft a state constitution that the group hoped would persuade Congress to approve statehood. (Most Democrats refused to participate on the grounds they had not received adequate representation.) Of those present, fourteen Republicans owned between them a total of 9,457,166 acres of land in New Mexico. With the prominent legislator J. Francisco Chaves presiding over the convention, a constitution was drafted containing provisions that were "highly satisfactory" to large landowners.[32]

Despite the political dominance exercised by big land interests at the 1889 convention, however, growing numbers of people were becoming aware of the shady maneuverings that had enabled huge chunks of New Mexico's public domain and grant lands to fall into the hands of a privileged few. As early as 1884, in fact, the first year in which land-fraud statistics were made public by the General Land Office, the territory had been shown to rank first with 827 cases of fraud, followed by California with 574 cases.[33]

The culminating decade in the early settlement and development period of southeastern New Mexico took place from 1890 to 1900 and was dominated by two trends that occurred simultaneously, and had the effect of altering the political and economic landscape of a frontier preparing to move beyond the pioneering stage and on to an era of social integration. Both trends involved the issue of people and power, or to put it another way, the issue of which individuals and which groups had the political means of voicing their concerns and protecting their interests in the emerging social matrix.

The first trend was one toward the growth of local government; growth of sizable communities with all their attendant institutions such as schools, churches, banks, commercial establishments, and newspapers; and growth of a nonagrarian middle class composed of professionals of various sorts and business people.

The second trend, arising out of the discontent inherent in the land-based monopolistic underpinnings of the southeastern frontier as well as out of grievances over the national economy as it affected agricultural producers, was a growing refusal on the part of small farmers and ranchers to allow their fate to be decided either by political bosses or big business.

The trend toward the growth of a nonagrarian middle class was centered in the eastern portion of southeastern New Mexico, as this area saw the rise of such towns as Roswell and Carlsbad. The trend toward a politics of protest, on the other hand, was centered in the mountain valleys of the western portion of the southeast region. There was no intrinsic parallel and even a degree of contradiction between the two trends, given the almost instinctively conservative orientation of town-dwellers with middle-class aspirations to prosperity and stability. The net effect of the two trends, however, was to mitigate, or at the very least create a political counterweight to, the great influence wielded up until that time by the large cattle and land interests.

Roswell's emergence as a viable townsite came with unexpected swiftness, following upon some fifteen years of almost static existence as a small outpost on the Pecos. The U.S. Census of 1880 listed Fort Stanton's population as 118; Lincoln's as 638; and White Oaks's as 268 (1,000 by 1883); but did not show Roswell, as it was too small for inclusion.[34] In June of 1885 there were but nine houses there.

The selection of Roswell as county seat of Chaves County in 1889 had an immediate impact upon the pace of growth. The first election in Chaves County was held in November 1890, with 318 votes cast, and the

CHAPTER FOUR

newly organized county government began to conduct official business on the first day of January 1891. A courthouse, costing $30,000, was completed soon after. A U.S. Land Office had been established at Roswell in 1889 by an act of Congress. The existence of local and federal governing agencies brought new people and a new need for commercial outlets.

Granville Richardson, who opened the first law office in the Pecos Valley at Roswell in April 1889, was soon joined by other lawyers. In the spring of 1890 the first hotel, called the Pauly, opened. In July 1890 the Bank of Roswell opened for business in a room of the Pauly Hotel. The first newspaper, the *Pecos Valley Register,* ran off its first two hundred copies in November 1888. Over the next few years other papers were organized, including the *Roswell Record,* which was started in 1891 by J. D. Lea and Lucius Dills. In 1902 H. M. F. Bear bought the *Record,* changed its political leanings to Democratic, and in March of 1903 made it the *Roswell Daily Record.*

In 1890 William Hale, owner of the first well-drilling machine in the valley, had been hired by Roswell resident Nathan Jaffa to dig a well on the lot where his home was located, in an effort to obtain clear water. At the level of 250 feet, deeper than any well previously dug, the drill hit porous limestone and pure water bubbled in abundance to the surface. This proof of the area's artesian water sources was used to promote the county and brought many hundreds of new settlers within the space of a few years. And the coming of the rail line in 1894 cemented the growth potential of this middle portion of the Pecos Valley, enabling farming to flourish with Roswell serving the consumer needs of an irrigated agricultural mecca.

If only because there was a growing consensus that the days of frontier outlawry were over, it came as a rude shock to Roswell townfolk to discover instances of embezzlement and theft of public funds on two occasions during the 1890s. In early 1893 Frank Lesnet, receiver of the Federal Land Office, disappeared; his accounts were missing $8,933.48. In the late spring of 1896, Sheriff Charles C. Perry vanished; a deficit was found amounting to $7,639.02. These aberrations notwithstanding, the community was one in which all the nationally prevailing notions of the social graces in dress, manners, and business comportment were much in evidence. The variety of architectural styles exhibited in the many new homes springing up indicated desire to bring southern and midwestern influences to the new commercial hub of the southeast frontier.

National influences were not always so benign, however, and certainly neither towndwellers nor agriculturists could escape the impact of the national economy. It was the national situation in combination with longstanding local grievances over land monopolies that produced Lincoln County's trend toward organized political protest.

The agricultural economy of southeastern New Mexico was becoming more integrated into the national economy. While such local products as alfalfa and corn were sold locally, the area's two big money earners—cattle and sheep—sold on regional markets that fed into the national supply-and-demand system. Throughout the 1880s the nation experienced economic expansion, although by the end of the decade large areas of the West were suffering depression as a result of low farm prices and the 1886–87 drought and its lingering aftermath.

As the 1880s ended, however, the political mood of voters nationwide was beginning to change from optimistic faith in unbridled capitalism to openly expressed concern over the economic and political control exercised by the railroad, manufacturing, land, cattle, and oil monopolies. There were few policy differences between the Democrats and Republicans during the early 1880s, neither party had responded to the plight of western and southern agronomists, and both parties promised in the campaign of 1888 to curb monopolies.

With bipartisan support, the Sherman Antitrust Act was passed by Congress in 1890. The act did not adequately define trusts and monopolies, however, and for at least a decade its injunction against trusts that had the effect of constraining trade was not enforced with any vigor. The antitrust act was a beginning, though, and serves as an apt symbol for the start of a decade that produced the greatest amount of political upheaval the nation had yet known in peacetime.

Like other farmers and ranchers in the West, Lincoln County producers were suffering not only from the drought and lower prices for their crops and livestock but also from the high prices they paid for manufactured goods, prices they believed were artificially high because U.S. industry limited foreign competition through import tariffs. The McKinley Tariff Act of October 1890 raised the general level of duties on imports even higher, from 38 percent to almost 50 percent. Anger swelled among many groups.

In 1892, with Republicans for high tariffs and Democrats for lowering them, Democrat Grover Cleveland was elected to his second term as president, defeating incumbent Benjamin Harrison. But Cleveland then proceeded to disappoint many who had voted for him by taking an extremely conservative position with respect to expansion of the money supply, an issue of paramount concern to many westerners, who were convinced that the best remedy for the nation's economic ills would be to have the government purchase more silver—produced in the West— and issue more money. Even after the onset of a severe economic depression, Cleveland failed to respond to the needs of farmers and other debtors. Repeal of the Sherman Silver Purchase Act by Congress only worsened the impact of a deflationary cycle that had caused prices for farm products to plunge.

Lincoln County agriculturists were in a fighting mood well before the 1893 depression began. In fact their discontent was fueled more by existing local conditions and the state of politics in New Mexico than by the national debate over silver, tariffs, and antitrust legislation. While all of these national issues were included in their proposed reforms, their deepest anger was reserved for the cabal of land, cattle, and railroad interests that worked hand in hand with a ring of powerful territorial politicians in Santa Fe. Together these economic and political powerbrokers exercised near total control in such bread-and-butter areas as water rights, railroad hauling charges, access to the public domain, and land prices.

Still, the lot of the small producer in the county undeniably was made even worse by the nationwide decline in prices for livestock, wool, and grains. The price per head of cattle raised in southeastern New Mexico was twelve dollars in 1886, below the national average, and just seven or eight dollars by 1889. "The drop in cattle prices hurt the small rancher, often a marginal producer, much more than the large operator. And these low prices, when added to the fear of monopoly, accounted largely for the agitation in the cattle-raising counties of New Mexico."[35]

In 1885 James Miller of Chaves County sold his wool in Las Vegas for sixteen cents a pound. In 1893 he had to go to New York, where he found that the best price he could get was eleven cents a pound. The following year he was forced to cut the wages he paid his herders from twenty-two dollars to fifteen dollars per month. In 1895 Miller had to look long and hard before he found a Philadelphia buyer willing to pay six and a half cents a pound for his wool. Market conditions were even more difficult for sheepmen in 1896. "Large wholesale merchants and banks refused to carry the sheep men and the broad prairie on the great mesa east of Las Vegas was covered with big fat wethers, brought there to be sacrificed for a little money to tide over their owners."[36] Wool producers in southeastern New Mexico derived some financial relief, however, from herd improvements that increased average wool yield per sheep from two pounds in 1883 to over four pounds in 1899.[37]

Prices for grains also fell sharply during the 1890s. The amount of cultivated farm acreage had expanded rapidly in the western states and territories; the supply of farm products was growing far faster than the population of the nation. At the end of the Civil War, wheat sold for one dollar and sixty cents a bushel, but by the 1890s it had dropped to forty-nine cents.

Acting on their belief that neither the Democratic party nor the Republican party was responding to the needs of agricultural producers, a group of farmers and ranchers formed a Lincoln County chapter of the Farmers' Alliance and Industrial Union, commonly referred to as the Southern Alliance. The Southern Alliance was active primarily in the southern states, and with one million or more members it was larger than the National Farmers' Alliance, known as the Northern Alliance and active in the western and midwestern states. While there is no record of the exact number of members in the Lincoln County chapter, the organization was functioning and holding regular meetings by 1888. Other chapters were forming in New Mexico at about the same time.

The Nogal Nugget, a newspaper published in the small community of Nogal, twenty-five miles northwest of Lincoln, was the official voice of the Southern Alliance in southeastern New Mexico. Its capable editor was J. E. Sligh, a newspaperman who also managed a ranch on the eastern slope of the San Andres Mountains. The paper had a readership of a little under one thousand. In one 1888 issue, twenty-two ranchers carried ads in the paper, including George W. Coe, who ranched along the Rio Ruidoso.[38]

When the Lincoln County Alliance organized its chapter in 1888, another member of the Coe family, Jasper N. Coe, had been named president; in 1890 when the alliance expanded its activities throughout the territory, Jasper Coe became president of the territorial alliance. It was in the natural order of things for members of the family to stand with those willing to challenge the existing power structure. For the Coe men had a history of displaying just the sort of gritty determination it took to survive as small ranchers in Lincoln County.

And small ranchers they were by any standard. Tax rolls for 1888 show that Jasper Coe had four horses and three cows, and that the value of his property was $940; the property of his cousin George Coe was valued at $1,528; and that of Frank Coe, Jasper's brother, was worth $2,537.[39] With twenty-two horses and eighty head of cattle, Frank Coe was the best-off of the three, although all went on to become established ranchers.

It was typical of the strong-willed Jasper Coe to write a letter such as that published by the *Nogal Nugget* on 16 August 1888, in which he strongly defended a special land agent attempting at some risk to himself to investigate land-fraud cases in Lincoln County. The Coes had been in the thick of things ever since their arrival in the Lincoln area in the early 1870s. All during that decade one band of violent outlaws after another entered the county. After one episode of killing and stealing in 1876 had ended with capture of the desperado who had stolen a valuable stallion from Frank Coe, justice was on the way to being served, with the prisoner under sheriff's escort and on the way to Fort Stanton. Frank Coe and a small group of cohorts waylaid the sheriff's party and lynched the prisoner.[40]

When the Lincoln County War in 1878 pitted the Murphy-Dolan faction against the McSween-Chisum faction, both Frank Coe and George Coe sided with McSween. The two Coes retreated into the mountains after their side was defeated. While they were gone, Dolan partisans burned the Coe ranch to the ground. Frank Coe and George Coe then went to the San Juan Valley of Colorado, where Jasper Coe joined them in a ranching venture. In 1882 Frank Coe returned to settle along the Rio Ruidoso. In 1884 Jasper Coe and George Coe also returned, and this time all three were there to stay; certainly they were ready by the late 1880s to organize politically, if that was what it would take to ensure the survival of the beleaguered stockmen and cropmen of Lincoln County.

The Lincoln County Alliance took a strong stand against what it saw as the unfair protectionism pursued by the powerful Cattle Association, whose membership consisted of the large cattle companies rather than small stockmen. The Republican Party in the territory, according to the alliance, consistently passed laws to protect the Cattle Association's monopoly of the public domain, showing no concern for the rights of settlers in the territory. Republicans also had protected the railroads from taxation and from demands for fairer hauling rates. Lincoln County Alliance members were particularly incensed by a territorial quarantine law that was said by legislators to be designed to keep cattle carrying Texas fever out of New Mexico, but which alliance members saw as a sham that actually was being used to keep new small stockmen out of the southeastern part of the state, thus leaving the public domain to the handful of giant companies that had dominated it for years.

The Southern Alliance was not a political party, and the Lincoln County chapter, though many of its members were Democrats, remained insistent that the membership was entirely free to vote for either of the major parties without any instructions or even suggestions from the organization. Rather than being apolitical, however, the Lincoln County Alliance, as well as the territorial association of alliance chapters, was focusing on issues still being avoided by the two major political parties. Thus it was only natural that Southern Alliance members should be among representatives of populist groups from thirty-three states and territories who met in Cincinatti on 19 May 1891 to create a national People's party, whose adherents quickly became known as Populists.

T. B. Mills of San Juan County, a former newspaper editor and a mine investor who had twice served in the territorial legislature as a People's party representative, issued the first call for a Populist party convention in New Mexico. It was held on 13 September 1894, in Albuquerque, with representatives from almost every county, including Lincoln County. Delegates adopted a platform calling for the free coinage of silver; abolition of the electoral college and direct election of the president and vice president; election of district judges, marshals, and postmasters; and popular referendums on all laws passed by the territorial legislature. This last item was a clear indication of the distrust Populists had of the normal political process as it worked in New Mexico.

In the 1894 election campaign, T. B. Mills was the Populist candidate for territorial delegate to Congress. Populists were active in numerous counties, including San Juan County in northwest New Mexico, where another Coe family member was involved in reform politics. Chosen as one of three members of the resolutions committee was Lou W. Coe, a cousin of Jasper Coe. With silver not yet the all-consuming issue it would be in 1896, Populists stressed the great disparities in wealth between the "producers" of wealth, who were the nation's farming and laboring people, and the "non-producers," who were the "capitalists and businessmen."[41] Republican candidate Thomas B. Catron, however, easily defeated the Democratic incumbent Antonio Joseph, while the Populist Mills took only 3.77 percent of the total vote in the territory.

Populists were never a strong force, certainly not a dominant one, in New Mexico politics. But by the time of the 1896 presidential election campaign, sentiment throughout the territory had swung strongly to the side of reform. Although New Mexicans, still living under territorial status, could not vote for Democratic and Populist presidential candidate William Jennings Bryan, so strongly did they support the cause of free silver that Catron was swept out of office by combined Populist and Democratic votes. The winner of the office of delegate to Congress was Democrat Harvey B. Fergusson, a lawyer of high integrity in an era prone to corruption and a man who firmly favored the free coinage of silver.

"Fergusson did particularly well in those counties where protest had begun in the late eighties."[42] In Lincoln County Fergusson won by a vote of 769 to 464. In Chaves County, separated from Lincoln County for seven years, he won by a four-to-one margin, a ratio almost duplicated in Eddy County, lying to the south of Chaves and also carved from Lincoln County. The Democratic victory across the territory had much to do with the Democrats having seized upon and made their own some of the issues closest to the hearts of the Populist reformers such as those in the Lincoln County Alliance. "In both Lincoln and Colfax counties it was the Democrats who spearheaded the opposition against monopolistic cattle barons and land-grabbers."[43]

Whether by simply speaking through the vote or by actively organizing themselves politically, many of the people of southeastern New Mexico had expressed their desire to throw off the yoke of land, cattle, and railroad monopolies. And as the century drew to a close, this sign of independent thinking may be seen as a fitting end to the pioneering period that lasted from the 1850s to 1900, despite the fact that the territory's identification with the forces of reform caused opposition to New Mexico statehood to resurface in a Republican-dominated Congress. For it showed yet again that, far from being a backwater where little of importance happened, the southeast quadrant was a place where development had proceeded in an atmosphere of competitiveness, entrepreneurship, ethnic and class organizing, and finally, political activism in the best of the American tradition.

By the year 1900 the United States was once again brimming over with recharged feelings of confidence, and this optimistic spirit was displayed as well in southeastern New Mexico. The nation had elected conservative Republican William McKinley rather than the populist Bryan in 1896. The tariff was raised to an average of 57 percent, the highest level ever, but one that enabled U.S. industry to expand again. Foreign crops failed, increasing demand for American farm goods. Prosperity had returned by 1898. The gold standard was adopted in 1900, but new gold discoveries abroad and use of the new cyanide process for extraction expanded the world supply of gold, making possible a growth in the money supply. Americans had flexed their muscles as a newly powerful nation by defeating Spain in the Spanish-American War of 1898.

The huge open spaces of southeastern New Mexico looked much the same as they had fifty years before, when they had been occupied only by Native Americans. Yet now there was a settler society in place; now there existed the institutional foundations for permanent communities. And there was a sureness that this far frontier was part of, not separate from, the mainstream of New Mexico's and indeed the country's historical momentum.

Quanah Parker, last great Comanche chief. Probably made shortly after the Army campaign of 1874 in which Parker and the Comanches he led were defeated and taken to a reservation at Fort Sill in Indian Territory, this portrait photograph dramatically illustrates the Plains Indians' pride, dignity, and way of life as expressed in buckskin and beautifully crafted decorative elements using feathers, beads, and leather fringe. (Courtesy, Archives/Library, Chaves County Historical Museum, Roswell, New Mexico. #1782-A)

The legendary Kit Carson of Taos as he appeared in his Army Colonel's uniform during the Civil War. This photograph by G. Grelling was made around 1862, not long before Carson was recruited by General James Carleton for the last great campaign against the Navajo and the Mescalero Apaches. (Courtesy, the Rose Collection in the Western History Collections, University of Oklahoma Library. #604)

Cattleman extraordinaire John Simpson Chisum as he looked during his early years in Texas. This photograph may have been made during the Civil War years when Chisum was a beef contractor for the Confederate Army. (Courtesy, Historical Center for Southeast New Mexico, Roswell, N.M.)

Seen here in the early 1870s after his move to southeastern New Mexico, John Chisum was in the process of acquiring the huge herds of Texas Longhorns that earned him the title Cattle King of the Pecos. (Courtesy, Archives/Library, Chaves County Historical Museum, Roswell, New Mexico. #604-D)

James J. Dolan (on left) poses in 1873 with Lawrence G. Murphy, the hard-driving, jovial ex-Army major who built a business fiefdom in southeastern New Mexico. When the alcoholic Murphy turned the business over to his feisty protége, it was Dolan's stubborn opposition to new competition that led to the infamous Lincoln County War. (Courtesy, the Rose Collection in the Western History Collections, University of Oklahoma Library. #2182)

A young Patrick F. Garrett seems to stare with a mixture of determined defiance and sorrowful regret into an unknown future in this picture made when the man who would one day kill Billy the Kid was still in his twenties, circa 1875. (Courtesy, the Rose Collection in the Western History Collections, University of Oklahoma Library. #1781)

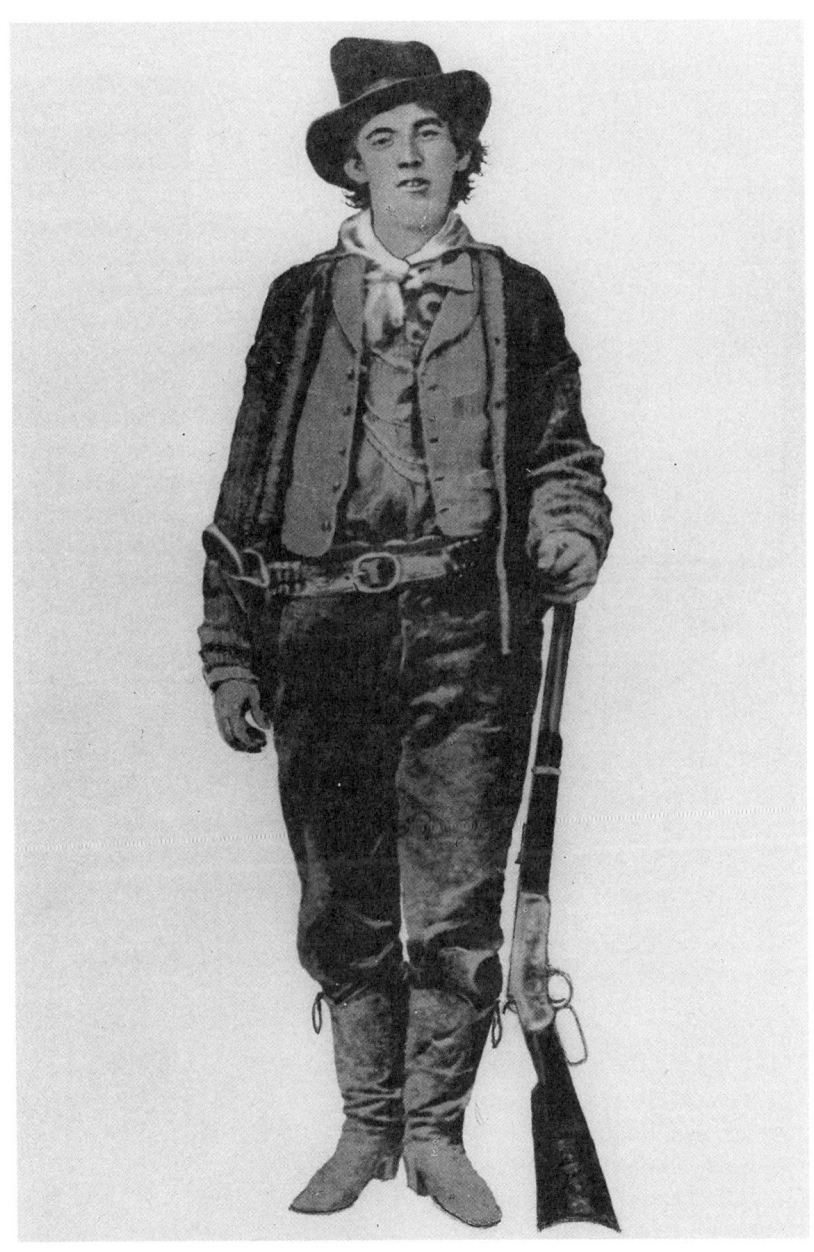

Familiar as it is, this photograph taken in Fort Sumner in 1879 is the only known photograph of Billy the Kid in existence that has been proven authentic. (Courtesy, the Rose Collection in the Western History Collections, University of Oklahoma Library. #2169)

Sallie Chisum Robert, niece of John Chisum, arrived with her younger brother and widowed father James at South Spring on the Pecos in December 1877. Spirited and intelligent, she is seen here in the early 1880s following her marriage to ambitious William Robert, who joined the Chisum cattle operation and won the affection of the aging Cattle King of the Pecos. (Courtesy, Archives/Library, Chaves County Historical Museum, Roswell, New Mexico. #494)

Captain Joseph C. Lea was the preeminent economic and political figure of the middle Pecos Valley when this picture was made in the early 1890s. His large ambitions for himself were matched by his equally grand goals for the region he helped develop. (Courtesy, Archives/Library, Chaves County Historical Museum, Cosgrove Collection. #495-A)

Located in what is now downtown Roswell, this adobe house with dormer windows, verandah, and "widow's walk" was constructed in 1867 by G. W. Hartman, sold to Van C. Smith in 1869, to Marion Turner in 1874, and to Major William Wildy in 1877. Wildy's son-in-law, Captain Joseph C. Lea moved with his family into the house in late 1877, and in 1878 Wildy deeded the house and a 480-acre tract of land to his daughter, Sally Wildy Lea.

In this November 1879 photograph showing Lea family friends and relatives, Lea's brother Captain Frank Lea is fourth from left in group, and his brother J. Smith Lea is sixth from right. The Lea house served as family home and local boarding house at this time. (Courtesy, Historical Center for Southeast New Mexico, Roswell, N.M.)

Amid the ornate trappings of a typical Victorian home, Joseph C. Lea poses for a family portrait in the early 1890s with his third wife, Mabel Day Lea, her daughter Willie, and his children Ella (standing) and Wildy. (Courtesy, Archives/Library, Chaves County Historical Museum, Rohr Collection, #2134-A)

PART II

THE IMPACT OF INDIVIDUALS

5

John Chisum, L.G. Murphy, James Dolan, and John Riley

SOME DOZEN OR SO UNIQUELY VIVID FIGURES STAND OUT IN THE saga of southeastern New Mexico, their names destined to be forever linked either with one of the starkly violent moments that punctuate the region's past or else with one of the pioneering economic efforts that set the region's future course of development. Some were men of education, like John Tunstall; or of professional status, like Alexander McSween. Some acquired wealth, like John Chisum; or possessed it when they arrived, like James J. Hagerman. Some were notable for their civic leadership, like Joseph C. Lea; some were fearless lawmen, like Patrick F. Garrett. Some, like Billy the Kid, began and ended their time in southeastern New Mexico as outlaws, while others, like Lawrence Murphy and James Dolan, freely mixed legitimate business activity with violations of the law and of ethical standards. Some are famous figures in the history of the American West; others merely infamous.

What they possessed in common was a certain toughness of physical and psychological nature that led them to act boldly in an environment so harshly primitive in its physical endowments and its social and political structure that a confident sureness of self was essential if one was to be a player in the no-holds-barred game of survival and advancement being waged. These were men who shaped their time and place, whether for good or bad; they both epitomized the spirit of their times and dominated the broad outlines of its chain of events.

Just as the characteristics of the land were shaping economic development, human characteristics were shaping the development of political relationships, that is to say political affairs in their broadest meaning of internalized rules governing the face-to-face dealings between individuals and between groups. If it is true that character is fate for the individual, so also is it true that the fate of a place is determined by the characters of the people who occupy it.

And yet character, or persona, is inextricable from the chain of events. Character is in fact revealed through events, although certainly it is true that in the early turbulent years in southeastern New Mexico events often took on a life of their own, drawing men of one type into concerted action with others possessing characters opposite to their own. In these circumstances character was seen to evolve under pressure and to be revealed in a particularly truthful way. Cattle baron John Chisum and cowboy-gunslinger Billy the Kid are striking examples of how character is revealed even as it is determining one's fate through a process of interaction with the existing set of realities.

Chisum was the quintessential cattle baron of the Old West. Rough-hewn, wily, but able to think big and to strategize, he forged personal links with a national ethos and built for himself a social place of both wealth and respectability. Billy the Kid was his mirror image. He, too, was rough-edged and crafty, but never seizing upon an opportunity to rise above his beginnings, he remained locked in a provincial world view, used violence to survive, and finally lost through acts of thievery and killing whatever claim to respectability he temporarily created by virtue of loyally avenging the death of John Tunstall, his one-time employer.

Both Chisum and Billy the Kid had in their basic characters a desire to be liked, and both possessed a certain charisma, or ease of communication, which made them likable. Billy the Kid was, perhaps, misled by his own likability; a sometime recklessness that led him to almost dare his pursuers to capture him seems to have been the result of more than just the sense of invulnerability possessed in general by the young, and more than just the result of his cocksure reliance on his skill with guns and his coolness under fire. The record of his friendly relationships with various people, from sheepherders to the townspeople of Lincoln and Fort Sumner to his fellow cowboys, indicates a personality that was capable of making well-adjusted connections with others. The fact that he felt himself to be part of, not alienated from, his community apparently was the cause for his decision not to flee from Lincoln County after his last escape from jail. And more importantly, his feeling of integration with at least certain elements of his society seems to have created in him a subconscious belief that no bad act of his could outweigh the overall good act of his having become part of the people, a person liked by many. Thus it may have been his very connectedness, in essence his own likability, that made the Kid feel invulnerable, at least as much as did his youth or his physical prowess.

Chisum, too, was a man connected with his society. Sardonically sarcastic in humor and demanding as an employer, Chisum nonetheless never regarded himself as socially above his cowhands, members of his family, or the settlers with whom he had contacts sometimes contentious in nature. Strong-minded but never arrogant, he was earthy and unpretentious, known to the end as a man who would get out and repair his own roof, set out new trees, or help work the cattle at roundup time. He was part of his community even while undoubtedly relishing his special role as a driving force in its development.

But for Chisum there was no self-delusion that he could or always would undo the designs of any real or potential enemies. His astuteness extended to the full realization that the forces arrayed against him, whether political enemies in Santa Fe or rustlers bent on stealing his cattle, might at any given time make it necessary for him to change course or take unprecedented action. Chisum was always ready with a variety of defensive responses. The Kid, on the other hand, representing what might be called the youthful underclass of his day, viewed violence as the only defense. But even for the Kid, with his admittedly smaller range of options than an older, wiser person might possess, there were in many instances options of response other than the violent ones he chose; in the end it was character that dictated his choices.

An answer to the question of what manner of men they were, these larger-than-life figures who left their marks in the history of southeastern New Mexico, may be found by looking at their characters as manifested in their actions. Knowledge about these men may, in turn, yield further understanding of the development period of a frontier region that experienced far more violence and economic and political fractiousness than many other similarly endowed frontier regions of the West.

During southeastern New Mexico's half-century as frontier country, a magnificently pristine landscape served as an exhilarating but harshly challenging backdrop to a small number of human inhabitants. The ruggedness of the land and the sparseness of the population were salient features of the environment that must not be overlooked in any recounting of deeds done by those whose impact was singular and lasting. For it is almost only in frontier environments of this kind that such essentially basic initiatives as the opening of commercial trade, the building of a transportation system, and exploitation of the land for production of livestock, crops, or minerals become noteworthy in and of themselves, allowing the people who undertake these enterprises to become leaders simply by virtue of having carried them through to successful completion.

The region underwent several changes in county status during the development period. Lincoln County was created in 1869. In 1878 the territorial legislature enlarged it with addition of land from Doña Ana County on the west, making Lincoln County geographically the largest county unit in the United States, with 27,000 square miles, stretching 180 miles from north to south and 160 miles from west to east, only a little smaller than the state of New York. A journey from Lincoln, the county seat, to Santa Fe, the territorial capital, took five days by horse and buggy.

During the 1870s and 1880s, Lincoln was the hub of commercial, legal, and social affairs for the entire area. The annual April session of the Lincoln district court brought a bustling crowd of attorneys, prosecutors, clerks, accused, jurors, onlookers, and traders into the town's single street. The Wortley Hotel was the place for eating and talking; the Montaño store on the other side of the street served as the town assembly hall and as the place where the biggest of the local bailes, or dances, were held. For these occasions the women of Lincoln and the surrounding countryside turned out in a fairly remarkable display of finery, and the dancing to lively fiddle music often went on til the small hours of the morning. By the early 1880s, Lincoln had its first Catholic church, a classically steepled building of adobe that served as a center for virtually all local ceremonial occasions.

In 1879 a mail-stage route was established from San Antonio on the Rio Grande and running through White Oaks, Lincoln, and Roswell. Fort Stanton had the area's only telegraph station, and until the late 1870s had the only available physician as well. An outbreak of smallpox in 1877 swept through Lincoln County almost unchecked, as no vaccine was at hand. Throughout the 1870s and 1880s, the town of Las Vegas, two hundred miles north of Roswell, was the supply center for most of southeastern New Mexico. Starting in 1874 a stagecoach ran three times a week from Las Vegas to the town of Lincoln.

Carlsbad, which began as a small settlement on the Pecos seventy miles south of Roswell under the leadership of Charles B. Eddy, was not an incorporated town until 1889. The total population of Lincoln County remained small and scattered. Nevertheless the vast size of the county and the inconvenience of travel to the county seat brought growing pressure to create new counties. The 1889 creation of Chaves and Eddy counties was followed by the creation of Otero County in 1899 and Roosevelt County in 1905, further diminishing the size of Lincoln County, but leaving unchanged the common fate of southeastern New Mexico as frontier country.

A difficult but eventually successful movement from a state of wild danger replete with Indians and outlaws to a state of community order and opportunity was the common theme for all of this quarter of New Mexico, whatever the county lines within it. Immense, silent, shimmeringly alive under the endless onslaught of changing winds, clouds, and temperatures, the land was a stage for pioneering struggles and triumphs.

John S. Chisum

When he died a lonely, painful death far from home at the age of sixty in 1884, John S. Chisum completed a life in which there had been few moments free of turmoil and little time for the pursuit of personal happiness. Chisum knew upheaval in every form, from Indian troubles to the Civil War to financial setbacks to violent range wars. And yet this man of little education and great natural ability not only built one of the largest cattle operations in the country but was known for his ready laugh, teasing wit, and pleasure in easy banter with men and women alike, for picking up a fiddle and turning out a fine tune, and in his last years at his adobe ranch home, for the peaceful joy he found in feeding cracker crumbs to the fish that filled a ditch running the length of the house.

A paradoxical man even during his lifetime, he became in the years immediately following his death a legendary figure around whom many misperceptions accumulated as a result of widespread falsehoods put forward by those who had opposed him. But even with the gradual setting straight of the historical record, much about Chisum remains unknown and open to speculation, if only because he himself chose throughout much of his life to keep to himself his plans, his strategies, and his beliefs concerning significant events and people.

What can be said with certainty is that he was a man born to the land and who for all his life remained bound to it by virtue of his instincts, temperament, and natural proclivities. Chisum embodied in his lifetime of entrepreneurial activity the very pulse of post–Civil War nineteenth-century America, as the nation sought to wrest from the lands of the trans-Mississippi West the resources that enriched individuals even as they helped build a new world power.

In the prime years of full maturity, when he was in his late forties and early fifties, Chisum was a handsome man of some presence. Of medium height and strong build, his movements bespoke a life of action and the outdoors. His slender, angular face with its high cheekbones, prominent nose, deep-set, grey-blue eyes and long, jutting chin, was weatherbeaten and sunburnt to the color of leather. He had thick brown hair, generally wore a heavy mustache, and photographs as well as accounts by contemporaries indicate that his demeanor was that of a shrewdly intelligent man, inclined to irony but basically straightforward, honest, even kindly in nature. And indeed, although his business success proves he was a man who always looked for and exploited the main chance, the record shows him also to have been a man who paid his debts, was fair in his dealings with others, and showed little inclination for personal violence of any sort.[1]

Chisum was born on his grandfather's plantation in western Tennessee on 16 August 1824. As a youngster he had ample opportunity to observe the management of land, slaves, and livestock. In 1837, when Chisum was thirteen, he moved with his parents, Claiborne and Lucy Chisum, to the new community of Paris, Texas, where his family became influential farmers. Although there is no record of Chisum ever having attended school, he acquired enough education in some manner to become county clerk of Lamar County in 1852. He also worked for a grocer and acquired real-estate interests. Always interested in cattle (his childhood nickname had been "Cow John"), he welcomed a chance to become partners in 1854 with easterner Stephen Fowler, who purchased $6,000 worth of cattle with which Chisum set up his first cattle operation on land north of present-day Fort Worth. His affinity for the cattle business manifested itself from the start; by 1860 Chisum's share in the partnership was worth $50,000.[2]

Only long after his death did it become known that during these early years in Denton County, Chisum as a bachelor in his early thirties had a love affair with a mulatto slave girl, a relationship that resulted in the births of two daughters in the years 1855 and 1857. Chisum had built a large house, a store, and a post office on the ranch property. One day a family of emigrants en route to California camped nearby. In need of cash, they prevailed upon Chisum to purchase their fifteen-year-old female slave for the sum of $1,400. Known as Jensie, the new household worker proved to be as able and intelligent as she was beautiful. While accepting the social sanctions against legalization of his relationship with Jensie, Chisum did not deny his paternity when children were born of the union.

When the Civil War broke out in 1861, Chisum voluntarily freed all of his slaves, including Jensie, and began paying regular wages to those who wished to remain as employees. As troops in the area were removed to fight in the war, Indian raids on cattle resumed, and Chisum decided to move his operation farther west. But before relocating to the confluence of the Concho and Colorado rivers in Coleman County in 1863, he found a home for Jensie and the two little girls in the town of Bonham, Texas, and provided money for their needs. On at least one later occasion he visited, leaving money for schooling. The children grew up knowing that Chisum was their father. By the 1890s there were numerous descendents of Meady, the younger daughter, living in the Fort Worth area, many of them business people and teachers.[3]

From the time Texas joined the Confederacy in 1861 until 1865 when the war ended, Chisum was a designated beef supplier under contract to Confederate forces, although the need for supplies lessened in the waning months of the war as less and less territory remained under the South's control. Even before the war ended, Chisum was looking for new markets. Change was everywhere and everyone had to respond to it. Tough, half-wild longhorn cattle were proliferating on Texas ranges even as growing numbers of farmers moved in to shrink the open range by staking agriculture claims under homesteading laws. Chisum seems always to have been a man who thought ahead; he was said to have "a good inkling" of what might be coming.

Sensing that the two things he needed most—a ready market and free public domain for grazing—were more likely to be found in New Mexico than in Texas, Chisum took his first herd across the Pecos in August of 1867, following the trail blazed not long before by Charles Goodnight and Oliver Loving. As his six hundred head were being sold off to the military at Fort Sumner throughout that fall and winter, Chisum observed the area and its potential for stock raising. In the spring of 1868, just before leaving the Bosque Grande site where Goodnight also had made camp, Chisum made a verbal agreement with Goodnight, whereby Chisum would send cattle from Texas to New Mexico, where Goodnight's trail outfits would take charge and drive them north to markets in Colorado and Kansas. This arrangement continued until 1871, with Chisum earning profits substantial enough to enable him in 1872 to make a permanent move to New Mexico and purchase from James Patterson the Bosque Grande ranch site.

CHAPTER FIVE

By late 1872 twenty thousand Chisum cattle, branded with the Chisum "long rail" line from hip to shoulder and also marked with the famous slit "jinglebob" ear, were grazing on public domain just south of Bosque Grande, located about thirty miles north of present-day Roswell. This Chisum operation formed the first large cattle ranch established in southeastern New Mexico, inaugurating a new era of freewheeling use of the Pecos Valley rangeland, which encompassed about ten thousand square miles.

Chisum's expertise with cattle became a matter of much comment during the years at Bosque Grande. He was known for his unerring accuracy in rapidly categorizing and counting cattle as they were brought in for marking and branding or preparations for shipment by trail west or north, and for his ability to quickly identify and root out the source of a cattle stampede.

Shortly after coming to New Mexico, Chisum had brought in a younger brother, Pitzer M. Chisum, a capable man who remained part of the operation until 1883. Pitzer was given charge of all range activities. The two brothers began looking at sites with better water sources and soon decided that a move farther south on the Pecos would be beneficial. In December of 1874 Chisum gave James Patterson twenty-four hundred head of cattle in exchange for a forty-acre site on the South Spring River, a large artesian stream that headed five miles south of Roswell and flowed five miles due east to the Pecos. Early in 1875 Chisum moved his entire operation to the new South Spring site, which included a fortresslike eight-room adobe house with an attached corral.

Chisum already displayed in full measure many of the traits that were to characterize him as a businessman until the end of his days. He was gruffly easy in manner, able to correct or discipline an employee without antagonizing him. He was slow to anger but extremely stubborn once he had taken a position. He was very concerned with the acquisition of money, and was preoccupied much of the time with business matters. But he employed a bookkeeper and preferred not to spend his time with accounting, and he also preferred to do business orally rather than in written form whenever possible. He was a frugal penny pincher in many small matters but was generous with friends and relatives. He often advanced wages to his cowboys, many of whom were from distant places and likely to be drifters. He gave credit on easy terms at his ranch commissaries and often provided free goods to new settlers. He gave frequent dances with plenty of food and drink, affairs attended by virtually every soul in the Pecos Valley. He traveled frequently, in the early years by horseback, later by horse and buggy. While on the range or at his ranch headquarters, he dressed as an ordinary cowhand; when traveling to St. Louis or points eastward, his more formal attire transformed him into a businessman distinguishable from city dwellers only because of his deeply tanned skin and his colloquial manner of speech.

By 1875, just before the move to South Spring, Chisum was the major economic power in the Pecos Valley and the largest cattleman in all southeastern New Mexico, grazing eighty thousand head on a hundred-mile stretch of public domain. It was during this period that Chisum's reputation spread, and newspapers as far afield as Denver and Phoenix began referring to Chisum as the Cattle King of the Pecos. In April 1875 the *Grant County Herald* of Silver City called Chisum "our stock king of New Mexico."

But in his usual state of prescience and caution, Chisum himself was aware of a growing trend toward smaller, more select herds rather than the type of herd represented by his thousands of leathery Texas longhorns. Demand for a better beef product was growing in midwestern markets, although Chisum was still finding good markets for his cattle.

In fact the route to Arizona used by his trail drivers became known as the Chisum Trail. It led west along the Hondo River, followed the Rio Ruidoso, and moved up through the White Mountains, then turned southwest along the southern edge of the White Sands, and from there crossed the southeast slope of the Organ Mountains to the San Augustine Pass, and then moved down the west side of the mountains. The herds forded the Rio Grande south of Las Cruces, then were trailed due west past Stein's Peak finally to reach beef markets in Arizona. During 1875 alone, more than ten thousand Chisum cattle moved over this route, while another twenty thousand head went to markets in Kansas, Missouri, and Colorado.

Even so Chisum was ready by the fall of 1875 to sign a carefully negotiated agreement with Hunter, Evans and Company, prominent beef contractors of St. Louis, Missouri, under which almost half of the Chisum stock would be transferred to the company, with the company holding title to all Chisum cattle as a bond pending final delivery of those cattle actually purchased. It was reported that Chisum was paid one-half cash down on the sale, the total sale price being $219,000.

Hunter and Evans were to take the cattle on a gradual, as-needed basis, in specific lots as the firm obtained government beef contracts. It was understood by both parties to the agreement that it would take a number of years to complete the actual transfer of so large a number of

CHAPTER FIVE

livestock.⁴ Thus it must be recognized that from this time forward the majority of the cattle grazed, rounded up, and shipped at various times by Chisum were no longer actually his but were under his management on behalf of the firm to which he had consigned them. At the same time, however, Chisum started new, more select herds in his own right.

Following the relocation to South Spring in 1875, Chisum's actions and decisions began to indicate a man wishing to put down roots, help develop a community, build something of permanence. For the first time since entering the cattle business back in 1854, he turned part of his attention to the raising of crops and set about digging irrigation ditches from the South Spring River to cultivate wheat, rye, millet, and alfalfa, often on an experimental basis to see what varieties would do best in the soil and climate conditions of the Pecos Valley. He employed Felix McKittrick, a nearby farmer, to oversee his farming projects, all of which were irrigated from an acequia with water capacity for one thousand acres.

Eventually another of Chisum's younger brothers, James Chisum, was given charge of the agricultural component of the Chisum holdings at South Spring. James Chisum, a widower, arrived at the ranch in December of 1877, bringing with him from Denton County in Texas his three children, Sallie L., Walter, and Will.⁵ The addition of a bright, pretty young niece and the two likable, hard-working young nephews brought added enjoyment and stability to Chisum's peripatetic life. For despite periodic rumors that the bachelor cattleman was in the midst of courting one or another of the area's relatively few eligible young women, Chisum never married, and there is no evidence that he ever came close to doing so. He was sometimes heard to remark in his typically self-deprecating, humorous way, "no girl has courted me long enough yet," or, "it's best I'm not married; no woman would put up with all my traveling."

The presence of Lincoln County's largest cattleman in the Roswell area had immediate impact on the fortunes of the small settlement lying just six miles northwest of the Chisum headquarters. Taking it as a sign that the area held potential for both farming and livestock endeavors, emigrants to the territory, both from Texas and elsewhere, began to file homestead claims southeast of Roswell and to start small cattle operations that utilized the public domain for grazing. Chisum was generally friendly to those setting up farms. He was particularly helpful to a Mormon group that settled near him. He was far less friendly when it came to incursions onto the public domain by incoming cowmen.

Chisum had staked out his turf along both sides of the Pecos; the smaller lots of new cattlemen inevitably got mixed in with the huge Chisum herds when out on the range, causing extra work at roundup time and opening the door to thievery of Chisum cattle by unscrupulous operators.

Cattle rustling, in fact, increased steadily to epidemic proportions during the 1870s and was the subject of much newspaper reporting and editorializing. Both local government authorities and cattle-owner associations made repeated, generally futile, efforts to stamp it out. Rustling was too easy and too lucrative to be easily eliminated. Lawmen were few and far between. Brands could be altered, often at secret camps set up for just such purposes. Good markets for stolen cattle existed south of the border in Mexico, in Arizona, or right in New Mexico, where such men as Pat Coghlin of Tularosa would receive stolen cattle at their ranches, pay off the thieves, then resell the stolen cattle to the beef contractors for Fort Stanton. With the government paying the same price for stolen cattle as that received for legally purchased cattle, the middlemen, contractors, and rustlers all made good profits on rustling.

While Chisum's concern over rustling was genuine, leading him to make several proposals to territorial governors that a comprehensive system of guarding against thieves be established, a large share of Chisum's ire was directed specifically at legitimate small cattlemen, who affronted him merely by having the temerity to challenge his longstanding claim to a vast range, including all of its frontage water. Chisum cowboys, often numbering as many as a hundred, went armed at all times; as the 1870s wore on, they were increasingly ready to use their arms to intimidate and even to kill invaders on the range where the Chisum herds grazed.

Chisum men also showed themselves on at least one occasion to be killers for no reason other than greed and possibly prejudice against Hispanos. It happened in the winter of 1877 on the Canadian range in the Texas Panhandle, and Chisum himself probably never knew about it. J. Phelps White was scouting the land north of Tascosa for his uncle, George W. Littlefield of Texas. White came across "five or six big mule wagons that had been burned." He investigated and found out that Chisum trail driver Frank McNabb and his outfit, who were delivering cattle to Hunter and Evans, "had run onto these wagons and a bunch of Mexican buffalo hunters. They killed the Mexicans in order to steal their work cattle, and burned their bodies with their wagons. They spared only one person, so an old Mexican told me later, which was a boy." By then McNabb had gone on to Colorado to sell the stolen cattle. "Then they came back to New Mexico and got killed themselves . . . during the Lincoln County War."⁶

The ongoing state of hostilities between Chisum and the small cowmen and renegade rustlers on the Pecos range was one of the elements contributing to the bloody episode known as the Lincoln County War. It was a war between two factions, each of which was competing in two important areas of economic activity.

One area was the cattle business; there was competition between small cattlemen and large cattlemen, with the small cattlemen often losing out to the larger ones who used force to control access to water sources. There also was competition for access to beef markets, with Chisum throwing himself directly into the line of fire when he refused to use the Lawrence G. Murphy firm in Lincoln as middleman purchaser of his cattle for supplying Fort Stanton. Chisum sought instead to make his own contract with the military by underbidding the Murphy firm. As a result of Chisum's threatening competitiveness, Murphy, as the beef subcontractor for a powerful Santa Fe government contractor, viewed Chisum as an enemy to be thwarted at every turn.

The second area of economic competition between the factions was mercantile trade and banking, an area that included a whole range of business activity, from the buying up of local agricultural production in Lincoln County, to the retail selling of farm supplies, clothing, food, and whiskey, to the granting of credit and cashing of checks. In this area, too, the Murphy firm held virtual monopoly until suddenly, in the year 1877, Chisum openly allied himself with new Lincoln residents Alexander A. McSween and John Tunstall. McSween and Tunstall opened a large new store, and with Chisum's backing they also organized the county's first official bank.

Thus the lines were drawn, with Murphy and his allies among small Pecos cattlemen on one side; Chisum and McSween with their allies among Lincoln area folk who had been hurt by the Murphy monopoly on the other side. The lines were drawn as early as 1877; the bloody denouement came in July 1878; the violent aftermath rumbled on until 1881 and may be said to have come to a fitful close with the death of Billy the Kid in July of that year.

Chisum had good reason for joining with McSween and Tunstall to create competition ending the Murphy firm's monopoly of commercial activity. Although Chisum obtained several beef contracts from Fort Stanton, "more than once, Chisum's bids for government beef contracts had been thwarted by Murphy and his Santa Fe allies."⁷ There can be no doubt that Chisum, McSween, and Tunstall all were economically motivated in joining as business partners and allies. Letters written by Tunstall and McSween clearly indicate that their goals were to make large sums of money and to substitute their own economic control for that of Murphy. Nevertheless it would also appear that Chisum developed a genuinely warm relationship with the young lawyer McSween and his vivacious, if equally ambitious, wife Susan. Although McSween's letters to Tunstall's family in England are recognizably self-serving, there probably was some basis in fact for McSween's statement to Tunstall's sister that Chisum always referred to his three Lincoln friends as "the family."

Such a friendship, with its economic implications for all concerned, not only aroused the enmity of Murphy and his partners but inevitably led to hostility toward Chisum from a figure far more threatening than the amiably unscrupulous Murphy, who after all was only a local kingpin. It was, in fact, the enmity of Thomas B. Catron of Santa Fe that brought trouble for Chisum. In the mid-1870s Catron was U.S. district attorney for New Mexico, president of the First National Bank of Santa Fe, a rancher, the owner of large amounts of land, and a bigtime land speculator; all this in addition to being head of the Republican party in the territory.

And as it happened, Catron held the mortgages on the Lincoln mercantile establishment run by Murphy and his young protégé, James Dolan, and on Murphy's cattle ranch thirty miles to the west. Murphy and Dolan also ran some two thousand head of cattle on the Pecos below South Spring; their camp at Seven Rivers was believed by Chisum and others to be a gathering place for rustlers. All too aware that Murphy and Dolan would not be able to repay their large debts to him if their complex business empire, including its shadier aspects, was ruined by a bigtime cattleman like Chisum operating in league with upstarts like McSween and Tunstall, Catron used every opportunity to damage Chisum either legally or financially.

There is nothing in the record, however, to suggest that Chisum was doing anything other than seeking to protect his own interests, not ruin Murphy, when he swung into action in the fall of 1876 to halt the Seven Rivers gang. Large numbers of his cattle were missing during months when he and his men were working day and night to put together cattle lots to be dispersed to Arizona or Kansas to fill Hunter and Evans contracts. Chisum personally went to El Paso and saw proof that cattle stolen from him were being sold there by men from Seven Rivers.[8]

CHAPTER FIVE

Following several months of simmering range war and several killings, in April of 1877 Chisum himself led a group of his men south to the Seven Rivers home of the Beckwith family, where a number of those believed to belong to the ring of cattle thieves were "holed up." The Chisum forces first removed the horses belonging to the men in the house, eliminating their means of escape. Then they hunkered down in the arroyos and brush around the adobe house and settled in for a tense siege, which lasted several days. Chisum offered to take the women and children in the house out to safety; they refused. Finally, with the eventual victory of the besiegers clearly inevitable, the two groups negotiated a temporary standoff, and the Chisum men rode away. Chisum had shown he meant business. But as a perhaps unintended result, the Murphy-Dolan faction became an "implacable enemy" of Chisum and all who associated with him.[9]

It proved to be a hard year for Chisum, for shortly after the Seven Rivers siege he came into contact with the smallpox virus and went into the crisis period of the disease while camped with one of his outfits far south on the Pecos. His friend, near-son, and employee, the black Frank Chisum, rode four straight days on horseback to and from Fort Stanton to obtain medical help for him. The Chisum cowboys put their boss in a special tent and assigned men to nurse him day and night. Frank Chisum returned and remained at Chisum's side through the most contagious period of open sores, rotting flesh, high fever, and heavy scabs. Then he, too, came down with the disease. The faces of both men were left deeply pitted by their bouts with smallpox.

By the end of 1877, Chisum was prepared to embark on an extended business trip to St. Louis, in the company of McSween and his wife. Chisum had been using the young lawyer to handle his legal affairs for several years. The two had first met shortly after McSween's arrival in Lincoln in 1875, their acquaintance beginning at the Hondo Valley ranch home of the Casey family, a favored overnight stopping place for many making the two-day trip from the Pecos Valley to the county seat at Lincoln. The trip now planned by McSween and Chisum was a natural expression of friendship and shared business convenience, with Mrs. McSween intending to see doctors while in St. Louis. The three left Lincoln County on December 18, intending to travel by buckboard to the nearest railhead, at Trinidad, Colorado, and continue from there by train eastward.

But upon reaching Las Vegas on Christmas Eve, the small party found its plans abruptly aborted. The travelers were forcibly detained by the sheriff of San Miguel County. James J. Dolan had obtained from W. L. Rynerson, district attorney for the third judicial district, an arrest warrant for McSween on charges of embezzlement of life-insurance proceeds McSween had collected on behalf of the heirs to Emil Fritz, the deceased former partner of Murphy. McSween, confident that the charges he believed politically motivated could be easily cleared, left under escort for the court at Mesilla, while Mrs. McSween was convinced by her husband and Chisum to continue her journey eastward for rest and medical care.

As for Chisum, he now came face-to-face with the kind of protracted legal complexities that could be set in motion by a determined political foe. Catron had found the ideal opportunity to attack Chisum in a court of law as the result of an attempt by Santa Fe merchant William Rosenthal to collect on a promissory note for $2,370.69, allegedly cosigned by Chisum when he was a resident of Texas. Catron had obtained a court order prohibiting Chisum from leaving the jurisdiction of the New Mexico courts, and he was placed in the county jail on charges on having resisted arrest.

The note in question was one of several acquired by New Mexico investors in the mid 1870s. Catron and his law partner, W. T. Thornton, "had as clients not only J. J. Dolan but certain other persons who were enemies of Chisum and who claimed to hold court judgments against him, including William Rosenthal, who had managed to secure old notes on Wilbur, Chisum and Clark, the meat-packing project in Arkansas."[10] A court in Texas had cleared Chisum in the matter, and the statute of limitations had ended the possibility of further legal action in that state; but the notes had nevertheless been sold as collectible securities to out-of-state investors. Rosenthal would have derived considerable benefit from a court judgment against Chisum, as Chisum most likely would have paid off the debt in cattle. Rosenthal could have made good use of Chisum cattle costing him nothing but his court expenses; he was badly in need of cheap cattle to meet his beef contract at Fort Stanton. Under terms of the contract, Rosenthal received a price per pound that was too low for him to make a profit after paying livestock producers.[11]

During the eight-week period from early January to early March of 1878 in which he was incarcerated at Las Vegas, Chisum broke from his usual custom of committing few thoughts to paper and wrote a lengthy statement presenting his side of the case, parts of which were published in various territorial newspapers. According to Chisum, he

CHAPTER FIVE

had been approached in 1867 by "Mr. Wilbur," a businessman who wanted to open a packing plant in Fort Smith, Arkansas, with a man named Clark. During discussions between Wilbur and Chisum, it was proposed that Chisum join the venture as a partner who would supply beef cattle. Chisum claimed that he never heard from Wilbur again, and that the plan was never formalized with his participation. Only later, he said, did he learn that the plant had opened and briefly operated, using his name on papers of incorporation and his forged signature on notes of indebtedness issued by the company.[12]

Catron later introduced as evidence in court a document said to be articles of incorporation bearing Chisum's name and a promissory note bearing a signature said by a witness for the prosecution to be that of Chisum. The case against Chisum was delayed in the courts, as no definitive answer could be found to the question of whether Chisum actually owned sufficient assets in New Mexico that could be attached should the notes be found valid.[13] Since 1875 legal title to the Chisum livestock had been held by Hunter and Evans of St. Louis. Chisum had presented only a short list of assets when requested to state his personal holdings while in jail in Las Vegas.

James Chisum went to Las Vegas and posted bond for his brother in early March. Chisum was released and the two men traveled together back to the South Spring Ranch. Along the way Chisum undoubtedly heard from his brother that during his absence McSween's business partner Tunstall had been killed in a brutal ambush by a sheriff's posse, and that scant weeks later McSween partisans had captured and killed two of the men accused of killing Tunstall.

A state of near anarchy now prevailed in the huge county. The only existing vehicle for law and order, the sheriff's office, was believed by many to be a corrupt agency acting on behalf of the Murphy-Dolan faction. Everywhere people were tense, angry, or simply afraid. Nearly every man, whether farmer, cowman, boardinghouse cook, or saloonkeeper wore a gun strapped to his waist. Wagons were being loaded with bedding and tools, as families prepared to leave a place where law and order had broken down. Every day the battle lines hardened as cowboys, drifters, small ranchers, and outlaws of various sorts joined one or the other of the opposing factions.

Chisum could have had no illusions that he could avoid the repercussions of the bitterness and rancor all around him. His very presence in the county was a powerful economic force; he hired many men, he bought large amounts of supplies, he sold supplies through his ranch stores, his cattle were the county's most lucrative export. And his own range claims were one cause for the choosing of sides, the killings, the hatreds. Not only could he not stand aside as a disinterested observer, but he already was a partisan in the battle being joined. Having been associated with McSween and Tunstall in several capacities for some time, there was no question of Chisum being neutral in actuality, or pretending to be neutral and getting away with it.

In fact as Chisum must have been informed immediately upon his arrival home from Las Vegas, the tough band of McSween partisans known as the "Regulators" had brought their prisoners, Frank Baker and William Morton, directly to South Spring after their capture. Only a day after leaving South Spring, the prisoners were killed.[14] The Chisum ranch, even in its owner's absence, already was being used as a battle post in the Lincoln County War. Sallie Chisum, then nineteen years old, wrote in her diary that Morton and Baker had been placed in a center room with no windows with a guard posted all night at the door.

A clear pattern of involvement had been set by Chisum's past associations, and despite the fact that the powerful cattleman never permitted himself to become drawn into the running gunbattles in the way that McSween eventually did, Chisum continued until after McSween's death to give sanctuary, material support, and quite probably his advice and counsel to the anti–Murphy-Dolan faction. No record exists of the talks between McSween, his men, and Chisum that must have taken place during the several occasions between March and July of 1878 on which McSween sought shelter from the turmoil of Lincoln at Chisum's place on the Pecos.

For instance while it is known that McSween was with Chisum at South Spring in the days preceding the 1 April 1878 killing of Sheriff William Brady and Deputy Sheriff George Hindman on the main street of Lincoln, there can only be speculation in the absence of evidence as to whether McSween alone, or McSween and Chisum together, had any hint that this action might be taken by the Regulators, or whether Chisum had advised McSween either to pursue or retreat from the steadily accelerating course of violence his associates were following. Perhaps all that can be said with certainty is that Chisum, on the one hand, did not back away from his support of McSween, but on the other hand, did not at any time participate in the open warfare finally joined by McSween as the climax neared. The only hard facts are that "many jinglebob employees joined the band" of McSween partisans, and that "on various occasions Chisum's headquarters on South Spring River was host to this roving constabulary."[15]

CHAPTER FIVE

Chisum traveled to Lincoln with the McSweens when it was time for the April court session to begin. The town was in an uproar over the shocking killings of Brady and Hindman that had just taken place. McSween was arrested immediately upon his arrival, even though he had been nowhere near the scene of the murders. McSween insisted that he and his wife be placed under custody at Fort Stanton rather than remain in the hands of a deputy sheriff who had served Brady and was now replacing him without legal authority to do so.

Judge Warren Bristol came from Mesilla, stayed at Fort Stanton, and was brought into Lincoln by military escort each day to conduct court. His docket was crowded with criminal charges, most centering around the numerous killings of recent weeks. Chisum was present in court to lend support to McSween. He also was there as an observer with a personal interest in the outcome of the charges against Murphy and Dolan.

A grand jury was selected and convened. A thorough job was done by the conscientious jury members. McSween was exonerated of criminal charges of embezzlement. Dolan men were indicted for cattle stealing. Members of the pro-Dolan Brady posse were indicted for the murder of Tunstall. Billy the Kid and other members of the Regulators were indicted for the retaliatory murders of Brady and Hindman. It seemed that justice might be done after all. Chisum attended a celebratory town meeting. Dolan announced that the store would cease doing business for the time being. He appeared to recognize a setback for the Murphy-Dolan faction.

Within a short time after the court session ended, however, it became clear that neither of the two factions considered itself defeated and neither intended to acquiesce peacefully to arrest warrants. New men, armed and dangerous, arrived in Lincoln and placed themselves at the disposal of the pro-Dolan forces. In the Pecos Valley to the east, men opposed to Chisum who previously had played no part in the hostilities now openly declared their pro-Dolan stance. And in the meantime, resentment mounted among McSween supporters, because those indicted for Tunstall's murder had been freed on bond, while arrest warrants were given for those accused of killing Brady and Hindman.

By late spring 1878 Chisum began to act on his growing apprehension. The seemingly endless round of revenge and open outlawry boded no good for sound business operations in Lincoln County. Governor Samuel B. Axtell favored the Dolan side; on May 18 he removed Sheriff John Copeland, Brady's successor, and replaced him with Dolan supporter George Peppin. Peppin deputized Marion Turner of Roswell, an enemy of Chisum. Chisum's cattle business was his life; he had no intention of risking its complete ruin. He made plans to move his cattle and headquarters to the Tascosa area of the Texas Panhandle.

But it was a complicated affair to pull up stakes and move a family, employees, and a large herd of livestock. He was still in the process of closing out the South Spring operation when on July 20 the terrible news of a five-day gunbattle and fire at Lincoln, ending with McSween's death, was brought to Chisum by Charles Bowdre, one of the Regulators. The plan to move was quickly finalized.

Pitzer Chisum remained at South Spring with a skeleton crew, while James and his children led the move northeast to the new site on the Canadian River. They traveled to Bosque Grande first and rested there for fifteen days, moved up to Fort Sumner, where they were joined by Chisum, and then moved northeastward.[16] Sallie Chisum drove one of the wagons carrying family goods. Before reaching the final destination, Frank Chisum escorted the three young people back over the trail to Anton Chico, in New Mexico, where they were enrolled in school.

Chisum had acted wisely in selecting the panhandle; the several thousand heifers he brought up from the Pecos did well on the new range. Chisum then made a business trip to the East, leaving James in charge.[17] There are few records of this episode in Chisum's life, but again actions spoke louder than words. Although his own abandonment of the Pecos Valley had prompted several hundred other settlers to follow suit, Chisum himself seems to have kept watch on events in Lincoln County. In February 1879 he told an interviewer in Mesilla that he had recently sold holdings in Arizona, after a trip through Colorado to California, and now intended to return to New Mexico. By summer preparations were under way in the panhandle for a move back to the Pecos. And in the fall of 1879, Chisum returned to the South Spring ranch headquarters. He personally supervised the return drive of a smaller herd.[18] It was probably more than mere coincidence that Chisum chose to return only after Axtell had been removed from office and replaced by Governor Lew Wallace, who had taken a personal hand in attempting to restore law and order to Lincoln County.

Ever a builder and doer, Chisum plunged into a round of ceaseless, and in many ways rewarding, activities upon his return to Pecos country. With Roswell beginning to show signs of permanent life, he developed strong social ties with its few leading citizens, including the upright and ambitious Joseph C. Lea and the staunchly civic-minded young

CHAPTER FIVE

John Poe. On 16 January 1880, the marriage of Chisum's twenty-one-year-old niece Sallie to William Robert at Anton Chico was cause for a happy celebration at the old jinglebob ranch. Chisum by all accounts liked Robert, and over the next few years he gave him important bookkeeping responsibilities and seems to have envisioned the new family member as a possible eventual successor to his own leadership of the cattle operation.

Other changes took place as well. Chisum was indisputably the driving force in the family's ranching, farming, and livestock marketing operations, and he continued to make all major decisions concerning capital, breeding of livestock, and sales transactions. But for reasons of his own, he had had title to the stock transferred to Pitzer Chisum when his arrangement with Hunter and Evans was concluded, shortly before the return to South Spring from the panhandle. James Chisum then was given a share in the business as well. And it was in the spring of 1880 that Chisum personally selected two hundred head of fine yearling heifers and gave them to Frank Chisum, his faithful longtime employee, in order that the black cowboy might have his own stake in the future.

This same period also saw a resurgence of cattle rustling, much of it under the leadership of Billy the Kid. A chance meeting in Fort Sumner between Chisum and the Kid sometime in early 1880 brought a demand that Chisum pay the Kid for what the Kid called his "services" on behalf of McSween and Chisum as one of the Regulators in the battles at Lincoln. When Chisum declined to accept the notion that he had ever hired the young outlaw to do anything for him, Billy the Kid walked away with a resentment subsequently translated into stepped-up stealing of Chisum cattle. Several newspapers also reported that the Kid had threatened to kill Chisum if he got the chance. Though Chisum never commented publicly on the matter, he undoubtedly was relieved to learn while in Santa Fe during July of 1881 that the Kid had been killed at Fort Sumner.

By late 1881 the Chisum cattle operation was thriving under a new type of defined boundary management, with range claims now extending along the Pecos only from about twenty miles north of Roswell to some forty miles south. John, Pitzer, and James Chisum, along with William Robert, all traveled frequently and participated in territorial livestock associations. Numerous improvements were made at the South Spring headquarters site. The old adobe ranch house and corral were torn down and a new house, quickly dubbed the "long house," was constructed just to the southeast of the old structure.

The long house, also made of adobe bricks, had a pitched roof and a verandah extending the length of the building. Facing west, it contained eight large rooms, four on each side of a wide central hallway. The gracious house, approached by a cottonwood-lined drive, was well furnished, with Chisum's bedroom on the north serving him also as a comfortable office with a desk and large dictionary stand. Chisum's friend J. Phelps White recalled Chisum's "good guest room with a bed fixed up nicely for anybody that came in. On one side of the room he had a fireplace, but he never slept in bed himself but would pull down some blankets and always slept on the floor."[19] The house cost twelve thousand dollars to build. To the east and south of the long house were buildings used as camp houses for the Chisum cowboys and for dances held at the ranch.

The Chisum household was a fairly large one, including not only Pitzer and James and his children, but Sallie's husband William Robert, several of the longtime cowhands, and a number of trusted servants who had long worked for Chisum as cooks or gardeners. Lilly Casey was the eldest daughter of Chisum's old friend Robert Casey, the settler on the Hondo who had been killed in 1875. She visited the Chisum ranch often as a girl and recalled in later years that hundreds of rose bushes had been planted around the house. Chisum clearly enjoyed the new house; Lilly Casey remembered watching him as he sat on the east porch in the cool of early mornings, cheerfully tossing cracker crumbs to the fish in the deep, clear ditch running the length of the house.[20]

With his vast experience in all aspects of the cattle industry, Chisum knew well how to make the most of whatever opportunities existed in regional markets at any given time. He was also an innovator, constantly on the lookout for the best new breeding stock. As a result his herd grew in quality as well as size during the early 1880s. In April of 1883 the *Denver Daily News* reported that Chisum had one of the finest herds in New Mexico, with "30,000 of the best graded cattle."

But even as all seemed finally to be falling into place for the indomitable veteran cattleman, new troubles loomed. Strains within the complex arrangement of family management came first. Pitzer Chisum was critical of the way his brother James was handling ranch affairs with the help of his son-in-law William Robert. Pitzer apparently believed the two were jeopardizing the ranch's future; with little direct experience in the cattle business, they were mortgaging ranch bulidings in order

CHAPTER FIVE

to expand. Sometime during 1883 Pitzer left South Spring and returned to Paris, Texas, where he married for the first time and lived out his days on the proceeds of his settlement with the family, which amounted to some $50,000, although his interest in the livestock was actually worth closer to $100,000.[21]

By late 1883 Chisum was facing his own private tragedy. A tumor had developed on his neck and continued to grow larger, causing him pain and eventually forcing him to hold his head far to one side. Though he sought medical help and tried to remain optimistic, he well understood the implications, since "his father and grandfather had died from the same trouble."[22] The fortunes of the cattle ranch suffered as Chisum was forced to turn over more and more of the daily management to James Chisum and William Robert. It was John Chisum, after all, whose expertise was vital in complicated cattle transactions.

After months of struggling to conceal his growing pain and anxiety, Chisum decided to seek the best medical treatment. Insisting that no family member accompany him, he left by carriage with a driver on 7 July 1884 and traveled to Kansas City, where he underwent surgery to remove the tumor on July 24. Told that the operation was a success, he started for home. But on reaching Las Vegas, he fell seriously ill again. Doctors advised that he go to the health spa at Eureka Springs, Arkansas, for further care and therapy. Chisum lived in a hotel there during the fall and winter months, the tumor returning and growing even larger than before. In December James went to stay with him. On 22 December 1884, Chisum died, his brother by his side. On Christmas Day he was buried in the family plot in Paris, Texas.

In accordance with Chisum's wishes, his brother James took charge of the cattle ranch, which was renamed the Jinglebob Land and Cattle Company. Without the astute leadership of Chisum, however, the ranch's new managers were not able to overcome the difficulties stemming from the drought of 1886–87 and the ensuing depression in the beef-cattle industry. Sallie and William Robert were divorced after the births of two children, and Robert left the company. Although James Chisum was able to get a large loan from a bank in Danville, Kentucky, the bank eventually had to foreclose.

Thus a pioneering enterprise in frontier Lincoln County died away within a decade after the death of its founder, a man whose character was uniquely suited to the opportunities and challenges of his time and place.

Lawrence G. Murphy, James J. Dolan, and John H. Riley

In the mid-1870s the two-story adobe Murphy-Dolan store in Lincoln was a thriving commercial center serving Hispanic residents, Anglo settlers, local military personnel, and reservation Indians. Nestled in seeming security in the narrow valley of the rushing mountain stream known as the Rio Bonito, the pitch-roofed building rose in perfect proportion against the piñon-covered hills and high mountain peaks that surrounded it. As shadows played across its heavy wood doors and the planked floor of its front porch, shaded by a second-story balcony, the store seemed to meld with its surroundings; the browns of wood and adobe were enlivened by the flickering green tracery of trees, the shifting blues of the nearby sky, and the pale dusty hue of Lincoln's main street. At sunrise and again at sunset, the mud-plastered walls of the sturdy structure were turned to burnished gold by slanting sunlight. Except for Fort Stanton, the store was the most imposing building in all Lincoln County. By those with urban standards of architecture, its pretentions to dominance would have gone unnoticed; but to those living in the raw frontier environment of southeastern New Mexico, it appeared an appropriate enough setting for what was widely recognized as the focal point of the region's economic and political power.

The three men whose names were most closely identified with the enterprise known as "the store" or "the firm" were Lawrence G. Murphy, James J. Dolan, and John H. Riley. Though they differed in style, they had much in common: all were of Irish descent; all were former army men; all were congenial and convivial in personality; all were bachelors during the store years at Lincoln; and above all else, all three were audacious and ambitious to the point of amorality if not immorality. All three were schemers, deal-makers, pragmatists devoid of lofty ideals. In their actions they expressed a conviction that the world rewards those who take whatever they can get.

Their careers represent a striking amalgam of two leitmotifs in American history from the end of the Civil War almost to the end of the nineteenth century. There was first the frontier dynamic, based on the widely shared belief that all things were possible in the new western land waiting for the determined, the tough, those with dreams. And then there was the increasingly influential business ethic, based on the notion that America's commercial and industrial sector, the key to a prosperous future, should be left unregulated, trusted to serve honorably as an engine of social progress. Frontiersmen and businessmen at one and the same time, Murphy, Dolan, and Riley were, each in his own way, as comfortable with a cow or a gun as with a ledger or a contract. Certainly they were ready to use any or all of these to ensure financial success.

Murphy was born in Ireland in 1831. After emigrating to the United States in his youth, he enlisted in the army in 1859. He was living in Santa Fe and no longer in the military when the Civil War started, but promptly signed up with the First New Mexico Volunteers. Serving under Kit Carson at the Battle of Valverde, in the battle to subdue the Mescaleros, and finally in the Navajo campaign, Murphy was promoted to captain and then major before being honorably discharged in 1866. For the remainder of his life the jovial Irishman was called "Major Murphy."

Almost immediately after his release from military service, Murphy used his contacts at Fort Stanton and Fort Sumner to secure the post of civilian sutler to four-company Fort Stanton.[23] With a partner, the German-born Emil Fritz, he opened a store, a brewery, and a saloon on the military property. The quiet, methodical Fritz was bookkeeper for the partnership, while Murphy utilized his own considerable skills in dealing with the public to build business. Even before they were given official sanction as post traders at Fort Stanton in April 1868, Murphy and Fritz "had discovered army contracting and received one-year contracts from September 1, 1867, to furnish both fresh beef and beef on the hoof for the Fort Stanton garrison." They also began to supply the fort with lumber, corn, and other supplies on a contractual basis.[24]

In 1869 Murphy decided to make Lincoln his place of residence, and he soon opened a branch store in the small settlement. In 1870 he was made probate judge and began playing a political role in local affairs. With his affable ways and air of business propriety, the red-bearded former military man cut an impressive figure, dressed in his customary formal black suit. Friendly to one and all, he was regarded by the people of Lincoln during these early years as a man of merit providing essential trade goods and community leadership. In 1871, with business growing, Murphy hired young Jimmie Dolan to work as a clerk for him at Fort Stanton.

Born in Ireland in 1848, Dolan had come to the United States as a child with his parents. He joined the army in 1863 and was posted to New Mexico in 1866. When he was hired by Murphy, Dolan brought more than clerking skills to the firm. Since his discharge from the army he had been operating a cow camp at Seven Rivers on the west bank of the Pecos. The military beef contract he held was a valuable addition to the Murphy operation. Only three years after he was hired, he was made a full partner in the firm.

The short, round-faced young Dolan was smart, aggressive, and almost entirely "devoid of principle."[25] He liked to talk, was convincingly sincere in manner, and was known as a persuasive negotiator. He was also something of a bully and a braggart, and his argumentative nature and hair-trigger temper earned him as many enemies as his Irish charm earned him friends. In 1873 a heated argument between Dolan and a Fort Stanton officer was a contributing factor in Murphy's dismissal from the post of sutler, after charges of intimidating federal agents at the Mescalero Indian Reservation were made against the firm.[26]

After selling his building at Fort Stanton for eight thousand dollars, Murphy moved his entire mercantile operation to Lincoln. It was at this time that the Murphy-Dolan store was built, complete with meeting rooms and second-floor bedrooms for use by the firm's partners. The building contained twenty-eight hundred square feet on each of its two floors and cost a little over seven thousand dollars to build.[27] Fritz had been spending most of his time at his ranch near Lincoln for some time. In the summer of 1873, he went back to Germany, hoping to recover from the tuberculosis he had contracted. He died in Germany in the spring of 1874. The Lincoln store was then operated by Murphy and Dolan as partners. Always looking to expand their possibilities for profit, the two men also acquired the government beef and flour contracts for the Mescalero reservation, acting as subcontractors for the Rosenthal firm.

John H. Riley, after clerking for Murphy for several years, was made a junior partner in the firm in 1876. Since 1873 Riley had been operating a cattle ranch west of Fort Stanton, specializing as a dealer who bought cattle on one market and sold them on another. It was Riley's access to cattle that prompted Murphy and Dolan to offer him an interest in the firm; he was in a position to help them meet their beef-subcontracting commitments. In July 1875 Murphy and Riley were named by William Rosenthal of Santa Fe as his beef subcontractors for supplying the Mescalero Indian Agency. In actuality the Murphy firm, even with Riley's knowledge of the cattle business, never was able to make a profit solely by buying cattle on the open market and then selling them to the government. Almost from the start the firm turned to stolen cattle, which could be obtained for five dollars a head, as a supply source, in addition to purchasing from legitimate stockmen who could not afford to sell the same class of cattle for less than fifteen dollars a head.[28]

CHAPTER FIVE

Born in Ireland in 1841, Riley had emigrated with his parents to the United States in 1853. He was in California when the Civil War started, and after enlisting in the Union Army, he was assigned to Carleton's California Column and entered New Mexico in 1862. Like Dolan, Riley was quick-tempered and had participated in a good many gunfights over the years. But as a partner in the Lincoln business, he tended to play the role of behind-the-scenes strategist, while Dolan acted as public spokesman and leader of the Murphy-Dolan faction. Shortly after Riley was made a partner, Jacob B. "Billy" Mathews was given an interest and made a "silent" junior partner. Mathews previously had farmed in the Roswell area.

Always a heavy drinker in an environment where whiskey was viewed as a natural part of daily life, Murphy, even in the midst of his growing prosperity, now began to fall victim to his personal weakness. He spent more and more time at his Carrizo Spring ranch home west of Lincoln and finally relinquished operational control of the store to Dolan and Riley, who bought out his interest in 1877, changing the firm's name to J. J. Dolan and Company.[29] Dolan and Riley mortgaged all of their personal property as well as the store in order to acquire Murphy's share in the business. It was Catron of Santa Fe who held the titles on the mortgage, eventually lending more than twenty thousand dollars to the two partners.[30]

Despite the name change, the Lincoln mercantile business continued to be commonly referred to as "the Murphy store," perhaps justifiably, for no changes took place in the firm's longstanding operational methods. Not even Murphy's gracious ways as a host on festive occasions had been sufficient in the end to conceal his hardfisted greed and his callous disregard for the rights of others. The tradition continued under Dolan and Riley's management, and understandably so. Not only had the firm's numerous underhanded schemes to maximize profits worked well in the past, but they were even more essential to the new ownership, due to heavy indebtedness as well as to the threat of new competition.

When an attorney of impeccable integrity, Frank Warner Angel of New York, was sent by Washington in 1878 to investigate troubled conditions in both Colfax and Lincoln counties, he accumulated a mass of documentation and numerous eyewitness accounts that added up to a stinging indictment of the Murphy-Dolan operation on charges of fraudulent business activity. Some were breaches of law while others were merely unethical.

From the start of their work as suppliers to Fort Stanton and the Indian reservation, Murphy and Dolan had lied to the government about how many Indians were being served, padding the numbers and consistently overcharging the government for beef, corn, and salt. The firm had delivered improperly milled corn and wheat. And although it was more difficult to prove that stolen cattle were being sold to the government, it was widely known that Dolan's cow camp at Seven Rivers was a holding place for stolen cattle and was run by a number of notorious cattle thieves.

The ordinary citizens of Lincoln and the surrounding countryside also suffered under the yoke of the firm's unscrupulous methods. Farmers and ranchers had no choice but to sell their beef, milk, corn, or vegetable produce to Murphy-Dolan: the store was their only available market outlet. The firm acted as middleman, selling these goods at the fort, the reservation, and the Lincoln store. Murphy-Dolan offered the farmers and ranchers below-wholesale-market prices for their produce, then charged them above-retail-market prices for the food, clothing, and other goods they had to buy from the store.

As most people had little cash, they had no choice but to accept the low prices offered and then go into debt to the firm as they purchased their family essentials. Murphy "held so many people in debt that he could dictate to almost anyone, as he did frequently."[31] There can be little doubt, however, that settlers and military personnel alike welcomed the generous terms of credit offered by Murphy. In fact while Murphy may have gained leverage over those who were in debt to him, his policy of operating as the local "mercantile capitalist" hardly served his business interests. Despite a large volume of sales, Murphy and Company was continually short of actual cash income. The firm's ledger shows that for the months of May through December 1871, sales exceeded receipts "by over $25,000, while in 1872 this difference came to more than $38,000."[32] Although "nearly everyone did make payments on their accounts," most settlers paid in produce such as corn, hay, wheat, barley, and occasionally cattle. Company records indicate the firm made most of its profits through its government contracts, and made perhaps its best rate of return on extra purchases made by the Indian Agency on a noncontractual basis for such items as sugar, coffee, and flour.[33]

Murphy was willing, however, to go to court against some of those in debt to him. McSween told investigator Angel that there were many cases in which a settler, driven into bankruptcy by Murphy, would abandon his homesteaded property in despair, only to have it illegally taken over by Murphy, who would rent it to some new settler unaware that Murphy was not the legal owner. If the settler discovered that Murphy did not hold title and refused to pay rent, Murphy would prosecute, resulting in "either the opposing party giving in or leaving the country."[34]

Murphy and Dolan were able to operate as they did in the economic sphere because their control extended into the political sphere. Murphy's readiness to take debtors to court, for example, stemmed from his confidence that the local sheriff, judge, and prosecutor would be responsive to his wishes. By 1877 Murphy and his associates "could install their henchmen in the county offices as easily as dealing a deck of cards and also see that they obeyed orders afterwards." In 1876 William Brady, former military officer with Murphy, took office for the second time as Lincoln County sheriff. It "was commonly recognized that Brady was a Murphy henchman and took his orders from the man who had been responsible for placing him in office."[35]

Murphy's political influence extended beyond the local level. The would-be frontier tycoon sought and won backing from territorial power brokers. William L. Rynerson, district attorney for southern New Mexico, was an ally of Murphy, whose words out of court and actions in court betrayed blatant partisanship. Catron, as U.S. district attorney and territorial attorney general, had close ties of business and friendship with Murphy and his partners. Governor Samuel B. Axtell displayed such tolerance for the corruption of Lincoln County government by Murphy and Dolan that he was removed from office in 1878. Axtell considered himself a personal friend of Murphy and in 1876 accepted a personal loan of eighteen hundred dollars from the firm made through Riley.

New Mexico's powerful group of wealthy politicos was known as "the Santa Fe Ring." The Ring "had largely Republican and Masonic affiliations" and was "dedicated primarily to gaining political and economic control of the Territory with a view to the financial enhancement of its members." Its origins lay in the "uniting of some of the leading politicians of New Mexico to secure control of old claims" to land grants and then have their own titles to these grant lands declared valid by territorial and federal courts.[36] Catron and Delegate to Congress Stephen B. Elkins were among the leading members of the Santa Fe Ring. Murphy and Dolan headed their own smaller ring in Lincoln County; the two groups "worked together as friends, as politicians, and as businessmen."[37]

A combination of favorable elements had created Murphy's success: a military fort, an Indian reservation, and a town all within an area small enough for one enterprise to serve: customers who had no other choice but to buy most of their goods from him; and political friends in all the right places.

But it takes change in only one of the elements comprising a situation to alter its overall configuration. Murphy retained his influential friends, and the customer base was still there; what changed was that a new man arrived in Lincoln, openly complained about what he saw of the Murphy operation, and finally found a partner who had the capital to build a store large enough to compete with Murphy. Customers were now going to have a choice of whether to buy from Murphy or not. The Murphy-Dolan firm was presented with the dilemma of how to respond. It chose to try to drive out the competition, first by legal harassment, then by gun.

The ensuing fight, a true war between civilians turned outlaw on both sides, was the Lincoln County War. It was fought simultaneously on several fronts. Each side had its store and fought for customers. Each side sought to sway public opinion by writing letters to newspapers. Each side used the legal system to fight its enemies. Each side used political influence in high places as best it could. Finally each side gathered gunfighters like a dirty snowball rolling downhill. And in the end both sides lost their assets, along with any claim to legal innocence, as the gunfighters took all down to ruin.

6

Alexander McSween and John Tunstall

*I*T WAS THE ENTRANCE ONTO THE LINCOLN COUNTY SCENE OF ALEXander A. McSween in 1875 and John H. Tunstall in 1876 that brought into play the final elements in Lincoln County's deadly drama of downfall and destruction. Its violent outcome was all but inevitable, given the characters of the principals and the nature of the environment in which they acted.

There were, first of all, fundamental differences in perception between Murphy and Dolan, on one hand, and McSween and Tunstall, on the other. The only traits the protagonists had in common were ambition, drive, and a view of themselves as destined for financial success and social position. Murphy and Dolan saw society in essentially secular terms. They accepted it as it was and sought to make gains by filling a niche within it. They were not out to help shape a society, but rather to occupy a privileged place within it.

McSween, with a strong religious background, needed a philosophical rationalization of his own behavior. Having left behind the Presbyterian ministry as a possible career and having chosen the law instead, he carried forward with him into the realm of law and business a world view in which the successful man could be, indeed should be, both money earner and model citizen. He openly sought to be a shaper of the society in which he found himself. Tunstall, still a very young man, embodied the values of a law-abiding society brought from his homeland, although he combined them with an entrepreneurial spirit as aggressively capitalistic as that of any American businessman. He learned to be tough in his adopted American West, but it was a toughness acquired primarily

CHAPTER SIX

because he recognized that his financial goals had no chance of being met if he were to allow himself to be bullied by a Murphy or a Dolan, and it was a toughness coupled with a certain amount of naiveté as to the effect his actions would have on his opponents.

Murphy and Dolan viewed the situation with a simpler, but to them compelling, logic. They saw their economic and social position in the mid-1870s as a fait accompli, won by hard work, deserving of respect, and certainly not something to be disrupted unnecessarily. What right, in the view of Murphy and Dolan, had a rabble-rousing newcomer like McSween to cause trouble, particularly as the Murphy firm had not, even by 1877, been at the top very long. In the view of Dolan in particular, the firm was only beginning what could be a long and uninterrupted reign of commercial dominance. McSween's truculence and loud complaints, followed by action in the economic sphere, jeopardized all that had been won and all that could be won in the future.

Perhaps it was inevitable that someone like McSween in impact, if not McSween himself, was bound to intrude rudely into the profitable little domain being nurtured by Murphy and Dolan. And yet it may well have been precisely the odd mixture of character traits in McSween himself that uniquely suited him to play the role of spoiler—and stubborn, naive spoiler at that. For McSween comes through in letters to newspapers and to friends, in reported conversations, in professional behavior as a lawyer, and in his actions as a pivotal figure in the Lincoln County blood feud as an intelligent, though not intellectual, man of unswerving moral earnestness, with a certain permanently fixed innocence as to the real nature of the world. His self-sustaining self-righteousness, genuine civic-mindedness, his religiosity and honesty all coexisted with an ambition for wealth and social position untroubled by scruples over whether his materialism was entirely consonant with his religious leanings.

Out of these traits arose a stubborn refusal to bow to an entrenched opposition. In McSween's view the Murphy-Dolan side could not be invincible, because there were levels to which even the Murphy-Dolan people would not stoop. McSween believed his side in the conflict was bound to prevail, because it was on the side of the angels and therefore almost precluded from being judged to have used immoral means to achieve its ends. McSween was not a man who found it easy to accept the ambiguities of human behavior.

Also contributing to the inevitability of violence was a startling amount of miscalculation by both sides in the conflict from start to finish. Murphy and Dolan counted on protection from their political allies, apparently believing that political influence would enable them to defy the law with impunity as well as use the courts to destroy their opponents. McSween seems to have been overly confident that the weight of public opinion and moral outrage would force Dolan and the firm into a weakened position as soon as all was made known through newspaper accounts and complaints to high officials at both territorial and federal levels. McSween also seriously underestimated the pervasiveness of the gun mentality in Lincoln County, and he failed to recognize the depth of the political corruption. Dolan, for his part, did not realize the degree of antagonism toward the firm that existed in the Lincoln area, an indignation that enabled the new Tunstall store to take away Dolan's customers and also fueled the gathering of gunfighters to McSween's side. Murphy and Dolan miscalculated in an even more serious way by failing to take into account the fact that even if Governor Axtell and U.S. Attorney Catron were willing to tolerate their cheating on government contracts, officials in Washington would not permit such violations of the law once they were known. As the feud escalated in intensity, each side recognized too late what the consequences of a previous action would be.

And finally the violent acting out of what was essentially an economic and political competition must be seen as a direct consequence of its having taken place in a society where individuals could freely buy, sell, own, carry, and use firearms. The Lincoln County War was a bursting into life of the ever-present latent possibility that civilians would form into armed groups fighting private wars for personal gain or to redress private hatreds and grievances.

After observing firsthand the effects of such a volatile mix of opposing viewpoints, misguided competitive strategies, and ready recourse to firearms, Lew Wallace said of the territory he served as governor from 1878 to 1881: "Every calculation based on experience elsewhere fails in New Mexico."[1]

The Newcomers

Alexander McSween was born in 1843 on Prince Edward Island, Canada. His parents were of Scottish origin; Alexander may have been their adopted child.[2] During his youth he studied for the ministry, but after deciding to become a lawyer he moved to St. Louis, Missouri, where he earned a license to practice law in 1873. In August of 1873 he married

CHAPTER SIX

Susan E. Homer, then twenty-seven years old, at Atchison, Kansas. Not long after their marriage the couple decided to settle in the Southwest, where they hoped to find a climate helpful for McSween's asthma. After starting the journey, they heard about open land and opportunity in Lincoln County, New Mexico. Immediately they set their sights for the territorial frontier, and in March of 1875 the young lawyer and his wife arrived in Lincoln by wagon from Las Vegas.

McSween began to take cases and soon was an established figure whose clients included Lawrence Murphy and John Chisum. Susan McSween had a strong personality and a flair for fashion and entertaining. The McSweens built a fine adobe house. Eventually its heavy Victorian furnishings included an ornately carved piano ordered from the Midwest. McSween charged high prices but nearly always won his cases. He did not hesitate to turn down cases he did not view as justified.[3] The nature of his work naturally led him to awareness of the fraud being perpetrated by Murphy on customers at the store, renters of property, and the military at Fort Stanton. He became active in politics, speaking at local Republican meetings and occasionally traveling to Santa Fe, where his abilities as an orator were noted. Party leader Tom Catron, hoping to be elected Territorial Delegate to Congress, was not pleased by hearing McSween spoken of as a potential candidate for the territory's highest elective office. McSween was in his early thirties when he came to New Mexico. As he built up his law practice and found a place for himself in political life, his future looked bright.

In 1876 he met John Tunstall in Santa Fe. The tall, slender young Englishman, then twenty-six years old, had been searching the West for a good investment opportunity. He was the only son of John Partridge Tunstall of J. P. Tunstall and Company, a mercantile firm in London. Hoping to improve the family's financial situation and particularly to help his three sisters, Tunstall had gone to Victoria, British Columbia, in 1872 to work for a firm in which his father had an owning interest. When the partners in Victoria made things difficult for him, Tunstall moved on to California, where he considered starting a sheep ranch. But after hearing that New Mexico offered even better grazing conditions, he decided to go there instead. After spending time in Denver, he arrived in Santa Fe on 15 August 1876, with a letter of introduction to Governor Axtell. A number of people whose advice he sought, including Catron, suggested Lincoln County as a ranch site. As Tunstall had written to his father, his intent was to find "well watered stock country."[4]

Tunstall and McSween met while staying at the same hotel and were soon on friendly terms, each seeing advantage for himself in the relationship. In November of 1876 Tunstall traveled to Lincoln, and early in 1877 he filed claims, first on land along the Rio Peñasco and then on twenty-three hundred acres along the Rio Feliz, thirty miles southeast of Lincoln. Tunstall's father was backing him with capital in the amount of five to six thousand pounds. McSween, acting as agent for Tunstall, purchased at bargain prices a small herd of cattle being sold by the widow of the deceased Robert Casey. Tunstall had a modest ranch home built on the Rio Feliz property. He hired young Dick Brewer as his ranch foreman, and his cowboy ranchhands included William Bonney, known locally as "the Kid," John Middleton, and Fred Waite. Brewer, a bachelor, also ran his own small ranch farther west on the Ruidoso.

For all his clipped British accent and well-educated manner, Tunstall had an open and engaging personality and a democratic approach in his dealings with employees and acquaintances; he apparently revealed only to his family his disdain for the Hispanic elements of New Mexico's frontier society. He was well liked in Lincoln, even, at the start, by the ubiquitous Major Murphy. Murphy's attitude changed, however, when McSween advised Tunstall to steer clear of the Carrizo ranch property that Murphy offered to sell to Tunstall. With McSween at his side giving advice as well as handling legal matters for him, Tunstall's eye opening in the matter of ranch buying was quickly followed by other revelations about how business was done in Lincoln County. Within a short time Tunstall became convinced that a new store offering more goods and better prices would be a financial success in Lincoln.

The Tunstall family wrote numerous letters back and forth between England and America, and John Tunstall's father came to understand the situation in Lincoln well enough to caution his son on more than one occasion about the possible dangers to himself involved in deliberately creating competition for the Murphy-Dolan firm. Tunstall wrote to his father that he was aware of the risk but confident. He intended to do well financially, he assured his elderly parents in an April 1877 letter, and he was not about to allow Murphy and Dolan to prevent him from meeting his goal of getting "the half of every dollar that is made in the county by anyone." Having concluded that every profitable activity in New Mexico was "worked by a 'ring,' " he confidently announced that he was "at work making a ring" of his own and had thus far "succeeded admirably."[5]

CHAPTER SIX

The store project absorbed more and more of Tunstall's time during the spring and summer of 1877. By August the store was open. No records exist showing the prices Tunstall charged his customers; but the company's records indicate that in late 1877 Tunstall was paying local farmers two cents per pound for corn or wheat. If Tunstall had had any contracts with Fort Stanton at that time, which he did not, he would have made a profit of one-half cent per pound. "All in all, John H. Tunstall probably offered no better value on produce than did Murphy's successor, J. J. Dolan and Co."[6]

The cautionary advice of Tunstall's father had not gone totally unheeded; the solid adobe store building, with a corral to one side and in the back, had extra thick walls and windows with double-thick wooden shutters and steel plates between the layers. The Tunstall store was across the road and less than one-fourth of a mile east of the Murphy-Dolan store; located on the north side of Lincoln's main street, the Tunstall store was close to the Rio Bonito, which ran past the back of the building. In addition to a large room for merchandise of all kinds, the new store building contained an office for McSween and a room intended for use as the Lincoln County Bank. Although the bank never operated, its organization was announced and letterheads were printed saying that Chisum was president, McSween vice president, and Tunstall, cashier. McSween had no financial interest in the new J. H. Tunstall and Company, but he worked as Tunstall's attorney, and it was agreed that part of his earnings would go toward accumulating an owning interest in the store and bank.

As if all this were not enough to provoke defensive measures from Murphy and Dolan, Tunstall now became outspoken in his criticism of the older firm and its founding members. On 26 January 1878 the *Mesilla Independent* published a letter from John Tunstall in which he charged that Sheriff William Brady, a close friend and political ally of Murphy and Dolan, had illegally allowed tax monies collected by Brady for the county to be used by Murphy and Dolan. Of twenty-five hundred dollars collected, fifteen hundred dollars was in the form of a check paid by McSween. Brady had jointly endorsed the check with John Riley of the Dolan firm. Riley had presented the check for payment and had then used the proceeds to pay for cattle. When the tax funds did not reach Santa Fe within the required time period, Catron covered the amount for the delinquent county official.[7]

McSween and Tunstall had, by early 1878, publicly criticized Murphy and Dolan, refused to buy their property, opened a new store, formed a new bank, and made a public charge of embezzlement of county tax funds. In addition McSween had refused to acquiesce to Dolan's claim on the proceeds from the deceased Emil Fritz's life-insurance policy. Although McSween with his professional manner and his piano-playing wife, and Tunstall with his cultured British air, had brought a certain nonfrontier mentality to territorial New Mexico, they had also, it appeared, fairly rapidly taken on the typically western attitude that fight was better than flight.

To Dolan, losing business to the new Tunstall store even as he was buying out Murphy's interest and taking on greater responsibility and new debt, the McSween-Tunstall alliance undoubtedly looked like deliberate provocation, if not outright conspiracy to ruin him.

The Round of Killings

Tunstall's boldly accusatory letter to the *Mesilla Independent,* one of the most influential newspapers in southern New Mexico, earned him the enmity of Sheriff Brady and confirmed Dolan's worst suspicions about his new rival. Dolan already had sought and found a vehicle for harassing McSween, and after the affrontery of the Tunstall letter, he undoubtedly was not averse to seeing Tunstall damaged along with McSween, as he carried out a scheme to use the courts in his struggle for supremacy in Lincoln County.

McSween's actions as the attorney hired by the brother and sister of Emil Fritz to collect the proceeds of their brother's life-insurance policy provided Dolan with the weapon he needed. The insurance company was in bankruptcy, but after traveling to New York, McSween was able to collect the ten thousand dollars of proceeds. He deducted expenses for himself and placed the remainder in his own bank account in St. Louis. Dolan claimed that the proceeds must be used to partially repay some fifty-one thousand dollars he said Fritz had owed the firm at the time of his death, rather than be given to Fritz's brother and sister as heirs. McSween obtained a court order permitting an inspection of the firm's books. Dolan refused to comply with the order, and McSween therefore refused to release the money to Dolan. After the McSweens and John Chisum set forth for St. Louis in December of 1877, Dolan induced Fritz's sister, Emilie Fritz Scholand of Las Cruces, to press a charge that McSween was in the act of absconding with the insurance funds. District Attorney Rynerson did not clear McSween of the charge, despite a lack of evidence in the case. McSween was released

CHAPTER SIX

on bail with the charge still pending and arrived back in Lincoln on 10 February 1878, under court guard.

The writ of bond issued by Judge Warren Bristol entitled Sheriff Brady to attach property belonging to McSween up to a value of eight thousand dollars.[8] It was the action taken to execute this bond order that led directly to the opening shots of the Lincoln County War.

Brady entered the Tunstall store and removed large quantities of goods, despite Tunstall's protests that McSween was not the owner of any of the store's merchandise. Furniture and other items from McSween's house were also seized. Altogether property "easily worth $30,000 to $40,000" was attached by Brady.[9] Tension was high; Tunstall was armed and angry. Outside the store Billy the Kid and Fred Waite were acting as armed bodyguards for their employer. Tunstall convinced Brady that horses and mules in the store corral belonged to him alone, but Brady insisted that the writ of attachment applied to the cattle at Tunstall's ranch on the Rio Feliz.

When a posse named by Brady and including many Dolan partisans arrived at the ranch, foreman Brewer told posse member Billy Mathews he would permit the cattle to be rounded up to see if any belonged to McSween, but none should be removed until the court had heard Tunstall's objection to the way the writ was being implemented. Mathews agreed to seek further instructions from Brady in Lincoln. A group of Tunstall cowboys, including Billy the Kid, also headed for Lincoln to inform Tunstall of the development. Tunstall said force should not be used against the posse; he was willing to let the court judge his claim to be the sole owner of the cattle. He set out from Lincoln for Chisum's South Spring ranch and discussed the situation with the older and more experienced cattleman before turning west again and traveling the sixty miles by horseback to reach his own ranch at about ten o'clock Sunday night, 17 February.[10]

Tunstall's men wanted to resist the posse if an attempt was made to remove the cattle. Tunstall said no. His decision not to use force against the posse probably was based in part on his knowledge that his men were vastly outnumbered by the Brady-Dolan forces. He decided to return to Lincoln with the horses exempted from the writ, leaving just one man at the ranch to await the return of the posse. At 8:30 A.M. on 18 February 1878, Tunstall and his men left the Rio Feliz ranch, heading north to the Rio Hondo. The group divided, Tunstall with a small group and the horses ascending a rough shortcut route leading to the Ruidoso to the northwest, the others keeping to the main trail. Tunstall was riding at the head of a single column in a canyon four miles south of the Rio Ruidoso when suddenly hoofbeats were heard. A posse of Brady-Dolan men approached from the south. Tunstall employees John Widenmann and Dick Brewer rode hard into the pine-covered hills above the canyon to make a stand. John Middleton shouted to Tunstall to take cover.

But Tunstall, according to an account given later by a posse member, stopped and sat his horse as the posse approached. Billy Morton, at the head of the posse, then raised his rifle and fired directly at Tunstall, hitting him at close range in the chest. Tunstall fell face downward onto the ground. Jesse Evans then took Tunstall's revolver and fired a shot into the back of his head. This account was given by a man named Albert Howe, who said these were the facts given him by posse member George Kitt. Howe gave the account during the investigation by Frank Warner Angel, five months later. No member of the Tunstall party was close enough to be an eyewitness to the shooting. It was late afternoon, cold, with winter darkness just beginning to fall, when the shooting occurred. Upon hearing the shots, the Tunstall men knew instantly what had happened and rode as swiftly as possible to Lincoln, arriving at 10 P.M. to report that Tunstall had been killed. Meanwhile the posse left Tunstall's body on a blanket and rode to meet Dolan, who was a member of the posse and waiting with other men at the Tunstall ranch. Dolan and other posse members, including Morton and Evans, claimed later that Tunstall had been killed because he resisted arrest.[11]

Tunstall was buried on 23 February in a simple ceremony just to the east of his Lincoln store. Sheriff Brady made no attempt to arrest those who had killed Tunstall or even to investigate the circumstances of his death. McSween was sufficiently unnerved by the chain of events and the brutality of his partner's death to write his last will and testament in late February, and in all likelihood it was at this time that he arranged for a ten-thousand-dollar insurance policy on his life.[12]

Determined to set the wheels of justice in motion at whatever cost, McSween sought and obtained arrest warrants for posse members from Justice of the Peace John B. Wilson. Wilson appointed Dick Brewer as constable and deputized Fred Waite, Billy the Kid, Frank Macnab, Doc Scurlock, Charles Bowdre, Henry Brown, and Sam Smith, all McSween-Tunstall supporters. Brewer was given the arrest warrants to execute and the new group, with wide support in Lincoln, began to call itself the "Regulators."[13] A number of Chisum cowboys had signed on with the Brewer forces by the end of February.

CHAPTER SIX

Dolan and Murphy asked Governor Axtell to come to Lincoln. On 8 March Axtell arrived at Fort Stanton, and on the following day he spent three hours in Lincoln. He did not conduct a formal investigation or ask questions of McSween or any other Tunstall employees about the death of Tunstall. He returned to Santa Fe within a few days.

On 9 March the Regulators ambushed and arrested Frank Baker and Billy Morton, both members of the posse that had killed Tunstall, at the junction of the Peñasco and Pecos rivers, south of Roswell. After spending the night with their prisoners at Chisum's place on the Pecos, the Regulators took them six miles north to Roswell and then headed west across the range, ostensibly to deliver Morton and Baker to the authorities at Lincoln. The truth about whether they ever intended to act as lawmen and actually turn the two over to Brady will never be known. As the group was riding single file through rough country approaching the mountain foothills, gunshots suddenly rang out and Baker and Morton were shot dead in their saddles by the Regulators.

Arriving in Lincoln with the bodies of their prisoners, the Regulator group that had carried out the capture and included both Billy the Kid and Dick Brewer unanimously agreed that Morton and Baker were killed as they attempted to escape.

On 9 March Governor Axtell had issued a proclamation pronouncing Brady the chief law enforcer and entitling him to call upon the military at Fort Stanton to help enforce writs and arrest warrants. The proclamation declared that the Lincoln County Commission's appointment of John B. Wilson as justice of the peace was illegal and the Brewer deputizations therefore invalid, despite the fact that one of the governor's earlier proclamations had stated that commissioners had the right to name new justices when a resignation or death occurred.[14] In the meantime U.S. Attorney Tom Catron was doing little to investigate Tunstall's death or to ensure that the judicial process worked properly in Lincoln County.

There is no evidence that McSween knew in advance that Morton and Baker would be killed. Together with the news that the Regulators were now operating outside the law as a result of the governor's proclamation, the killings threw the McSween camp into confusion. Brewer returned to his ranch, while the McSweens went to the South Spring ranch and remained with John Chisum, just released from jail at Las Vegas, until early April, when they all traveled together to Lincoln.

A sullen uncertainty hung over the town of Lincoln as the April session of the district court approached; everyone knew how high the stakes were for all those who were to be charged with crimes. It was thought that Judge Bristol would open court on 1 April. About nine o'clock that morning, Sheriff Brady and deputies George Hindman, Billy Mathews, George Peppin, and John Long walked down the dusty main street from the Murphy-Dolan store to the courthouse building to the east. Upon discovering that court would not convene for at least another week, they started back.

As the group passed the Tunstall store, the tranquil silence of a clear spring morning was shattered by rifle shots fired by some of the six Regulators hidden behind the gates of the Tunstall corral. Brady was hit by numerous bullets and fell dead. Hindman staggered a few steps after a single shot hit him and died moments later. The others scattered to take cover. Billy the Kid, one of the Regulators who had been firing, stepped into the street and leaned over Brady's body to retrieve the rifle that Brady had confiscated from him some time earlier. A shot came from a house, wounding the Kid in the upper leg. Billy Mathews later said it was he who had shot the Kid. Billy got care for his wound before leaving Lincoln; the other Regulators rode out of town immediately after the shooting.

Deputy Sheriff Peppin called in soldiers from Fort Stanton. The assassination of Brady, who left a wife and nine children, stunned the people of Lincoln. Peppin arrested a large number of people, including McSween when he arrived from South Spring several days later. Also arrested was McSween's brother-in-law, David Shield, who had been in the McSween home when the shooting occurred. Shield, an attorney who had come to practice law with McSween, was married to Susan McSween's sister.

Both McSween and Brewer publicly condemned the Brady and Hindman killings. The renegade Regulator group, which was known to have stayed in the Tunstall store the night before the killings, seems by all the evidence to have acted independently of the Regulators' own acknowledged leaders, Brewer and McSween. The fact that McSween did not make a clean, irrevocable break with the group after Brady's death is probably attributable to two factors: first, McSween and his wife felt the need to have protective allies; and second, there was, for all the gunslinging of the Regulators, a common bond of deeply felt grief and anger over what was seen as the cold-blooded murder of Tunstall, a man who had treated his employees with a decency they repaid by considering him as much a friend as an employer.

CHAPTER SIX

On 2 April Lieutenant Colonel Nathan A. M. Dudley arrived at Fort Stanton from Fort Union to take over as commanding officer. Although he was not particularly intelligent, the bewhiskered Dudley was a dedicated career military man who took himself and his duty very seriously. Extremely conscientious in attempting to carry out orders, including those to submit complete briefings to Washington on the state of affairs in Lincoln County, he was impeded in the proper implementation of his orders only by his arrogance and his heavy consumption of whiskey. Dudley immediately became embroiled in the upheavals of Lincoln County and remained a key figure in the conflict, as each of the factions sought his protection or intervention at various stages of the struggle.

On 4 April a gunfight took place at Blazer's Mill, located west of Lincoln on the Mescalero Indian reservation. Andrew "Buckshot" Roberts, generally believed to have been among the posse that killed Tunstall, went to the mill about noon that day, reportedly on a tip that the killers of Brady would be there. Blazer's Mill was being used as Indian Agency office and living quarters by the agent Frederick Godfroy and his wife. When Roberts arrived, Brewer, Middleton, Bowdre, and Billy the Kid, accompanied by Frank Coe and his cousin George Coe, were eating a meal prepared by Mrs. Godfroy. They said they were on their way to retrieve stolen Tunstall cattle that they believed were being hidden at the Shedd Ranch across the mountains near Tularosa. Roberts was among those for whom the Regulators had an arrest warrant, although the warrant had been made invalid by Governor Axtell's proclamation. Roberts, for his part, knew he could collect a two-hundred-dollar reward for killing or capturing any Regulator being sought in the Brady-Hindman killings.

Frank Coe tried to talk Roberts into allowing himself to be arrested but failed. Roberts started across a meadow toward the Blazer house, but as he reached the doorstep he was shot by Bowdre and fell wounded, pushing himself just inside the door for protection. From that vantage point he blazed away at the Regulators, who were now crouching behind a low building a short distance away. He shot off George Coe's trigger finger, wounded Middleton in the chest, and grazed the Kid's arm. Brewer raised his head slightly above the building. That was enough for Roberts; when Brewer raised his head again, he was struck squarely between the eyes by a clean shot from the dying Roberts. Brewer was killed instantly.[15]

While some of the Regulators were cowboy drifters and others were outlaws, Brewer was neither; twenty-seven years old at the time of his death, he was the most capable and sober-minded of the gunfighters on the McSween side. His death left McSween with perhaps only his wife and John Chisum to turn to as the battle worsened and the lines between legality and outlawry on both sides were all but obliterated.

Meanwhile a battle of words over the meaning of the events in Lincoln County was carried on with passionate partisanship in newspapers throughout the territory. Governor Axtell, Catron, Murphy, Dolan, and Riley found support for their interpretation in the *Santa Fe New Mexican*, while the *Cimarron News and Press* of Colfax County, where Axtell was held in low regard, was willing to express views openly critical of the governor's partisan response to the strife. During March and April of 1878, all of the central figures in the conflict, McSween most notably, wrote lengthy letters and reports, which appeared in the Santa Fe and Cimarron papers as well as in the *Mesilla Independent* and the *Las Vegas Gazette*. The Cimarron paper took the position that Judge Bristol of the third judicial district was a partisan of the Santa Fe Ring and incapable of objectivity in regard to the Lincoln County cases.

And in fact when on 14 April 1878 the annual court session finally opened in Lincoln, Judge Bristol's address to the assembled grand jury members was pointedly critical of McSween, while barely touching on the murder of Tunstall. The jury, composed of local citizens, was too aware of the real situation to be deterred from doing its duty conscientiously. McSween was cleared of embezzlement charges in the Fritz case; Jesse Evans and four others were indicted for the murder of Tunstall, with Dolan and Mathews named as accessories; Billy the Kid, Middleton, Waite, and Brown were indicted for the murders of Brady and Hindman.[16] The grand jury reported that it found strong evidence of fraud by Indian Agent Godfroy and strong evidence that the Murphy-Dolan firm was dealing in stolen cattle.

At the same time the relatively objective voice of the grand jury was being heard, a new element was being introduced into the Lincoln County equation: the administration in Washington was beginning to take notice of the state of near anarchy that existed in parts of remote frontier New Mexico. Charges that Governor Axtell was aiding members of the Santa Fe Ring in their attempt to control the huge Maxwell Land Grant in northeast New Mexico's Colfax County had reached Washington in early 1877, when a lengthy petition citing the governor's manipulation of federal and territorial agencies was forwarded to President Rutherford B. Hayes by reform-minded Mary McPherson, mother-in-law of William Raymond Morley, a Maxwell Land Grant Company executive who objected to ring member Stephen B. Elkins's unethical leadership of the Dutch-investor-owned company. Reports concerning the explosive events in Lincoln County only heightened pressure on the Hayes administration to take action.[17]

The British Embassy was pressing Washington for a formal investigation of British citizen John Tunstall's death. Letters filled with detailed allegations of fraud in the management of the Indian reservation, written by McSween and others, were reaching the Department of the Interior. And finally Secretary of the Interior Carl Schurz, among the ablest and most influential of President Hayes's cabinet members, began to take a personal interest in the events in Lincoln County as a result of several impassioned and highly informative letters he received from Dr. Mantague R. Leverson, an acquaintance whose views and integrity he respected.[18]

The president, along with Schurz, was the recipient of letters from Leverson, a British citizen who had arrived from Colorado during March and who stayed with Chisum while considering various sites for a group of American and British settlers. Leverson accepted an invitation to accompany Chisum and the McSweens to Lincoln for the April court session. Arriving just days after the Brady killing, Leverson observed with shocked indignation the abrogation of constitutional rights by local officials and the gun-enforced political rule exercised by the Dolan faction. He promptly put pen to paper and provided a graphic description of the prevailing lawlessness for his powerful Washington friends.

In fact the tactics used by ring members in seeking to control Lincoln County had been "clearly foreshadowed" by tactics used in Colfax County just a short time earlier.[19] The administration's response was too slow and too encumbered by layers of bureaucracy, however, to halt the momentum toward violence. In a sense the two factions had become substitutes for legitimate political parties at the local level, the only difference being that once in office, a faction partisan regarded it as his right to harass the other faction by gun and any other means at hand. After Brady's death the county commission named John H. Copeland sheriff. Copeland was cooperative, even friendly, toward McSween. The Dolan faction disliked him. On 28 May Governor Axtell removed Copeland from office, on the grounds that he had failed "for more than 30 days to file his bond as collector of taxes."[20] The governor appointed as sheriff George W. Peppin, a friend of Murphy and Dolan. Like them Peppin was an ex–Civil War soldier. He had come to New Mexico with the California Column. Peppin was the builder of the Murphy-Dolan store and had served as deputy under the pro-Dolan Brady. As far as determining actual events on the ground in Lincoln County, the appointment of Peppin was far more meaningful than the arrival in May of Frank Angel, even though the naming of the highly respected New Yorker as special investigator for the Department of Justice was a clear signal that all the voices raised in protest had at last caught the ear of Washington.

With assistance from deputies at Seven Rivers and a posse headed by Marion Turner at Roswell, Sheriff Peppin set about with a vengeance to exercise the warrants for the arrest of Brady's killers. Billy the Kid was singled out as the most elusive and dangerous among those charged. All up and down the Pecos area of lower Lincoln County, men with a grievance against Chisum saw the Peppin-led hunt for specific Regulators as the perfect chance to make life difficult for Chisum by assisting the anti-McSween forces. During June three Chisum cowboys were killed while on the range. In early July McSween was staying at Chisum's ranch with about fourteen of the men who supported his side, leading to an attack on the well-fortified old ranch homestead by a large Dolan-Peppin force, which began on 4 July and continued without letup for an entire day and night.

The siege ended without the taking of any McSween or Chisum men, but left McSween deeply shaken; a lawyer, a man with political ambitions, a man who had brought to Lincoln its first Protestant minister, a man who saw himself as a professional of innate civility, McSween now realized how deeply he was mired in what could only be termed gang warfare—surely a far cry from his original intent when he sought wealth and a modicum of reform in his newly chosen place of residence. On 13 July McSween began the return trip to Lincoln, having decided there was no alternative to making a stand. Chisum men accompanied the group, acting as bodyguards for McSween. More and more riders joined the group as the two-day journey progressed.

Gun skirmishes had been taking place for several weeks at San Patricio, a McSween stronghold on the Rio Ruidoso south of Lincoln, and it was known that Jimmie Dolan had sent riders to Doña Ana County to the west to bring back gunmen looking for action at good pay. The outsiders were deputized by Peppin upon arriving in Lincoln. Altogether the Peppin-Dolan forces numbered about forty, almost equal to the number of men who rode into Lincoln at sundown on 14 July with McSween.[21]

CHAPTER SIX

The Peppin-Dolan men made the Wortley Hotel west of the McSween house their headquarters. McSween and between twelve and fourteen of his men stayed in his house, barricading doors and windows with adobes, drilling shooting holes through the walls, and preparing for the worst despite the presence of Mrs. McSween, her sister and her sister's children in the house. The other McSween men, including about twenty-five Hispanos, were dispersed in the nearby Ellis house and a small store belonging to José Montaño. Shooting began on the morning of the sixteenth in the nearly empty town; of the approximately forty families who lived in Lincoln, all but about twelve had fled for their lives as the gunfighters rode in over the course of several days.[22]

Ten miles west of Lincoln at Fort Stanton, Colonel Dudley was kept informed of the deteriorating situation. But his hands were tied. On 28 June he had received word from Washington of a new order from Congress barring the use of troops in civil disturbances. In Lincoln County the effect of the policy was to give a free hand to the two opposing forces, as they gathered men for a final showdown. Dudley had been friendly toward Dolan, for whom he had on more than one occasion provided shelter at the fort. And he took the position that Peppin represented the legitimate legal authority in Lincoln. But he was aware of the criminal backgrounds of many of the outsiders brought in by the Dolan-Peppin forces, and he had been repeatedly importuned over the preceding weeks by terrified citizens to halt the assaults on non-Dolan supporters carried out by Peppin. His concern for women and children in particular was genuine, and he finally "persuaded himself that a carefully neutral military posture in Lincoln" might protect civilian life "without violating the orders."[23]

Dudley had about one hundred men under his command, including a regiment of black troopers and another company of white infantry troops. Taking thirty-five troops and all of his officers, he marched into Lincoln at midmorning on Friday, 19 July 1878. Lending greater credibility to this show of force, Dudley also brought in a Gatling gun with two thousand rounds of ammunition and a mountain howitzer. The military marched through Lincoln and set up camp at the east end of town between the Ellis house and the McSween house, aiming the Gatling gun directly at the Montaño store.[24] Dudley told leaders of both sides that he was not there to support either side, only to protect civilians and prevent property destruction. He then told Justice of the Peace Wilson to issue a warrant for the arrest of McSween, on the grounds that one of his soldiers had been fired upon by a McSween man. There was no evidence the bullet had been fired by a McSween gunfighter, and McSween denied the charge.

The course of the battle changed with the arrival of Dudley. After being told by Dudley that the cannon and full force of trooper fire would be turned on the McSween house and those inside it if a soldier were to be hit by a McSween gun during the course of the fight, the McSween forces were constrained from firing out to the street and forced into an essentially defensive stance, unable to take the offensive for fear of accidentally shooting a Dudley trooper.[25]

Shooting was fierce throughout 19 July. Short periods of eerie quiet were quickly broken by furious spates of whizzing bullets. No one walked the single long street. Eyes watched from behind barricaded windows. Figures crouched behind adobe walls. Any man who went outside to care for the horses in the corrals became an instant target for the enemy. The McSween group had taken some comfort early on in the fact that they had the better marksmen and more men of individual courage, but as the vicious battle of bullets entered its fourth day, reasons for anxiety began to multiply. Rendered ineffectual by the Dudley weaponry, the group led by Martin Chavez left the Montaño store en masse and crossed the Rio Bonito; not long afterward, the gunfighters in the Ellis house also gave up the fight, among them Bowdre, Scurlock, and Middleton. That left only the group in the McSween house, and it was becoming clear that the Peppin-Dolan plan was to keep this last McSween stronghold surrounded day and night and force a surrender that, if it did not end with death for those in the house, would end with the arrest of many of the Regulators inside, including Billy the Kid. And for these McSween men in particular, it remained a central, galling fact that while they were hunted by a sheriff who openly sided with their archenemy Dolan, the men charged by the grand jury with Tunstall's murder remained free on bail and in effect safe from the arm of the law.

Shortly after noon on 19 July, Peppin men slipped into the kitchen in the east wing of the McSween house and started a fire with kerosene poured on the floor. The blaze was discovered and put out with buckets of water. Less than an hour later Peppin men returned, this time using wood chips and planks piled against the rear door of the west wing to start a larger fire. McSween men were prevented from extinguishing it by a constant hail of gunfire. Slowly the fire began to smolder and flames spread from room to room, burning rafters, floors, and furniture, and creating dense smoke even as the thick adobe walls stood resistant. Susan McSween courageously opened the front door and slipped out into the street, assuming no one would shoot a woman alone, and went to Colonel Dudley. They argued, she asking him to prevent the destruction of her home, he telling her that an angry earlier note from McSween meant it was possible McSween had set fire to his own house. She returned in despair.

It is not known for certain whether McSween took up a gun himself in this last showdown. But it is known from Mrs. McSween's later recounting that he was seized by an enervating depression, which rendered him unable to provide the leadership required under such desperate circumstances. With McSween crumpled in numbed silence, Billy the Kid, though the youngest of the cohort in the house, stepped forward with a coolness of manner and came up with a last-ditch plan for an escape attempt.

Just before dark fell at the end of a hot summer day, Susan McSween and the women and children of the Shield family left the house and joined the family of the Reverend Taylor Ealy staying at the Tunstall store. They were escorted by Dudley troopers to a place of safety at the unoccupied Juan Patrón house. When darkness finally came, a little before 9 P.M., the Kid's plan was put into effect. The group gathered in the east-wing kitchen. Billy the Kid and several others made a mad dash into the darkness, running under a hail of bullets from Peppin men down to the Rio Bonito. The Kid was among those who survived, while several men fell wounded or dead.

McSween and the others were supposed to make their escape while the Peppin gunfire was diverted toward the Kid's group. No one lived to tell the details of the final moments; apparently McSween hesitated a moment too long. He was shot down in his back doorway, his body riddled by five bullets, as the house crumbled in a smoldering blaze around him.[26]

The Peppin-Dolan forces celebrated throughout the night by looting what remained in the Tunstall store. The following day a coroner's jury reported on the five bodies retrieved from the demolished McSween house. McSween was buried unceremoniously near Tunstall, his wife afraid to come to the grave of her husband.

The Aftermath

Tunstall and McSween were gone. Those of their gunfighters who were not dead or being sought on murder charges retreated, still fearful of retribution, to homesteads and ranches, or else resumed their hard lives as cowboys for hire. Victory by gun belonged to the Peppin-Dolan side, and by extension to the interests in Santa Fe that had backed it with political support. But the aftermath of the violent episode showed the gun to have been the least effective of all possible weapons for use in a battle for commercial dominance and political control. Not only did the winners of the gunfight lose ground financially, but in the end they were defeated on the political front as well, as reform prompted by their blatant misuse of power gradually took hold.

Lawrence Murphy was in Santa Fe as the climactic events in Lincoln unfolded, only dimly aware of what was happening and too weakened by his losing battle with the effects of alcohol to be able to participate even by offering counsel to his protégé, Jimmie Dolan. In the days following the burning of McSween's house, Dolan went to Santa Fe and spent time with the older man who had given him a chance to realize his ambitions. Murphy died on 20 October 1878. He was heavily in debt to Catron and the First National Bank of Santa Fe at the time of his death. To recover its capital, the bank sold Murphy's Bar W Ranch to British investors for $225,000 and the ranch became the core of the huge Carrizozo Cattle Company with five hundred thousand acres of land in Lincoln County.

Catron sent his brother-in-law, Edgar Walz, to Lincoln to reopen and manage the Dolan store. Although the firm continued to fill government beef contracts for the military, the store operation experienced an irreversible decline. Catron became its owner when Dolan was unable to make payments on the mortgage held by Catron.

Dolan was back in Lincoln by December of 1878, struggling to rebuild his business career. In 1879 he married Caroline Fritz, the daughter of Emil Fritz's brother Charles. In December 1882 Charles Fritz purchased the Tunstall store, and a short time later Dolan became the store's proprietor, managing the property until its eventual sale to the Rosenthal firm of Santa Fe.[27] And strange as it seems, he managed to acquire the Tunstall ranch as well, making it his family home as the Flying H Ranch. After holding posts as county treasurer and territorial senator in the 1880s, Dolan unexpectedly died in Roswell on 26 February 1898. He had had two marriages: the first to Caroline Fritz; and the second, as a widower, to Maria Eva Whitlock, in 1888.

John H. Riley left Lincoln County after the showdown fire and fight. He never returned, settling first in Las Cruces, where he homesteaded and jointly owned cattle with W. L. Rynerson, later helping to build a Colorado railway, and eventually moving without his family to

CHAPTER SIX

Colorado Springs, where he ranched for a number of years before his death in 1916.

Special Agent Angel had begun laying the groundwork for political reform in New Mexico when he arrived early in 1878 to conduct an investigation for the Justice Department. By the time he reached Lincoln on 14 May, the diligent young lawyer already had formed an unfavorable impression of Governor Axtell as a result of his investigation of conditions in Colfax County, where the governor had complied with a Justice Department request for cooperation only to the extent of denying all allegations made against him while refusing to provide any substantive information.[28]

Although Angel was unable to influence the events in Lincoln County that led to the 19 July gunfight, the federal representative completed a thorough report within two months and presented it to President Hayes in mid-August. The three-hundred-page report provided clear evidence of corruption at both county and territorial level. While the fraud perpetrated by Indian agents, government contract holders, and local law officials was clearly documented, special attention was paid to the behavior of Samuel B. Axtell as governor of the territory, including his highly partisan actions on behalf of Murphy and Dolan. "It is seldom that history states more corruption, fraud, mismanagement, plots and murders, than New Mexico has been the theatre of under the administration of Governor Axtel [sic]," said Angel in his report.[29] "He was a partisan either through corruption or weakness."[30]

On 4 September 1878, Secretary of the Interior Schurz removed Axtell from office. Knowing he would be removed along with Axtell, Catron resigned as U.S. district attorney and was replaced by S. M. Barnes. President Hayes offered the post of New Mexico governor to General Lew Wallace, a man of national stature who after some thought accepted the challenge of trying to bring order out of chaos in a western territory he had never seen.

When Wallace arrived in New Mexico on 30 September 1878, he was fifty-one years old and had a record of accomplishment in several fields. He had served as an officer in the Mexican War and the Civil War. He had studied law and maintained a law practice in the Midwest. He had been a member of the military commission that tried the assassins of Abraham Lincoln. He had published a novel; when he came to New Mexico he was in the process of writing *Ben Hur*, the great historical novel set in biblical times that eventually earned him world fame as one of the best-selling authors of all time.

Wallace's first months in office were not easy, as he attempted to carry out his mandate from the president to end corruption in the administration of territorial affairs and reestablish law and order, particularly in Lincoln County. Living alone in the ancient Governor's Palace, since his wife, Susan, had not yet arrived to join him, Wallace received troubling reports of ongoing warfare between partisans of the Dolan and McSween factions. A desire for revenge and retribution was perpetuating instability. The men being sought on murder charges were being protected by their respective factions. And new gangs of outlaws from Texas, led by such notorious gunmen as John Selman and John Kinney, were terrorizing all of Lincoln County with a series of murders, rapes, and thefts of livestock. More than two hundred members of these armed bands roamed the countryside.

Wallace responded with two initiatives. During October he obtained from President Hayes an executive order declaring that a state of insurrection existed in Lincoln County and permitting the use of military troops to enforce the law and reinstate civil order. And on 14 November Wallace issued a proclamation offering amnesty to all those in Lincoln County charged with crimes committed between 1 February and 13 November 1878. The amnesty offer did not apply to those already under indictment.

The governor's amnesty order was intended to quell the old hatreds and promote a return to peaceful ways. But with Peppin still in office as sheriff and Dudley still at Fort Stanton, the McSween forces continued to do battle in the belief that nothing had changed. Susan McSween kept alive the flame of indignation by hiring a hot-headed young lawyer named Huston J. Chapman to bring suit against Dudley for his role in the death of her husband and destruction of their property. Chapman denounced Dudley and Peppin as supporters of the Catron-Dolan alliance, prompting renewed antagonism from the Peppin forces, who were still harassing those who had sided with McSween.

Even after Peppin resigned in December, on the grounds that he had not been paid by the bankrupt county, and had been succeeded by George Kimball, a capable man who had remained neutral during the troubles, unrest continued. So many people in the Lincoln area sided with the McSween faction that Kimball was unable to round up a posse to control the cattle-theft ring allegedly being led by Billy the Kid. In fact the Kid and a group of fellow Regulators rode into Lincoln during December and used their local support to make themselves at home

CHAPTER SIX

without fear of challenge from the authorities. As 1878 drew to a close and members of both factions continued to defy the law even with their respective leaders dead or in disarray, New Mexico's new governor was forced to conclude that it would take more than proclamations to end the strife.

7

Billy the Kid and Pat Garrett

*I*T WAS SUSAN MCSWEEN WHO INADVERTENTLY SET IN MOTION THE events that resulted in Wallace's acquaintance with Billy the Kid and Pat Garrett, the two men who above all others were to become central figures in the lingering aftermath of the Lincoln County War. Alone, virtually penniless, and a woman on her own in a society dominated by men, Mrs. McSween nevertheless showed herself in the months immediately after her husband's death to be as feisty and fearless as she had been during his lifetime. She did not return to Kansas; she did not fade away into obscurity; and it was her persistent attempt to redress what she perceived as an outrageous injustice that led to the governor's personal involvement in the affairs of Lincoln County.

Susan McSween was thirty-three years old in 1879, healthy though prone to attacks of illness brought on by emotional stress, and had no children. Even in the difficult conditions of frontier strife, she maintained high standards of Victorian fashion and propriety, to the extent that some in the town of Lincoln faulted her for pretentiousness. No one doubted her fortitude, however, or her passion in giving voice to her grievances. She appears to have had the same mixture of high-minded idealism and worldly self-interestedness that marked her husband: in the wake of his death, she wrote skillfully worded letters to John Tunstall's father in London in a successful attempt to claim money she said Tunstall had owed her husband, and in an unsuccessful attempt to have herself substituted for John Widenmann as executor of Tunstall's estate.[1]

But she was undoubtedly genuine in being incensed by what she

CHAPTER SEVEN

believed Colonel Dudley had done to her husband and to her own life and property. There was a case to be made, and Mrs. McSween vehemently made it, that Dudley had stood by in deliberate partisanship while her home burned and McSween people were killed, despite the fact that women and children were inside the home and Dudley himself had explicitly declared his purpose to be the protection of innocent civilians and property. When she chose the young, one-armed lawyer Huston Chapman to represent her in a court suit against Dudley, she doubled the impact of her inflammatory charges, for Chapman, intemperate by nature, proved to be as capable of provoking antagonism by overheated rhetoric as his client. His charges of a Dudley-Dolan conspiracy were given wide publicity in territorial papers, and he wrote several letters to Governor Wallace demanding justice in the courts.

Then, with shocking brutality, Chapman was shot dead in Lincoln as he walked alone and unarmed on the cold, snowy night of 18 February 1879, returning from a conference with Mrs. McSween to his hotel. It was the murder of Chapman that finally brought Wallace to Lincoln, after months of trying to deal with the crisis of authority by fiat from the territorial capital.

Other factors were involved in his decision as well. He had received many letters urging his presence, and the *Mesilla Independent* had printed disturbing news of a meeting between Jesse Evans, one of the outlaws who allegedly had killed Tunstall, and Billy the Kid, accused murderer of Sheriff Brady, at which the two desperados agreed to cease fighting and help each other evade arrest in view of the tough law-and-order stance being taken by Catron's successor as U.S. district attorney, S. M. Barnes.[2] But it was Chapman's death that was the final straw for the governor; occurring one year to the day after Tunstall's murder, it was so clearly cold-blooded and vicious that it could not be dealt with from afar, symbolizing as it did the wanton disregard for human life rampant in Lincoln County.

Wallace arrived in Lincoln by horse-drawn buggy on 5 March 1879 and remained until 18 April. Traveling with him from Santa Fe was Colonel Edward Hatch, the capable and highly regarded commander of army forces in New Mexico. Wallace established his headquarters in rooms provided by merchant José Montaño at his Lincoln store. Within days of his arrival, the governor had Hatch remove Dudley from his post as commander at Fort Stanton.[3] Not only had charges of a serious nature had been brought against Dudley in a civil suit, but the governor had concluded that Dudley was failing to comply with President Hayes' executive order authorizing the military to execute arrest warrants as a means of restoring civil authority. Despite the known presence in and around Lincoln of many of the leading gunfighters charged with crimes, neither the sheriff nor Dudley had made any move to arrest them. The governor also had been informed of circumstantial evidence indicating Dudley may have known in advance that Chapman was to be killed. After an acting commander, Captain Henry Carroll, was named at Fort Stanton, Wallace gave him a list of thirty-six people to be arrested, "almost a muster roll of the principals in the feud."[4]

Often working until late at night by kerosene lamp, Wallace made himself available to all sides in the Lincoln County troubles. The bearded, bespectacled governor, looking scholarly while at the same time exuding an aura of military discipline, listened patiently to numerous versions of the cause for strife, and he attended a town meeting at which area residents expressed their grievances and pleaded for an end to the factional violence.

Wallace may have delayed for too long his personal assessment of the situation in Lincoln County, but once there he seems to have made a good-faith effort to deal with it. Not only did he insist upon implementation of outstanding arrest warrants, but he also supervised the dispatch of cavalry troops to search ranches whose owners were suspected of harboring stolen cattle. And to further insure restoration of civil authority, he named Juan B. Patrón, Lincoln tavern owner and former speaker of the territorial House of Representatives, to form a citizens militia to be called the Lincoln County Rifles.

There was criticism of Wallace in several territorial newspapers for using the military to control cattle rustlers without a declaration of martial law. And the governor's offer of amnesty was widely believed to have had the unfortunate effect of encouraging outlaws to remain in Lincoln County without fear of prosecution for known criminal acts committed in the recent past. Nevertheless the mere fact that a serious effort now was being made to restore order was enough to bring renewed emigration to the Roswell area of the Pecos River valley. Governor Wallace himself did not underestimate the amount of criminal activity requiring control, noting in his journal that there were nearly 200 indictments in a county with a total voting population of 150.

Wallace left no stone unturned; his effort to restore law and order brought him face-to-face with the teenaged outlaw called "the Kid," and Pat Garrett came to his attention when cattleman John Chisum wrote the governor recommending Garrett, then a resident of Fort Sumner,

CHAPTER SEVEN

as the ideal man to head an antirustling force to patrol the rangelands and conduct searches in the White Oaks area where Billy the Kid, among others, was selling stolen cattle.

The dramatic encounter between Governor Wallace and Billy the Kid, bringing together in a frontier setting two men representing near polar opposites along the spectrum of American society, took place at the initiative of the young outlaw and was but one example of his resourcefulness when confronted with threat to his own freedom. The Kid was in hiding near Lincoln when the governor arrived. Within days arrests were being made, and there were more to come; the Kid knew the dragnet was closing in on him.

But he also knew that the governor was particularly interested in seeing to it that the men who murdered Chapman be tried in a court of law. To achieve that end, the governor needed witnesses to identify and then testify against the men—Jesse Evans, James Dolan, Billy Mathews, and Billy Campbell—who had accosted Chapman and shot him at such close range that burning gunpowder set fire to his clothes as a rifle bullet tore through his chest. Billy the Kid had been nearby on the street that bitterly cold night, he and other Regulators having just finished celebrating the truce with Jesse Evans by drinking whiskey with their former enemies. It was close to midnight when the Kid, who as a nondrinker remained sober and clearheaded, saw Chapman killed by the inebriated group. As a witness to the crime, he knew he had something to offer Wallace, and he knew what he wanted in return for giving testimony at a trial.

He wrote a letter to Wallace and sent it by a messenger, who waited as the governor read the Kid's offer to give testimony if indictments against him were lifted. "I was present when Mr. Chapman was murdered and know who did it, and if it were not for those indictments I would have made it clear before now," wrote the Kid. "It is in your power to anul those indictments."[5] Wallace sent a note back to the Kid, telling him to come to Justice of the Peace John Wilson's home at 9 P.M. on 17 March.

As recounted later by the governor, the Kid knocked at the door at precisely the appointed hour. Only after being assured of his safety and the complete secrecy of the meeting did the wary gunfighter consent to lay down the rifle he held in one hand and the pistol he carried in the other. The governor sat down and talked at length with the youthful outlaw he described as slender and of medium height, with brown hair worn long, dressed in boots, pants, western shirt, vest, and broad-brimmed hat, and appearing no older than the nineteen years he actually was. Because it was widely assumed that those accused of killing Chapman would try to kill anyone ready to testify against them, it was agreed that the governor would place the Kid under arrest, a phony arrest intended to protect him until Dolan, Evans, Campbell, and Mathews were safely in custody. In return for the Kid's cooperation as a witness, Wallace promised he would issue a governor's pardon should the Kid be convicted on any of the charges against him.

The first phase of the scheme was implemented within days. The Kid was placed in detention in Lincoln, first in a dungeon-like underground cell, then was transferred to a more relaxed form of imprisonment, in which he had daily visitors who sometimes included the governor. And in April when Judge Bristol again presided over the annual court session in Lincoln, the Kid's testimony helped secure indictments against the Chapman killers, even in the face of the lenient attitude toward them displayed by District Attorney W. L. Rynerson.[6]

Billy the Kid

Only enough is known of the early life of Billy the Kid to raise questions that can never be answered. Might the child who was intelligent, lively, good-humored, and though spirited not a troublemaker have become a law-abiding member of society had he not lost his father early on, his mother to tuberculosis at age fifteen, and subsequently been given no parental guidance by his stepfather? Would the boy so capable of communicating and so eager to be in the thick of things have developed a different pattern of behavior had he not come under the influence of the code of the West, with its double standard of condemning yet romanticizing the gun? If the identity of his father were known, would it be discovered that the Kid's readiness to cheat and steal marked the father as well? And finally, was it mere immaturity or a permanently embedded attraction to criminal activity that in each of several instances kept the Kid from acting on an expressed desire to settle down as a law-abiding homesteader in the upcountry near Lincoln where he felt at home?

It can with some fairness be said that the answers to these questions are irrelevant, particularly as thousands of other people have arisen from the same environmental circumstances and become neither thieves nor killers. If the questions arise at all, it is only because of two realities that emerge from the known record of Billy the Kid. First he was not stupid, not mean-spirited, not cruel, not under the influence of whiskey; his

CHAPTER SEVEN

potential was apparent to many of his contemporaries. And second, there was a troubling incongruity in his sentence to hanging, in view of the fact that by normal legal standards of his time he was not given a fair trial, would not under normal circumstances have been found guilty of first-degree murder, and under normal conditions of law and order would not have been the only one of several dozen men involved in the Lincoln County War to pay any penalty under the law.

In the absence of documented evidence, it is not possible to reconstruct his background in any depth. The few facts there are indicate that his childhood was one of dislocation and struggle, with little in the way of privilege or advantage, although its hardships were not uncommon in the society of his time. He was born Henry McCarty, probably in 1859, most likely in the state of New York. His mother, Catherine McCarty, was left a widow to raise Henry and a younger son, Joseph. The small family moved westward and lived in Wichita, Kansas, and Denver, Colorado, before coming to New Mexico. On 1 March 1873 Catherine McCarty was married in Santa Fe to William H. Antrim, a man younger than herself, with whom she and her boys had been friends since their days in Kansas. Henry McCarty, though a minor at the time, was apparently given permission to stand as a witness to his mother's marriage, for his name is shown on the marriage record. William Antrim moved his new family to the small mountain community of Silver City, in southwest New Mexico.

In Silver City young Henry was sometimes called "Billy Antrim," the name of his stepfather. Henry McCarty attended school in Silver City; teachers remembered him as bright, while friends later said he liked to read books and also loved to sing and dance. On 16 September 1874 Catherine McCarty died of the tuberculosis that had prompted the family's move to New Mexico.[7] Not long after his mother's death, Henry left Silver City, after his first scrape with the law for stealing clothes from a laundry, and at the age of sixteen was on his own; there is no evidence that he retained family ties with his stepfather, although he may have had occasion to see his younger brother. From Silver City, Henry McCarty, an auburn-haired, slightly buck-toothed boy who told people he would also answer to the name Billy Antrim, went west and began working as a ranchhand in southeast Arizona, where the U.S. Army operated several military posts, including Camp Grant, where Henry was frequently seen.

His boyish appearance already was prompting people to call him "the Kid," and he was already becoming a practiced hand with the gun, the horse, and the lariat, all accoutrements of the drifter-cowboy life he had stumbled into as the only avenue open to him, but for which he seemed suited by instinct and desire. He seems to have wanted to excel at whatever it was he was doing; by 1877 he had brought his skills in riding and shooting to a high level from constant practice and had become fluent in speaking the Spanish language. All these skills were later employed by him in his New Mexico years, though mostly outside the law rather than in the pursuit of honest work.

It was in Arizona that the Kid first demonstrated another pattern of behavior, one that remained central to his life until it ended. He could kill a man, usually in circumstances that in another kind of man might have provoked anger but not murder. He could rationalize the act in his own mind, always finding a reason it could not be avoided. And he could and would employ a high degree of cunning and bold defiance in escaping after being jailed for his crime. It began in August 1877, when he got into an argument with a big burly blacksmith named Francis Cahill, who was known to be a bully. Finally after Cahill had verbally taunted him and physically assaulted him, the Kid grabbed the man's gun and shot him. Cahill died the following day. By the time a coroner's jury had charged him with murder, the Kid had made his way across the border into New Mexico. In retrospect it was a fateful event, for it made him an outlaw, a fugitive from justice, from that time onward, and it was his headlong flight from the likelihood of punishment that brought him to Lincoln County.

The Kid's first place of relative refuge after fleeing Arizona was the town of Mesilla, on the Rio Grande in central-southern New Mexico. There he became acquainted with the notorious Jesse Evans, leader of a horse- and cattle-theft gang. The Kid had stolen a few horses himself while in Arizona and was now displaying a tendency to outlawry of a type common in the frontier territories. In October of 1877 the Kid traveled with Evans and his gang, called "the boys," up the Mesilla Valley, east across the Rio Grande, and on into Lincoln County. Moving up into the high country, the Kid and Evans passed through the town of Lincoln and continued east down into the Pecos Valley, reaching Seven Rivers, below Roswell, in mid-October. "The boys" were put up at the Beckwith ranch, while the Kid boarded with Heiskell Jones, the early settler now ranching near Seven Rivers and raising a family of eight sons and a daughter.

The Kid used a new name in Lincoln County, telling people he was "William Bonney." Why he chose the surname Bonney is not known;

there is no evidence indicating that it had familial or personal relevance. Though the use of an alias beginning at this particular time would appear to be a deliberate attempt to find a new identity, that was not quite the case. Not only was it fairly common practice among the cowboys and gunmen of the time to use aliases as they moved from one place to another, but it is also true, and only puzzling if the Kid were trying to escape his real identity, that he would always add that he was sometimes called Billy Antrim or Henry Antrim and would answer to those names as well. The new William Bonney was still commonly referred to, however, as "the Kid." And at the Jones ranch, the Kid was made welcome, fed, and supplied with a horse, no questions asked. Although he usually spoke little of his early experiences, the Kid spoke fondly of "Ma Jones" after the 1877 visit, and he returned in friendship even though some of the Jones boys ended up on the Dolan side in the Lincoln County War.

In November the Kid joined some thirty members of the gang who went to Lincoln to free Jesse Evans and three others who had been arrested at Seven Rivers and jailed in Lincoln by Sheriff Brady for stealing horses owned by John Tunstall and Dick Brewer. When Evans and the others went back to Seven Rivers, the Kid stayed in the Lincoln area, boarding with Dick Brewer and sometimes with the cousins Frank and George Coe. He liked these new friends, and in addition may have been hesitating about committing himself to open outlawry with Evans.[8]

The Kid was friendly to everyone in the Lincoln and San Patricio area. He worked hard, was always in good spirits, and soon was a popular figure at local bailes. He drank little if any whiskey and did not use tobacco. He loved to gamble, enjoying poker and the game of monte. Guns and horses were his passion; he was known for never failing to provide well for his horses and never abusing them. He was never condescending to anyone, a trait much appreciated by Hispanos in particular. He was intelligent and able to make good use of his grammar-school education, as his letters attest. Physically he was agile as a cat. Mentally he was able to focus instantly and totally when a contingency arose that demanded fast thinking. In general he had personality traits as well as mental traits that would have stood him in good stead in any of a number of professions other than that of cowboy-gunslinger in which he found himself. Side by side with these positive traits, however, there existed in the Kid a flash-point temper that was lethal when aroused and that ultimately undermined the surface stability of his persona.

When Brewer became foreman of Tunstall's ranch on the Rio Feliz in early 1878, either he or Tunstall himself hired the Kid to join the crew of cowboys and ranchhands Brewer was putting together for the young Englishman. Billy the Kid was still a boy among men, just eighteen years old and not likely to have grown to physical maturity yet, when he signed on with Tunstall. The land, with its rough mountains, foothills, canyons, and vast bowls of grass-filled range sheltered in between, demanded endurance and strength from those who worked it on horseback. Physical comforts were few. But to the Kid, a footloose near-vagabond without resources, already alienated from what family was left after the death of his mother and already in trouble with the law, the new life as a Tunstall hand must have seemed good. He was part of a group. He was paid regular wages. Most of the men, including Tunstall and Brewer, were unmarried, and there was a degree of comradeship, a rough kind of unspoken friendship, among them. The Kid became good friends with Fred Waite, a Choctaw Indian from the Indian Territory; they talked about one day farming together on the Rio Ruidoso. Godfrey Gauss, a kindly German who cooked the cowboy fare of beans, beef, biscuits, and coffee for the Tunstall outfit on the Feliz, provided a homelike atmosphere the Kid had known only for brief periods in his youth. Looking at the situation from what is likely to have been his viewpoint, it makes sense to conclude that the Kid probably liked the job and place enough to want nothing more than to be as grittily tough as the men around him. And with no way of knowing what course future events would take, the Kid would only have welcomed the chance to prove his toughness further when his new job as a cowboy suddenly meant doing duty as a gunmen as well.

Within weeks of Billy's hiring, it was clear that Tunstall men would be used for more than cattle roundups and ranch chores. The Tunstall store in Lincoln, opened in August of 1877, was by January of 1878 offering a variety of merchandise ordered in by Tunstall and drawing business away from a fuming Jimmie Dolan at the Murphy store down the street. With his lawsuit against McSween on embezzlement charges serving as the perfect pretext to harass Tunstall as well, Dolan actively participated in Sheriff Brady's attachment of Tunstall property, on the grounds that Tunstall and McSween were partners. Dolan was a member of the posse that went to Tunstall's ranch home on the morning of 18 February 1878. While Dolan waited at the ranch house, part of the posse, led by Jesse Evans, went after Tunstall, who was peacefully leading his men back to Lincoln. Billy the Kid saw the posse coming

CHAPTER SEVEN

and was above it in pine country when the shots came that signaled Tunstall's death.

It could have been the end of a job for the Kid. Certainly it was the end of regular wages; McSween gave the Tunstall men and other McSween fighters only food and ammunition, no money payments, after the death of Tunstall. But the group was too caught up in common purpose, held together by the tightening bond people feel when confronted by common threat, to think of dispersing as former employees in the normal way. Then, too, the ranch was still there and the store was still there, being run by a Tunstall employee, with both store and ranch now part of the estate of the dead Tunstall and perhaps viable as economic enterprises. All was fluid; events moved rapidly; nothing could be foreseen. Yet clearly the idea of securing justice, and even more the idea of taking revenge, was the glue that kept together the Tunstall men who formed the core group calling itself the Regulators.

Though never a leader of the Regulators, Billy the Kid was among its most openly aggressive adherents. Challenging and belligerent, he publicly derided the law establishment of Lincoln County as represented by Sheriff Brady. He took part in the arrest and killing of posse members Baker and Morton on 9 March, in the killing of Brady on 1 April, and was a participant in the gunfight at Blazer's Mill that ended the lives of Buckshot Roberts and Dick Brewer on 4 April. He was at the center of the countless skirmishes and shootouts that punctuated the period from April to July of 1878, and he was with McSween at the end on 19 July, escaping in a hail of bullets only as fire consumed the McSween house. Along with John Middleton and Henry Brown, the Kid was indicated in April 1878 for the murders of Brady and Hindman. Middleton and Brown fled New Mexico and were never seen again in the territory.

The Kid, for whom an arrest warrant was issued, managed to evade being served until 14 April 1879, when during the annual court session he was again indicted and made himself available for arrest by Sheriff George Kimball, in accordance with his bargain with Governor Wallace. Billy the Kid upheld his part of the bargain by giving testimony against the killers of Huston Chapman; in return he expected the governor to pardon him if he were convicted of Brady's death or any other capital offense. District Attorney Rynerson obtained a change of venue to Doña Ana County because of strong sentiment in Lincoln in favor of Billy the Kid. The Kid pleaded not guilty to the Brady murder charge, with no attorney to represent him in court. But Rynerson made it clear that he did not intend to allow William Bonney to testify against Dolan at the upcoming trial for Chapman's murder, and also stated publicly he did not believe the governor had the authority to promise a governor's pardon to the Kid.[9]

Sitting in jail in Lincoln during May of 1879, with the governor now gone back to Santa Fe, Billy the Kid could not have failed to recognize that the bargain he had made to protect himself had not turned out to be as ironclad as he hoped. And the Kid was interested in self-protection above all else. The exact details of how he managed to escape are not known. But on 17 June, with help from friendly locals, he rode off into the surrounding countryside, determined to remain free and no longer trusting in the governor's ability or willingness to help him do it.

The Kid gradually resumed the life of crime he had led during the period from July 1878 until his incarceration at the hands of Wallace. He knew every corner of the land and made good use of hiding places, which included caves along the bluffs of the Pecos River. A number of similarly inclined young outlaws sometimes helped him carry out raids, alter brands, and market stolen cattle, although the Kid never headed an organized gang. Pat Garrett later said that the Kid would not steal from those who were his friends, although he was not above occasionally cheating his fellow cattle thieves when dividing up the profits.[10]

In the larger scheme of things, Billy the Kid could be categorized as simply a cattle rustler, a drifter cowboy, and a gunfighter in a pattern common throughout much of the West at that time. Nevertheless his participation in the turbulence of the Lincoln County War undoubtedly played a part in his psychological development and altered his own perception of his behavior. For the fact is that his passage from adolescence to manhood took place in a context providing the sanction of quasi legality and the cover of a cause larger than self for what were essentially violent, lawless activities. The experience may have, all unconsciously, reinforced submerged antagonisms toward authority existing in Billy the Kid since childhood. After the Lincoln County War, having accustomed himself to the role of one who stands outside the law but views himself as on the side of people being abused by those in power, he probably refused at some subconscious level to recognize the purely criminal nature of his activities. The citizenry in general, and Pecos Valley cattlemen in particular, had no such problem in seeing his thievery for what it was. The hue and cry for his capture grew louder by the day as the year 1879 drew to a close.

CHAPTER SEVEN

Pat Garrett

At the very time Billy the Kid was confirming with every new act of theft that he had resolved the ambiguities of the Lincoln County War in favor of lawlessness, a cowboy named Patrick F. Garrett, who was nine years older than the Kid, and had proven himself just as skilled with a horse and a gun, was gaining public acclaim as defender of the law on the wide-open range. While Billy the Kid was seen by 1879 as a tough cowboy gone over to the bad side, Pat Garrett of Fort Sumner was seen as a cowboy combining toughness with incorruptibility. Only for a few years in the late 1870s and early 1880s did the lives of these two men intersect. But because each seemed to personify some aspect of a morally simplified American West, their brief but fateful encounter propelled both into that strange limbo of posthumous fame that feeds on a mix of folklore and fact.

There was a certain rough symmetry in the life patterns that drew the Kid and Garrett into their respective roles as outlaw and sheriff. Each began as cowboy pure and simple. The Kid entered Lincoln County from the west, already moving into a life outside the law. Garrett came into the county from the east, moving with seeming inexorability into the life of exemplary lawman. In their clear embodiments of powerful, stereotypical frontier images, the two seemed unconsciously to be preparing themselves for the mythologizing that would occur after they had vanished from the scene.

Pat Garrett was born on 5 June 1850, in Alabama. His family moved to Louisiana, where his father ran a small plantation. Garrett acquired only a grade-school education. The family holdings never recovered from the ravages of the Civil War, and at the age of nineteen Garrett left home to look for work. His first job was as a cowboy in Dallas County, Texas, in 1869. After working ranches for six years, he went to the south plains of Texas, where he was a buffalo-hide hunter from 1875 to 1877 and may have joined in local military campaigns against the Comanche. Early in 1878 Garrett went to Tascosa, in the Texas panhandle; by the fall of 1878 he had moved on to the Pecos Valley in New Mexico, settling in at Fort Sumner, where he became acquainted with a variety of people frequenting the town's lively saloons and attending its Mexican bailes, among them wealthy sheep rancher Pete Maxwell, cattleman John Chisum, and William Bonney, otherwise known as "the Kid."[11]

Garrett was six feet four inches tall, lanky and slender. He had blue eyes, dark brown hair worn parted on the side, a straight nose, high cheekbones, a determined set to his mouth, and wore a mustache. Garrett was sociable, easygoing and gregarious by nature, relishing a game of poker as much as the next man, although he usually knew how to enjoy himself without overindulging in whiskey. Within a short time he was known among the leading stockmen of the area as an able man whose common sense and work experience made him too valuable to ignore. Many of Fort Sumner's Hispanic residents also found Garrett likable, particularly as he showed little of the unreasoned prejudice characteristic of many former Texans. Hispanos called Garrett "Juan Largo" (Long John).

At the suggestion of Chisum and other cattlemen, Garrett moved to Roswell in the fall of 1879 and was appointed deputy sheriff by Lincoln County Sheriff George Kimball. Operating from the county seat at Lincoln, Kimball was hard pressed to control the large county; a reliable Roswell deputy was needed. Garrett bought land just east of Roswell, which became the nucleus of a farm and ranch eventually covering eighteen hundred acres. On 14 January 1880 he married Apolinaria Gutierrez, of Fort Sumner. Garrett had a two-story adobe house constructed on his Roswell property.

There were now more small cattleman and more homesteaders and farmers in the Pecos Valley. Their numbers had been growing since Governor Wallace's effort to restore order began in the spring of 1879. Chisum was rebuilding his herd on the Pecos range. But the very numbers of cattle grazing along both sides of the Pecos, including large numbers of Chisum stock, presented a tempting target for cattle thieves, stimulating a sharp rise in the amount of rustling. One of many examples occurred in January 1880, when a Chisum range outfit found over eighty head of their cattle hidden in Canyon Cueva, one hundred miles north of the South Spring ranch, with brands and jinglebob earmarks crudely altered in preparation for illicit sale. A high proportion of the most audacious of the cattle thefts were believed to be the work of former McSween partisans, most notably Billy the Kid. Public rancor against Sheriff Kimball grew as he proved unwilling or unable to muster the force required to bring the Kid to heel.

In 1880 Democratic Party leaders chose Pat Garrett as candidate for sheriff. He ran on a law-and-order platform against his old boss, Sheriff Kimball. Garrett was elected in November 1880, with strong campaign support from leading citizens J. C. Lea, Chisum, and George Curry, and strong support at the polls from Hispanic voters as well as Anglos. So dire was the rustling situation considered that Garrett was pressed into service even before taking office. He immediately began a series of posse searches, making use of tips about hideouts and ranches where stolen livestock was being held.

Garrett's strength as sheriff lay in his activism and personal leadership in the saddle and on the range, gun at hip. His weakness was the office work, which at that time included tax collecting; for these duties of office Garrett later employed erstwhile postmaster, school teacher, justice of the peace, and journalist extraordinaire Ash Upson, who proved himself an able and devoted aide. A sheriff's use of such a clerical assistant was a common occurrence at the time. Garrett knew well, however, that nothing would suffice to prove himself in office but to capture Billy the Kid; no other action could be a substitute. By late November 1880, with the Kid still at large though tantalizingly close and seen publicly coming and going in Lincoln, Fort Sumner, and even White Oaks, where he was intensely disliked, Garrett decided personally to lead the posse that would track him down.

The Crossing of Two Lives

Billy the Kid was an avid reader of newspapers whenever he could lay hands on them, and he also had personal contacts who told him what was going on. He knew he was regarded as the chief criminal in the southeast quadrant, especially now that some of the Texas outlaws had returned to their home state. Learning that Garrett was aiming for his capture, the Kid wrote a lengthy letter to Wallace. Dated 12 December 1880, the letter said in part, "Deputy Sheriff Garrett acting under Chisum's orders went to Portales and found nothing. J. S. Chisum is the man who got me into trouble and was benefited Thousands by it and is now doing all he can against me." The letter was implicit evidence of how important in the Kid's eyes had been the meeting between himself and the governor; certainly for him the contact had more import than it had for Wallace. And in flinging baseless charges at Chisum, the Kid revealed that he immaturely needed the delusion of believing he was being unfairly persecuted in order to avoid recognizing that there was no justification for his criminality.[12] On another level, of course, the Kid's wild accusations were no more than an inept attempt on the part of a woefully unworldly young hoodlum to pull the wool over the eyes of the governor. The governor made no response to the Kid, choosing instead to offer a five-hundred-dollar reward to anyone who would deliver Bonney to the sheriff of Lincoln County.

Garrett, himself the newly elected sheriff but not due to be sworn into office until January 1881, was not waiting for the Kid to be delivered to him. He calmly prepared to close in on the county's most-wanted outlaw whenever an opportunity presented itself. In early December a rash of horse thefts was blamed on the Kid. Garrett took a posse to Fort Sumner, where members of the gang, said by the *Las Vegas Gazette* to have from forty to fifty members, had been seen.[13] In his letter to the governor, the Kid had in fact announced he had "been at Sumner," making his living by "gambling" since the Lincoln County War ended. Garrett and his posse were in Fort Sumner by mid-December, joining forces with another twenty men led by Frank Stewart, detective for the panhandle cattlegrowers' association. Meanwhile the *Las Vegas Gazette* was complaining that the governor's reward was insufficient and a "purse of $5,000" should be raised as an incentive to bring in Billy the Kid.

As dark fell on the stormy night of 19 December 1880, the Kid rode in toward Fort Sumner in the company of his close friends Tom O'Folliard, Charles Bowdre, and several others. The group was met just outside town by Garrett and his men, who demanded surrender. All but O'Folliard, who was shot and died several hours later, managed to get away in the confusion. The Kid and his friends found refuge of sorts in a deserted stone sheepherder's house located east of Fort Sumner at a place called Stinking Springs.

It was bitterly cold and heavy snow blanketed the isolated, uninhabited countryside. The men inside the small stone structure had no fuel and no food. The Kid took his prized gray mare inside the house, and there was just enough room for the horse of one other man. The other horses were tethered to vigas outside. Garrett and his posse had followed the outlaws and stationed themselves within shooting range in a nearby arroyo. When Bowdre opened the door of the house to go out and feed the horses, he was instantly killed by Garrett, who mistook him for the Kid. Bowdre had been earning an honest living and attempting to get straight with the law. His death was regretted by everyone, including Garrett.

On 23 December, hungry, nearly frozen, and with no hope of escaping from the well-provisioned lawmen doing relay duty outside, Billy the Kid and the others with him in the stone house gave up. Garrett had shot away the ropes holding the horses outside. One horse, shot by the deputies, was blocking the doorway, so that a dash on horseback from inside the house was impossible. The Kid and his friends were brought outside, manacled, fed their first meal in days, and taken back

CHAPTER SEVEN

to town as prisoners. Garrett took Billy the Kid and two others to Las Vegas, then on to Santa Fe by train on 28 December.

Garrett had gotten his man; he was given the five hundred dollars in reward money and took on the status of celebrity. Billy the Kid would finally stand trial on one or more of the major charges against him, thanks to the tall, staunch sheriff from Lincoln County. The capture was big news throughout the territory, with the *Las Vegas Gazette* putting out an entire extra edition as soon as its enterprising editor learned the Kid was being brought in by Garrett.[14]

And yet the situation was not without its anomalies. Billy the Kid presented a jauntily hopeful face to the world, confident that all would yet be well, that he would be freed in some manner. There was a certain logic to this assessment of his predicament. Though indicted for the murder of Brady, the evidence was circumstantial, as there was no way of proving whose bullet had hit Brady when any or all of six men might have been shooting. Other indictments for killings were even less substantial. The charges of cattle and horse stealing were lesser charges that could bring a jail term but not hanging. And then there was the governor's specific promise to the Kid of a pardon.

A Gazette reporter interviewed Bonney at the Las Vegas jail. The Kid was, the paper reported, a nice-looking boy, asking with pretended nonchalance how bad the Sante Fe jail was, keeping his spirits up with a show of bravado, friendly to everyone, and rather enjoying the public attention. "I don't blame you for writing of me as you have. You had to believe others' stories; but then I dont [sic] know as anyone would believe anything good of me, anyway," he said. "I really wasn't the leader of any gang. I was for Billy all the time."[15]

From a jail cell in Santa Fe, the Kid continued to indicate he believed he was being unfairly singled out for past acts in the Lincoln County War for which others should share the blame, and he continued to contend he was not the ringleader of the cattle thieves. Both contentions contained a fair amount of truth, although no one was listening to the Kid's side at the time. Over a period of three months, from January through the end of March 1881, the Kid wrote notes and letters to Wallace asking, demanding, and finally pleading for, an indication from the governor that he would provide some kind of protection from what the Kid gradually saw looming before him: a trial at which his side would not be presented fairly. "I guess they mean to send me up without giving me any show," he wrote the governor on 4 March 1881, from his jail cell.[16]

The plight of Billy the Kid was of little concern to the governor, who by now had dismissed him as a brazen young outlaw beyond redemption. The governor may have felt he had done what he could by asking attorney Ira Leonard to meet with the Kid shortly after the governor and Bonney made their bargain in Lincoln. The Kid had failed to appear at the meeting place to talk with Leonard. In any case Wallace's attention was on things other than New Mexico in the spring of 1881. He had completed *Ben Hur*, which received its first printing in November 1880 and was greeted with reviews favorable enough to deeply gratify its author. He also was expending considerable energy in trying to profit from a number of mining ventures in which he had invested. And now, having supported newly elected President James A. Garfield in the 1880 campaign, he was seeking appointment as an ambassador abroad. On 9 March he submitted his resignation as governor of New Mexico, and on 17 March the president accepted it, naming Lionel A. Sheldon of Ohio as Wallace's replacement. Wallace left Santa Fe on 30 May by Pullman car on the Santa Fe Railroad whose building into New Mexico he had welcomed during his tenure as governor. As he departed, newspapers of every political persuasion united in praising him as one of the ablest and most honest governors ever appointed to administer New Mexico. In June the U.S. Senate confirmed his appointment as ambassador to Turkey, and Wallace embarked by ship with his wife for the Middle Eastern lands that had been so much on his mind even while serving in a frontier territory of the American West.

At the end of March, Billy the Kid was taken under heavy guard to Las Cruces by train and on to the county seat of Mesilla by coach. The Kid was the only one present of nine defendants under federal indictment for the killing of Buckshot Roberts at Blazers Mill. Judge Warren Bristol presided over the court. Bristol was the subject of much controversy for his arbitrary manner in dealing with lawyers, witnesses, and evidence. Many considered him lacking in sufficient knowledge of the law. Bristol had dealt for several years with the criminal charges growing out of the Lincoln County War. He was tired of the whole affair and convinced in his own mind that the fault lay with the Tunstall-McSween side in the feud. After dismissing the Roberts case on grounds that the federal court had no jurisdiction on the Blazers Mill property where the killing had taken place, the judge decided that Billy the Kid would be tried instead in district court, on the charge of having murdered Sheriff Brady. Again the Kid was the only one present of three defendants in the case.

CHAPTER SEVEN

The court appointed the law partners A. J. Fountain and John D. Bail to defend Billy the Kid. Bright, ambitious, and somewhat flamboyant in manner, Fountain was known as an honest man and a crusader for justice. In 1896 he was to lose his own life in a murder never solved. Fountain and Bail were not given sufficient time to prepare an adequate defense for the Kid. They did not have a single witness for the defense to call.

The jury was largely unaware of the economic and political implications of the factional violence surrounding the Brady killing. Judge Bristol made it clear in his instructions to the jury that he considered the Kid guilty as charged, and he failed to present to the jury instructions that would have laid forth possible grounds for reaching a verdict of guilty on a lesser charge than first-degree murder. The case was called on 8 April. Isaac Ellis, B. F. Baca, and J. B. Mathews were witnesses for the prosecution. There were no witnesses for the defense. On 9 April the case went to the jury, which wasted little time before returning a verdict of guilty. On 13 April Judge Bristol sentenced Billy the Kid to be hanged at Lincoln on 13 May.

Shortly before he was taken in iron shackles to Lincoln in a closely guarded armed convoy, the Kid was interviewed by the *Mesilla News*. The paper "created prejudice against me," said the Kid. Asked whether he expected a pardon from the governor, he replied, "considering . . . the friendly relations that existed between him and me, and the promise he made me, I think he ought to pardon me. Don't know that he will do it."[17] As enterprising as ever in his own cause, the Kid had written a letter from the Mesilla jail to an attorney in Santa Fe, asking him to arrange the return of the gray mare taken from him at Stinking Springs in December 1880. Although the posse member appropriating it had given it to a woman at Las Vegas, the horse still legally belonged to the Kid. With no financial resources of any kind, the Kid wanted the horse to use as payment to Fountain, as the attorney had agreed to appeal the verdict if funds could be found to sustain the legal expenses.

On 21 April 1881 Billy the Kid was imprisoned at Lincoln. His jail cell was in the old Murphy-Dolan store, which had been purchased by the county in 1880 to serve as a public courthouse and jail. As no alterations had yet been made to the building, Garrett had to assign personal guards for the Kid after placing him in the northeast corner room on the second floor. Deputy J. W. Bell, a decent man liked by everyone including the Kid, and Deputy Marshall Robert Olinger, a sadistically bullying man with a history of feuds with the Kid, were chosen to provide round-the-clock guard. Garrett's office was just to the west of Billy's confinement quarters. The two had several conversations during the days the Kid was confined. "He appeared to have a plausible excuse for each and every crime," Garrett said, except the killing of a man named Jimmy Carlisle near White Oaks, about which the Kid said, "there's more about that than people know of." In their talks, according to the sheriff, "he would sometimes seem on the point of opening his heart, either in confession of [sic] justification, but it always ended in an unspoken intimation that it would all be of no avail, as no one would given him credence, and he scorned to beg for sympathy."[18]

While it was true that Bonney was the only principle in the killings engendered by the factional troubles to be condemned to death, or even to be brought to trial, it was equally true that the bullets fired by the Kid and those with him were intended to kill Brady. The act was deliberate, whether a momentary impulse because the opportunity presented itself or an event planned during the previous night spent by the Regulators at the Tunstall store, and therefore deserving of punishment on its own merits, regardless of whether the perpetrators of other, related murders were caught or not.

As he confronted the prospect of his own death by hanging, however, Billy the Kid would most likely have singled out as even more important than his unique status as the lone condemned man the fact that it was Sheriff Brady's men who had fired the first shots in what was literally a war for control of Lincoln County, and that in openly siding with the Dolan side, Brady had vacated his role as objective lawman and made himself a participant in a confrontation in which he bore as much blame as all the others who so recklessly traded rifle and pistol shots. But if that indeed was William Bonney's view, albeit one not given full verbal expression, of the killing for which he was scheduled to hang, it was a rationale that could only be accepted as satisfactory were the feuding of 1878 to be granted the status of war, that state in which the normal rule of law is superseded by the law of the battlefield. And certainly there was in Billy the Kid's time no definitive answer to a question that had scarcely been formulated about the nature of a particular frontier conflict.

On 28 April, eight days after being placed in the Lincoln jail, Billy the Kid escaped. Precisely how he did it will never be known, as he killed the only witness to his first daring move. Billy's own account as given to a friend named John Meadows after the escape may in the end be the most reliable of several renderings. During the afternoon Olinger

CHAPTER SEVEN

took several prisoners across the street for a meal at the Wortley Hotel, leaving Bell to guard the Kid. Bell took the Kid downstairs to the corral at the back of the courthouse, where a privy was located. As they returned Billy the Kid was ahead of Bell. He reached the landing at the top of the stairs faster than Bell, and for a few moments was hidden from Bell's view. The Kid slipped free of a handcuff, something he always could do because his wrists were larger than his hands.

When Bell reached the landing, the Kid knocked him down by swinging with his cuffed wrist. In the scuffle the Kid obtained Bell's gun. Bell stumbled back down the stairs. The Kid knew all was lost if Bell got away. From a prone position on the second floor landing, the Kid shot down at Bell just as the deputy sheriff reached the bottom of the twelve-step stairway. Mortally wounded, Bell stumbled blindly out into the area near the corral, falling into the arms of courthouse caretaker Godfrey Gauss and expiring within seconds.[19]

Olinger had heard the single shot. Rushing back from the hotel, he was met at the front gate to the courthouse by Gauss with news of Bell's death. Olinger did not have time to move farther. As he reached for his own gun, Billy the Kid took aim from the northeast corner window on the second floor with a double-barrelled shotgun belonging to Olinger that he had taken from Garrett's office, killing Olinger instantly with eighteen buckshot. The Kid then came out onto the balcony and fired down on Olinger again. Stunned townspeople were cautiously gathering in the street outside the courthouse, awed by the brutal display of determination to escape, uncertain of what to do. There were no other lawmen available. Sheriff Garrett had ridden to White Oaks on official business on the previous day. The bodies of Bell and Olinger were left where they had fallen.

The Kid did not rush away from the mountain community where central events of his short life had taken place. After both deputies were dead, he used a file thrown up through a window to him by Gauss and spent an hour removing one of the shackles on his legs. Unable to remove the other, he tucked the dangling end into his belt. He took a Winchester and two revolvers from the armory. He commandeered the fast pony owned by Lincoln resident Billy Burt, promising to send it back, then had two blankets tucked behind the saddle.

Finally, as cool winds hastened the end of a spring day, he galloped west out of Lincoln. He then turned north to the Capitan Mountains, where he found friends and shelter before moving south across the Rio Ruidoso and Rio Peñasco. Advised to go across the border into Mexico, he seems to have considered it. But in the end he turned north again toward the Pecos country around Fort Sumner, country where he could count on being kindly protected by some and ceaselessly pursued by others, in the scenario mixing familiar domesticity with dangerous risk that seems to entice the individual whose psyche is part insider, part outsider. Late on the day after the Kid's escape, Billy Burt's horse wandered back into Lincoln, its rope dangling behind.

In Santa Fe on 30 April 1881, two days after the escape he did not yet know about, Governor Wallace wrote out in his own hand and signed the death warrant for William Bonney, alias Billy the Kid. Upon learning shortly afterward from a telegram that the Kid was again at large, the governor immediately posted notice that a five-hundred-dollar reward would be paid for the capture and delivery of Billy the Kid to the authorities.

As the man who had captured the Kid, and more importantly as the county official responsible for keeping him under lock and key until the time came for him to swing from the gallows, Garrett received news of the Kid's escape with a show of steely calm that masked a sense of personal failure. He had failed, he later said, in not providing adequate guard for one so "daring and unscrupulous" he would have "killed a hundred men" to escape the fate of being hung.[20] Informed by a letter brought to White Oaks on the twenty-ninth, Garrett was back in Lincoln on the thirtieth. Attempts to follow the Kid's trail proved futile. For the next two and a half months, Billy the Kid wandered as a fugitive through the Pecos country, moving from sheep camps east of Fort Sumner to caves along the river farther south. "He had many friends who were true to him, harbored him, kept him supplied with territorial newspapers."[21]

In early July Garrett asked John Poe, theft investigator for Canadian River stockmen, and Deputy Thomas McKinney of Roswell to accompany him on a reconnoitering trip to Fort Sumner, where the Kid was rumored to be spending time. The three met in Lincoln, went east to Roswell, then up the Pecos on 10 July. On the thirteenth they waited to meet a man who had said he knew where the Kid was hiding. When the man failed to appear, Garrett sent Poe, who would not be recognized as looking for the Kid, into Fort Sumner.

Poe returned to La Punta de la Glorieta, four miles north of Fort Sumner, reporting he had found one individual who was convinced "the Kid was about." Garrett decided to talk to Pete Maxwell, someone he felt he could trust. As the three rode toward Maxwell's home place, a

CHAPTER SEVEN

gracious pitch-roofed adobe building that had been built for army officers when the fort was occupied, they stopped at a shepherder's camp and while there observed from a distance a man in shirt sleeves and vest who spoke in Spanish before moving on in the direction of Maxwell's house. Garrett said he later came to believe that this man was the Kid.

Late that night, the fourteenth of July, Garrett and his colleagues made their way in the dark to the long verandah of the Maxwell house. Poe and McKinney waited at one end of the porch, twenty feet from the door of Maxwell's bedroom, which opened on to the porch. Garrett entered the bedroom anad sat down on the edge of the bed where Maxwell was sleeping. Garrett asked Maxwell "as to the whereabouts of the Kid." Startled into wakefulness, Maxwell replied, according to Garrett's account in his later book, that the Kid had been around but he did not know if he was still in the vicinity. "At that moment a man sprang quickly into the door" and called twice in Spanish, "Who comes there?" Upon receiving no answer, the man proceeded into the room and came close to the bed as he asked, "Who are they Pete?" apparently referring to Poe and McKinney seated outside.

Maxwell whispered to Garrett, "that's him," and as the man retreated rapidly backwards across the room, having sensed the presence of someone besides Maxwell, Garrett drew his revolver and fired from a sitting position, then threw his body sideways and fired again. Struck by the first bullet, the man fell dead.

Garrett said later he had known instantly upon hearing the man's voice that it was Billy the Kid. He had seen a pistol in one hand and a butcher knife in the other; Garrett, Poe, and McKinney all claimed to have heard three shots fired. Garrett believed the Kid had fired one shot between his own two shots. But no bullet holes were found indicating any shots were fired other than those from Garrett's gun, and Garrett conceded he had been mistaken.[22] As the tumultuous events of the night proceeded, and Billy the Kid's body was identified and prepared for the coroner's jury that gathered the following morning, Poe and McKinney said they had seen the Kid enter the room but did not recognize him. Upon hearing him speak in Spanish, they had concluded he was a Hispanic employee of Maxwell.

Garrett's bullet had struck Billy the Kid just above the heart. "It will never be known whether the Kid recognized me or not," Garrett said.[23] The inquest held on 15 July found the shooting to be justifiable homicide in self-defense by an officer of the law. Billy the Kid was buried in the military cemetery at Fort Sumner later on the same day the inquest was held.

The Kid was twenty-one years old at the time of his death. He had probably killed six or seven men in his lifetime, including a man named Joe Grant, who had turned on the Kid during a drinking bout in a Fort Sumner saloon; Bell and Olinger during the escape from Lincoln; Bob Beckwith during the flight from the burning McSween house; Brady; possibly Morton and Baker, the posse members hunted down by the Regulators after Tunstall was killed; and possibly White Oaks resident Jimmy Carlisle, during a gunfight involving a number of men. In the cases of Brady, Hindman, Morton, Baker, and Carlysle, the Kid's gun was among several being fired at the same time.[24] To the list should be added the Arizona blacksmith shot dead in 1877, although a case could have been made that Francis Cahill was shot by the Kid in self-defense.

Garrett Goes On

Garrett received a substantial amount of public praise for having killed Billy the Kid. But he also came in for a fair amount of criticism. For some the manner of the Kid's death—in a darkened room, caught unaware—left room for questions of fairness, even courage, on the part of the sheriff. And though there was little basis in reality for the criticism, as Garrett had neither planned for nor wanted a dark-of-the-night killing of the Kid, it nonetheless stung the lawman to the quick. Garrett was, after all, a man of limited education, who had quite literally created himself as the ever-upright, trustworthy frontier sheriff. He had made for himself a place in a settler society, built a public career, and its very underpinning was his own integrity and credibility. Pat Garrett, lawman, could not finish with Billy the Kid, outlaw, until he had set the record straight and presented to the public his version of the death of the Kid.

The book Garrett published in April 1882, with the assistance and writing skills of Ash Upson, had a profound impact upon future interpretations of the life of Billy the Kid, despite the 137-page book's limited circulation. Although the chapters of the book dealing ostensibly with the childhood and early life of Henry McCarty were patently the product of Ash Upson's imagination, the later chapters of the book are written as a first-person narrative by Garrett himself, and the information concerning the Kid's capture at Stinking Springs, his trial, imprisonment at Lincoln, the escape, and his death at Fort Sumner has been proven by later historians to be essentially sound.

CHAPTER SEVEN

Although Billy the Kid was but one of many renegades, desperados, and outlaws roaming the West in the last quarter of the nineteenth century, it quickly became apparent there was something about the boyish-looking Kid, with his oddly affecting quality of light-heartedness, his sometime openness, his friendships and loyalties, his participation on the corruption-battling side in the Lincoln County War, and his daredevil escapades, that lent him just enough ambiguity, just enough romanticism, just enough of the quixotic in nature, to render him a tantalizing subject for the popular "dime" novels of the day. Some eight of these potboilers offering sensationalized versions of Billy the Kid already had been published by 1882, when the *Santa Fe New Mexican* press printed the first edition of Garrett's account. The newspaper lacked the means to distribute Garrett's book properly, but it nonetheless became the basis for many future accounts, beginning with Charles Siringo's widely read 1885 work, *A Texas Cowboy*.

In 1882 began a testing of the character of Garrett that was to last in one form or another for the rest of his life. New forces were emerging in the Old West, forces promoting community, commerce, and civil order, and requiring of leaders abilities different from those that had been requisite in the earlier era, when cattle barons and gunfighters dominated the scene. Garrett would now find himself moving back and forth between a political arena where party organization was increasingly important and a business arena in which managing money was increasingly important; he was never to prove completely comfortable in either world, although he continued to be a determined player in both.

When his term as sheriff was up in 1882, Garrett was not nominated again by county Democrats, who instead selected his deputy, the solidly competent John Poe, to bear the party standard. While Poe ran and won, Garrett turned to ranching and farming. He retained ownership of his Roswell property but ranched near Fort Stanton as well and then accepted the captaincy of a Texas Rangers company in the panhandle. After several months in Texas, he returned to Lincoln County to be manager of the Kirby Ranch. That, too, proved a short-lived venture, and by 1885 he was back in Roswell, concentrating on his Pecos Valley holdings and acquiring more land.

But it was not in Garrett's nature to settle into the unspectacular if relatively secure life of the small agriculturist and rancher. Even if no longer in the spotlight of political office, he could and did use the contacts he had made as sheriff to further his business interests. It was with high hopes that Garrett became a partner of Charles B. Eddy, and together with fellow investors Charles Greene, G. B. Shaw, General Bradley, and R. W. Tansill formed the Pecos Valley Irrigation Company in 1881. The company constructed the first large-scale irrigation project in the Pecos Valley, taking a large ditch from the east side of the river to irrigate a tract of land on the Eddy ranch, located between Seven Rivers and the town of Eddy (present-day Carlsbad).

In 1889 the company began a second project, the Northern Canal, which took water from the Rio Hondo on Garrett's farm, four miles east of Roswell. The canal was dug in a southeasterly direction from the river. Requiring expensive machinery as well as intensive labor, the work on both projects absorbed large amounts of capital, which the investors were unable to supply after the initial work began. Neither ditch functioned without silting problems and neither attracted enough emigrants to offset high costs. By 1890 the company was failing, and its remaining assets were bought out by industrialist J. J. Hagerman, who made it the nucleus of his own much more ambitious irrigation schemes.

Garrett wanted to become the first sheriff of newly created Chaves County badly enough that when Democrats chose a Poe-backed candidate instead of himself for the November 1889 election, he ran as an independent candidate for sheriff. Poe's candidate and the entire Democratic ticket were elected. "Garrett was deeply hurt by his defeat."[25]

Just how severe the blow was to his pride may be measured by his response. Admittedly Garrett's irrigation investment had not gone well. But he had been in the Pecos Valley since 1878, owned a considerable amount of land, and was raising a family that eventually included eight children, the third of whom was the blind Elizabeth, born in Roswell in 1885. Though never entirely domesticated and ever a man who craved risk of some kind, Garrett was in his way a devoted family man. His slender, dark-eyed wife, Apolinaria, who survived her husband and died in 1935, spoke English with some difficulty, as she more often used the Spanish language; Garrett was at all times a willing and kind interpreter on her behalf. He lavished time and attention on small Elizabeth, frequently taking her with him on his horse and giving her as normal a childhood as possible.

But in a mood of bitter disillusionment after the 1889 defeat, Garrett uprooted his family, sold his farm and ranch, and moved to Uvalde, Texas. Ash Upson, who had become a close friend while living at the Garrett home and helping with the writing of Garrett's book, followed Garrett to Uvalde and remained, until his death in 1894, with the Garrett family. Garrett started a horse ranch near Uvalde, met with a de-

CHAPTER SEVEN

gree of financial success, enrolled Elizabeth in the Texas School for the Blind in Austin, where she received a music education, and served a term as an elected county commissioner. Among the numerous friends he made in Uvalde was a young lawyer named John Nance Garner, who shared Garrett's passion for fine quarter horses.

Garrett by now knew well the hazards of the political realm. Even so he was drawn to it repeatedly, perhaps needing public recognition in self-confirmation, certainly never seeming to find complete fulfilment in private business pursuits. When men of influence in southern New Mexico's Doña Ana County wrote letters to him in the wake of A. J. Fountain's mysterious disappearance in early 1896, Garrett answered their summons to take up once again the duties of a lawman by packing up family and possessions and going west into the ruggedly beautiful land where mountains, Rio Grande River, and the White Sands of a wind-swept desert formed another frontier as replete with Old West drama as had been that of Lincoln County, lying to its east.

Garrett arrived in Doña Ana County in 1896 and was appointed deputy sheriff. In April he was named sheriff to replace Numa Reymond, who resigned under pressure from Republicans demanding action in solving the shocking presumed murder of the well-known Fountain. In 1898 Garrett ran for the office as an independent and was elected to a two-year term as sheriff.

For virtually the whole of his tenure in office as Doña Ana County sheriff, Garrett's energies were focused on the Fountain matter, which took on aspects of a personal cause for him, almost as though it was a testing of his manhood in the same sense confronting Billy the Kid had been those many years before, in 1881.

But here it was different. Although Garrett needed a known villain, there were only suspects. Although he needed bodies to prove a murder had been done, none were found. Although he needed public consensus that he was pursuing the guilty man, there was none, and the man he sought to capture and convict as the killer of Fountain was supported by a substantial portion of the public and by some of the powerful political figures in the territory. Garrett was again the tall man in the white hat, but instead of the clear show of unassailable competence he wished to present, the result of his second episode as sheriff was a public image even more blurred by contradictions and ambiguities than had been the case when he shot and killed Billy the Kid.

Soon after assuming his duties at Las Cruces, Garrett became convinced that Fountain and his small son were the murdered victims of a cunning conspiracy perpetrated by tough and unscrupulous Texas cattlemen who engaged in rustling along with legitimate ranching after they emigrated to New Mexico's Tularosa Basin. At the center of this conspiracy Garrett placed a cattleman named Oliver M. Lee. Only days before his disappearance, Fountain had obtained indictments against Lee and several of his friends while acting as special prosecutor in cattle-theft cases during a court session held in the town of Lincoln.

Even in a territory where such energetically talented and politically ambitious men as Albert Bacon Fall, Thomas Benton Catron, and Harvey B. Fergusson rubbed shoulders, Albert Fountain stood out as a man of many talents with enough ego, drive, and confidence to exploit them all. Born in New York in 1838, Fountain had attended Columbia College and survived a series of remarkable adventures in Europe and Asia before arriving in San Francisco to become a journalist in the late 1850s. While in California he studied law and passed the bar exam. When the Civil War started, he joined the Union Army and marched to New Mexico with Carleton's California Column. He fought Indians under Carleton, served as collector of internal revenues in Texas, was a Texas state senator, then returned to New Mexico in 1875. He opened a law practice, headed an Indian-fighting militia, and in 1888 served in the territorial legislature, where he was elected speaker of the House. Over the years he wrote numerous articles for territorial newspapers. In 1896 he was serving as special prosecutor for rustlers and other chronically troublesome outlaws.[26]

When the January 1896 court session ended in Lincoln, Fountain was told that death threats were being made against him. Responding that he had a rifle to protect himself and his nine-year-old son Henry, who was accompanying him, Fountain left for the return trip to Las Cruces by buckboard, a new pony for Henry tied to the back. On 31 January the father and son were traveling along a lonely stretch of road when they were attacked at a point forty-five miles from Las Cruces. Within days of their disappearance, searchers, who included an older son of Fountain, located the buckboard and found signs of struggle, a pool of blood, and a footprint believed to be that of little Henry. Hoofprints and horse tracks leading in the direction of the Organ Mountains also were found near the scene, although they were impossible to follow more than a short distance. Despite intensive searching, no bodies were located and no conclusive clues were uncovered.

If Garrett was convinced that Oliver Lee had a hand in the Fountain murders, Oliver Lee was for his part equally convinced that Garrett was out to kill him in cold blood. Garrett obtained arrest warrants for Lee and his colleague Jim Gilliland in April of 1898. He had relied heavily on testimony from one man, Jack Maxwell of Tularosa, who claimed to have been at the Lee Ranch the night the Fountains were attacked. Maxwell said Lee and Gilliland were not there all night, but came riding in the next morning in exhausted condition.

Garrett made elaborate plans to serve his warrants in a surprise attack on Lee while he was visiting another ranch. But the early dawn raid on the sleeping Lee was badly bungled; Garrett was forced to lay down his arms and retreat, leaving one of his deputies wounded and dying. After that Lee kept his guard up constantly at his own ranch, scanning the horizons for Garrett and prepared to fight the lawman he considered to be pursuing a personal vendetta. But Garrett never went to the Lee Ranch, and his reluctance to make a move gave Lee's political supporters time to act.

Albert Fall rammed through the territorial legislature a bill creating a new county including the land where the Fountains had disappeared. Fall obtained Governor Miguel Otero's signature on the bill by naming the new county for Otero. The Fountain case was removed from the jurisdiction of Doña Ana County when Otero County was created in 1899, and Lee agreed to surrender to the new county's sheriff, George Curry, and stand trial.

A change of venue took the case to trial in the mountain mining town of Hillsboro in Sierra County. Tom Catron was special prosecutor for the territory, while Albert Fall and Harvey Fergusson were lawyers for the defense. Lee and Gilliland were codefendants. Each side, prosecution and defense, had its witnesses housed in its own camp at opposite ends of the town. Reporters from territorial and national newspapers thronged the streets. Support for Lee was strong and emotional. It was as much a political as a legal affair, pitting the territory's most powerful political foes against each other in the courtroom. The widely sensationalized trial was a showdown of sorts between Catron and Fall, the two men who were to become the state of New Mexico's first U.S. senators, in 1912.

Garrett was a star witness for the prosecution. But he had no more hard evidence to offer than when he first began to investigate, and his appearance on the witness stand failed to live up to its advance billing. The evidence presented by Maxwell, the man who claimed to know Lee was away from home the night when the attack on the Fountains took place, proved to be evidence tainted by a written contract in which Garrett agreed to give two thousand dollars for testimony that would convict Lee.[27] Lee's mother, Mary Lee, testified that her son had been at home on the night in question. In the absence of conclusive evidence and helped by a powerfully dramatic final summation by a drained but fiercely convincing Fall, the jury took but a short time to bring in a verdict of not guilty. Lee walked away a free man; Garrett had not gotten his man this time. Oliver Lee went on to live a long life, respected and holding several positions of responsibility in the community.

In 1901, out of office as sheriff, Garrett decided to seek a presidential appointment as collector of customs at El Paso, a much-sought-after post traditionally held by a New Mexican, as the post of El Paso covered all of New Mexico but only the western portion of Texas. Garrett was one of several men who actively campaigned for the job by having friends and supporters lobby President Roosevelt through personal appeals, letters, and telegrams of recommendation. Among the most influential of those who supported Garrett were Fall; former governor Wallace, who personally visited the president on Garrett's behalf; and John Nance Garner, the rising politico who one day would be Franklin D. Roosevelt's vice-president. Garrett also was on good terms with New Mexico's delegate to Congress, Bernard S. Rodey, who forwarded a large number of telegrams favoring Garrett to the president's office.

It was clear that choosing Garrett would be unusual, for as the *El Paso Herald* noted on 13 December 1901, Garrett was a registered Democrat until he registered as a Republican following his 1898 election as sheriff. Even the Republicans who had supported him when he ran for sheriff said "he accepted the office as a Democrat . . . and was taken up by the Republicans solely to secure his aid in the Fountain case."[28] Roosevelt, however, had a soft spot for strong lawmen of the West, and he liked what he heard from Garrett's friends. On 16 December 1901 the president sent Garrett's name to the Senate for confirmation. Garrett was then in Washington and met the president for the first time.

He returned by train to El Paso in time for a jubilant Christmas celebration with his family. It was a high point in Garrett's life. He was confirmed in January and immediately took over the duties of his office, occupying customs quarters in a federal building in central El Paso. Garrett relished the high visibility of his new post, which suited his penchant for socializing and dressing well. But he took the job seriously, especially its large responsibility for assessing the value of cattle being brought across the border.

CHAPTER SEVEN

Almost immediately Garrett began to have strong disagreements with the Treasury Department over his interpretation of various regulations pertaining not only to customs assessments of cattle but the assessment of valuables brought across the U.S. border by tourists. The secretary of the Treasury received letters critical of Garrett, and he was also charged with lack of "politeness" and "tact," according to the *Houston Post* of 11 March 1903. During 1903 he further eroded his reputation with his superiors by getting into a highly publicized fistfight on a downtown street corner with a man named George Gaither, who had been discharged by Garrett after serving as special cattle assessor, a job Garrett preferred to do himself. Gaither thought Garrett could have and should have given him a permanent position. Garrett had accepted him for thirty days only because ordered to do so by the Treasury Department. Although it was Gaither who had confronted Garrett, both men were assessed fines for disturbing the peace, and Garrett was sharply rebuked by Washington.

Garrett further damaged himself in 1905, when he recklessly allowed a saloonkeeper friend named Tom Powers to be presented to President Roosevelt in the patently false role of big-time cattleman during a Rough Riders reunion in San Antonio, where Garrett was a special guest of the president. Several photographs appeared in newspapers showing Roosevelt seated across a table from both Garrett and Powers. Garrett's detractors lost no time informing the president that he had been duped by his New Mexico appointee.[29]

When rumors told him in December 1905 that Roosevelt was about to replace him with one A. L. Sharpe, recommended by the secretary of the Treasury, Garrett went to Washington "in a last ditch effort to save his job."[30] He saw the president on 11 December and was coldly received. On 13 December the *El Paso Herald* reported that Roosevelt had decided not to reappoint Garrett. In a mood of deep depression far different from his elation of four years earlier, Garrett again made the long train ride back to El Paso. His term expired on 2 January 1906.

Roosevelt denied in letters to such Garrett supporters as the author Emerson Hough that the Tom Powers incident was relevant, claiming that he chose not to reappoint Garrett because of reports that he was "inefficient."[31] Despite the negative impact of his man-about-town ways, however, and even granting that he ran the customs office with strong-minded adherence to his own interpretation of regulations, there is no evidence to suggest that Garrett did anything other than a credible and honest job as customs collector.

Out of office once again, Garrett returned to his Doña Ana County horse ranch, about twenty-five miles east of Las Cruces in the Organ Mountains. The restlessness, irritability, and increased drinking displayed by Garrett during the last years of his life may have been caused by his growing financial problems. On the other hand, it may be that his business affairs suffered because Garrett was feeling submerged yet very real frustrations at having in one way or another failed to succeed in each of the political positions he had held over the years since 1880. Now in his fifties, still lean and muscular though slightly bowed in posture and grey of hair, Garrett seemed in his occasional belligerence toward acquaintances and business associates to be a man still not sure of, or satisfied with, his place in the world. He always "believed that his fortune lay just around the next turn on the race track or in the mine shaft or in the next deck of cards."[32]

By early 1908 Garrett found himself in financial circumstances more precarious than ever. He wrote his friend George Curry, now serving as territorial governor, "I am in a hell of a fix. I have been trying to sell my ranch, but no luck. For God's sake, send me fifty dollars." Curry promptly sent the money.[33] Certainly Curry owed Garrett a favor, for back in 1890 Garrett had cosigned with Curry and another individual on a one-thousand-dollar loan to Curry. As the loan had not been repaid by Curry in 1896, when Garrett moved to Las Cruces, the Albuquerque bank that had made the loan took Garrett to court and attached his property, instigating legal and financial problems that lasted until Garrett's death.[34]

A few days after receiving Curry's check, Garrett left his ranch and set out for Las Cruces by horse and buggy, accompanied by business acquaintance and friend Carl Adamson. As Adamson later recounted it, Garrett stopped the buggy and got out at a point along the road, rifle in hand, to relieve himself. While Garrett stood in the brush along the side of the road, a man named Jesse Wayne Brazel, who had ridden up from behind the buggy, began haranguing Garrett. The two men knew one another well, and at that time Brazel was renting part of Garrett's land for grazing purposes. Garrett and Brazel argued heatedly at the back of the buggy. Adamson was not in a position to see exactly how it happened, but suddenly shots were fired. Garrett lay dead on the road and the only logical conclusion seemed to be that Brazel had shot and killed him.

The evidence showed clearly that Garrett had been shot in the back of the head with a .45 bullet and again in the back of his body. Garrett had not fired his rifle and was wearing a glove on his right hand. His gun was four feet from his body when found. Brazel turned himself in to the sheriff and confessed, saying the two had argued because Garrett was asking Brazel to remove his goats from the land Brazel leased from him in order that cattle could be brought in for another lessee named Jim Miller.

The murder of Pat Garrett was never satisfactorily resolved. Some believed that Brazel was hired by supporters of Oliver Lee to kill Garrett in retaliation for his actions as sheriff. The Texan named Jim Miller who supposedly caused the argument with Brazel by insisting that the goats be removed to make way for his cattle proved never to have had any cattle. And even if it were a simple argument over how fast to get a few hundred goats marketed in time to clear land for cattle, murdering Garrett would seem to have been a grossly disproportionate response, in view of the evidence that Garrett had not pulled a gun and had his back turned to Brazel when shot.

In 1909 Brazel was tried before a jury and acquitted on grounds of self-defense. The prosecution failed to adequately present the overwhelming evidence that self-defense was not involved in the crime.[35]

Pat Garrett was buried in a cemetery in Las Cruces. Fifty-eight years old at the time of his death, Garrett had lived into the first decade of the twentieth century and been a witness to the social and economic changes driving territorial New Mexico into a more ordered and settled existence.

Yet he himself remained, by virtue of his temperament and abilities, a nineteenth-century frontier lawman. It was during the last quarter of the nineteenth century that western lawmen and outlaws most closely matched one another in the quick-shooting, hard-riding, cool-witted methods that were the tools of both their trades. Garrett personified the singularly American archetype of frontier lawman precisely because he possessed in unsurpassed measure the skills needed on the open range. And it must be remembered that there were, over those decades of rampant lawlessness on untamed frontiers, more than a few instances where men were lawmen in one period of their lives and outlaws in another, and sometimes both simultaneously, blotting out the clear line that should have divided integrity from criminality.

Garrett, however, embodied in his very being an unspoken but thoroughly internalized commitment to the community standards of his time; he had none of the outlaw's alienation from society, indeed wanting nothing more all his life than approval from the established elements of society in every form, be it social or political. Whatever his human fallibilities, he had in fact chosen adherence to the law as his vehicle for achievement, and he remained squarely on the side of the law as his life passed through its several phases. For that he may well deserve the role of man in the white hat assigned him by at least some of the mythmakers of the West.

Mescalero Apache schoolchildren with their teacher in 1892. Located on 40 square miles of land in the Sacramento Mountains of southcentral New Mexico, the Mescalero Indian Reservation was established by the U.S. government in 1873. With only a small portion of the land suitable for farming and lacking the resources for timber or other large-scale ventures, the Mescaleros found themselves living in poverty and dependent upon the government for food subsidies as well as schooling. (Courtesy, Archives/Library, Chaves County Historical Museum, Olive Tracy Collection. #1886-B)

John and Sophie Poe on their wedding day, May 5, 1883. The couple was married in the Roswell home of Captain Joseph C. Lea. John Poe was sheriff of Lincoln County at the time of his marriage, responsible for keeping law and order in the largest county in the entire country. (Courtesy, the Rose Collection in the Western History Collections, University of Oklahoma Library. #469)

John W. Poe, lawman, rancher, banker. In this early 1900s photograph taken long after his buffalo-hunting days and service as the gun-toting sheriff of huge Lincoln County had ended, John Poe the banker shows the same air of calm strength and incorruptibility that had brought him the respect of Sheriff Pat Garrett when they first met at White Oaks in 1881. (Courtesy, Historical Center for Southeast New Mexico, Roswell, N.M.)

A roundup crew around the campfire on the Pecos range, 1892. With the vast darkness of the rugged range looming all around and the silence of the night broken only by the howling of coyotes, the sometimes boisterous, sometimes mournful, singing of cowboy songs around the campfire brought comfort, conviviality, and a sense of community to isolated, lonely cowboy camps. (Courtesy, Archives/Library, Chaves County Historical Museum, Olive Tracy Collection. #1890-C)

Cowboy chuckwagon and crew at roundup time in 1893 in Eddy County. The rough, tough outdoor life of the cowboy in the arid Southwest changed little over the years. Fast horses, lariats, broad-brimmed hats—and eating meals of beef, beans, and biscuits from a plate on the ground—were essential elements of an enduring lifestyle. (Courtesy, Archives/Library, Chaves County Historical Museum, Olive Tracy Collection. #1890-A)

Standing among the fine old trees that graced the South Spring Ranch where he resided from 1900 until his death in 1909, the great industrialist James J. Hagerman has the world-weary demeanor of a man who has been through the wars of a boom-and-crash economic cycle in this 1905 photograph. (Courtesy, Archives/Library, Chaves County Historical Museum, Roswell, New Mexico. #1204)

Ella Lea. The first Anglo child born in Roswell, Ella was the daughter of Captain Joseph C. Lea and his wife, Sally Wildy Lea, who died three years after Ella's birth in 1881. This photograph, signed and dated in her own hand by Ella, was taken in August of 1899 when she was eighteen-years-old. A much sought-after belle known for her love of dancing, Ella was married in 1901 to attorney Hiram Dow, who subsequently was elected to several political offices and became state lieutenant governor in 1923. (Courtesy, Archives/Library, Chaves County Historical Museum, Roswell, New Mexico. #1893)

The miracle of water. Captain Joseph C. Lea (on right) watches as a new artesian well sends a gusher of underground water to the surface on land near Roswell in 1893. The first artesian well had been drilled in Roswell in 1890, bringing a rush of homesteaders to a new agricultural mecca. (Courtesy, Archives/Library, Chaves County Historical Museum, Olive Tracy Collection. #1888)

Pecos Valley cattleman and landowner J. Phelps White in the years of his maturity, circa mid-1920s. Nephew and business partner of the legendary George Littlefield of Texas, the entrepeneurial White built a flourishing network of ranching and farming enterprises and played a key role in developing the valley's lucrative cotton industry. (Courtesy, Western Collection of J. Phelps White III, Roswell, N.M.)

The first train into Roswell moves north from Carlsbad in 1894. James J. Hagerman was hailed as a hero when his Pecos Valley Railroad linked the fertile Pecos Valley with the outside world. Begun in 1890 in Pecos, Texas, the rail line was completed in 1899 with a linkup with continental routes in Amarillo, Texas. (Courtesy, Archives/Library, Chaves County Historical Museum, Olive Tracy Collection. #1885)

Turn-of-the-century life in the typically Western frontier town of Artesia on the Pecos below Roswell featured a wide variety of modes of transportation, as this 1905 scene indicates with its Main Street mixture of horse and buggy, wagon and team of horses, and state-of-the-art new automobile. (Courtesy, Historical Center for Southeast New Mexico, Roswell, N.M.)

8

Joseph C. Lea, Martin Corn, and John Poe

As a man of prominence and wealth in his later years Joseph C. Lea may well have paused at times to remember earlier days, when upon hearing that a pioneer family was passing near the fledgling settlement of Roswell, he would drop his work and ride forth to courteously but persuasively convey to the travelers how good life could be in the middle Pecos Valley. It usually took but little to convince his listeners at least to partake of a home-cooked meal at the Lea home and boarding house, where young Sally waited with as welcoming a manner as that of her enterprising husband. More than one emigrant family over the years decided to homestead on the southeastern plains as a direct result of Lea's friendly advice, which was often followed by help and support for the newcomers.

Martin Corn was an altogether different kind of man than Lea; sunburnt, stocky, with piercing dark eyes, he was a man forever engaged in the earth-centered labors of a farmer born and bred. But he, too, saw his own fortunes as bound up inextricably with the development of communities on the southeastern New Mexico frontier. And he, too, had a host of memories to turn to in the culminating years of his long life. He might have remembered the time the cottonwood saplings arrived and he walked the dirt lane that bordered his irrigation ditch, placing the slender sticks one by one every few feet along each side. In the eye of memory he might well have seen them some years later, reaching high and leafy green, their branches touching like a roof across the country road in the fullness of summer foliage. To that gift of beauty for the

CHAPTER EIGHT

land he added the practical gift of ample harvests of corn, wheat, and alfalfa, melons, pumpkins, and squash, to say nothing of the beef cattle and milking cows he raised as well. To some, gruff and kindly Martin Corn seemed living proof that Lea had spoken nothing but the truth about the Pecos Valley.

And big John Poe, when he traveled the world or sat a respected figure among fellow bankers in his older years, must with some tenderness have looked back if but once or twice to the early days, when he met and courted Sophie Alberding at country dances held at Lea's adobe house. It was a rare thing in those days for a pretty girl, unattached and spunky, gentle and full of gaiety, to appear in the remote frontier world peopled largely by cattlemen and cowboys. The dignified elderly Poe would perhaps have smiled inwardly recalling how quickly he'd decided to ask Sophie to be his bride.

Contemporaries and friends, Lea, Corn, and Poe each arrived in Lincoln County in the late 1870s. Each made the Roswell area his home for the remainder of his life, and each survived until past the turn of the century, having participated in the transformation of the area from untamed wilderness to established agricultural and livestock center.

While each of these men was possessed of the same raw ambition that fueled those who had sought commercial dominance in the Lincoln township area to the west, and each was as determined to succeed as the cattle barons who ruled the ranges, ambition in each was tempered by belief that life on the frontier should be governed by the same legal, social, and moral conventions that prevailed in the rest of the country; they saw the frontier as a place in process of becoming like the rest of the country, rather than as a place exempt from normal traditions because of its territorial, frontier status. None viewed violence, abuse of whiskey, or gunfighting as inevitable byproducts of life on the frontier. Each exemplified in his own way the new type of setttler who gradually supplanted the bold frontier figures who had dominated the decade of the 1870s.

Yet the new-model citizen settlers, whether Lea and Poe or any of a number of others who played leading roles, were as driven by private motives as had been their colorful counterparts who lived by the law of the gun. In addition these new men were every bit as imbued with the nineteenth-century social prejudices that separated people into ethnic and economic groups, and they were equally imbued with the mystique of the American frontier as a place of unlimited possibilities.

The difference was that the new settlers saw a violently competitive free-for-all as inimical to their own prospects and, in contrast to some of their predecessors, saw safe and prosperous towns surrounded by small ranchers and farmers as the setting best suited to their own pursuit of success. Their attitude denoted the arrival on the southeastern New Mexico frontier of the age-old ethic whereby the private gain of the individual is made to seem synonymous with, or in fact actually becomes synonymous with, the good of the community as a whole.

Even as the turmoil of the Lincoln County War was proceeding and being resolved, from 1877 through 1881, pioneering by this somewhat different type of settler had been taking root in the middle Pecos Valley, leading to a development of economic strength that gradually enabled the eastern portion of Lincoln County to take precedence over the mountainous area to the west in terms of population numbers and commercial activity. This did not occur all at once, and indeed throughout the 1880s and into the early 1890s the gold mines of White Oaks and the large cattle companies of the upper Hondo Valley lent superior economic strength to the western portion of southeastern New Mexico. Nevertheless the foundations for permanence and economic viability were being laid on the range-and-valley portion of the Pecos Basin during these same two decades, and the creation of Chaves and Eddy counties as separate entities in 1889 may be seen as tacit recognition of that fact by the territorial legislature.

By 1890 a clear pattern of economic activity was visible as the basis for both town and rural population growth. The cattle and sheep industries were primary revenue earners, followed by fruit, alfalfa, and grain crops in irrigated portions of the valley. The emergence of Roswell and the surrounding area as a center for settlers was not inevitable. It occurred for a number of reasons, some related to the natural environment, others having to do with the leadership provided by some of the area's earliest settlers. But a case can be made that without the promotional efforts, civic leadership, political involvement, and private economic initiatives of a number of the new settlers, the fate of the Pecos Valley might have been significantly different.

Joseph C. Lea

Joseph Callaway Lea was born on 8 November 1841 in Cleveland, Tennessee, the son of Dr. Pleasant J. G. Lea and his wife, Lucinda Callaway Lea. In 1849 the Lea family, now including several children, moved to a small new community in Missouri, which soon became

CHAPTER EIGHT

known as Lea's Summit. Although young Joseph worked on farms, he essentially was raised in comfortable circumstances, as the son of a physician who intended to see to it that each of his sons got as good a start in life as possible. But the Lea family was destined to become one of the many whose fortunes were altered by the cataclysm of the Civil War. Joseph Lea, twenty years old when war broke out in 1861, was among the thousands of young men who survived the war but found their lives moving in directions they might not have taken had the war not intervened.

Lea's mother was a northerner; with political passions at fever pitch in the border state of Missouri, the Leas decided at the outbreak of hostilities that it would be best if she returned to the north until peace was restored. Soon after her departure, Dr. Lea was forced to confront an angry crowd that had gathered in front of his house. The doctor was taunted for his seeming neutrality. He was accused of lacking commitment to the southern cause. The crowd became a mob, irrational and violent. Dr. Lea was shot dead as he attempted to speak from the front porch of his house. With the war and the death of his father aborting all thought of further education for the moment, Joseph Lea joined the Confederate Army and served until 1865 with the Sixth Missouri Regiment, Shelby's Brigade. He attained the rank of captain, then colonel in 1864, but for the rest of his life was known as "Captain Lea."

When the war ended, Lea went to Georgia, where he found employment on farms and railroads. In 1867 he married the widow of a man named Douglas Burbridge. This first of Lea's three marriages ended with the death of his wife in 1871. Once again Lea was a young man in search of place and social position. Photographs of Lea from this period show a handsome youth with thick hair, brooding eyes, and even features. Leaving Georgia in 1871, Lea went to Louisiana and started a farm. After two years he moved on, this time to Yazoo County in Mississippi, where shortly after his arrival in 1873 he became acquainted with Major William W. Wildy of Satartia and was accepted as a family friend. On 3 February 1875 Lea married Wildy's twenty-six-year-old daughter Sally.

With the backing of his new and supportive family, Lea decided to take the risk of seeking a better opportunity than farming by trying ranching in the West. Not long after the marriage, he traveled to New Mexico, leaving Sally in the care of her father, and started a ranch in the gold-mining area in Colfax County. Despite the known rigors of life on the rugged ranges of northeastern New Mexico, Sally wrote to her husband that she preferred to face the hardships of the prairie than be without him.¹ Early in 1876 Sally joined Lea in New Mexico. Their first child, Harry Wildy Lea, was born in Colfax County on 3 April 1877.

The year 1877 also brought Major Wildy to New Mexico. Looking for investment opportunities, the Mississippi cotton planter traveled through the Pecos Valley and immediately responded to its potential for cattle raising, crop production, and town building. From Roswell resident Marion Turner he purchased some 480 acres of land, including a house and several smaller buildings. Part of this land, located in what is now central Roswell, had first been claimed by Van C. Smith in 1871, when the settlement near the juncture of the Hondo and Pecos rivers was called Rio Hondo. When he started a post office in 1873, Smith officially renamed the place Roswell, his father's first name. A notice in the *Daily New Mexican* of Santa Fe on 25 May 1872, however, shows that Smith already was referring to the settlement as Roswell at an earlier date.²

Although Smith went into partnership with Aaron Wilburn, opened a merchandise store, and undertook several improvement projects, he neglected to travel to Mesilla and pay the filing fee that would have made the land legally his. Thus the quit-claim deed he gave to Tom Catron in 1874 in exchange for a thousand dollars was in effect only for the buildings and improvements. Having spent much of his time at the racetrack he built from his store to the Hondo River, Smith was losing money. He had no choice but to mortgage the property to Catron. In 1874 Turner paid Catron eight hundred dollars for the buildings, and he later correctly paid the two-hundred-dollar filing fee and acquired title to the land, enabling him to sell the land to Wildy in a legal manner.

Encouraged by glowing reports of the area's attractiveness from Wildy, Joseph and Sally Lea sold their holdings in Colfax County and traveled by wagon south to Roswell in the late autumn of 1877. With them came several employees and their families, as well as sheep and a small number of cattle. Lea immediately filed on a 160-acre tract just west of his father-in-law's holdings. He moved his family into the two-story, pitch-roofed adobe house located on the property owned by Wildy. Called the Old Adobe Home, the structure was the first permanent building in Roswell and had been built by G. W. Hartman in 1867, with glass for its windows transported by wagon from Fort Sumner. Hartman had sold the house and a small parcel of land to Smith in 1869, when Smith was preparing to file claims on additional land. When the Leas moved into the house, probably in the winter of 1877, it was still the only house

CHAPTER EIGHT

in the settlement of Roswell. And during the first cold months of 1878, even on into the spring and summer, it looked as if it might remain the sole imposing building of Roswell. Settlers were in fact fleeing from the area, as the Lincoln County War violence escalated, the killings mounted in number, and word of the area's instability spread by word of mouth and territorial newspapers.

As tensions rose and men began choosing sides in the Dolan-McSween conflict, following Tunstall's murder in February 1878, Lea faced what might for many men have been a dilemma without a satisfactory solution. He had established friendly relations with John Chisum and might plausibly have sided with Chisum and his allies as they opposed the Dolan forces. On the other hand, he and his family had invested heavily in their new location; to see it torn by dissension, as the Lincoln area was, clearly would hinder settlement and prospects for prosperity. Yet Lea was a newcomer who had no way of being sure any effort he made to avoid being drawn into the conflict would not result in direct attacks on him by some of the partisans who were active in the Pecos Valley, among them the very Marion Turner who had sold Wildy his property.

Lea's response as he contemplated the worsening situation provides insight into the basic traits that characterized him throughout his life. His friendship with Chisum notwithstanding, he promptly took a firm stand that the settlement of Roswell was and would remain neutral territory; fighting there between partisans of Dolan and McSween would not be tolerated. As 1878 wore on, Lea had even more reason to protect his interests, for on August 1 of that year Wildy deeded over his 480-acre tract to Sally Lea, making the Leas owners of the entire village of Roswell. Throughout this period Lea displayed a calm determination that had its intended effect in restraining for the most part any overt attempts to conduct sieges or shootouts in the immediate vicinity of Roswell.

By 1880, as settlers once again began to trickle into the area due to Governor Wallace's use of force to pacify cattle rustlers and other outlaws, Lea had attained the status of a local leader, his influence surpassing even that of longtime local power John Chisum. Lea's leadership was based on on his economic position and also on his personality traits, among them his steady, low-key manner and his diplomatic tact. All of his actions, in fact, from his choices in marriages to his business activities to his political role, indicate a man of restraint and reserve who kept his emotions well under control. As he matured these traits led to his emer-

· 200 ·

gence as a solidly dependable, if not charismatic or colorful, establishment figure, respected by his immediate neighbors as well as by officeholders and wielders of economic influence at the territorial level.

Lea's business activities extended in several directions almost from the start of his residence in Lincoln County. In addition to running a boardinghouse and store, he grazed sheep, improved existing adobe corrals, and gradually acquired more cattle, which were grazed west of the village proper. He improved the building where the store and post office were located, starting this expansion of merchandising capacity shortly after he and Sally came into possession of the property in 1878. Although several members of the Wildy family came to Roswell during these early years, they retained their holdings in Mississippi and periodically returned to work there. In 1879 Lea became postmaster of Roswell, taking over from Ash Upson, who had held the post since 1877. Lea was postmaster until 1884. In 1880 Lea's personal support for Pat Garrett helped ensure Garrett's nomination for sheriff by the Democratic party and confirmed Lea's political role as a local power broker.[3] In 1881 C. D. Bonney bought an interest in the Lea store, and the name was changed to Lea and Bonney.

The early 1880s were happy but hard times at the Lea home and boardinghouse. Despite Lea's landownership and mercantile interests, frontier conditions prevailed. Isolation necessitated cooperation among the few hundred residents in the area. The care of cattle, sheep, and horses, precious commodities all, as they provided income, food, and transportation, took top priority. Activity was ceaseless at the Lea establishment. Long wooden tables and benches occupied one portion of the first floor. Anyone traveling along the Pecos route could expect meals and lodging at minimal cost. More than twenty cowboys who worked for Lea also took most of their meals with the family. There was no doctor available. Weather conditions had unavoidable impact, sending men into the fields or onto the range whatever the time of day or night, as they sought to protect their livelihood from the severe snowstorms that could sweep in from the mountains to the west, or the flooding of the Hondo, or the day-long dust storms that drove dirt in menacing swirls at stinging speed.

For Sally Lea it was a life of almost constant work. Even with the aid of a hired cook, much of her life was taken up with pots of stew and pans of cornbread, the sweeping of dirt-floored rooms, the airing of bed linens, the patching of endless numbers of torn shirts. In 1881, when she was thirty-two years old, Sally Lea had her second child, a baby

CHAPTER EIGHT

girl whom the Leas named Ella. Ella Lea was the first Anglo child born in Roswell. A few months after the baby's birth, Sophie Alberding arrived at the Lea home. She was the nineteen-year-old sister of Lea ranchhand Fred Alberding, and she recalled in later years how glad Sally Lea was to have her join the household.[4]

Sophie was a keen observer of the social scene she encountered in the frontier outpost. Privacy was scarce, luxuries nonexistent. But there was a spirit of family, and the Lea house was the site of numerous community social events. Country fiddle dances were regular affairs. The parlor room on the ground floor was lit by coal-oil lamps. Two or three fiddlers stood in one corner, tapping their feet and nodding their heads, as they gave forth with one after another of well-known cowboy tunes, Irish jigs, Spanish fandangos, and polkas and walzes. Everybody two-stepped, walzed, twirled, stomped, and sweated. There were never enough women to go around, so cowboys danced with fellow cowboys, unable to resist the sawing rhythms. Best finery appeared on everyone; women in fullest crinolines and newest lace collars, men in polished boots, vests, and bold-colored neckerchiefs. The dancing went on most of the night. Toward morning a full-course meal of eggs, fried chicken, biscuits, vegetables, coffee, and a variety of fresh-baked pies was served to everyone.

On 20 February 1884 Sally Lea died. Although her health had been failing for a number of months, her death was a deep shock for Lea. Yet another phase of his life began. He kept his seven-year-old son Wildy in Roswell until he was nine, then sent him each school term to military school in Fort Worth, Texas. Three-year-old Ella was sent to California, where she lived until 1889 with Lea's friend Horace Thurber and his family. Lea, now in his early forties, began to take on the physical attributes that distinguished him as he grew older. His forehead was high and domed, his eyes dark hazel and intense, and he wore a goatee and mustache. A slender man, he stood well over six feet in height. As he continued to acquire land in and around Roswell, he was ever the conservative, diplomatic, astute but ambitious businessman.

Several of Lea's brothers came to the Pecos Valley, among them Alfred E. Lea, who came from Denver in 1885 at the request of Lea to survey and plat Roswell into streets and blocks. Lea filed his plat with the county on 1 November 1885. Frank H. Lea, another brother, moved permanently to Roswell. Among other posts he held, he was probate clerk after Chaves County was organized. His son, Joseph D. Lea, started the *Roswell Record* in 1891, in partnership with Lucius Dills. In 1892,

Dills married Gertrude Lea, daughter of Frank Lea.[5] In 1891 yet another brother, J. Smith Lea, was elected to the new Roswell board of trustees and named treasurer.

The year 1885 brought not only the platting of Roswell but also the prominence of Lea as a cattleman, backed for the first time by corporate power. On 20 April 1885 the Lea Cattle Company was incorporated in the Territory of New Mexico. The corporation investors were Horace K. Thurber, John C. Delany, Joseph C. Lea, and Charles S. Thurber. Horace Thurber was a powerful tycoon who had made a fortune in the wholesale grocery business, getting his start in New York City. Lea Cattle Company was incorporated at $1 million, with ten thousand shares at $100 each. For Joseph Lea, who had built his own cattle herd to nine thousand but needed big capital to make the breakthrough to bigtime cattleman, the incorporation was a benchmark measuring not only how far he had come in the ten years since marrying Wildy's daughter in 1875, but also how much farther he planned to go.

Lea Cattle had its main office in Roswell. It eventually grazed upwards of forty thousand head of cattle on rangeland stretching west and northwest from Roswell for a distance of some fifty miles, to the eastern slope of Mount Capitan, where the ranch headquarters was located. When George Curry, as Lincoln County assessor in the late 1880s, conducted a survey, he found that "the largest ranch in Lincoln County was what was known as the Lea Cattle Company, of which Captain J. C. Lea of Roswell was general manager." With forty thousand head of cattle, Lea had more livestock than any other ranch in New Mexico at that time.[6] The company also owned an impressive amount of waterfrontage land. Lincoln County assessment rolls for 1888 show Lea Cattle Company as the owner of 16,500 acres. "Most of this land, which extended along the entire Rio Hondo to its juncture with the Pecos, was purchased by the enterprising Lea during the period from 1879 to 1885."[7]

Having achieved the financial security and social position he had aimed for since his days as a penniless youth at the end of the Civil War, Lea turned part of his attentions in the years between 1888 and 1893 to two issues in the public arena. While Lea's efforts in both cases were intended in part to further his own interests, the fact remains that his actions on these issues were to prove his most important and lasting contributions to the development of southeastern New Mexico. His leadership had direct bearing on the region's county-government boundaries and on its higher-education resources.

CHAPTER EIGHT

Lea well understood the linkage between economic and political power in territorial New Mexico. In an economy based on the primary production of commodities, economic advantage accrued in direct relation to favorable action by the territorial legislature in such areas as taxes, land law, and water policy. And as new mines opened, new agricultural land came under the plow, and new towns sprang into existence during the quarter-century of intensive pioneering from 1875 to 1900, there also was constant pressure on territorial lawmakers to bestow the benefits of county government upon communities that hoped, though sometimes in vain, to become thriving centers of growth. County-seat status was seen both as a confirmation of existing strength and a catalyst for further development. In 1880 territorial New Mexico had twelve counties; in 1890 it had sixteen; by 1910, on the eve of statehood, it had a total of twenty-six, with five counties carved in whole out of the former Lincoln County. The once-vast county also contributed parts of its land to the making of three other counties on its western and northeastern borders.

It was Lea who initiated the process of carving up Lincoln County. When he got himself elected to the territorial House of Representatives in 1888, he did so with the firm intention of introducing a bill creating one or more new counties in eastern Lincoln County. He had support from many of his constituents, among them such notables as former sheriff Pat Garrett. Also favoring the new county notion was Charles B. Eddy, irrigation-project partner of Garrett and energetic promoter of emigration to the lower Pecos Valley. Together Garrett and Eddy gathered signatures for a petition asking for new counties and then accompanied Lea to Santa Fe in January of 1889.

In addition to presenting the petitions, the two lobbyists joined Lea in making the case to legislators that new counties were justified. Aware that the sparse population of the Pecos Valley in and of itself hardly justified the expense of new government, they chose to emphasize the inconvenience caused plains-and-valley residents by being forced to travel two days over rough roads to reach the county seat at Lincoln in order to conduct business pertaining to property or court matters.

Of equal if not more importance than these lobbying efforts was the personal impression made by Lea on his fellow legislators. He was liked and respected by many, including such influential figures as Speaker of the House José Francisco Chaves and Major William H. H. Llewelyn, a Republican from Doña Ana County. Llewelyn was familiar with Lincoln County, having served in the early 1880s as Indian Agent for the Mescaleros.

On 25 February a bill creating Chaves and Eddy counties was passed by the legislature. Together the two new counties took away from Lincoln County all of the rangeland and valley land extending from east of the mountains to the Texas border. The bill was signed into law by Governor Edmund G. Ross, a reform-minded Democrat who on other occasions had found himself in sharp opposition to bills presented for his signature. During discussion of the bill in the House, suggestions were made that the new county whose seat was to be Roswell should be named for Lea.

But Lea modestly declined and proposed instead that the new county be named for Chaves, without whose firm support the bill would have had slim chance of passage. George Curry, a resident of Lincoln County when the bill was passed, was among those who were unaware that 'Chaves' was the correct spelling of the Speaker's name. In later years Curry wrote that "advocates of Chaves County, most of whom had come from Texas, insisted that the name [of the county] be spelled with an 's' instead of the final letter 'z' " that occurs in the name of the man; Curry thus lent credence to a rumor that had no basis in fact.[8]

Soon after the creation of Chaves County, Lea donated land for the county's first courthouse, a wooden structure located across the street from the Lea home. In 1917 Llewelyn, speaker of the House, named a newly created county in the extreme southeast corner of the state for Lea, honoring posthumously the man he remembered as an effective and self-effacing leader.

The man for whom Chaves County was named is one of the most illustrious historical figures of the territorial period. The friendship and alliance formed between Lea and Chaves is noteworthy, for even granting their commonality of interests as large landowners, the backgrounds of the two men could not have been more different, and their opposing political affiliations might as easily have resulted in a lack of personal affinity as in friendly relations. What they had in common would appear to have been no more than the fact that just as Lea typified an elite minority of Anglos who became wealthy after moving westward, Chaves typified an elite minority of Hispanos who dominated their ethnic group's poorer members by controlling access to land and livestock.

In all other respects Lea and Chaves were different: Lea a Protestant and a southerner who had fought for the Confederacy, Chaves a Catholic who had been intensely pro-Union, anti-slavery, and fought in the Union Army; Lea a Democratic Party stalwart of the old southern school, Chaves a highly partisan Republican activist who held virtually every post his party had to offer over the years; Lea a resident of the territorial region with the least direct knowledge of the three-hundred-year-old Hispanic tradition of New Mexico, Chaves born and bred of that tradition. Despite these differences, however, the friendship between the two men was a genuine and lasting one, based on a mutual respect that went beyond mere recognition of one another as fellow members of an elite propertied class.

Chaves's career epitomized the symbiotic relationship between Anglos and Hispanos that distinguished New Mexico from other western territories. Chaves represented the educated and office-holding Hispanic settlers with whom the conquering Americans formed a working alliance after the invasion of 1846. He was born in 1833 on a hacienda south of Albuquerque. His father was Mariano Chaves, a wealthy man who had served as governor under Mexican rule. Chaves's grandfather, Francis Xavier Chaves, also had been governor.

When barely into his teens, the bilingual Chaves was pressed into service as an able translator for General Stephen Watts Kearny during the entry of American troops into Santa Fe. In 1853 the young Chaves took twenty-five thousand sheep to California, where they were sold in the booming gold-mining camps and towns. Chaves was educated in St. Louis, Missouri, where he attended St. Louis University. From there he went on to New York, where he studied medicine.

At the start of the Civil War, he returned to New Mexico and joined the Union Army. Serving under Kit Carson in the New Mexico Volunteers, he fought at the Battle of Valverde in February 1862 and later followed Carson on the Navajo campaign. Starting in 1865 he won three consecutive elections for territorial delegate to Congress. After returning to New Mexico from Washington, he studied law and was admitted to the bar. He was a tough and capable district attorney in the early 1870s. In 1875 he was elected to the territorial House of Representatives, beginning the first of eight terms served in either the House or the Council, which was the territorial equivalent of a senate.[9]

Chaves played a strong role in territorial Republican politics and was generally viewed as a full-fledged member of the group of power manipulators known as the Santa Fe Ring. In 1896 he backed Catron for delegate to Congress at the party convention and was made convention chairman. His adroit management enabled Catron to win the party's nomination despite strong support from many Republicans for free-silver Republican L. Bradford Prince, a former territorial governor who also was seeking the nomination as delegate. Named superintendent of public instruction in 1901, Chaves vigorously implemented the 1898 Fergusson Act establishing a public-school system, traveling ceaselessly into the most remote, rural areas of the territory to start schools where none had previously existed. In 1903 the legislature appointed him to an additional post as territorial historian.

His death came under tragic, still unexplained, circumstances in November of 1904. Dining with friends at his hacienda ranch home at Pinos Wells in Torrance County, he was shot and killed by an unknown assailant, who fired through an open window. Although the murder was never solved, speculation centered around Chaves's fearless opposition over the years to the unscrupulous tactics of various politicians and his ruthless pursuit and prosecution of cattle rustlers during his years as a district attorney. By odd coincidence the life of Lea ended in the same year as did that of the staunch friend for whom he had named Chaves County.

Returning to Roswell from Santa Fe at the end of the 1889 legislative session, Lea must have felt a quiet satisfaction at having accomplished his self-imposed mission of county creating. He had little time to savor his triumph, however, as an important change was about to take place in his personal life. For some time he had been discreetly courting a Texas widow named Mabel Doss Day. On 28 April 1889 the two were united in marriage at the ranch home of Mrs. Day, with her young daughter, known as Willie, present at the ceremony.

The new Mrs. Lea was the owner of a 77,500-acre, fenced ranch. But as her first husband had died without leaving a will, his relatives contested the right of his widow to take control of the property. After lengthy legal proceedings, which continued for some time after the marriage of Lea and Mabel Day, a major part of the Texas ranch was lost to other heirs. In the end Kentucky investors ended up as owners of much of the holdings.[10] Lea's wife, however, not only retained a substantial sum of money even after her large losses, she also brought with her to her new home in the Pecos Valley her considerable expertise in the business of cattle ranching.

Mabel Day Lea was a short, somewhat round-faced woman of calm capability. She became mother to Lea's children, twelve-year-old Wildy and eight-year-old Ella, who was brought back from California after her father's marriage. Mabel Lea's mother moved to Roswell and became owner of local land in her own right. The Leas were involved in virtually every land transaction that took place in Roswell throughout the 1890s. Lea had owned all of the original town and had continuously expanded his holdings since his first land claim in late 1877. Therefore when blocks were divided into lots and new residents wished to build houses, it was to Joseph Lea they most often went to purchase a lot.[11]

As a landowner Lea was aware of the assumption made by such fellow landowners as Catron and Chaves that statehood would have the immediate effect of increasing land values by a substantial percentage, in some cases making land worth three dollars per acre rise to a market value of five dollars per acre.[12] When the Springer Omnibus Bill was passed, New Mexicans supporting statehood were disappointed by the last-minute exclusion of New Mexico from the legislation, which granted statehood to the Dakotas, Montana, and Washington in February of 1889.

Hoping to demonstrate New Mexico's desire for statehood in a way that would renew congressional action on the territory's behalf, statehood supporters elected delegates to a constitutional convention held in the summer of 1889. The constitution of 1889 produced by this body included numerous provisions that were highly favorable to large landholders and railroad companies. The constitution was submitted to territorial voters for approval or rejection in a special election held on 7 October 1889. Although it was rejected by a vote of 16,180 against to 7,493 approving, with opposition to its big-business slant strong in southeastern New Mexico, Lea probably favored the constitution both for its concessions to landowners and because it enhanced the chances for statehood; there is no evidence to indicate that he joined other local Democrats in opposing it.[13]

Setbacks for statehood notwithstanding, Lea continued to play a forceful role in the development of southeastern New Mexico. He was among the original purchasers of stock when E. A. Cahoon organized the Bank of Roswell as the area's first financial institution in 1890. And in the same year he took steps that led to an advance in the cause of education for the region. Lea's establishment of a military school in Roswell ranks second only to his leadership in creating new counties in his legacy of accomplishments in the public realm.

Only 343 people resided within the boundaries of Roswell in 1890. Many more people lived on outlying farms and ranches, and a one-room public school had been started in the farming area southeast of Roswell. A public school did not open in Roswell until the fall of 1891. Since 1886 Lea's son and several other Roswell boys had been enrolled in Fort Worth's military school. Travel to and from the private academy was costly and difficult. The Roswell students traveled by buckboard

160 miles to the nearest rail point, at Pecos City, Texas, and from there by train to Fort Worth.

After visiting the school, Lea was sufficiently impressed by its commandant, Colonel Robert H. Goss, to extend an invitation to him to spend the 1890 Christmas holiday in Roswell. During the visit, Lea proposed to Goss that he move to Roswell and establish a military school similar to the Fort Worth institution. Goss agreed to the proposal, and Lea promptly donated five acres of land in Roswell for a school building.

The Goss Military Academy opened on 3 September 1891 with thirty-eight students, including several girls, Lea's own daughters among them. The cost was three hundred dollars per year for tuition, board, light and fuel, books, a uniform, and one bath suit. By 1892 there were sixty students.

But it soon became clear that the school would need territorial financial aid to remain viable, and its supporters sought help from the legislature, which passed a bill signed into law by Governor L. Bradford Prince on 23 February 1893, making the institution a territorial military school. The bill was written by Roswell residents Lucius Dills and E. A. Cahoon and introduced in the territorial House of Representatives by Chaves County representative James F. Hinkle. Although Lea and Goss both were named to the first board of regents of the school, renamed the New Mexico Military Institute, Goss soon after left Roswell, in apparent disagreement over the goals and methods being adopted.

Between 1895 and 1898 the school was inoperative, while government funds were being channeled and a new campus was being constructed on a forty-acre site on a hill in north Roswell, contributed by J. J. Hagerman. The new campus opened in 1898, its building designed by I. H. and William Rapp, the noted architects who also designed the 1900 Territorial Capitol Building and La Fonda in Santa Fe. The Institute, with its yellow-brick, military-gothic-style buildings set on low green hills became a prominent regional landmark, a fully accredited military junior college attracting students from a wide area.

In the troubled economic climate of the 1890s, it may have been easier to establish a college than to sustain the profitability of a large cattle company. Not even Lea with his unflappable equanimity and persistent air of optimism could escape the impact of the overriding circumstances affecting the fate of the West, and of farmers, ranchers, miners, and railroad men in particular. The American frontier was closing; after the census of 1890 was completed, it was announced that a frontier line no longer could be identified. The vast prairies and semiarid lands lying to the east and west of the Rocky Mountains had become overstocked and overgrazed by cattle and sheep. The Panic of 1893 dried up sources of business capital, placing further stress on the livestock industry.

Lea's official position with Lea Cattle Company was western manager. From that perspective he saw prospects for growth in a rapidly developing frontier area, and renewed possibilities for monopolizing land and cattle range even as neighboring small operations struggled or went broke. Horace Thurber, on the other hand, was financial manager and banker for the company. He operated out of eastern cities, where the nation's money centers were located. Thurber's stance was that of a cautious investor responsible for large sums of money. The differing perspectives of the two men are reflected in their voluminous correspondence. Conducting most of his business with Lea over the years by mail, Thurber wrote letters that increasingly showed outright exasperation with Lea's endless stream of proposals for expensive ranch improvements.[14] He turned down many of Lea's requests for additional capital, hoping to keep the company afloat with prudent management.

Nevertheless, burdened by its size and overhead, Lea Cattle Company slowly became a losing proposition; perhaps the time for such large operations had passed. Despite a general recovery in the fortunes of cattlemen, farmers, and mine owners in New Mexico by the year 1900, it was too late for Lea Cattle. The well-known firm was liquidated in 1898, leaving Lea financially sound but shorn of the enterprise that had once symbolized his climb to prosperity on the southeastern New Mexico frontier.

The demise of Lea Cattle Company scarcely diminished Lea's influence. He maintained close contacts with powerful figures in the territorial capital. He closely followed every matter affecting Chaves County, writing, for example, to Governor William T. Thornton that he had been concerned about Sheriff Charles C. Perry even before the lawman absconded with county funds in June of 1896. Along with other citizens, he told the governor, he had "anticipated the sheriff's misconduct" in view of his recklessness, heavy drinking, and association with unsavory characters.[15]

When Roswell's population reached forty-five hundred, in 1903, Governor Miguel Otero issued a proclamation authorizing Roswell to incorporate as a city. Lea seemed ready to take on new public duties; he was elected Roswell's first mayor at a special election held in December 1903. But early in 1904, shortly after being sworn into office, he was stricken with a severe case of pneumonia. His illness was sudden and brief. On 4 February, at the age of sixty-three, the man known to all as Captain Lea died.

Chaves County was still part of a sparsely settled frontier. Roswell was still a cow town on the Pecos where gamblers seemed to outnumber churchgoers and dirt streets lined with hitching posts became muddy impasses when the Rio Hondo overflowed its banks. Even so, both county and city were fixed features on the map of southeastern New Mexico, due in no small part to the actions of Lea, a man who had combined amiability with ambition, the pursuit of private gain with a sense of public duty, and who just happened to have heeded his father-in-law's advice about where to settle back in 1877.

Martin Corn

A wholeness and symmetry can be seen in the life of Martin Van Buren Corn, bound together as it was by themes of family, land, work, and integrity that represented some of the young American republic's most cherished notions about itself. As a pioneering farmer, Corn embodied an aspect of the American experience that remained central to the national self-image long after it was no longer the predominant reality.

The opening of the West after the Civil War was viewed as a means of realizing the Jeffersonian ideal of independent, land-owning agriculturists whose productivity would feed and clothe the nation as well as their own families. Both farmers and nation would prosper as the Homestead Act and the Timber Culture Act enabled enterprising Americans to acquire land and tame the nation's frontiers.

But as the nineteenth century wore on, farmers found their position undermined by setbacks in this idealized plan. The very success of a Martin Corn, achieved only at the cost of ceaseless work, constant innovation, and willingness to forgo the easy profits that tempted others of his generation, attests to the precarious position of late-nineteenth-century farmers even when they demonstrated flexibility and tenacity, and even when they met with a certain amount of good luck in their choice of location.

For even as a successful crop and livestock producer never broken by debt or driven into tenancy, Corn lived a life that was never free of struggle. Attending to his daily chores in a remote corner of a vast nation, certainly far in distance from the world capitals where major events were set in motion, Corn nevertheless was affected by sweeping economic and political changes that accelerated as the twentieth century approached.

CHAPTER EIGHT

Between 1870 and 1900, the number of acres under cultivation in the United States expanded from about 500 million to almost 850 million. The number of farm families grew from 1.5 million in 1860 to over 6 million in 1910. With steady growth in commercial farming and tripled investment in farm machinery, the production of farm goods increased far faster than demand. The index of wholesale farm prices dropped from a high of 140 at the end of the Civil War to 89 in 1876, 71 in 1890, and 52 in 1896. Farm debt grew rapidly, and farm tenancy increased everywhere, but particularly in the South, Texas, and the plains states. It is against this background that the accomplishments of Corn must be seen.

Martin Corn was born on 16 October 1841, in the state of North Carolina. He was the oldest of ten children born to John R. and Mary Elizabeth McMinn Corn. As small farmers the Corns belonged to that large group of southern whites who sometimes owned one or more slaves but who in general benefited little from the slave-based plantation economy that dominated the South. Seeking a fresh start, John and Mary Elizabeth Corn moved to Georgia after the birth of their first two children. In 1860 the growing family pulled up stakes again and trekked west to Texas, where John Corn and his sons began farming near Kerrville, in the south-central part of the state.

Several times Indians raided Corn livestock being grazed on the open range. And the advent of the Civil War disrupted operation of the fledgling farm with even more serious consequences. Young Martin Corn was one of several family members who fought for the South. He enlisted as a private soldier in Wood's regiment of the Texas Cavalry on 29 March 1862, furnishing a horse and equipment valued at $145. John R. Corn and one of his sons died while serving in the Confederate Army. Martin Corn was discharged in August 1865 and returned to Kerrville to help his mother, now a widow with nine children from eight months old to twenty-four years old. In addition to farming, Corn served in 1867 on the Kerr County Commissioners Court.[16]

Corn was twenty-six years old when on 13 April 1867 he married Mary Jane Nichols Hampton, a young widow whose son James he adopted and raised. Martin and Mary Jane Corn had ten children, the first born in Texas in 1868 and the last in New Mexico in 1882. All of the children survived to adulthood except for the third child, a daughter who died at two months and was buried in Kerrville.

Farming in the arid conditions of Kerr County became increasingly difficult as competition for land and water intensified in the 1870s.

Encouraged by favorable reports about New Mexico and Arizona after the opening of the Goodnight-Loving Trail in 1866, some of Corn's neighbors began to look west for cattle-marketing and settlement opportunities.

In 1878 Corn decided to go west himself. He joined a caravan of six wagons and several families who intended to settle in either Arizona or New Mexico, depending on which site looked most promising. Corn owned two of the heavy-wheeled wagons. Mary Jane Corn's brother, J. L. Nichols, owned another, and Martin Corn's sister Zilpha and her husband William Holliman also joined the group. A number of cowboy bachelors signed on with the caravan and were assigned the job of looking after some five hundred head of cattle and one hundred horses that were moved along with the families and their possessions.

After departing from Kerrville in the fall of 1878, it took the caravan three weeks to travel from Kerrville to Horsehead Crossing on the Pecos River. Several more weeks were spent moving up the west bank of the river to Seven Rivers, the outpost on the Pecos and a place that only months earlier had been the scene of bloody shoot-outs between Dolan and McSween partisans. Probably knowing little of the particulars of the Lincoln County War, the caravan leaders felt relief at reaching a known resting place on the long trail and decided to leave the women, children, and younger men at Seven Rivers while they went on to explore sites north and west.

Although Corn traveled with the other men into Arizona, a visit to Chisum's South Spring ranch convinced him to settle in the Pecos Valley. Settlers already were moving into the fertile area southeast of Roswell, and the Chisum operation was easing their farming endeavors by granting credit at the ranch commissaries and buying their corn crops at good prices.

The Chisum brothers made an offer to assist the Corn group as well, stipulating only that the new settlers should not file homestead claims on land south of South Spring River, where they were developing crop acreage. In return the Chisums agreed not to file on land north of South Spring River.[17] After making this oral agreement, Corn and the others went back to Seven Rivers to bring the families north to their new homesite. During their absence, a killing had taken place; ironically enough it was caused by a dispute between two of the young men tending the caravan's cattle, rather than by partisans in the Lincoln County range wars.

In a 1927 letter Corn's daughter Mary Elizabeth vividly recalled the

CHAPTER EIGHT

hardships of the long cold winter of 1878–79 spent camping on the new family land southeast of Roswell. The 160-acre homestead site filed on by Corn was located a mile and a half southwest of the ranch home of Pat Garrett. Determined to be prepared for their first spring planting season, the men spent most of their time building a dam and irrigation ditch north from South Spring River. The dugout used in the first months for shelter was replaced by a sod house. No timber was available for a frame house.

When Chisum returned from the Texas panhandle to remain permanently at South Spring, he and Corn became firm friends, and Chisum granted Corn the right to run his cattle freely on the range with Chisum stock and have them looked after by Chisum cowboys at no cost. This is the only known instance in which Chisum made such an arrangement.[18] After getting his seed planted in the spring, Corn purchased a small gristmill and installed it at the mouth of Spring River, where it served to grind corn and wheat for his own family and for neighbors. A few years later, G. F. Blashek built a larger mill on the North Spring River near Roswell, and Corn ceased operating his own mill.

In October 1881 Corn wrote to a brother-in-law in Kerrville that he was raising good crops and a mile of ditch was completed. His house was not yet finished, but he expressed satisfaction with the outcome of his move to New Mexico. He expected to get four to five cents a pound for his corn, ten to twelve dollars apiece for his stock cattle, and between twenty and twenty-three dollars for each of his beef cattle.[19]

All of the Corn children put in long hours at farm labor; Clarence Corn remembered his father as a man who "strongly believed in discipline and hard work, both for himself and his children."[20] But education was not neglected. In 1881 the children began attending the adobe one-room school built three miles east of Roswell. The first teacher was a man named Asbury Rogers. After 1885 the Corn children attended a somewhat larger school built to replace the earlier school. Its first teacher was Miss Sara Lund, who subsequently married early settler C. D. Bonney.

Hard work and childbearing took a heavy toll of many of the early women pioneers. Not long after the birth, on 25 August 1882, of her tenth child, a boy who was named George Washington Corn by his parents, Mary Jane Corn died. With unexpected suddenness Corn found himself a widower with nine children and a stepson. On 14 October 1886 Corn was married again, this time to a young woman who was to be with him for the remainder of his life.

Julia Miller McVicker was just sixteen years old when she married Corn, who was then forty-five years old. She had been orphaned a few years earlier while living in Missouri. Her uncle, James Miller, brought his young niece with him to New Mexico in an ox wagon. Miller bought sheep from Lea and became one of the territory's largest sheep ranchers. Julia Corn became stepmother to Corn's children from his first marriage, and Martin and Julia Corn had eleven children of their own, including eight boys and three girls. The first of their children was born in 1887, the last in 1913.[21] The Corns named their tenth child, born in 1909, Poe W. Corn in honor of John Poe, a family friend for whom Corn had deep respect.

In 1888 Corn made several changes in his landholdings, perhaps as a means of strengthening his resources at a time when the economic effects of the drought of 1886–87 were still rippling through the farming and ranching settlements of southeastern New Mexico. On 27 September 1888 he paid the fee of four dollars and filed a claim under the Timber Culture Act for 129.5 acres of land lying just to the east of his original homestead claim. A large stand of cottonwood trees was planted on the newly acquired land to comply with the terms of ownership.

In November of 1888 Corn sold Pat Garrett 45 acres of land. The price paid by Garrett, according to the court record of the sale, was $1 and "other valuable considerations." In December of 1888 Garrett sold the land under the same terms to the mercantilist Charles Ilfeld of Albuquerque. In July of 1891 Ilfeld sold the land to John Poe for $650.[22] Poe was at that time putting together and managing large landholdings based on the old Chisum properties on behalf of J. J. Hagerman, whose involvement in the Pecos Valley was even then changing the pace of development. In fact the changing ownership of that single 45-acre land parcel may be taken as symbolic of a whole process of change in personalities, leadership, and types of entrepreneurial activity that took place between the time of Chisum's death in 1884 and Hagerman's move in 1990 to the South Spring property once owned by Chisum.

Corn and the other settlers in what came to be known as "The Farms" raised principally corn in the early years but also some wheat. Corn was among those who were always experimenting, however, and ready to try new crops or methods. When the ready market for their corn diminished with the demise of Chisum's cattle operation in the late 1880s, many area farmers began putting more of their acreage into alfalfa. Although small plots of alfalfa had been tried in the late 1870s and early 1880s, it was not until after Poe successfully raised 400 acres of alfalfa in 1887 that the green-grass crop that became quality hay became a mainstay of Pecos Valley agriculture. Corn was a leading alfalfa producer, using a substantial portion of his irrigated acreage to raise several crops of alfalfa each year.

Fruit trees also had been proven to grow well in the valley's irrigated areas, and in 1891 Corn established his own fruit orchard. To finance the new project, he mortgaged his 129 acres of Timber Culture land to the Stark Brothers Nursery of Hannibal, Missouri. The company in turn supplied Corn with most of his apple tree stock, and the rest he ordered from nurseries in Arkansas. The young trees, their roots carefully packed in soil-filled bags, were transported to the Corn farm by rail across Texas, west to Carlsbad where the line ended, and then north by wagon. Under the terms of the agreement with Stark Brothers, Corn was to pay $238 at 6 percent interest within ten years. He had paid the debt by 1895.[23]

Corn probably acted for a number of reasons when, in 1894, he moved his family and all of his farm and ranch operations to a new site, still in the valley but in a far harsher environment, in a setting where pioneering efforts were once again necessary. Corn himself always said he was prompted to move by his asthma, a condition he was convinced was caused by his many years of breathing alfalfa dust in the fields.

But it is also true that he was presented with an opportunity to sell his farm, an opportunity that undoubtedly sharpened his sense of direction. There is also little reason to doubt that this vigorous man who had been a natural leader during the caravan drive from Texas to New Mexico still possessed a spirit that relished the challenge of building anew. In deciding to turn most of his attention to cattle instead of crop raising, Corn also may have been influenced by declining prices for corn, difficulty in finding markets for apple crops, and the fact that the cattle business in southeastern New Mexico was beginning to recover from the drought, oversupply, and overgrazing problems associated with the late 1880s and early 1890s.

Hagerman was still living in his luxurious Colorado Springs mansion when in April of 1894 Martin and Julia Corn sold him their farm and their interest in a large irrigation ditch for the sum of $14,989.59.[24] But in that same year, Hagerman's Pecos Valley Railroad was built north from Carlsbad to Roswell, creating new development possibilities, and Hagerman was amassing the land on which he would later build his new home and which he would develop with thousands of fruit trees and other crops.

Hagerman's purchase of the Corn farm gave Corn the chance to respond to the lure of a new settlement being proposed for uninhabited dry land located along North Salt Creek, also known as Arroyo Acequia, some twenty miles north-northeast of Roswell. North Salt Creek lay on the north side of the Capitan Mountains, fifty miles west of Roswell. Every year it sent floodwaters coursing down from the foothills during the spring and summer runoff season. There was heady talk among Corn, his older sons, and other families about using these waters for a whole new irrigated cropland area. Corn made plans to build a reservoir for irrigation purposes and for livestock watering. He was the first to settle in the valley of North Salt Creek, and he was considered the community leader by the small number of other families who followed the Corns' example.

Corn's hopes were expressed in the name he gave to the several hundred acres on which he filed claim—Eden Valley Ranch. Another name commonly used for the swath of rangeland cut through by the sometimes dry, sometimes overflowing, creek was Macho Draw. It was a treeless, barren place. But to Corn it represented just the right mixture of challenge and potential. At the age of fifty-four, Corn experienced a renewed zest for life as he commenced building a dugout to shelter his family while a rambling house of stone was gradually constructed between stints of family labor on the reservoir and a ditch. The house was ready for the large family to occupy by the spring of 1895.

Nothing was easy in the scattered little settlement that took Eden Valley for its name even beyond the confines of the Corn ranch. Wolves abounded in the area and preyed on the livestock. It took most of a day to reach Roswell by wagon. Led by Corn the settlers built a one-room school. The teacher lived in Corn's house, and Corn paid the teacher's salary of thirty dollars per month out of his own pocket for the first two years, until Chaves County took on responsibility for the school.

The reservoir did not provide enough water for continual irrigation, as the creek proved an unreliable source of surplus mountain moisture. Almost all of the few other settlers moved away. Corn remained but concentrated more intensively on cattle raising and eventually prospered at the new site. He bought some of the claims abandoned by his fellow settlers and more than doubled the size of his holdings. Although cattle and a small number of sheep were his mainstay, Corn was a master of the soil, who until the end could not resist putting seed into the ground and watching it grow to harvest. The abundant crop of large watermelons and pumpkins he raised at Eden Valley was loaded each year onto long deep wagons pulled by six horses. Corn and his sons annually drove their wagons north sixty miles to Fort Sumner to sell these readily desirable products of their labor. The grain crops raised at Eden Valley mostly went to feed Corn livestock. Cattle, wool, and live sheep were sold through markets in Roswell.

Clarence Corn, basing his conclusion on testimony from his older siblings as well as his own memories, saw his father as a man whose tough exterior was balanced by his innate common sense. He was moderate in his political views and never a strong partisan of any political party, although he voted as a Republican in his later years. He adhered to the basic tenets of the Southern Baptist tradition in which he had been raised, but made daily life rather than weekly church the focus of his simple ethics. It was work itself, the actual physical labor of building, planting, harvesting, even planning, that was the single most passionate cause in Corn's life, according to his son. Despite steadily worsening respiratory problems, Corn worked daily until very near the end of his life. At the end, his attacks of asthma became more frequent, lasting, and severe. He died at the Eden Valley Ranch on 30 September 1915, just sixteen days before his seventy-fifth birthday. He was buried on his own land in a community cemetery located one-half mile from his house.

In a very real sense, Corn began and remained a pioneer. The world's first great modern war involving airplanes and mechanization was well under way when he died. The automobile, first produced in the United States in 1893, already had wrought great change in the social landscape of America. But Corn was still pioneering, still using horse-drawn wagons, still using a mule-pulled plow, and doing it in deliberate choice as he stubbornly, independently, tamed his own piece of the Western frontier.

John Poe

The significance of John Poe's long life stems from his participation in more than one of the interlocking pioneering episodes that brought successive waves of fur trappers, explorers, Indian scouts, cavalry troops, buffalo hunters, miners, railroaders, cattlemen, and homesteaders pouring onto the plains, into the deserts, and up into the mountains of the vast continental interior. Poe was a particular type among men of the West, one of those who in the early years easily met the demands of a daunting social and natural environment, but for whom feats of physical prowess were no more than a means of removing obstacles on the road to an underlying goal of personal prosperity in a traditionally structured society. What Poe and the many others like him wanted was the satisfaction of making a new life in a new land. They were ready to pay whatever price was demanded by a West they intended to claim as theirs.

John William Poe was born on 17 October 1850 on the tobacco farm in Mason County, Kentucky, owned by his grandfather and father. Set amid rolling green hills, the farm offered a secure livelihood and a safe, if predictable, future. After the Civil War, black field hands continued to work the long straight rows of lush tobacco plants in much the same manner as during the slave era. Poe's family planned for him to achieve an education and then take over the reins of the family enterprise.

But from an early age Poe showed signs of resisting the direction in which his life was supposed to move. He heard talk about the West. He read the Waverly novels of Walter Scott and wanted to experience personally some of the challenge and excitement conveyed to him in the books. To an idealistic young farm boy, it seemed clear that in America such romantic adventure could be found only on the western frontier, certainly not in the bucolic setting of the rural South. Strongwilled, stubborn, and capable of keeping his plans to himself, Poe quietly prepared for his own getaway by saving the earnings he received as a country fiddle player at local dances and weddings. His family discouraged all talk of his leaving, and his grandfather offered to pay his way through college if he would remain close to home. But after a first abortive attempt to run away with a friend, Poe made a final move on his own. On a warm spring night in 1870, he climbed down a ladder from his bedroom window and made his way to Kansas City.

He took whatever work he could get. For a time he dug potatoes on the farm of an old French farmer. He laid rail for the Santa Fe Railroad, quickly proving himself a hard worker. He avidly read the newspapers, pamphlets, and books provided by the company for its employees. He saved his money and showed little interest in going to saloons. He went home for a visit but left after three months, more convinced than ever that his future lay in the West. Hired again by the Santa Fe, he laid track with a crew in Topeka, Kansas, where he made friends with one Dan Hudson and with him decided to travel to Fort Griffin in Texas.

Moving through the Indian Territory and down into West Texas, Poe saw the West of his dreams finally take shape before his eyes. Arriving in Fort Griffin in 1872, Poe and Hudson found it to be a rough, tough frontier outpost enlivened day and night by the ceaseless activities of cowboys, gamblers, buffalo hunters, and military men. A six-company army fort stood on a bluff overlooking the town site located on a flat plain adjoining Clear Fork Creek, which fed into the Brazos River. Fort Griffin was a collection point for buffalo hides and a supply center for cattlemen driving their herds from south Texas north to markets in Kansas.[25] While his traveling companion found the wild ways of Fort Griffin to his liking, Poe recoiled from the whiskey-imbued atmosphere of violence that nightly resulted in one or more killings and drunken brawls. Parting from Hudson, Poe moved on into the open range west of the town. At the James Barton ranch, he learned that a fellow Kentuckian by the name of John Jacobs was farming nearby and immediately went to meet him.

Jacobs was an engaging young fellow bent on saving up enough money to marry. He and Poe became friends and farming partners. When the corn crop they struggled to bring to harvest was destroyed in a single day by a horde of locusts, the two young bachelors dusted themselves off and rode back to Fort Griffin, where after searching out every available work prospect and rejecting the notion of buffalo hunting for the time being, they accepted a military contract to supply Fort Griffin with 1600 cords of wood for winter fuel at one dollar per cord. They spent the spring and summer of 1872 living on the land, cutting timber ten hours a day, and brought the wood in as scheduled in the fall.

Buffalo hunting had become a major economic enterprise. Hunters were moving from Kansas onto the southern plains despite the Indian threat. While the Indians took only enough buffalo to meet their subsistence needs, the white hunters made a thoroughgoing commercial enterprise out of the great buffalo kills that continued through most of the 1870s. The obliteration of vast herds was rationalized by the white hunters as a means of eliminating the Indians from areas where whites wished to settle. Extermination of the buffalo was seen as necessary to allow for a rapidly growing beef-cattle industry. And while buffalo skin was too porous to make good shoe leather, whole buffalo hides brought prices of from one dollar to three dollars for use as robes and blankets.[26]

Poe and Jacobs invested their profits from the wood contract in buffalo-hunting equipment; they bought a wagon, rifles, ammunition, mules, and food supplies and hired a buffalo skinner. From 1873 until 1878 they spent the better part of each year moving from camp to camp on the rugged plains, shooting altogether an estimated twenty-thousand buffalo. The kills were group efforts and highly organized. Poe's specialty was the accurate, single-shot kill with a high-powered Sharps rifle, which had a range of a mile or more. As relentlessly bloody as this work was, the buffalo-hunting experience undoubtedly honed Poe's ability to cooperate with others in a venture requiring discipline and dependability on the part of everyone involved. Skinned from the slain animals, the hides were cured in the sun for ten days; every camp was surrounded by buffalo hides stretched flat on the dry ground. The hides were then scraped clean of remaining flesh, stacked in huge piles and loaded onto wagons for sale in Fort Griffin, from where they were transported to the marketing center in Fort Worth.

In their first six months of buffalo hunting, Poe and Jacobs took eleven hundred buffalo; in other years, with the help of three skinners, they took much higher numbers. Evenings around the camp fire were spent cleaning empty shells and preparing molten lead in fifty to eighty pound batches to pour into bullet molds for the next day's hunt. At one camp Poe and Jacobs built a winter tepee nine buffalo hides thick as protection from the cold and from Indian raids.[27]

Competition for the dwindling numbers of buffalo grew fierce; by 1878, the year buffalo hunting reached its highest level of activity, Poe had had enough. He and Jacobs delivered their last seventeen hundred hides in the spring of that year and invested their money in fourteen hundred sheep in San Antonio. Jacobs married and set up a sheep ranch, while Poe returned to Fort Griffin to accept a position as deputy U.S. marshal and simultaneously the post of town marshal, or chief of police.[28] Having taken part in the controversial, if perhaps inevitable, buffalo-hunting episode that forever altered the ecological balance of the West, Poe now found a new role in the increasingly necessary business of imposing law and order in those parts of the West where it was absent.

Physically hardened by years of outdoor living, Poe at the age of twenty-eight in 1878 was a strongly built, compact man standing five feet eight inches tall. His face was broad and his demeanor serious; his manner was generally calm and somewhat reserved, although he had proven himself a good sport during the frequent prankster-type joking that accompanied the comaraderie of buffalo hunting. As a lawman he manifested a no-nonsense attitude and credible probity that made him an effective peace officer. Certainly his mettle was tested in Fort Griffin, a place where lawmen battled outlaws on one hand and violence-prone vigilante groups on the other.

In 1879, having proven himself a capable lawman and discovering that he liked the work, Poe gave in to his urge to find newer frontier country and moved on to Wheeler County, dominated by the cattle empire of George D. Littlefield. Hired as a peace officer, he was soon persuaded by townfolk in Wheeler to run for sheriff. His defeat in the November election by one vote was generally attributed to overconfidence on the part of his many supporters. Poe declined to contest the election and instead took a position as stock detective with the Canadian River Cattlemen's Association.

Still wearing the deputy marshal's badge that allowed him to make arrests, Poe rode the ranges hunting down rustlers and gathering evidence from altered brands. Texas cattlemen were losing stock daily; recognizing they could not eliminate rustlers, their hope was to bring the worst of them under control. Until his December 1880 capture by Garrett, Billy the Kid was thought to be one of the worst.

The Kid was evidently slipping over into West Texas and driving small groups of cattle across the border into New Mexico, where he would sell them to one of several contacts extending from Portales, close by the border, clear over to the western slope of the Sacramento Mountains and Sierra Blanca, where Pat Coghlin bought stolen cattle at his Tularosa Basin ranch. But even during the period from January to April 1881, when the Kid was being tried and convicted, cattle continued to disappear from the Texas range, sometimes reappearing in New Mexico.

Poe entered New Mexico in the spring of 1881, determined to identify some of the buyers of the stolen Texas cattle. Coghlin was a key suspect, as his name had been part of rustling lore for years. Poe had the good fortune of discovering hides with Texas brands drying on a fence at Coghlin's ranch, evidence that eventually helped bring about an indictment and trial for the ruddy-faced rancher who, while otherwise an upstanding citizen, had lined his pockets over the years with gain from trading in contraband.

During the month of April 1881, Poe was often in White Oaks, at that time the largest and certainly the liveliest of southeastern New Mexico's towns. While staying at the town's hotel, Poe met and talked with Lincoln County Sheriff Pat Garrett.[29] The Kid was forty miles to the east in the Lincoln jail, awaiting hanging. Poe and Garrett, with their shared interest in arresting cattle and horse thieves and their shared knowledge of exactly how these outlaws operated, quickly found they could be of use to one another.

Thus it was only natural that when word reached White Oaks on April 28 that the Kid had broken loose only days before his scheduled hanging, Garrett would talk things over with Poe. And it was equally natural that when Poe some weeks later was given a believable tip that the Kid was living in and around Fort Sumner, Poe would take the story to Garrett, telling him he thought it a serious enough message to deserve being acted upon. Not only did Garrett act on the tip, but when he rode north to Fort Sumner for his final, fateful, dark-of-the-night encounter with the Kid, Poe was one of the two deputies who accompanied him.

Poe did not return to Texas when his 1881 investigations in New Mexico were complete. He had found in the rugged and richly varied terrain of sparsely populated Lincoln County the true frontier he had sought since leaving home in 1870. Working as a deputy under Garrett, he fast became a respected lawman in the huge county. So respected was Poe, in fact, that he unexpectedly found himself supplanting Garrett as sheriff. Despite Garrett's success in ending the criminal career of Billy the Kid and his subsequent fame as a lawman—or perhaps because of it—the Democratic Party in Lincoln County chose Poe rather than Garrett as candidate for sheriff in the November 1881 election. The strained relations between the two unavoidably caused by this development only worsened when Garrett lost his bid in the election for a seat on the Territorial Council, while Poe was easily elected sheriff. A dispute during 1882 over a land transaction exacerbated the tensions between Poe and Garrett, and they never renewed their friendship.[30]

In truth the seeds of discord between the two men were present almost from the start of their working relationship. Garrett was freewheeling and idiosyncratic in style, less businesslike in his handling of the affairs of office than the sober-minded Poe, with his methodical way of dealing with every problem. And eventually a residue of misunderstanding accumulated between them, as a result of Garrett's defensiveness about his tactics in hunting down and killing Billy the Kid. Poe always stood firmly by his story that he had put Garrett on the trail to Fort Sumner at the right time. Garrett, on the other hand, never emphasized Poe's role, preferring to see the final closing-in as a natural outcome of his own persistence.

Early in 1882, however, shortly after Poe took office as sheriff, the mutual respect between Poe and Garrett was still strong enough to prompt Garrett to lend his presence and encouragement when J. C. Lea decided to suggest John Poe as an appropriate suitor to a young woman who was a member of Lea's household. The nineteen-year-old Sophie Alberding to whom Poe was introduced soon after that tactfully conducted conference was, like Poe himself, a newcomer to Lincoln County; she too had responded to the bold majesty of its sweeping landscapes and its challenging frontier status. Traveling by buckboard south from Las Vegas into the hamlet of Roswell for the first time, her fears of the unknown had given way to exhilaration as she observed the piercing blueness of the sky and "a glorious panorama of mesa and mountains . . ."[31]

Sophie Alberding was born in 1862 in Petaluma, California, one of five children of Frederick and Rosanna Alberding. Her father was a civil engineer, a horse breeder, and an ambitious speculator who changed jobs often. In the early 1870s he took his family to Nicaragua and started a ranch. When he died there in 1872, the mother and children returned to California and struggled to earn a living on a chicken farm. The mother died of tuberculosis within a year, and the children were sent to live with relatives in rural Illinois. Young Fred Alberding found work as a ranchhand for J. C. Lea in Colfax County in New Mexico and moved with him to the Pecos Valley in 1877.

In 1881 Fred wrote to his sister Sophie that he would like her to come for a visit. Although Sophie had not seen her brother since she was twelve years old, she eagerly accepted the invitation. There was a connection between her family and Captain Lea; Sophie's aunt in Lea's Summit, Missouri, was married to Stephen A. Lea, a cousin of J. C. Lea. Traveling alone and wearing her blonde hair in a long braid down her back, Sophie took a train from Kansas City to La Junta, Colorado, where she changed trains and went south to Las Vegas, New Mexico. Her brother had come to meet her. The five-day trip from Las Vegas back to Lincoln County gave the two a chance to become reacquainted and gave Fred a chance to explain some of the customs of frontier life to his sister.

Even with the help of her brother's advance warnings, Sophie was at first taken aback at the undisguised and sometimes boisterously humorous advances made to her by the unsophisticated but disarmingly chivalrous cowboys who gathered around Lea's dinner table. She soon came to enjoy her popularity, developed a genuine friendship with Sally Lea, and found a warmly supportive surrogate mother in Mrs. Lea's widowed sister, who had joined the household with her two children.

By the time Lea introduced Poe to Sophie in 1882, she had become an experienced helper in running the Lea boardinghouse; Lea himself acknowledged her expertise in broiling venison steaks over a mesquite wood fire. She had gone on country buckboard rides and attended country dances with a number of would-be suitors. She enjoyed a charmingly gentle friendship with the idiosyncratic but always fatherly and gallant John Chisum, who upon taking a fancy to Sophie, drove her one day down to his South Spring ranch for a week of country walks and talks, peppered with typical Chisum teasing and wit. Despite the presence of servants, Sophie insisted on lending a hand and had one of her most interesting conversations with the Cattle King of the Pecos while feather-dusting his bedroom-office.

Once she had met Poe, however, Sophie had not a doubt that she had found the right man for her. Poe's work kept him on the move and away from Roswell much of the time, but he had given Sophie clear indications of his intentions and feelings from the first day they met. A year of letters between the two cemented the courtship, and early in 1883 Sophie accepted Poe's proposal of marriage.

Poe was thirty-three years old and Sophie twenty-one when they were married on 5 May 1883 in Lea's house. The cottonwoods, adobe corrals, water-filled acequias and hollyhocks surrounding the structure's honey-colored walls lent a lyrical grace to the 5 A.M. ceremony performed by Justice of the Peace Edmund Stone, there being no priest or minister within a two-hundred mile radius of Roswell. After a wedding breakfast, the sheriff and his bride set forth on the journey to the county seat at Lincoln, Sophie's trunk strapped to the buckboard. It was Sophie's first venture into the mountainous western portion of southeastern New Mexico.

The Poes boarded for a month with longtime Lincoln resident Isaac Ellis before moving in June into the sheriff's living quarters on the second floor of the Lincoln County Courthouse. The Poe's bedroom was the northeast corner room that had served as Billy the Kid's jail quarters during his brief imprisonment. Sophie Poe found it unsettling that blood stains still marked the stairway where Deputy Bell had been killed by the Kid during his escape. Space on the first floor was rented out as a store by the county. With Poe traveling on frequent forays to pursue outlaws, the county jail was left in the charge of deputy J. Smith Lea. Prisoners were kept in the Lincoln jail after arrest and during trial; those convicted were taken to Leavenworth, Kansas, as New Mexico had not yet built a prison.

Although Lincoln still had a population larger than Roswell's, with some seven to eight hundred inhabitants, Sophie chose in January 1884 to make the arduous trip to Roswell in order to be with the Leas as the time drew near for the delivery of her first child. When she went into labor in the first days of February, complications developed, and the Dr. North who was in attendance sent a messenger on a nonstop horseback ride to Fort Stanton to bring back the fort surgeon. Unable to leave a woman in similar circumstances at Fort Stanton, the surgeon sent back special instruments that were used to help deliver Sophie's baby. Within hours of its birth on 4 February, the baby boy died. He was the only child born to the Poes. After several weeks of slow recovery, Sophie was taken home to Lincoln by her husband, lying on blankets in the back of a horse-drawn wagon.[32] Poe was just beginning his second term as sheriff, having been reelected in the November 1883 election.

During 1885, while Poe was still sheriff, the couple moved from the courthouse to an adobe house at the large VV Ranch that Poe had purchased, about fifteen miles southwest of Fort Stanton. Both in Texas and eastern New Mexico, Poe had been a close observer of the thriving beef-cattle industry. He now felt ready to enter it himself, hoping to achieve in some measure the financial success of such men as Lea and Chisum. By the end of 1885, he felt sure enough of his new direction to submit his resignation from the office of sheriff to the territorial governor, who named Roswell deputy Jim Brent acting sheriff in accordance with Poe's recommendation.

Poe was not yet a settled man, however. It was in his blood by now to be constantly on the move, either out on the land with the cattle or traveling on business and always, always, ready to make the most of new opportunities. Foreign investors, English and Scottish in particular, were eagerly buying up Western properties in the 1880s. Poe saw a chance to acquire sizable capital when he was approached by a Scotsman interested in moving to the VV Ranch with his family. Although the sale of the ranch worked to create new options for Poe—and for his wife, who often had felt isolated at the ranch—the Scottish family never felt comfortable in the rough social environment of the frontier West and returned to Scotland after a few years.

Poe in the meantime was pursuing a new idea, one that showed just how strong in him was the urge to move on to fresh fields. Cattle ranching in Argentina seemed to offer intriguing possibilities. After talking it over with J. Smith Lea, Poe decided to do an on-scene investigation of the South American country. First he and Sophie enjoyed their first vacation, traveling by train to a resort in Arkansas.

Then in early 1887, Poe and Lea went together to Argentina, Brazil, and Paraguay. Arriving in Buenos Aires, they spent several weeks traveling by rail across the pampas, where they saw cattle, horse, and sheep ranches, and toured vineyards. Near the Andes Mountains in the interior of Argentina, they found good grazing land for 25 cents an acre. Prospects for a large cattle ranch appeared promising. Poe arrived back in New Mexico in midsummer 1887. He seems always to have been a man who thought out his decisions without seeking the advice of his wife—or possibly anyone else. He told Sophie that, having given the matter much thought, he had decided not to leave New Mexico, a place he now was convinced offered "plenty of opportunity for a man seeking his fortune."[33]

The journey to South America was something of a watershed event in Poe's life. It seems to have given him fresh insight into the simple reality that sometime, somewhere, he must make a choice to stay in a place, leave aside a mentality based on possibilities just beyond the next horizon, and build out of the materials at hand. The trip also may have allowed Poe time to reflect on how best to combine his own particular abilities with his available options in order to move toward that goal of financial prosperity that had taken on increasing importance for him, although it had certainly been a latent motivation from the day he left Kentucky.

The steps he took almost immediately upon his return to the Pecos Valley in 1887 indicate that, whether consciously or not, he had decided to use his agricultural heritage and experience and apply it to his new surroundings, stamping his efforts with the business acumen he had discovered to be one of his traits. For even as a lawman, Poe had been recognized more for his sound management than for his bravado.

Poe had an almost uncanny instinct for moving into areas of economic activity just as they were taking on importance or entering the early growth stages. The artesian wells that would later make the middle Pecos Basin famous as an agricultural center had not yet become a factor when Poe in 1887 purchased a large tract of land five miles southeast of Roswell. But the irrigation ditches taken from Pecos tributaries already had created a mixed-crop farming base that was making an extended oasis of green and gold along land lying between Roswell and the Pecos River some fifteen miles to the east. Poe was not an innovator, but he was an astute observer of trends. Chisum, Corn, and even Garrett before him had experimented with the mixed raising of livestock and crops in this irrigated area. Poe now took this concept and combined it with the new trend toward fenced ranching.

He made his land into what was probably the territory's first genuine stock farm. He used only selectively bred cattle and kept them all under fence, an idea still only in the process of gaining acceptance. In addition to his initial acquisition of 350 highbred cattle, Poe bought 150 quality brood mares. Although small plots of alfalfa had dotted the valley for some years, Poe (influenced by his observations of large-scale alfalfa farming in Argentina) planted about 400 acres of alfalfa. With four cuttings a year, a yield of four tons per acre, and bringing ten dollars a ton, the alfalfa acreage proved so successful that it became a model for the area's other farmers. Poe's 571.86 acres included some of the valley's finest agricultural land, irrigated by the earliest and largest of the ditches taken from the South Spring River.[34]

In 1888 Poe entered a partnership with J. Smith Lea and William H. Cosgrove in buying out and operating the J. C. Lea and Bonney mercantile business. The store's name became Poe, Lea and Cosgrove. After a few years Poe and Lea sold their interests to Cosgrove, but later Poe bought the land where the store stood; in 1905 he built a group of new stores on the property in central Roswell. And in 1889 Poe demonstrated his political muscle by opposing the candidacy of Garrett for sheriff; the man backed by Poe won the election.

In 1890 Poe showed yet again that beneath the calm exterior was a somewhat restless nature, a desire both to seek new work and make new money. Still owning his land and also serving as manager of Hagerman's local properties, he went into banking with E. A. Cahoon, when he started Roswell's first bank. Poe was elected president in 1893, and although he continued for another year to act as manager for Hagerman, he and his wife moved into a large new home on one of Roswell's finest streets in 1895. In 1897 Poe sold all of his landholdings to Hagerman and concentrated his attentions on the bank, still the only one in all of southeastern New Mexico.

When the bank reorganized in 1899 as the First National Bank of Roswell, Poe resigned his presidency and the following year organized a new bank, the Citizens' Bank of Roswell, capitalized at fifty thousand dollars. Poe was the bank's president. In 1921, with Poe still president, the bank absorbed the American National Bank of Roswell and became Citizens' National Bank of Roswell.[35]

During his years as a banker, Poe held a number of public positions. From 1890 until the time of his death he was a member of the board of regents of the New Mexico Military Institute. From 1915 to 1917 he was president of the State Tax Commission. During World War I he was fuel administrator for New Mexico. In 1907 the Poes made an extended tour of Europe, and in 1913 they traveled around the world from Pacific to Atlantic. In 1919 Poe's recollection of the killing of Billy the Kid was published in *Wide World* magazine, then republished in 1923 as a booklet called "Billy the Kid, Notorious New Mexico Outlaw."[36]

The John Poe who began his western days laying railroad track and ended them as a banker of local prominence is representative of numerous other self-made men who also transformed themselves from youthful adventurers to staid establishment figures in a West in the process of integrating with the rest of the nation. In addition Poe became part of an emerging social structure particular to southeastern New Mexico, where settlements and communities grew in tacit accordance with traditions of ethnic separatism influenced both by a southern legacy of white dominance and by notions of the superiority of Anglo culture over the indigenous Hispanic culture.

At the apex of the local Anglo-dominated establishment were found men like John Poe who, while undeniably deserving of their success, did not challenge a prevailing ethos that arbitrarily set ethnic and racial criteria dictating which people would even have a chance to vie for the kind of success they had achieved. These attitudes of cultural separatism were deeply rooted. In 1883 Poe, telling his wife about "the Mexican population of the Southwest," noted "their respect for an office, and their peculiar—and primitive—ideas of law."[37] There was little recognition that the legal and other traditions of those whom Poe called the "original citizens" of New Mexico had their own legitimacy.

But then John Poe took the world and his society as he found them. Within that context he played his role with intelligence and integrity, perhaps instinctively recognizing that frontiers exist only at odd intervals in the course of human history, offering unique chances for at least some individuals to make of themselves whatever they might have in them to be. By the time of his death, on 17 July 1923, he could justly claim to have been one of those who helped close out the frontier era of southeastern New Mexico. Ironically enough he did not die a wealthy man; several investments made in his last years proved unprofitable and greatly reduced the estate he left to Sophie Poe, who survived until well into her eighties in the 1940s.

9

J.P. White and J.J. Hagerman

BY 1912, THE YEAR STATEHOOD WAS GRANTED, SIGNS ABOUNDED in southeastern New Mexico that the pioneering era was over. The rapidly developing region was contributing leadership as well as resources to the welfare of New Mexico. William C. McDonald, a lawyer who began his New Mexico career in White Oaks in 1880 and went on to acquire the flourishing Bar W and Block ranches near Carrizozo, was inaugurated in January 1912 as the first elected governor of the new state. Both George Curry and Harvey B. Fergusson, the state's first two congressmen, had entered public life while living in southeastern New Mexico.

Newcomers to the region, along with such imported goods as brick, glass, and lumber, arrived almost daily by train in Pecos Valley communities located along the rail line that ran from Pecos, Texas, across the border to Carlsbad and north via Roswell to Amarillo. And a small number of Model T Fords could be seen briskly navigating the rough roads of Roswell and such turn-of-the-century new farming settlements as Dexter, Hagerman, Lake Arthur, and Artesia, all south of Roswell in the middle Pecos Basin.

In Lincoln County, along the western rim of the southeast region, adjustments in attitudes and goals had been made in response to the decline in gold production that depopulated White Oaks and to the naming of the railroad town Carrizozo as county seat, a move that robbed the old town of Lincoln of its courthouse-generated air of excitement and left it home to a small base of longtime residents often combining the best of the western and Hispanic traditions. Cattle and sheep ranching continued to be a primary economic activity in the mountain valleys and foothills.

However undeniable the steady integration of southeastern New Mexico into the general economy of the new state, the fact remained that a distinctive mix of environmental and cultural features made the region noticeably different in a number of ways from the rest of New Mexico. There was, for one thing, the region's ongoing cultural and economic link with Texas; settlers originating in that state comprised a higher percentage of the population than those from any other part of the country, and it was not by accident that southeastern New Mexico's principal rail line began and ended in Texas.

Another factor affecting the overall tenor of life in the southeast quadrant was the critical importance of water; its availability in an essentially arid land determined the location of communities, the level of emigration, and the quantity and quality of land-based production. In fact despite the buoyantly boastful promotionalism that characterized many local newspaper accounts, the path to the postfrontier era had not proceeded smoothly onward and upward at all times. The years between 1890 and 1912 saw the initial euphoria following the discovery of underground water resources and the damming of the Pecos turn to sober-minded realism when the artesian water showed signs of depletion, the dams flooded, and gypsum in the soil eroded major irrigation canals.

The land was still making known its inherent limits in 1912 when, after five years of steadily declining capacity, the grandiose Hondo Reservoir scheme finally had to be abandoned. First conceived in 1888 when there seemed no limits to irrigation potential for the Pecos and its tributaries, the Hondo Reservoir was completed under strong local pressure by the U.S. Reclamation Service in 1907. Created by a large dam, it was intended to provide irrigation for one hundred thousand acres of cropland along the Rio Hondo about ten miles southwest of Roswell. No more than one thousand acres were ever irrigated, for the gypsum underlay of the dam made the reservoir "nothing more than a giant sieve."[1] Despite the project's tremendous cost to taxpayers, it was a complete failure.

Life in southeastern New Mexico also was marked by the rigid social and economic segregation along ethnic lines that had become a distinctive regional feature by the time pioneering days had passed. Underlying prejudices were frequently revealed in editorials such as the one that appeared in the *Hagerman Messenger* and was quoted on 30 May 1906 by the *Santa Fe New Mexican*. Comparing the "dilapidated" Hispanic part of the territory unfavorably with the thriving southeastern sector, the writer attributed the area's good fortune to the fact that "the magic wand of the Anglo Saxon is over it, and that means development, progress, enlightment [sic] and power . . . over the greaser . . . who is too lazy to keep up; and smells too badly to be endured."[2]

And finally southeastern New Mexico was notable for the domination of its politics and its economy by a handful of locally powerful men, often wealthy landowners. A number of these leading figures, however, played decidedly positive roles in regional development. They participated in ventures that strengthened the local economic base, spurred emigration, and created the infrastructure necessary to end frontier isolation. J. P. White and J. J. Hagerman were among those who brought about enough change to help negate the decades-old congressional charges that New Mexico was too poor in people and in resources, too much an uninhabited backwater, to deserve the status of statehood.

James Phelps White

Perhaps it was a portent of things to come that the small town of Gonzales, seventy-five miles east of San Antonio, already was being called the cattle capital of Texas when James Phelps White was born there on 2 December 1856. For within a generation, several members of the extended family of cotton planters into which White was born were to become leaders in the industry that put Texas and New Mexico on the map as one of the great cattle-producing regions of the world. During the course of a long and fruitful partnership with his uncle, the empire-building cattleman George W. Littlefield, White himself was to play a key role in opening new ranges, developing new markets, and ushering in the era of fenced ranching and selective breeding.

Before becoming related through marriage, both the Littlefield and White families owned cotton plantations in the state of Mississippi. In 1841 Fleming Littlefield, the son of Panola County cotton planter Philip Littlefield, married Mildred Satterwhite White, the widow of John Henry White. At the time of her marriage, she was mistress of a large plantation left to her by her late husband and had five children including a daughter and four sons, one of whom was Thomas Jefferson White, later to become the father of James Phelps White.

Fleming and Mildred Littlefield resided on the White plantation after their marriage, and it was there that George Washington Littlefield,

CHAPTER NINE

the first of their three children, was born on 21 June 1842. Feuding between Satterwhites and Littlefields intensified over the years, and in 1850 Fleming Littlefield left Panola County and went to Gonzales County in south Texas, where he bought land on the Guadalupe River and established a cotton plantation. The following year his wife, their children, several of the White children, and a large number of Littlefield slaves joined him at the new location.[3]

The plantation in Gonzales County was soon producing good cotton on twenty-one hundred acres of rich bottomland, and Fleming Littlefield also bought an interest in a store in the town of Gonzales, fifteen miles downriver from the family home. In January 1853 Fleming Littlefield died of pneumonia, and in accordance with his will the livestock and equipment were divided among his heirs, but the land was kept intact. Thomas Jefferson White went to Mississippi to marry and returned with his bride to live in a new house built for him by his mother. It was there that his first child, James Phelps White, known as "Phelps" throughout his life, was born in 1856.[4]

George Littlefield, having received his early schooling from a tutor, attended Baylor University at Old Independence from early 1857 to October 1858. Mildred Littlefield presided as mistress of the plantation, exercising a matriarchal authority over family members and slaves alike. All of her sons, including George Littlefield and his half-brother Thomas Jefferson White, joined the Confederate Army when the Civil War began. The family was fiercely loyal to the southern cause; they had brought with them to Texas the mores and customs of the Old South, and even when the war was over and slavery no longer a legal institution, they continued to believe the slave-holding system had not been without merit.

George Littlefield, only nineteen when he signed up to fight for the South, saw action in several states and despite his youth rose quickly to the rank of lieutenant colonel. His only respite from active duty came when he took time to marry Alice P. Tiller, whom he had courted since school days, on 4 January 1863, in Houston.[5] In eastern Tennessee on 26 December 1863, Littlefield was knocked from his horse by a fragment of a bursting shell that "carried away the fleshy part of his left hip and left a terrible wound."[6] His superior officer promoted him to major on the field of battle.

Given little hope of recovery, he was slowly brought back to health by his personal slave, "Old Nath." But still badly crippled and on crutches, Littlefield was forced to resign and reached home in late September

1864. On 4 October he took charge of the family plantation, his brother Bill having proven to be an irresponsible manager. Although the South was now cut in two and the military situation was worsening rapidly, Texas plantations were still producing and selling large quantities of cotton, corn, beef, and pork.[7] Nevertheless by the time the war ended, the Littlefields had lost much of their money. When a copy of orders from a federal official was placed in her hands, Mildred Littlefield bowed to the inevitable and told the family's slaves that they were free to leave. Many of them chose to remain and work on the Littlefield farms for low wages.

Phelps White was still a small boy when his uncle returned from war. He spent much of his time over the next few years under the informal tutelage of Littlefield. "I was with him a great deal . . . I used to ride behind him as he went about his work," White recalled in later years.[8] Establishing a pattern that would last as long as both were alive, Littlefield was mentor and guide to White in a relationship based on implicit trust on both sides. It is interesting to note that White was born fourteen years after Littlefield and died exactly fourteen years after him.

Using the labor of former slaves, Littlefield made the family holdings efficient and productive even in the turmoil of the immediate post–Civil War years. In the summer of 1868, he bought the land of Thomas Jefferson White, when his half-brother was forced to declare bankruptcy. He also bought out the interests of several other brothers by canceling out their indebtedness to him.[9] But in 1869, having taken on these additional properties, including six hundred cattle and thirty horses previously owned jointly with a brother, Littlefield began to experience setbacks. After borrowing to finance planting, drought and worms diminished the harvest. Then a flood in July 1869 swept the bottomlands, killing people and destroying the cotton fields. Another flood wiped out the 1870 crop. Littlefield was left with debts and no money to pay them. In the words of White, Littlefield saw that "nothing could be made by farming at that time. Then he decided that something could be made with cattle."[10]

During 1871 Littlefield began building a herd to market in Kansas, where large stockyards facilitated the trade between buyers and sellers of beef cattle. Phelps White long remembered the day Littlefield rode up to the White farmhouse and told Phelps and his younger brother Tom he was giving away his calves and they could have as many as they could catch. "We caught nine of them, and that was my start in the cattle business."[11] In 1872 Littlefield drove his first herd of twelve hundred head to markets in Kansas and returned with enough profit to pay his debts. He never again acted as his own trail driver. Instead he spent his time obtaining cattle and organizing drives. He was always on the scene when his cattle arrived at their market destination, ready to finalize prearranged sales and find buyers for any cattle not yet taken.

He rapidly became one of the bigtime holders of government beef contracts. He used subcontractors in Texas to supply him with the cattle he needed to meet his commitments, buying on credit and paying for the cattle after the government paid him. The beef he sold the government went to Indian reservations in the Dakotas. The subcontractors bought local cattle "at their own prices, as the lower cowmen in Texas never realized that the prices were any higher than in 1866."[12] This trade, lucrative for the contractors if not the smallholders, continued until 1877, when the government began to curtail the number of contracts, leaving Littlefield with twenty-three thousand cattle on the trail.

"The Major," as Littlefield was now called by friends and business associates alike, realized he needed a permanent holding place for his livestock, to allow him flexibility in finding buyers. During 1877 he bought out his business partners. He then went to Phelps White, twenty years old at the time, and said to him: "It looks like I'm going to make a pretty good profit. I wonder if you'd like to go to ranching with me." Without a moment's hesitation, White answered: "Sure. I'll go anywhere with you."[13]

Driven by his determination to maximize the profitability of cattle, Littlefield, and White along with him, thus entered fully into the making of the hybrid Texas culture—part southern, part western. For Littlefield's attention was inexorably drawn westward as he considered alternative sites for a ranch. He selected the high plains of the panhandle in West Texas. In that dry ecological environment were found grasses that, unlike winter grasses in eastern Kansas and other locations, retained their nutritional value year-round. Southern though he remained in his own outlook and lifestyle, Littlefield came to depend on the lands and cattle-raising traditions of the West for a significant portion of the income that sustained his growing business empire.

With his seemingly simple decision to start a ranch, Littlefield also was doing something else; now in sole control of his operations, he became a patriarchal figure within his own family, and when he took on young Phelps as an associate, he was beginning a custom he would repeat often over the years as he found places on various farms and ranches for a number of nephews. He always bluntly assessed their capabilities and temperaments, placing them where he felt they were best suited to be, and he gave none of them any authority unless they earned it. Having lost his own three children in infancy, he found a way to play something of a father's role by helping various members of his extended family. Phelps White proved to be the nephew who most fully met Littlefield's high expectations, becoming "the Major's most cherished and dependable nephew."[14] He also was the nephew who emerged from his uncle's tutelage as a strong business leader in his own right.

When White "went to ranching" with Littlefield in 1877, he was essentially an untried farm boy, familiar with every aspect of farming but unfamiliar with the world that lay beyond the confines of damp, humid south Texas. Of average height and stocky build, he had a physical capacity for hard work and already showed signs of the self-discipline, moderation, and congeniality that marked him during later years. He was not much given to unnecessary talk.

His first test came in the form of several long cattle drives from Gonzales through Fort Worth and on to Dodge City, Kansas. He was given considerable responsibility, although he was not the trail driver. At the end of each drive, Littlefield was waiting. Not only were all the cattle dispersed to buyers but the horses as well. New horses were purchased for the return trip to Texas, as "horses were very cheap at that time."[15]

By the fall of 1877, a Scotsman named John Holicott, who had been hired by Littlefield, had scouted out a ranch site in the panhandle. White was assigned the task of moving 3,000 cattle, "2,200 of them choice she cattle," to the selected site "five or six miles below Tascosa," along the Canadian River. Wintering on the new range without benefit of a ranch headquarters meant constant hardship, as the men from more southerly climes endured ice storms, snow, frostbite, and scarcity of fuel while living in a dugout shelter. Nor did the isolation of the place mean an escape from the smallpox epidemic sweeping the Southwest. "We kept nine men that winter and all had the smallpox. Seven of us were down at one time. Lots of Mexicans died from it at . . . Tascosa, Salinas, and Boquillas."[16]

White searched the area and in 1878 bought a small piece of land north of Tascosa, where a ranch headquarters was built. He found three other big outifts running cattle nearby and made verbal agreements with their owners about where range boundaries on the public domain would be established. All of the thirty to forty miles of riverfront range used by the new LIT Ranch was public domain, simply claimed for Littlefield by White. LIT cattle ran on both sides of the river. "There were some

Mexicans on the south side, but very few cattle—more horses than anything else. The Mexicans gave us no trouble, as most of them were good people."[17] There were still plenty of buffalo in the panhandle while the LIT was organizing, with hunters working mostly to the east of the LIT range. But within a year most of the buffalo had been taken.

During the years of LIT cattle ranching, 1877 to 1881, Littlefield "moved to Austin and made it his headquarters." He came to the Canadian range about once a year, bringing new cattle up from south Texas.[18] The LIT Ranch was 600 miles northwest of Gonzales and 250 miles from the railhead at Dodge City. The LIT outfit was known for having fast and determined cowboys who would go to great lengths to bring back cattle that drifted away during storms. The outfit also acquired a reputation for frugality; its cowboys got the rather mediocre pay of from twenty to twenty-five dollars a month, wagon bosses got fifty dollars a month, and food rations were not overly generous.

In the late summer of 1878, not long after the July burning of Alexander McSween's house that marked the beginning of the end in the Lincoln County War, Billy the Kid appeared in Tascosa. Everyone there knew the Kid was being sought for horse stealing. Arriving on the Canadian, "he had what he called a race-horse with him. He hadn't been there an hour when he matched a race with old man Rhinehurt's horse, 'Spider.' He was a race-horse and we knew it. We didn't mean to beat him so badly, but when we found out that it was Billy the Kid we thought we'd better beat him good so there would be no squabble." White was one of the judges for the race. "Fred Wait [sic], a Kid man," was the other. Waite claimed a foul when he saw how badly the Kid had been beaten. "But the Kid said, 'Give it up, Fred. We're beat.' We had all bet some money as well as some horses on the race. The Kid and his outfit stayed around there about six months but never made any trouble."[19] While there the Kid became friendly with Dr. Henry E. Hoyt and gave him a fine horse, one of the presumably stolen horses he had come to the panhandle to sell.

By 1881 the panhandle was filling up with cattlemen, and foreign investors were paying good prices for both land and livestock. Littlefield himself had been approached by deal-makers suggesting that he buy the public domain he was using in order to insure it would remain under his control. He had refused. But when given the opportunity to sell the LIT cattle, ranch headquarters, and grazing rights to a group of Scottish investors, he accepted the offer of $248,000, of which $100,000 was paid in cash. Eventually it was discovered that the middleman who brokered the sale had cheated the investors, and they actually paid twice the amount received by Littlefield. In 1885 the case went to court, and with the aid of written testimony given by White, the broker was forced to pay back the excess charges.[20]

Although Littlefield had cattle on numerous ranges scattered throughout Texas at the time he closed out the LIT, his actions indicate that even at the time of the sale he was planning to expand rather than retrench. Almost immediately he began buying more cattle, and by the fall of 1881 White was searching out a new ranch location, this time in New Mexico. The Pecos Valley and its adjacent range was now known to be ideal cattle territory, possessing water, grass, available public domain, and cattle trails to markets and railheads. White first saw the Pecos Valley in "a year of plentiful moisture and lush green range."[21] Convinced that the environment was right for his purposes, White negotiated to buy the Bosque Grande ranch property thirty miles south of Fort Sumner on the Pecos that once had been occupied by John Chisum. "There was no one at Bosque Grande at that time, but the land had been filed on by A. C. Rogers. He had sold it to Mrs. Ella Calfee, a sister of Capt. J. C. Lea, and I gave her ten dollars an acre for the one hundred and sixty acres. She had a good four-room house and a stable that had belonged to John Chisum. That was a good price for the land, but we wanted the location."[22]

With this transaction, White "launched the last and most extensive of the Littlefield ranching ventures upon its long and successful career."[23] Tom White had joined his brother at Bosque Grande, and together they went to Kyle, Texas, where Littlefield was holding a large number of cattle he had bought in Louisiana for "a dollar and a half a head . . . My brother Tom and I bought about four thousand of them at eight dollars a head." These cattle were the basis of the herd they drove to the Pecos in 1882, going from Kyle "out by Fort Griffin, the Double Mountain Fork, and up Running Water, and across to the Pecos at Fort Sumner." In the meantime Littlefield took another twenty-two hundred cattle to Dodge City, but when he failed to sell them, White went to Kansas and bought them for the Pecos herd, arriving back at Bosque Grande in September 1882. In the spring of 1883, these cattle were driven to Deer Trail, Colorado, and sold "for twenty dollars a round."[24]

To build up the herd, additional cattle were acquired. "I bought a herd of a little over a thousand head from Roger Sikes, of Colorado City, Texas." Sikes had wintered the cattle on the Taiban River in eastern New Mexico and was heading south with them when White caught up with him near Seven Rivers and made a deal to buy the herd for fourteen thousand dollars. White gave the cattleman the one thousand dollars in cash he had with him. Then "he and I went down the Pecos to Pecos City, and from there over the railroad to Colorado City, where we were to wait until I could catch the Major, who was out receiving cattle. I was getting pretty uneasy about the matter, as I was still just a boy. But finally one of my messages got to him, and he caught a train and came right up and paid Sikes the thirteen thousand dollars for the cattle and thirty-five head of saddle horses that went in on the deal." Then "a herd came up from Texas that the Major had bought, and we put everything into the LFD brand, an abbreviation of Littlefield."[25]

In the spring of 1883, Littlefield made the long trip to Bosque Grande. He sat down with Phelps, Tom, and a senior trail driver judged deserving of a voice in the new operation. By this time Littlefield knew he could trust Phelps White, and he named him manager of the LFD. In also giving both Phelps and Tom a financial stake in the ranch, he was undoubtedly aware that he was increasing their zeal to make it profitable. Tom had $250 in cash assets; Littlefield said he could have $18,000 in stock. Phelps was told he could use the $10,000 assigned him under terms of the sale of another ranch and acquire $60,000 in stock.[26] With Littlefield, Phelps and his brother then organized the Littlefield Cattle Company as a partnership. "We intended to incorporate it, but the laws of New Mexico would have caused us so much red tape that we decided to operate as a partnership." White considered that under the terms of the partnership, "Tom and I owned a quarter each, and the Major owned a half interest."[27]

From his palatial Victorian brick house in Austin, Littlefield sent frequent letters to White at Bosque Grande. Written quickly and in unpretentious style, the letters were not aimed at telling White how to run the LFD but were intended to tell him everything possible to know about the business of breeding, raising, and selling cattle. For his part young White was now a true cowman. He loved the dusty, dirty, brawling business of running range cattle and was a fully involved member of his cowboy outfit, even acting as blacksmith for the ranch's many horses. There was no room for elitism when the job was handling livestock. White proved eminently suited to running the LFD precisely because, in spite of his family connection and the capital to which it gave him access, he had not been educated out of the requisite ability to immerse himself in the culturally insular world of roundups and cattle drives, a world that in return for the potential profit it offered demanded exhausting attention to every detail in the lives of calves, steers, and "she-cows."

The LFD claimed range that extended some "twenty to twenty-five miles up and down the river on both sides," including Pecos land from six miles north of Bosque Grande south to Lloyd's Crossing, about fifteen miles north of Roswell.[28] By 1882 the Chisum and the LFD ranches "were the two largest cattle operations in the Pecos Valley."[29] South of Roswell the range was dominated by the Anderson Cattle Company, which ran the Diamond A Ranch, and the Eddy and Bissell Live Stock Company, operating on the east side of the Pecos across from Seven Rivers. These companies were well financed by "stockholders who lived outside the territory."[30]

The LFD Ranch generally kept about fifty-thousand cattle on its range. Littlefield came to the Bosque Grande headquarters each year to consult with White. "We bought herds, kept them a year or two, and then sold lots of steers to Montana and Dakota buyers."[31] Including cattle from the LFD, Littlefield annually had as many as thirty thousand head on the trail going to markets at Abilene, Kansas City, Council Bluffs, and Dodge City.

When the drought of 1886–87 struck southeastern New Mexico, it spelled doom for many cattlemen. But the LFD survived and grew even larger when the worst effects of the drought had abated. Not only was White a careful manager, but Littlefield provided the financial resources needed to sustain the enterprise when profits temporarily declined. And White just happened to have established an experimental ranching project in 1883 that proved so successful it served as an immediately available alternative site when the drought hit and rendered the previous site untenable.

The experimental project began when White grew curious after hearing stories of buffalo hunters making use of four lakes they had stumbled upon in 1878 out on the Llano Estacado east of the Pecos Valley. Prior to the 1880s, there was virtually no cattle ranching in the barren southeastern New Mexico portion of the grassy high plains that extended westward from Texas. Before the early 1880s, the only cattle on the Llano Estacado "were those which wandered out on the plains in times of lake water from John Chisum's Pecos Valley range on the west; a few which had drifted or been driven away from the C. C. Slaughter and other ranches along the eastern Cap-rock a hundred miles or more to the east . . ."[32] By 1880, however, most of the Indians had been forcibly removed to reservations, and a few small Texas cowmen began entering the area, staking homestead claims and running their livestock on the public domain.

Not long after he first heard camp-fire tales about lakes on the prairie in the fall of 1882, White sent a scouting party to search the area southeast of Bosque Grande. About sixty-five miles due east of Roswell, the LFD men located the series of shallow alkali ponds that had been known as Four Lakes since buffalo-hunting days. And more important, they quickly realized that these valuable watering places were set in the midst of a vast, unspoiled prairie grassland that was "the finest cattle range in southeastern New Mexico."[33] With approval from Littlefield, White sold some of the ranch's saddle horses in Las Vegas and used the money to buy four hundred head of cattle, which were driven to Four Lakes.

Under the care of one lone LFD cowboy, the small herd was the start of a new venture. Over the next few years, Littlefield followed his instincts for expansion and for protecting his competitive edge. He had White buy out several surrounding small ranches, even sending his trusted one-time slave, 'Old Nath,' to occupy one particularly good site northwest of the lakes. Any rancher or homesteader occupying one of the rare spots on the Llano Estacado where surface water was even seasonally available was likely to find himself under economic siege from the LFD. "The LFDs continued to expand by buying watering places from small ranchers or settlers."[34] And even before drought became apparent, White dug water wells and put up windmills; they were the first to appear in southeastern New Mexico. By 1885 the area east and south of Four Lakes, toward the Texas border, was beginning to draw cattlemen, among them the Cowden brothers of Texas as well as a number of Scottish and British investors.

The 1886–87 drought had a devastating impact on the Pecos River. The movement of cattle toward the river in a desperate search for water could not be stopped by cattlemen operating on an unfenced range. Thousands of cattle stampeded headlong toward the river's edge as they caught the scent of moisture after weeks of wandering waterless. Bloating themselves after long deprivation, they died within hours. As the drought worsened, the swollen carcasses of dead cattle filled the Pecos, maggots feeding on their decomposing bodies. The waters of the Pecos became brackish and polluted; if a cowboy put a cup into the river and drew out water he found it undrinkable, unfit even for brewing coffee. Some cattle raisers left; some waited out the years of hardship. Some went bankrupt; many sold out.

The Littlefield Cattle Company simply put its Four Lakes Ranch into high gear. In 1886 "Uncle George, who was the money man of this operation, acquired six townships of land on the plains east of Roswell, with the headquarters being the Four Lakes Ranch."[35] Between fifteen and twenty thousand head of cattle were moved out to the range in 1886 and 1887; until 1894 White kept a portion of the LFD herds along the Pecos. Four Lakes "was a windmill ranch, and I developed it. We probably had forty or fifty miles square in our ranch, and had forty-five mills. Our headquarters was at Four Lakes, and our ranch ran down [southeast] to Lovington."[36] The windmills, spaced about ten miles apart, were bought in Midland and Amarillo and transported to the range by wagons pulled by long teams of mules.[37] The first windmills were twenty-two feet high; later ones were forty feet high. One cowboy served as full-time mechanic, keeping the windmills oiled and in working order.

The use of underground water to insure watering holes made the Llano Estacado range dependable for cattle ranching for the first time. The example set by White on his range of about 1.5 million acres was rapidly followed by other cattlemen. The LFD operation at Four Lakes generated profits that enabled White to invest in irrigated farmland in the Pecos Valley beginning in 1890. But the cattle business was where his heart was. He told his friend C. D. Bonney that he could think of "no more delightful situation" than sitting on the porch of his ranch house at Four Lakes "watching white-faced yearlings" come in to drink at the earthen water tank nearby.[38]

While White was diversifying with farm investments, Littlefield in 1890 was diversifying by opening his own bank, the American National Bank of Austin. The idea had first come to him as the result of numerous cattlemen asking his Gonzales store clerk to hold the heavy bags of gold and silver coins, often in amounts of fifty thousand dollars or more, that were the normal trading method as herds changed owners on the trail. Once he had incorporated his "cattlemen's bank," however, Littlefield quickly realized how many options it provided him in managing his financial affairs.

Littlefield's new role as banker was one of the factors facilitating his enormous purchase in 1901 of three hundred thousand acres of land in West Texas at two dollars an acre. The land he acquired was part of the three million acres owned by the Capital Land Company syndicate, which had established the XIT Ranch in the 1880s. Littlefield's purchase included the XIT headquarters, known as the Yellow House Ranch, and named for the yellowish limestone bluffs in the area later organized as Hockley County. The bluffs and Yellow House Canyon had been used by Indians, buffalo hunters, and Mexican traders before being acquired by investors intent on cattle raising.

The addition of the Yellow House Ranch to the Littlefield holdings had an immediate and permanent effect upon the life of Phelps White, who was named manager of the Texas property. His responsibilities were vastly increased. His wealth was increased. And for many years he would divide his attention and time between New Mexico and Texas.

He might, perhaps, even have considered relocating his primary residence to the West Texas ranch had it not been for a happy change in his personal life. When Phelps White first met dark-eyed young Lou Tomlinson in the Roswell post office where she was working during the 1899 Christmas season, he was a seemingly confirmed bachelor of forty-three, while the refined young lady who drew his attention was twenty years old. She was the daughter of successful building contractor David Tomlinson, who had moved his family to Roswell from Texas in 1898.[39]

White courted Lou Tomlinson for several years, and even before their marriage in June of 1903 she had brought new warmth and spirit to his life. After honeymooning at the Brown Palace Hotel in Denver, the couple returned to Roswell and for a number of months divided their time between the Tomlinson residence and the Four Lakes Ranch.

The operations of the LFD under White illustrate the manner in which the cattle industry of southeastern New Mexico maintained its equilibrium even through times of drought and market fluctuations. The system was characterized by a continuous process of small cattlemen entering the area; small cattle operations being bought out by the big cattle companies; and cooperative arrangements among cattlemen large and small pertaining to roundups and range boundaries. This informal system provided options and a measure of security for participants in an enterprise inherently frought with risk.

In an overall sense, southeastern New Mexico's cattle industry was dominated by a handful of giant concerns. But the existence of the corporate ranches often served to open up new rangeland and test new methods, such as windmills and selective breeding, that could be adopted by smaller operations after being proven practical. And the financial strength of the big companies enabled them to act as buyers for the cattle of small ranchers who found themselves in trouble. On the other hand, their monopoly of the best land and water sources, as well as access to capital, allowed the big companies to drive out their smaller competitors in times of economic difficulty, even when the independent operators would have preferred to stay in business.

For both large and small cattle operations, however, open-range ranching on the public domain presented problems that ultimately proved insoluble, contributing to a gradual shift toward fenced ranching and the leasing or purchasing of rangeland. Open-range ranching meant that when a cattleman committed his livestock to a buyer, he could never be sure of rounding up the promised numbers. A cattleman who wanted to improve his herd with good breeding bulls quickly discovered that his fellow cattlemen derived as much benefit as did his own enterprise. And during drought or severe winter storms, the cattleman could not get to his cattle to protect them.

During the 1890s cattle ranchers found an ingenious way to circumvent the federal law prohibiting enclosure of the public domain with fences. A rancher or farmer could fence only the 160 acres allowed him under homesteading rights. "But since a 'drift fence,' stretched something like a tennis net across the south edge of a ranching company's range, didn't really 'enclose' anything, most of the major outfits had some such fence by the turn of the century." Spread about forty or fifty miles apart, the drift fences "were as important to the next range south as to the outfit whose cattle they caught."[40] Cattlemen paid little attention to one side effect of drift fencing: large numbers of antelope were caught along the lines, attracting hunters who had only to lay in wait and then shoot the animals in large numbers, pile them on wagons, and cart them away for sale as meat.

Useful as drift fencing was to ranchers, however, the Interior Department eventually concluded that it violated the principle of open public land, and in 1902 orders went out from Washington to remove the barriers. The LFD rolled up its fences along with other big companies, and the impact may have been a factor in the LFD's eventual leasing of 150,000 acres of public land controlled by the territorial government.

Not long after the fencing went down, southeastern New Mexico cattlemen received a jolting reminder of just how risky open-range ranching was. During a severe blizzard in February 1903, many thousands of New Mexico cattle were driven into Texas by fierce winds and heavy snow. Even with tremendous effort from experienced cowboys, many ranchers never recovered cattle lost during the storm. Tom White, younger brother of Phelps White, took the lead in coordinating an inventive response to a situation that was causing consternation and even anger among local ranchers.

Garrulous and extroverted, Tom took naturally to politics and in 1903 was an elected commissioner of Chaves County when the blizzard struck. Having "conceived the idea of a county having the right to fence any county road or highway," Tom explained the idea at a Four Lakes barbecue for ranchers from all over southeastern New Mexico. He circulated a petition that was subsequently used to obtain a county road from the southeast corner of Chaves County, on the Texas line, to the west and then north to Roswell, along which fencing was constructed.[41]

As much as any other big cattle outfit, perhaps more, the LFD Ranch gave rise to stories that became the stuff of small legends. Repeated, enlarged, sometimes made into camp-fire songs, the homegrown lore always reflected the hardbitten humor, laconic stoicism, and respect for gritty and even careless bravery that marked the culture of cow country. A man's worth on the range was measured by his rapport with the speedy mustangs he could not survive without. The cowboy wanted his horses as near to wild as possible; they were faster and tougher that way. Every morning as the men gathered around the chuck wagon, a fresh test of wills was reenacted as the cowboy in charge of the *remuda* of horses went in to rope out the mounts selected for the day.

A black LFD cowboy known to everyone as "Nigger Add" was the acknowledged master of the remuda and the subject of many stories. The intrepid horseman, employed as first assistant to the LFD range boss, had grown up on the Littlefield plantation and been trained in every aspect of managing cattle and horses. Add was better than anyone at roping horses "out of the remuda which always consisted of two hundred or more, and about half of them just young, half-broke broncs."[42]

But it was a policy inaugurated by White and held to throughout his years at Four Lakes that gave rise to the most lasting stories. "An admirable characteristic of the LFD people was their willingness to let the boys whom they worked as regular hands have a brand of their own and run it on LFD range free of charge until they acquired as many as three or four hundred cattle at which time they were usually asked to put down a watering place." A good many men chose to work for White precisely because of the opportunity he offered, and over the years close to twenty of these cowboys went on to become lifelong ranchers, raising families on their own ranches as a result of the LFD policy.[43]

The same spirit of largesse did not extend to outsiders, as the LFD simultaneously pursued a fairly ruthless policy of keeping range country free of those called "nesters," settlers who filed claims with the intent of farming on the Llano Estacado. Nearly all of the land purchased outright over the years by the Four Lakes Ranch represented sections that had been filed on by settlers who were subsequently bought out by White.

Even as top man for two sizable cattle operations, Phelps White often found himself facing the same hazards encountered by the hundreds of ordinary cowboys under his employ. One day in the fall of 1904 when he was at the Yellow House Ranch, he and his ranch foreman looked west across the undulating prairie where their cattle grazed and on the horizon saw a raging prairie fire moving eastward across a wide front. The plains were green and the grass was high after good summer rains; high winds were driving the fire forward at a rapid rate. White instantly recognized that the fire, probably started by lightning on New Mexico grasslands, would advance unchecked through his range unless something could be done to stop it. Traveling in a buckboard with a team of mules pulling them, the two men "decided to go and try to help put it out."[44]

With Lou White at home in Roswell expecting their first child, White may have regretted the decision and realized the attempt was futile when he saw how fierce the fire was, extending without break across three or four miles and leaping ahead hundreds of yards at a time. But suddenly there was no way to outflank the fire or retreat from it. White moistened a bandana with water from his canteen and tied it over his face, leaving a slit for his eyes. Then he whipped up the terrified mules and drove straight through the fire.[45] Both men and all the mules were severely burned. "A ranch doctor had to be brought from Plainview by horseback. The doctor was unaware of the severity of the case, and covered my father with vasilene [sic], which was a terrible mistake. When this was removed, it pulled the top skin along with it, and as a result, my father never had feelings in his hands and other parts of his body. I don't think he ever rode a horse, of any consequence, after that," one of White's sons later recalled.[46]

After recovering from his burns sufficiently to travel, White returned to Roswell in time for the birth of his first son, named James Phelps White, Jr. He bought a house from a family named Peacock on a new street lying west of the central part of Roswell. There three more children were born: Zoa Elizabeth in 1906 and the twins Tom David and George Littlefield in 1908.

In 1910 White asked David Tomlinson, his wife's father, to build a new house for the White family. The Peacock house was removed and in 1912 the Whites moved into a three-story, brick house built on the same corner lot where the old house had stood. The house reflected White's wealth and position in the community. It was based on the solidly imposing Prairie Style developed by Frank Lloyd Wright, its exterior dominated by a wrap-around porch with stone columns, a wide beveled-glass front door, and a gently sloping roof of red shingle tiles. Inside the house fine woods were used for lavish woodwork and paneling, and the furnishings included numerous pieces imported from Europe. The library housed many hundreds of volumes, including a collection of works on the life of Napoleon that White purchased from the estate of J. J. Hagerman.

Although he continued to spend part of each year at the Yellow House Ranch, and the White children usually spent their summers there, White was now making a transition from cattleman living on the range to businessman based in town, more dependent upon accountants and lawyers to keep track of a variety of properties and investments.

Even White's cattle operations underwent a major change in the years after 1912. After several decades of steady movement toward fenced ranching, the era of open-range ranching finally ended about the time statehood came to New Mexico. White's response to changing circumstances was to sell the Four Lakes Ranch in 1914 to Roswell investors Ballard and Armstrong, then start a new LE Ranch based on properties along the Pecos River formerly owned by Hagerman. About this time he also invested heavily in the LFD Farm he owned east of Roswell, where irrigation enabled intensive crop raising.

Tom White, the hearty and much-loved bachelor brother of Phelps, died unexpectedly in 1914 at the age of forty-one from an unknown infection. The family buried him in Texas. The father of Phelps and Tom, Thomas Jefferson White, had been living in Roswell for several years. When Tom died, he fell into a grief so deep that "he never recovered and died himself only two weeks after his son died."[47] Sadly Phelps White made the trip to Texas for yet another burial at the family plot near Gonzales.

Not long after Tom's death, White bought his interest in the Yellow House Ranch. At about the same time, Littlefield and White decided to make a permanent division of the entire West Texas property. Under terms of the division, according to his eldest son, "Father owned 3/7 of the ranch, and Uncle George owned 4/7 . . ." White got the rougher west portion, which included three big salt lakes. "He actually acquired more acreage . . . but it was of less value."[48]

White continued to manage both parts of the ranch, the value of which was increased by a new rail line that ran through its northeastern corner. He ran the entire ranch until 1925, when he sold a major portion of his land to a newly formed Yellowhouse Land Company. He retained ownership of the Yellow House Ranch home and its surrounding property. During the late 1920s, much of the western portion of rangeland allotted to White under the original settlement was sold by the land company to incoming farmers in individual sections.

By 1920 White was indisputably the wealthiest man in the Pecos Valley. A thoroughly establishment figure by now—stocky, balding, attired in business suit and wearing eyeglasses—he nonetheless remained accessible and modest in manner, revealing himself still a cattleman to the core by his very manner of conversing. He was an active Democrat, lending his support to such local figures of political prominence as James F. Hinkle, the fellow cattleman and banker who was Roswell's first full-term elected mayor, and who became state governor in 1923. White never chose to run for office himself, preferring to serve as a regent at New Mexico Military Institute, where his three sons graduated and where he paid the costs for several other young men who attended the school.

He increasingly put his money into projects intended to develop the middle Pecos Valley and Roswell. In 1919 Dr. A. N. Crile planted ten acres of cotton along the Berrendo River just north of Roswell. By the next year one thousand acres in the area were planted in cotton. In 1921 White, Crile, and other investors built Roswell's first cotton gin just east of the railroad tracks. By 1922 cotton had surpassed alfalfa as the leading crop of the county.[49] In 1926 White purchased the Allison Building in Roswell, added three stories, and renamed it the J. P. White Building.

The fortunes of White and Littlefield continued to be entwined even after the death of Littlefield in the winter of 1920. He had been ill for a number of years, and White had upon one occasion taken his family to Baltimore to see Littlefield at the Johns Hopkins Hospital.[50] Phelps White was named executor of the Littlefield estate, along with H. A. Wroe, president of the American National Bank of Austin, and Whitefield Harold, a close friend and business protégé of Littlefield. An estate valued at some $10 million was left by Littlefield, who also left a detailed will listing the people he wished to benefit. But because much of the wealth was held in such assets as land, livestock, and buildings, White and his fellow administrators found themselves involved in a lengthy and complex process as they sold property in order to divide the estate among some 150 heirs.

There is no record of White's assessment of whether he was treated fairly in the will of the man who had played so powerful a role in his life. But his eldest son was convinced his father did not benefit "to the extent he should have," no doubt having in mind the fact that throughout Littlefield's career White was a totally dependable colleague who carried out each assigned task with remarkable success and was in actuality a contributing factor in Littlefield's own success.[51]

Phelps White died of cancer at the age of seventy-eight in 1934. From the beginning of his years in the cattle business, he had more access to capital, more options, more security, than did his fellow Texas cattlemen turned New Mexico ranchers on the virgin plains of southeastern New Mexico. Yet the differences between White and the average cowman were always ones of degree, not kind. White came out of the Texas–New Mexico cattle culture and to the end of his days he remained part of it—in outlook, temperament, even in his abiding love for the rough-and-tumble, land-based business of raising the beef cattle that made his corner of New Mexico a richer place in terms of incomes, government revenues, and export production.

James J. Hagerman

Only for twenty years was James John Hagerman involved in the affairs of southeastern New Mexico, and only during the last nine years of his life did he actually reside in the spacious valley he helped make fertile. Yet Hagerman's actions dramatically affected the pace of development in the Pecos Valley, and his name is central to the history of the region.

Hagerman was born on 23 March 1838, on a farm near Port Hope, Ontario, Canada. His father, James Parrott Hagerman, was of German and Dutch ancestry, and his mother, Margaret Crawford Hagerman, was a native of Belfast, Ireland. The couple had two daughters when James John, their last child, was born. Shortly after his son's birth, James Parrott Hagerman left his family with his wife's relatives and went to Galveston, Texas, to open a sawmill with a partner. Returning north after his partner cheated him, he stopped in Newport, Michigan, and decided to open a ship's carpentry shop in the thriving harbor community. In June of 1843, his wife and children joined him in the town, which had been renamed Marine City; subsequently all became U.S. citizens.

James J. Hagerman's father was a strong-willed, domineering man, well over six feet in height and powerfully built. He had little education, worked constantly, and was demanding and uncompromising. He drank heavily in early years, then became extremely religious; his drinking stopped, but his hot-tempered disciplinarianism did not. Although young Hagerman's mother did her best to mitigate the harshness of her husband's behavior, she was unable to prevent him from frequently beating his son with a strap.[52] Throughout his childhood, Hagerman worked twelve-to-fourteen-hour days in the various businesses started by his father. He ran machinery in the furniture-building shop and as a teenager traveled along the lakefront taking orders for new furniture and collecting on bills. He worked in the family gristmill for grain. His schooling was never for more than a few months at a time. There were compensations: sailing on the lakes in summer, hunting and fishing trips in the glorious wooded areas of the north, and stolen hours of treasured reading time, using books loaned him by a bright young employee of his father.

By the time his father moved the family to a farm, when Hagerman was in his late teens, Hagerman had long since determined that he wanted an education and a life far different from that proposed for him by his father. So different were the natures of father and son that Hagerman had once run away in desperation, only to return almost immediately as he thought of his mother and her concern for him. But the unrelenting rigor of farm labor finally drove him to a bitter break with his father. Defying his father's adamant insistence that there was no money for an unnecessary college education, Hagerman borrowed a small amount of money from an uncle and enrolled at the University of Michigan at Ann Arbor in 1857.

He worked part-time in the winter months and throughout each summer for a Captain Ward, who ran a shipping business on the Great Lakes. Hagerman repaid his uncle and paid all of his own expenses through the next three years as he pursued a college degree. By the time he graduated in June of 1861, he had risen from the job of clerk on sidewheel steamers to a position as a trusted colleague of Ward, carrying out contract negotiations with wealthy shippers on behalf of his employer. During this period he made contacts with powerful men who later joined him in mining and railroad investments.[53]

In 1865 Ward began building rolling mills to manufacture railroad iron and named Hagerman manager of the new company. On 12 June 1867, Hagerman and Anna Osborne of Detroit were married. They had met when she was a passenger on one of Ward's lake steamers. Hagerman and his wife moved to Milwaukee, where they built a large house. Both of their sons, Percy Hagerman and Herbert Hagerman, were born in Milwaukee. Hagerman continued his lifetime habit of reading widely in history and literature as well as business and economics, and in the late 1860s he avidly perused every source of new technological information on the manufacture of steel.

The United States was still using domestically produced iron rails for railroads at a time when Britain had converted to steel rails. When the United States placed a tariff on imported rails in 1869, Hagerman knew there was an opportunity for U.S. manufacturers to develop a steel-rail industry, and he began to search for ways to supply the iron needed by U.S. steel makers. Already a man of substantial wealth as a result of his partnership with Ward, the future appeared assured for a businessman so well prepared to exploit the rapid growth of American industry.

But in 1873 Hagerman fell seriously ill, and when a diagnosis finally was made it was discovered that he had an advanced case of tuberculosis. Nevertheless, when Ward unexpectedly died in 1875, Hagerman carried out a complex negotiation whereby he gained control of what few assets remained of Ward's business interests in the wake of the severe financial troubles of 1873. In 1876 he acquired mineral rights to rich iron-ore fields located in the northern peninsula of Michigan. In that same year he and his family first saw Denver and Colorado Springs, during a western trip made to benefit Hagerman's health.

In 1877 Hagerman's new Menominee Mining Company began shipping iron ore to blast furnaces in Pennsylvania. Tonnage shipped from the Michigan Iron Range increased from 10,000 tons the first year to 240,000 tons in 1878, when a profit of over four hundred thousand dollars was realized. Hagerman personally participated that year in the discovery by his company of a rich new vein of ore. Additional mines were dug by Menominee. By 1908 the area had produced 14 million tons of iron ore.

Under Hagerman the mining venture was a tightly managed, solidly profitable enterprise employing many thousands of people and operating company stores in the rugged mining communities of the far north. Among those buying Menominee iron were Thomas and Andrew Carnegie. Hagerman's wealth increased exponentially, and he became a well-known figure of industry and philanthropy both in Wisconsin and Michigan.[54]

But he was losing the battle against tuberculosis. In 1881 his lungs hemorrhaged so severely during a business trip to Cleveland that he remained for several months at the home of Mark Hanna, the millionaire industrialist and Republican Party stalwart who was one of Hagerman's closest friends. In 1882 Hagerman and his family made an extended tour of England, Switzerland, and Italy, during which Hagerman consulted with medical specialists and rested enough to regain some of his former strength. Upon returning to the United States, Hagerman decided he could no longer endure the climate of the upper Midwest, and after completing a highly profitable sale of his mining company he moved his family to Colorado Springs in 1884, with the intention at the age of forty-six of living a semiretired life of cultural pursuits and leisurely rest, sustained by his accumulated wealth.

As Hagerman emerged financially triumphant from his years as a participant in midwestern industrialization, he typified in many ways the nineteenth-century American business tycoon. Certainly he was as dedicated to the accumulation of a family fortune as any of his fellow giant industrialists, and he was as convinced as they were that the individual accumulation of riches exemplified capitalism working at its best. Nevertheless, to a degree not shared by many of the bigtime, self-made entrepreneurs, Hagerman also was convinced that it was not only socially and morally essential but entirely within the realm of the possible to acquire wealth and be a winner in the brutally competitive world of big business without resorting to lying, cheating, or stealing.

Of course Hagerman would not have accepted the case made by some reformers that railroad companies, for instance, were indulging in a form of cheating when they accepted bonuses and favorable land and tax concessions from the federal government. But by his own standards, as well as those of the many Americans who accepted a society of vast differences in economic standing and believed probusiness government policies benefited the society as a whole, Hagerman was an idealistic, at times even altruistic, man. A characteristic Hagerman had in common with many other self-made millionaires of the Victorian era was his fascination with the world of culture, particularly as manifested in the European paintings and art objects that graced his own as well as many other newly built American mansions.

Firmly committed in political philosophy and social outlook by his midforties, Hagerman also had a distinctive personal style. Ever courteous though bluntly direct in his assessments of people, he tended to be formal in manner. He was absorbed in the financial details of contracts, stock and bond issues, and buyouts and sales of various corporate entities, maintaining a disciplined daily regimen as he conducted his business affairs. He drove himself as relentlessly as had his father before him, although without the father's need to dominate the personal lives of those around him. If Hagerman was notable for any single trait, it was without doubt his persistence; he would not give up on a goal, be it a loan or a land purchase, no matter how great the odds at the outset or how many rebuffs he encountered along the way. So consistently persistent was he in pursuit of his objectives that in the end it would appear that their achievement ultimately meant as much or more to him than the financial benefits derived.

Certainly a stubborn kind of pride was one key to his character. In fact, as his own memoirs record, he had early on made some of the captains of industry with whom he had contact his personal role models, convinced by his dealings with them that a business leader could be "broad, fair and generous and honest."[55] A proud young Hagerman had set up for himself an internalized image of the man he wished to be, and whether or not that image corresponded to the reality of the financial kingpins later called "robber barons" by some, Hagerman had from that time onward pursued the realization of what he saw as the "compleat man"—the man who succeeds at what he sets out to do no matter how great the effort or risk involved, and who without resort to chicanery contributes to the wealth of his nation by building infrastructure and producing goods while acquiring wealth for himself and his family in the process.

Colorado Springs, a town of five thousand inhabitants lying sixty miles south of Denver, was situated on open grasslands just where the dominance of the Great Plains was abruptly ended by the looming chain of Rocky Mountains that barred the way to the remaining western third of the continental United States. In those mountains, high along the jagged, snow-capped peaks of the Continental Divide, had been found vast riches in gold, silver, lead, and coal, which were fueling a feverish rush of investors, bringing thousands of men into the region seeking their fortunes, and prompting railroad companies to vie for the right to haul the precious loads of ore to markets in distant cities.

James and Anna Hagerman had in all sincerity chosen Colorado Springs for its dry and healthful climate, and because they had found its wealthier citizens more genteel than those in Denver. Nevertheless by the time Hagerman completed his grand new house in Colorado Springs in 1885, he was being tempted back into active business involvement. He built a bank in Colorado Springs. He became a benefactor and trustee of Colorado College, donating two large campus buildings. And he invested heavily in silver and gold mines near Aspen as well as in several extensive coalfields. The man referred to by one of his local competitors as "a rich, ambitious, restless invalid" was discovering how difficult it was to deny his innate proclivity for playing the high-stakes game.[56]

While mining boomed to its west, Colorado Springs itself was in an economic slump. Hagerman noted that when he arrived, "the town was as dead as Julius Caesar. The old-timers were blue and discouraged."[57] Townspeople feared that unless a railroad was built from Colorado Springs to Aspen, the bulk of ore production would soon be routed through Denver by the aggressive Denver and Rio Grande Railroad Company, which was planning a mountain extension of its line. In 1883 a group of Colorado Springs businessmen had formed the Colorado Midland Railway Company to build a railroad from Aspen to Colorado Springs. But in 1885 it remained a paper organization without tracks, equipment, capital, or leadership.

When desperate directors of the Midland approached Hagerman and offered him the company presidency, his decision to accept the position undoubtedly was influenced by his own need for transport other than pack animals to carry the silver and coal being produced at several of his mine properties. And his subsequent research indicated there was tremendous potential for a handsome profit for a railroad that could haul huge amounts of coal; coke and coal were in strong demand for use by local ore smelters, and there was also a growing market for coal in such power-hungry growth centers as Kansas City and St. Louis. Under Hagerman's direction, the company set its sights on a 240-mile standard-gauge line from the Aspen-Leadville mining district to Colorado Springs, where it would connect with track owned by either the Atchison Topeka and Santa Fe or the Denver and Rio Grande, both of which had north-south lines passing through Colorado Springs.

Hagerman plunged with his usual confidence into the daunting task of enlisting working capital, buying steel rail and railroad ties, obtaining engineering surveys, and even signing up in advance the future freight customers for his railroad. Perhaps he was buoyed by news that the Giant Mine near Aspen in which he owned an interest had struck "a large deposit of ore containing about 40 ounces of silver to the ton, and 38% of lead."[58] Hagerman wrote hundreds of lengthy letters in his own hand to investors, engineers, bankers, company directors, and political leaders concerning the railroad and his proposals for it.

Writing to his longtime associate John H. Van Dyke of Milwaukee in July of 1885, Hagerman, who at that very moment had his agent in London negotiating for a $7 million British investment, said, "If we get the money, we propose to show that at least one R.R. can be honestly built in Colorado. It would be unique in the history of the state, if we except the C.B.&Q . . ."[59] Although he was constantly on the lookout for a "good typist" who would be "pleasant to have around," Hagerman usually kept the ones he hired for only a few days before returning to writing his own letters.[60]

Even with some success at raising money among American investors, it was a disheartening blow when it became clear in the fall of 1885 that the British investment had fallen through. One by one each of Hagerman's agents had failed to put together the sufficient number of backers for the Midland. In January 1886 Hagerman went to New York himself, traveling by private railroad car. He remained in the city through the end of March, staying at his customary lodging, the Fifth Avenue Hotel, and holding meetings day and night. Succeeding where his men had failed, he secured commitments for $1.5 million, which would pay for half the initial track. By April he had raised another $7 million, an amount sufficient to commence construction.[61] Among the investors was Charles A. Otis, Cleveland steel manufacturer and Hagerman's lifelong friend. Otis also invested with Hagerman in silver mines and in Hagerman's later railroad and irrigation projects in New Mexico.

Following complex negotiations concerning coalfields and rights-of-way, construction of the Midland began. By December of 1886 three miles of rail had been laid west of Colorado Springs, and grading near Leadville was under way. The Midland was geographically the most difficult to build of any railroad in the country up to that time, requiring numerous long tunnels and bridges through and across treacherous high country, all built under harrowing weather conditions and mostly with backbreaking manual labor. By early 1887 Hagerman felt enough progress was being made to place orders with the Pullman Palace Car Company of Illinois for one thousand freight cars, thirty-five passenger cars, and many heavy locomotives with the most powerful engines being built.[62] Several engines would be needed to pull one train up the steep curves of the new rail line; Hagerman knew, of course, that the need to use extra fuel and more than one engine per train would take its toll on the profits of the Midland.

On 1 September 1887 the Midland began to run trains on a regular schedule between Colorado Springs and Leadville, 135 miles to the west.

On 3 November, as work continued on the last section into Aspen, Hagerman wrote the company's Washington attorney, "when the last rail is driven I will rejoice. The task of building the Midland has been very absorbing, and very hard on a man who came to Colorado for his health."[63] By February of 1888 the line was finished to Aspen. In twenty-three months a total of 238 miles of rail line had been laid through some of the highest mountains in the nation.

The Midland was the first standard-guage railroad to cross the Continental Divide in Colorado. The first passenger train made the trip from Colorado Springs to Aspen in the scheduled time of exactly twelve hours, covering a distance of 216.2 miles. The train crossed the Continental Divide by means of the 2,164-foot-long Hagerman Tunnel, built just 500 feet from the top of the pass, at an altitude of 11,528 feet. Hagerman was ill with exhaustion by the time of completion, and for all his feeling of satisfaction at having done what he set out to do, the edge was taken off his victory by his longtime rival, the Denver and Rio Grande, which had beaten the Midland to Aspen in November with a narrow-guage line built from Denver.

Although Hagerman declined for health reasons to accept the company's request that he continue serving as president, he remained on the board of directors as one of the largest stockholders and had a deciding voice in the railroad's management. The Midland made money from the start. Even so, its profits did not meet Hagerman's high expectations, and as early as 1889 he concluded "the greatest profit for himself and his associates would come from the sale of the road to a big railroad system."[64] The market for railroads was strong, particularly for profitable lines with assurance of silver, coal, and coke freight. For the year ending 30 June 1890, the Colorado Midland paid $556,437.69 in interest and taxes and had net earnings of $558,943.21.

After months of bargaining that resulted in a stock-buyout transaction meeting Hagerman's requirements, the Midland was bought by the Atchison Topeka and Santa Fe Railroad Company in early 1890. In order to avoid a sale to the Denver and Rio Grande, which he feared would raise freight rates on mining production, Hagerman agreed to a stock purchase that favored him and the original Midland investors while paying less per share to later investors. Hagerman justified this arrangement as a necessary sacrifice, if he was to honor the commitment made by him to those who risked capital at the start of the venture.

CHAPTER NINE

INTO NEW MEXICO

Hagerman took the initial steps that led to his involvement in the Pecos Valley of southeastern New Mexico at the very time he was tenaciously pursuing an advantageous sale of the Colorado Midland Railway Company. But with a variety of lucrative mining investments still requiring his attention even after conclusion of the railroad-building episode, he was hardly a man on the lookout for investment opportunities. In fact his first moves in the direction of New Mexico were cautious ones, for in 1889 Hagerman knew little of the territory and its history, politics, land, or economy.

Even so his considerable entrepreneurial energies had been aroused immediately, when almost by accident he was introduced in mid-1889 by his friend Robert Weems Tansill to a singularly persuasive promoter by the name of Charles B. Eddy. Tansill, who had made his fortune manufacturing the famous "Punch" cigar in Chicago, already had invested in the fledgling irrigation company on the Pecos headed by Eddy in partnership with Pat Garrett, the would-be businessman and erstwhile lawman who even then was in the midst of what would prove to be a losing campaign to become the first sheriff of the new Chaves County.

With his company's irrigation projects half completed and funding all but depleted, the ever-bold Eddy had traveled to Colorado Springs looking for more capital. It was Tansill's idea to bring Hagerman and Eddy together on the off chance that the deep-pocketed industrialist might be interested in a new venture. The first meeting between Eddy and Hagerman may well have taken place in the ornately furnished, book-lined office study of the millionaire's three-story stone mansion, a setting that could only have reinforced Eddy's hope that here at last might be the pot of gold at the end of his rainbow.

Just thirty-two years old when he met Hagerman, the dapper and loquacious Eddy was a native of New York who already had made his mark by organizing one of New Mexico's biggest cattle companies, the Eddy Bissell Live Stock Company. Well financed by eastern investors, Eddy controlled more than twenty thousand acres of riverfront range in Lincoln County, and as a participant later that year in New Mexico's 1889 Constitutional Convention he would help territorial Republicans write tax and land provisions insuring favorable treatment for the giant cattle concerns in the event statehood were granted.

But none of that was enough for Eddy, a restless man who had no intentions of settling down permanently as a bigtime cattleman, even one with political influence. A lifelong bachelor who never put down real roots in the West, Eddy traveled incessantly to meet with capitalist backers, dressed in suits and stiff white collars even when conducting his affairs in Pecos country, and was at heart a schemer and a dreamer, whose strength lay in designing business projects and convincing others to finance them rather than in managing them once they existed.

When he sat down to talk with Hagerman, a man almost twenty years his senior and light-years ahead of him in solid business accomplishments, Eddy ostensibly was seeking only some relatively modest backing for an irrigation project. But in reality Eddy was by 1889 obsessed with something far larger and more audacious; he was convinced that simultaneous construction of railroads and large-scale irrigation projects would transform the wilderness of the Pecos valley range almost instantaneously into a mecca of prosperous towns, farms, and ranches. Taking full advantage of the rare opportunity to share his scheme with a man of Hagerman's experience and wealth, Eddy managed over the course of his stay in Colorado Springs to convince Hagerman that he should see the broad valley of potential riches for himself.

Anna Hagerman, an attractive woman of lively intelligence who shared her husband's devotion to reading and the arts, was far from being a mere silent partner in their marriage. Although she was by nature intensely loyal and had fully supported her husband as he struck out in new and sometimes risk-frought directions during the course of his career, she found herself beset with previously unknown concerns as she quietly observed Charles B. Eddy and took note of his affect upon her husband. Unhesitatingly she expressed her reservations about the man himself and about the risks associated with the projects he proposed. Addressing her husband by his middle name, John, as that was the name she had always preferred and used, she cautioned against a journey to the Pecos Valley, admitting that Eddy was unsurpassed as a salesman but noting there might be a touch of "Svengali" in him. John listened; then he made his decision.

In the fall of 1889 he boarded a train and went south as far as Toyah, Texas. There he was met by Tansill and Eddy, and together the three men traveled by horse-drawn buggy a hundred miles up the Pecos River to the Seven Rivers headquarters of the Eddy cattle ranch.[65] The baking heat of the summer months had given way to the gloriously calm coolness of a typical southern autumn, the kind rarely spoiled by the hints of raw winter that can mar fall days in more northerly climes. The landscape of river, plain, and mountain shimmered with the delicately muted

CHAPTER NINE

colors of a semiarid Southwest that was an entirely new experience for Hagerman. The visual impact of the journey was reinforced by a constant flow of information, all favorable, and a steady stream of verbal imagery, all future-oriented, coming from Hagerman's enthusiastic host.

Hagerman's response to the opportunities he saw in the partially completed irrigation projects on the Pecos was to present Eddy with a forty-thousand-dollar check for investment in the Pecos Valley Irrigation Company. It was the first of some $5 million that Hagerman would eventually sink into his southeastern New Mexico development efforts. Shortly after he returned to Colorado Springs, company stockholders met in Chicago and voted to move the company headquarters to Colorado Springs. Hagerman was elected president and Eddy vice-president. Pat Garrett was not given an executive position and from that time onward played little role in project management.

Hagerman reorganized the company as the Pecos Valley Irrigation and Improvement Company and raised a large amount of additional capital through the issuance of corporate stock and bonds. By the end of 1890 he was by far the largest stockholder in the rapidly expanding company, having invested his own capital to control the majority share of its securities. During this same period, he also directed construction of several large new canals in the southern portion of the Pecos Valley near the new town of Eddy, and he organized the Pecos Valley Railroad Company, which laid rail from Pecos, Texas, to Eddy in time to inaugurate train service in December of 1890.

Properties taken over from the old Eddy-Garrett company included the six-foot-deep, forty-mile-long Northern Canal, extending from the Hondo River near Roswell south to Lake Arthur, as well as several irrigation ditches along the east side of the Pecos that had been built on Eddy's land. Hagerman added to these resources the Eddy Dam and Reservoir; the Southwest Canal south from the Eddy Dam on the west side of the Pecos; the Southeastern Canal south from the Eddy dam on the east side of the Pecos; the Hagerman Canal on the river's east side, twelve miles south of Eddy; and the Pecos Land and Water Company Canal taken from the Pecos near the New Mexico–Texas border and intended to serve settlers on both sides.[66]

Writing in later years about the atmosphere of optimism prevalent during the construction of these works, Hagerman's son Percy said: "The amount of land to be irrigated by these canals was stupendous; I think that everybody concerned, including government and other engineers, Mr. Eddy and the other original promoters . . . all honestly and sincerely believed that it was all possible."⁶⁷ Hagerman himself believed so deeply in the viability of the canals and dams he was underwriting that he went to Washington from July to August of 1890 to personally oversee passage of legislation reversing an attorney general's ruling he thought would do irreparable damage to his Pecos Valley enterprise if left unchallenged.⁶⁸

At first glance Hagerman's commitment seems to represent a sharp break from his previous business ventures. For the first time he was providing managerial leadership, financial expertise, and personal capital in a region where he had no ties of residence. For the first time he was undertaking agricultural development and using methods that remained unproven in the environment in which they were being tried. And he was risking all on the assumption that large-scale emigration of new settlers would make his projects pay for themselves.

Despite these apparent breaks with the pattern of his previous investments, there was an element of natural progression in Hagerman's involvement in the Pecos Valley. There had always been an element of pioneering risk in his entrepreneurial career; he had opened up the Michigan Iron Range, built a railroad where none had gone before, and helped create a mining boom in the state of Colorado. In New Mexico he seems to have seen something larger and finer to do; in the Pecos Valley he had a whole region awaiting transformation, an empty canvas on which to place people, towns, irrigated agriculture, railroads, and commerce. There was the tantalizing possibility of altering the very landscape itself, of affecting the destiny of one of the nation's last frontiers. His overriding sense of confidence was fueled by his powerful ego, by his past record of successes, and by the general prosperity of the nation, of its financial movers and shakers in particular, as the decade of the 1890s began.

By 1891 the extension of the rail line to Eddy and the existence of irrigation canals had prompted a rapid increase in new settlement. Under Eddy's management the Pecos Valley Town Company sold plots of land to newcomers for $10 an acre, with water rental costing an additional $1.75 per acre. A twenty-eight page booklet published by Hagerman entitled "The Pecos Valley, the Fruit Belt of New Mexico," extolled the virtues of the area and showed pictures of flourishing crops of apples, onions, cotton, sorghum, and sweet potatoes.

A Swiss national named Henri Gaullieur scouted the area and spearheaded settlement by several hundred Swiss farmers in the lower Pecos Valley. Swiss investors placed $500,000 with the Pecos Valley Irrigation and Improvement Company in 1891. As settlers began farming, the

CHAPTER NINE

water flow from the Pecos River and a small amount of storage at Lake Avalon proved insufficient to keep the canals full. A larger reservoir was needed. Construction of MacMillan Dam on the lower Pecos near Eddy began in 1892 and was completed in January 1893, assuring a larger water supply.

Profits from Hagerman's gold and silver mines in Colorado were funding the Pecos Valley enterprise. Among Hagerman's properties was an interest in the Mollie Gibson Mine near Aspen. Hagerman owned about 33 percent of its stock in early 1891, when engineering reports indicated the strong possibility of striking a rich new vein of silver ore in one portion of the mine. Hagerman laid these reports before J. B. Wheeler, a fellow mine investor, when he visited him in New York in February. After several weeks of hard bargaining on both sides, Wheeler sold all of his stock in the Mollie Gibson to Hagerman for $.90 per share. In a statement released to the public in 1892, Hagerman claimed that it was Wheeler who first proposed selling his stock, and that Wheeler had been informed of the mine's potential. Wheeler by then had claimed, in a lawsuit filed but eventually dropped, that Hagerman had concealed the truth from him in order to gain control of the mine.

When "bonanza silver" was struck in March of 1891, Hagerman and his associates owned the majority of Mollie Gibson stock. Hagerman had paid $50,000 out of his own pocket for the water dredging that enabled miners to reach the new lode of silver ore. With silver selling for $1.29 per ounce and the Mollie Gibson soon producing "the richest silver ore ever shipped in such large quantity from any mine in the United States," Hagerman began to reap fabulous dividends in hard cash, while at the same time the paper value of his stock also leaped upward.[69] The stock Hagerman had bought from Wheeler for $.90 was now worth $10 per share.[70]

In late 1891, following a bout of pneumonia, Hagerman again took his family to Europe for a rest. And in 1892, with his interests in the Mollie Gibson Mine alone worth between $3 and $4 million, he began to acquire land in the Pecos Valley. Selecting an area already made fertile by artesian water and already well settled by earlier pioneering figures, he first purchased John Poe's large stock farm and all of its livestock southeast of Roswell for fifty thousand dollars.[71] He also purchased all of the remaining Chisum property at South Spring from the Kentucky corporation that had owned it since 1890. Poe was named manager of these properties, with the Pecos Valley Irrigation and Improvement Company listed as legal owner.

Although moving to the Pecos Valley was the furthest thought from Hagerman's mind when he bought the Chisum properties in 1892, the purchase is clear evidence that he was not seeking to end his involvement in the area. Even clearer proof came when during this same period a British syndicate proposed buying all of the infrastructure projects on the lower Pecos; Hagerman agreed to the highly profitable sale, which eventually failed to materialize due to a British bank failure, but "absolutely refused to include all his stock in this deal, although the price was considerably over par."[72]

By early 1893 Hagerman had, in fact, taken two steps intended to strengthen the Pecos Valley enterprise. He raised an additional six hundred thousand dollars in capital with the issuance of new bonds. And he formed the Pecos Valley Company as a holding company for all the stock of the railway, irrigation, and land companies. The reorganization was intended to end the increasingly frequent disputes between managers of the various corporate entities. Eddy's leadership on the scene had proven to be erratic, sometimes bordering on irresponsible. The holding company's board of directors was instructed to resolve conflicts of interest between the divisions and set clear administrative policy.

THE CRISIS YEARS

No actions taken by Hagerman, however, could have lessened the devastating impact of the events of 1893. Some were national in scope, others local. But none could have been foreseen in time to avert their consequences given the existing tools of analysis.

Democrat Grover Cleveland was elected to his second term as president in November 1892. Almost simultaneously with his inauguration in early 1893, a series of financial disasters began to sweep the country; the Panic of 1893 had begun. Its causes included the overbuilding and overinvestment of the 1880s, particularly by railroads and large industry; the sharp decline in purchasing power of the large farming population due to low farm prices; a decline in U.S. exports; and the withdrawal of gold by foreign investors.

The silver question had been avoided during the campaign by the two major parties. The third-party Populists, who endorsed free silver—the unlimited coinage of silver by the U.S. Treasury—won only the electoral votes of a few scattered states, including the four votes of mining-dependent Colorado. The nation had rejected free silver, but many Democrats still expected Cleveland to protect farmers and other debtors by maintaining a currency standard including a proportion of

CHAPTER NINE

silver-backed money. Bankers and other conservative interest groups, on the other hand, argued strongly that the Sherman Silver Purchase Act, authorizing the use of silver for monetary purposes, threatened massive inflation. Cleveland, always opposed to the silver compromise act, agreed with their analysis. In July 1893 he called a special session of Congress and used his powers of patronage to induce a Democratically controlled Congress to repeal the Sherman Silver Purchase Act.

Almost overnight the market for silver collapsed. "Before the Panic of 1893 occurred, it is believed that Hagerman took more than $5,000,000 in dividends from the Mollie Gibson."[73] But without government demand to bolster silver prices, production from the rich mine dwindled rapidly after mid-1893, and the dividends paid to stockholders fell to miniscule levels as the mining company struggled to stay afloat. Worth between $3 and $4 million in 1892, Hagerman's stock in the Mollie Gibson shrank in value by "at least $2,500,000" within a month after repeal of the Sherman Silver Purchase Act.[74]

Hagerman's name had become a symbol of progress in the Pecos Valley, with a new community south of Roswell even naming itself Hagerman in his honor. But as he conferred with his advisors in Colorado Springs, staring at the bleak financial reports scattered before him, Hagerman was forced to the grim conclusion that the millions of dollars in future capital he had counted on to fulfill the expectations of settlers would not be available. And with eastern capitalists and bankers suddenly unwilling to provide money for western development schemes, he accurately foresaw a period of trial by fire, during which the only financial resource left to him would be his dwindling reserve of personal wealth.

The time of testing began suddenly and without warning, when on 5 August 1893 the swollen, roiling Pecos flooded over its banks and burst through Avalon Dam. It was the kind of flood said to occur no more than once a century in essentially dry country. But the unpredictable river that had been called thoroughly treacherous by as knowledgeable an observer as the old Texas cattleman Charlie Goodnight had not yet completed its destruction. Even as farmers and townspeople on the lower Pecos coped with the heavy losses incurred by the August onslaught, a fresh bout of flooding in October wreaked even greater havoc. High waters crashed through the large Eddy dam and totally destroyed it. The extensive network of canals and ditches was ruined, either wiped out entirely or left dry and useless without the dam to assure water flow. Many miles of railroad track also were washed away.

Hagerman did not hesitate before responding. Immediately after being informed of the first flooding, he announced that all dams and canals would be rebuilt. Water rent charges were canceled pending reconstruction. As the damage mounted, he issued a strong statement that the rights of settlers would be protected and all projects, including the railroad, would be rebuilt as soon as possible. With their crops ruined and no way to replant without the irrigation network, several thousand settlers had been preparing to leave the area; Hagerman's assurance that help would be forthcoming prevented a mass exodus.[75]

In the months that followed, Hagerman proved himself as good as his word. Eddy, on the other hand, even while continuing to serve as a vice-president in each of the holding company's subsidiaries, sold all of his stock in the Pecos Valley Company soon after the flooding, as did a number of other investors. In the words of Hagerman's son Percy, "By February 1894 the dam had been restored and the canals were again in operation. The repairs cost about $150,000 and most of it came out of my father's pocket though it required great sacrifices to get it."[76]

Both for Hagerman and the Pecos Valley in general, the period from 1894 to 1990 was a time of completions and adjustments, retrenchments and consolidations. With responsibility for the fate of the Pecos Valley Company resting more squarely than ever on his shoulders, Hagerman began the year 1894 by taking steps to improve the company's management.

Tension between Hagerman and Eddy had been building for some time, and even while repair work on the irrigation projects was being done the two men were in open disagreement over management practices. The association between Hagerman and the man who first introduced him to New Mexico finally came to an abrupt end, when Hagerman announced in a statement to stockholders on 22 April 1894 that Eddy had resigned from all of his corporate positions.[77] Shortly afterward Eddy severed all ties with the Pecos Valley and left the area to seek fresh ground for his promotional abilities; in 1899 the town of Eddy renamed itself Carlsbad.

The role played by Hagerman in Colorado's infamous Cripple Creek Strike of 1894 is relevant to his activities in New Mexico, if only because it illustrates the nature of the man and his place within the broader business context. Hagerman owned major interests in several gold mines that were producing well in the mid-1890s, including the large Isabella and Zenobia mines at Cripple Creek. Growing numbers of miners were joining the Western Federation of Miners, although the union had not

CHAPTER NINE

yet achieved recognition as bargaining agent at any mine. Hagerman and other mineowners strongly opposed unions and bitterly resented the disruptive activities of the union organizers who were infiltrating the mining district.

Hagerman was still a man of great wealth in 1894. But a large portion of it was held in the form of such assets as coalfields, buildings, banks, stocks, and bonds; these investments yielded little cash flow in the wake of the Panic of 1893. Gold mining was Hagerman's single most reliable source of cash income, and the last thing he wanted was a labor dispute and a halt in gold production. Yet Hagerman was among the mineowners who, without consulting the miners, posted notices at mine entrances in January 1894 stating that henceforth all miners would work nine hours a day in order to receive the three dollars previously paid for an eight-hour day. New workers were arriving daily in the booming Cripple Creek area, creating a labor surplus that tempted mineowners to try for a cut in wages that were considerably higher than the national average.

Work stoppages, walkouts, and sporadic violence began almost as soon as the notices were posted. Within weeks virtually all gold mining had ceased. The 1894 Cripple Creek Strike remains one of the most protracted, bitter, and violent strikes in the history of Colorado. Several thousand members of the state militia as well as an untrained army of outsiders deputized by the sheriff of El Paso County fought pitched battles with stubborn, angry miners often armed with homemade weapons, rocks, and beer bottles.

From the beginning Hagerman was an articulate advocate for the mineowners' position. Throughout the strike, which lasted from January to June, he adamantly held to the view that while union men could be hired, there could not be any discrimination against nonunion men. In other words he would not compromise to the extent of accepting union organization of mines.

And yet despite Hagerman's outspoken antiunionism during an episode in which the union was the single channel for effective redress of miners' grievances, the miners and their union leaders accepted Hagerman when he was named bargaining representative for the mineowners in early May. Even among miners his credibility was unquestioned. Mineowners, for their part, chose Hagerman, not the biggest mineowner among them, because they had confidence in his ability to negotiate with intelligence and integrity and knew he would compromise only as it became necessary to end the bloodshed and restore gold production.

Davis H. Waite, the Populist governor of Colorado, was accepted by the miners as their bargaining representative, even though he had called out the state militia and supported efforts to arrest strike leaders alleged to have broken the law. Tempers flared and the tension was palpable during the long days of negotiations at Colorado Springs in late May, which finally led to a tortuously worked-out agreement between the two sides.

Even after the document was signed on 4 June by Governor Waite and Hagerman, a hate-filled force of more than one thousand sheriff's deputies marched on Cripple Creek, threatening to attack miners, while in Denver and Colorado Springs Waite and Hagerman offered differing interpretations to the press of what the settlement meant. But its central points were that miners would be paid three dollars for an eight-hour day with a twenty-minute lunch break, and that there would be no discrimination in the hiring of either union or nonunion miners.[78] While miners had won on the pay issue, the mineowners represented by Hagerman had won on the union issue. The truce Hagerman helped negotiate resulted in relative labor peace for the mining district for nearly a decade.

Hagerman, ever adept at juggling more than one business ball at a time, was building his Pecos Valley Railroad north from Eddy to Roswell even while working in Colorado Springs to preserve his capital flow from gold mining. The town of Roswell, which still had shown only 343 residents in the 1890 census, although probably more than twice that number lived on surrounding farms and ranches, eagerly awaited the coming of rail service. Local merchants had paid a bonus to the railroad company, and when the first train pulled into the new Roswell station on a sunny day in mid-October 1894, its engine named for Hagerman's loyal colleague Charles A. Otis, euphoric citizens turned out in their Sunday best for a platform ceremony attended by city and county officials as well as Territorial Governor William T. Thornton, a Democratic appointee of President Cleveland and a popular figure in southeastern New Mexico.

Shipment of cattle, hides, wool, fruit, and vegetables to the Texas railhead at Pecos City began immediately but nobody, least of all Hagerman, believed it would long suffice for transportation to move only in one direction from Roswell. Full development of the southeast quarter would come only with connection to a northern railroad linking the Pecos Valley to a transcontinental rail line.

"No sooner had the Roswell line been opened than plans began to be made for a further extension to the Santa Fe or the Rock Island in the Texas Panhandle . . . my father gave it his almost undivided attention from the beginning of 1895 until well into 1899," according to Percy Hagerman, who played a leading role in overseeing the project on behalf of his father.[79] Even after completion of the rail line to Roswell, the Pecos Valley Railroad Company consistently failed to show a profit; after it went into receivership in 1896 it became a matter of some urgency to save the railroad by linking it with a national route.[80]

No better proof of Hagerman's commitment to the Pecos Valley exists than his response to the railroad company's precarious situation. Still troubled by his own health, as well as deeply aware of record-high 12- and 13-percent interest rates on borrowed money and the general shortage of investment capital, he nevertheless embarked on what would prove to be the most arduous, harrowing, even humiliating, ordeal of his career as industrialist and developer.

When he went east in 1896, he initially was confident that his numerous contacts among major bankers and investors and his high repute in business circles would enable him to overcome any obstacles stemming from the economic depression gripping the country. But he soon found himself going from bank to bank, hat in hand, put off unceasingly from one day to the next. And as the weeks stretched into long months of waiting for some favorable response, some beginning of a deal to finance his railroad, his despair only deepened when he discovered that he had a fierce competitor in Charles B. Eddy for the limited amount of capital funding likely to go to the sparsely populated Territory of New Mexico. On more than one occasion, Hagerman and his old nemesis found themselves in the same outer office of a powerful banker, each awaiting his assigned appointment; long-existing tensions between the two were hardly lessened by the experience.

Eddy had formed a railroad company that was seeking funding for a line from El Paso northeastward. Part of his plan was to develop coal reserves known to exist south of White Oaks and simultaneously develop timber resources in the mountains. While Hagerman was still encountering rejection, Eddy secured enough funding to enable construction of the El Paso and Northeastern Railroad to begin in 1897.

The line went from El Paso to Alamogordo to Carrizozo to Santa Rosa and joined the Rock Island line at Tucumcari in northeast New Mexico. The company also built from the Phelps Dodge copper-mining area in Arizona to El Paso; and after Eddy bought the Dawson Ranch in northeast New Mexico's Colfax County, the company built another line to connect the ranch's large coalfield to Phelps Dodge smelters in Arizona. The fortune Eddy reaped from this venture was largely lost in later mining investments in Mexico.[81]

Hagerman's dogged search for funds continued until January of 1898, when the Santa Fe Railroad, the Pullman Car Company, and a number of eastern financiers committed themselves to capitalizing a newly reorganized Pecos Valley and Northeastern Railway Company at $9,486,000.[82] When he received the first infusion of $2 million, a jubilant but drained Hagerman wired news of his success to John Poe in Roswell. Hagerman's Pecos Railway Construction and Land Company was hired to build the extension from Roswell to Amarillo, the city that had been chosen as the railroad's terminus after offering a right-of-way and a $20,000 bonus. Construction began on 1 May, and the line reached Amarillo on 11 February 1899, completing a railroad that extended 372 miles from Pecos City, Texas, through eastern New Mexico, to Amarillo.

Completion of the railroad revived emigration to southeastern New Mexico, resulting in a near stampede for lands in the Roswell area. But no amount of emigration could offset the serious problems that had been plaguing the irrigation projects on the lower Pecos River some seventy miles south of Roswell. Low farm prices had a particularly harsh effect on farmers paying for every drop of water they used. Cotton, for example, grew well, but farmers refused to plant it because prices were so low. Sugar beets were planted, and Hagerman built a processing factory in 1894, only to see it destroyed by fire in 1896.

These setbacks were minor, however, when compared to the underlying conceptual flaws that ultimately rendered the entire system of dams and canals untenable, at least in the form it then existed. Unlike the middle Pecos Basin area near Roswell, where tributaries and underground water resources enabled irrigation to be less dependent upon the Pecos River, the lower Pecos Valley near Eddy relied solely on Pecos water. The river proved to be an unreliable source, and the reservoirs created by the dams often lacked adequate water supply. The canals had the capacity to water 200,000 acres; in 1897 only 12,500 acres were under cultivation. Sinkholes sometimes developed in the gypsum strata beneath the reservoirs, draining away precious water. In addition the high salt content of Pecos water had a seriously detrimental effect on soils that already were poor in quality and contained harmful gypsum. And last but not least, all of the canals leaked water from the bottom, causing nearby croplands to become waterlogged and useless.

CHAPTER NINE

After the 1893 floods, the Lake Avalon Dam was sold to the U.S. Reclamation Service for fifty thousand dollars. From that time onward, Hagerman and Otis poured their own money into the Pecos Valley Irrigation and Improvement Company subsidiary of the Pecos Valley Company, in the hope of sustaining it until such time as it became financially solvent.[83]

But in 1898, with ever-larger amounts of money being drained away to maintain the company, Hagerman was forced to declare bankruptcy and allow the projects to go into receivership. Foreclosing bankers sold all of the lower Pecos Valley infrastructure to the U.S. Reclamation Service. Hagerman came forward with fifty thousand dollars and retrieved ownership of the Northern Canal on the Hondo River as well as the extensive acreage southeast of Roswell he had accumulated in previous years.[84]

By 1899 the nation's economy was once again growing. Hagerman was able to sell all of the bonds issued by the Pecos Valley and Northeastern Railroad and use the proceeds to pay the creditors whose loans had financed the building of the line from Roswell to Amarillo. Hagerman owned 72 percent of the profitable railroad's stock shares, while Otis controlled the remaining 28 percent.

BITTERSWEET FINAL YEARS

At sixty-two years of age in 1900, Hagerman was a gray-bearded man with wise eyes and a straight set to his mouth, who looked older than his years. After four decades of effort to reach goals always set for himself by no one other than himself, he was ready to rest, or if not to rest, at least to use more of his remaining energy to enjoy his family, his scholarly pursuits, and the land of the West he had come to love.

The Hagermans sold their Colorado Springs home and moved to the South Spring Ranch in the Pecos Valley. He sold much of the land he owned south of Roswell, retaining only the six thousand acres on which Chisum's old ranch at South Spring was located. And reluctantly, according to his son Percy, he decided he no longer was strong enough to bear all the daily responsibility entailed in running the Pecos Valley and Northeastern Railroad.

In December of 1900 he sold the line to the Santa Fe for "a fair price," and accepted a portion of the settlement in the form of Santa Fe stock as well as scrip.[85] The sale of the railroad did not, however, preclude him from keeping a luxurious private railroad car parked on a siding at South Spring ready for his use, a practice much commented on by the townfolk of Roswell six miles to the north. After the sale of the railroad, Hagerman was left with about $250,000 "clear and in cash," in addition to his considerable assets in land, stocks, and bonds.[86] In 1902 Hagerman replaced Chisum's adobe long house with a new three-story, twenty-room brick residence.

Although the Hagermans maintained their habit of avoiding the limelight and any sort of ostentatious social activity, they quickly proved themselves to be genuinely interested in their new community. Anna Hagerman was a gracious, witty, unpretentious hostess. The Hagermans' circle of friends included Roswell lawyer Harold Hurd and his wife; Anna Hagerman was godmother to the Hurds' older son, born in 1906 and named for his father. When the boy at an early age changed his name to "Peter" Hurd, the kindly godmother sat him down for a little talk about the seriousness of changing one's given name.[87] Hagerman gave forty acres of land he owned in north Roswell as a new campus for the New Mexico Military Institute, and he helped pay for Roswell's first Carnegie library. At the same time, however, Hagerman was not quite able to squelch his businessman's nature. In 1902 he was using Santa Fe scrip to buy up property adjacent to his ranch site. And at the same time, he formed the South Spring Ranch and Cattle Company, which, because Hagerman knew next to nothing about cattle, steadily ate away at his remaining cash reserves for the rest of his life.

Still the years spent in the bucolic setting of the old Chisum ranch brought Hagerman more peace and more pleasure than he had known at any other time in his life. He was held in high regard by the people of the Pecos Valley. For them he was a father figure, the builder of a railroad seen as the linchpin of future development, and a famous man who had chosen their valley as the place he wanted to be in his declining years. Perhaps the esteem accorded him assuaged the hurt of his much-diminished stature as a man of wealth; perhaps it eased his inevitable sense of failure, as he faced up to the fact that he had chased a pipedream when he tried to harness the wayward, erratic, salty Pecos for irrigation. Altogether he had invested some $5 million in the Pecos Valley; $2.5 million of that sum was lost in failed projects. But the genuine equanimity with which he accepted the twists and turns of fate probably stemmed above all from the perspective he had acquired over the years from his reading and his introspective life-style.

Hagerman was, nevertheless, destined to undergo one more testing of his strength in these last years. It was an ordeal that caused a particularly personal kind of pain for this most private of men, for it involved for the first time a member of his family and the issue of integrity in politics.

Hagerman had been an unwavering supporter of the Republican party throughout his career. Having welcomed the 1896 election of William McKinley, whose ascendancy to the nation's highest office owed much to Hagerman's close friend Mark Hanna of Ohio, Hagerman also lent his full support to Theodore Roosevelt, when he became president following McKinley's assassination. Regarding Roosevelt as a personal friend, Hagerman was particularly gratified when his younger son, Herbert Hagerman, was appointed territorial governor of New Mexico by Roosevelt early in 1906.

Roosevelt had his own reasons for naming the politically inexperienced, thirty-four-year-old Hagerman to the sensitive post. First Roosevelt wanted a governor who would be amenable to the idea that New Mexico and Arizona should be admitted to the union as one large state, rather than be granted separate statehood. Republicans feared the possible election of four new Democratic senators from two sparsely populated western states and regarded joint statehood as the ideal solution to a thorny issue. Roosevelt had recommended jointure in his December 1905 message to Congress. But Governor Miguel S. Otero, a McKinley appointee, had continued to campaign vigorously for single statehood. Before naming Hagerman governor, Roosevelt presumably obtained some kind of assurance from him that he would not oppose joint statehood.

Roosevelt also hoped to end the incessant squabbling and power grabs that plagued the territorial Republican party. The feisty and strong-willed Otero had made bitter enemies of such party leaders as Tom Catron of Santa Fe and Bernard S. Rodey, New Mexico's jointure-supporting delegate to Congress.[88] So determined was Otero to dominate territorial politics that he engineered the nomination and subsequent election as delegate to Congress of William "Bull" Andrews, the president of the Santa Fe Central Railroad and a newcomer to New Mexico. Andrews's defeat of Rodey eliminated a strong voice on behalf of joint statehood, but Rodey joined party leaders in Washington in urging Roosevelt to replace Otero. In young Hagerman, Roosevelt saw a man who had never participated in New Mexico politics, was not associated with any of its feuding factions, and would be able to stand above the fray as a unifying force. As it happened, Hagerman acquitted himself in a manner more to Roosevelt's liking on the statehood issue than on that of the feuding factions.

Before his apointment as governor, Herbert Hagerman had spent three years in Russia as assistant secretary of the American legation at St. Petersburg. Not even this exotic experience, however, could have fully prepared him for the tumultuous political scene he encountered upon taking office in Santa Fe. In June 1906 a bill granting joint statehood to New Mexico and Arizona was signed by the president. The legislation called for a single state to be called Arizona, with its capital at Santa Fe. But an amendment to the bill called for a referendum in each territory; if either rejected joint statehood, it would not be imposed. Arizonans were virtually unanimous in opposing jointure. Most New Mexico leaders, all of its newspapers, and many ordinary citizens opposed joint statehood as well.

But Hagerman "had been asked by Roosevelt to do all he could for joint statehood and the record indicates he did."[89] The referendum on 6 November 1906, showed Arizona against joint statehood but New Mexico favoring it by a vote of 26,195 to 14,735. The southeastern counties of Chaves, Eddy, and Lincoln all voted in favor.[90] New Mexico was saved from jointure by Arizona's vote, which permanently ended the movement.

Political factionalism proved to be a far more intractable problem. As a "reform governor" who "had the initial backing of the President against certain territorial leaders whom the new executive labeled members of the 'machine,' " Hagerman did not hesitate to act decisively in cases involving corruption by public officials.[91] He fired Holm Bursum, a powerful Republican leader, from his post as superintendent of the Territorial Penitentiary at Santa Fe, following charges of discrepancies in the prison accounts for which Bursum subsequently paid the territorial treasury five thousand dollars.

Even after public opposition to Hagerman began to grow, and he was accused of supporting a voter reapportionment bill favoring large corporations, the young governor did not back down. His political enemies included Max Frost of the *Santa Fe New Mexican,* an ally of Bursum; Delegate to Congress Bull Andrews; and Major William H. H. Llewellyn, U.S. attorney for New Mexico. Hagerman had the approval of the *Albuquerque Morning Journal*. Tom Catron wrote Roosevelt endorsing the new governor. But Catron later broke with Hagerman over the reapportionment measure and joined the ranks of the opposition.[92]

Unfortunately for Hagerman, he had early on sown the seeds for his own downfall with a decision he made regarding the sale of public lands. Once the powerbrokers of the territorial political establishment had turned against Hagerman, they seized on the governor's questionable ac-

CHAPTER NINE

tion and made it a cause celèbre both in the territory and in Washington. Without doubt the Pennsylvania Development Company matter provided ample ammunition for Hagerman's foes.

In August 1906 Hagerman acceded to the Pennsylvania Development Company's request that deeds for property on which it had acquired options be given to the company following deposit of a ten-thousand-dollar bond to secure the transaction. The land that the company was purchasing included ten thousand acres of public timberland in Valencia County, and the sale was for three dollars an acre. The 1898 Fergusson Act restricted sale of public land to one-quarter of a section per person or corporation. Bull Andrews, who with his associates had organized the company, had found a way to get around this provision after the Board of Public Lands had turned down the company's first offer to buy. Responding to the suggestion made by territorial officials that the "offer be modified," Andrews had a large number of individuals file applications for the land, each asking for not more than one-quarter of a section.

After W. S. Hopewell, representing the company, had deposited the bond and had the deeds recorded in the Territorial Land Office, he went to Governor Hagerman and asked that all the deeds be turned over to him. Hagerman gave Hopewell the deeds in the governor's office at the Palace of the Governors.[93] He did not question the fact that one man, representing one company, had deposited the bond for numerous supposedly individual purchasers and was now taking control of all the deeds.

Early in 1907 Hagerman's enemies began to use the land-deed transaction to discredit him. Even Bull Andrews, the man responsible for the illegal scheme, joined the attack and called the governor's action fraudulent. In March the Bursum-controlled Territorial Legislature appointed a committe to investigate the charges. Hagerman called the proceedings unfair. The chairman was a man Hagerman had removed as district attorney for Santa Fe County. Hagerman's message to explain his side of the affair was ruled out of order by the speaker of the House.

The committee report was highly unfavorable to Hagerman. Forwarded to the Department of Justice, the report "eventually reached the President."[94] Andrews spread the word in Washington that the Republican party in New Mexico was in grave jeopardy as long as Hagerman held office.

Hagerman was called to Washington to explain his failure to uphold the law. On 13 April 1907 he was presented with a damaging report on his role in the matter by the assistant attorney general. A few hours later he saw Roosevelt. The president "appeared visibly shocked." He asked Hagerman for his resignation, having previously written the governor telling him he considered the August 1906 transaction "illegal and improper."[95] Hagerman had no choice but to resign.

He subsequently defended himself in "a series of long letters that passed between him and the President." Hagerman contended that he had turned over the deeds to Hopewell to get compensation for timber already cut. The Justice Department responded that giving Hopewell the deeds merely gave the company a defensible title to the land. Hagerman also claimed that a suit against the company by the territory would have been of "doubtful efficacy," to which the Justice Department replied that the territory had "ample power under the statutes."[96]

Although Hagerman's forced resignation clearly stemmed from a mixture of political, legal, and ethical factors, James J. Hagerman and his son were convinced that it was politically motivated. And in the weeks and months following Hagerman's abrupt removal from office, evidence emerged showing that the embattled Hagermans were more right than wrong in stressing the political motivations behind the affair.

An affidavit signed by James F. Hinkle of Roswell and forwarded to the president by Herbert Hagerman stated that Llewellyn had told Hinkle he had known six weeks before Hagerman's resignation, well before the legislative committee report had reached Washington, that George Curry was to be appointed governor. And in a Roswell speech on 6 August 1907, Curry himself stated that he was offered the post in February 1907, while in the Philippines.[97]

In truth Roosevelt had become disillusioned with Hagerman's handling of territorial politics some time before he learned of the land-deed transaction. "Hagerman is a good fellow, but has made an impossible Governor," the president told one listener.[98] Hagerman's decision to give the Pennsylvania Development Company the deeds to which it had no right revealed the young governor to have been at the least insufficiently aware of the law or else guilty of its outright violation, providing Roosevelt with a specific reason to remove him from office.

Inevitably the president's action ended the good relationship that previously had existed between James J. Hagerman and Roosevelt, particularly after the president claimed in a letter to Herbert Hagerman to know of charges against his father "in connection with his land transactions in the past."[99] The son strongly defended his father's unblemished record, but it was a sad ending to an episode that shadowed the sunny peace James Hagerman had found in the Pecos Valley.

CHAPTER NINE

As if setting his house in order, Hagerman sat down in the summer of 1908 and wrote out a memoir of his life, describing in some detail his youth and its hardships, the beauty of the Great Lakes region, his determination to get an education, and his activities in mining, railroading, and irrigation projects. Recalling the years from 1893, when the silver market crashed, to 1897, when the shroud of economic depression that hung over the country finally began to lift, he said, "how I lived through those years is more than I can understand."[100]

In 1909 the Hagermans traveled by train to the East Coast and embarked by ship for a European vacation. In Milan, Italy, Hagerman suffered a stroke and died on the fifteenth of September at the age of seventy-one. He was buried in Milwaukee, Wisconsin.

Hagerman remains a unique figure in southeastern New Mexico history, something of an anomaly when seen in relation to its other pioneering figures of note. He was one of a kind, for no one preceded him in the particular kind of efforts he made, and no one followed him in attempting the transformation he had so optimistically supported. And unlike many of those who pioneered the region, Hagerman did not arrive early in his career, did not earn his principal wealth there, and did not share the cultural perspective that bonded many in the area.

He was, however, very much the embodiment of the self-made man in nineteenth-century America, with all that implied in the way of raw ambition, grand and sometimes sentimentalized rationalizations of behavior and goals, and the drama inherent in building a fortune that might or might not last into the next generation.

Certainly the most interesting aspect of Hagerman's character and career is his unrelenting but never totally successful attempt to reconcile his equally strong desires to be both a man of substantial wealth and accomplishment and a man of absolute honesty and integrity. In the year 1892 J. B. Wheeler of New York was unable to find evidence to take to court to prove that Hagerman had kept knowledge of the Mollie Gibson mine's riches from him; the fact remains that Hagerman wanted majority ownership of the mine's stock shares before the great silver strike was announced, and he got what he wanted. Perhaps Hagerman compromised his integrity in the cause of pursuing wealth, perhaps not.

On the other hand Hagerman compromised his desire for wealth for the sake of making good on personal commitments, when he poured his money into the Pecos Valley projects even after all hope of monetary return was gone. If only because the integrity that kept him from cutting his losses and abandoning the Pecos Valley was a major cause of his own fortune failing to survive into the second generation, it may be fair to conclude that all in all Hagerman was a man who chose integrity over money when the two could not be reconciled.

Still the factor of ego, even hubris, must not be counted out of the equation, for Hagerman had in common with self-made men of any time an overreaching self-confidence in his own ability to succeed at any enterprise he initiated. Indeed it was in southeastern New Mexico, after a lifetime of hard-won victories, that Hagerman finally had to recognize that some projects, like taming a whole region and a great river, were beyond the scope of any one man in one lifetime. In the end the Pecos Valley changed Hagerman, just as he changed the fate of its people.

10

The Land Endures

NO ELEMENT OF THE GREAT MORALITY PLAY OF THE WESTWARD Movement is missing from the saga of southeastern New Mexico. It begins with the land, a primeval portion of the earth cut by river in one place, heaved upward into mountains in another. For untold thousands of years it was homeland to tribal descendants of those who first entered and peopled North and South America. The Native Americans had no need or desire to institutionalize their presence with either monumental buildings or governing structures; they lived as the land itself lived, responsive to the forces of nature. Europeans began to stake claims to southeastern New Mexico in the sixteenth century, but until 1850 the region remained empty of their imprint, the Spanish and their successors in Mexico having lacked the resources to occupy a vast place where the indigenous people traveled and fought at will. With United States control in 1846 came a military prepared to expend the force necessary to make the American hegemony meaningful.

Into the region during the 1850s came small groups of Hispanic settlers, followed closely by the army troops who built Fort Stanton and ushered in the era of Anglo settlement. The Indians were moved aside and confined on a mountain reservation. The Hispanic settlers, though American citizens, were gradually relegated to secondary economic status. Audacious Anglo men carved out commercial and ranching fiefdoms and fought among themselves for supremacy. Outlaws abounded, working sometimes for themselves, sometimes for the power seekers. Small homesteading ranchers and farmers formed alliances to protest the lawlessness of both the land-grabbers and the common outlaws.

CHAPTER TEN

In the end these small ranchers and farmers joined with growing numbers of town dwellers to form a numerically superior group of citizen settlers identifying with America's burgeoning middle-class values. And the need for local law and government, for commerce and transportation and irrigation, was met by those who were stabilizers and builders.

In its bare framework, this sequential series of events echoes themes that resounded in one form or another through much of the West as the American frontier advanced, repeatedly absorbing those who needed a chance to succeed, a fresh opportunity, or a great adventure unobtainable in settled regions east of the Mississippi River. Southeastern New Mexico also did its work as a safety valve for America's demographic and social tensions, even as it demonstrated as convincingly as other frontiers that inequity was not abolished, only recreated in new shapes, in frontier society.

But, and in this lies the fascination of history, the episode set apart for historical purposes as the southeastern New Mexico settlement period is, like every similarly separable episode delineated by time and place, ultimately nonrepeatable and unique in itself. Nowhere else was there quite the same mix of interacting forces in quite the same proportions. Nowhere else did the same cast of characters influence the interplay of existing forces.

Among the factors that produced the region's unique pattern of development, several are of particular importance. First the Mescalero Apaches who controlled the land at the midway point of the nineteenth century were a true nomadic raiding people, meaning that they not only regarded the land as theirs but that they were ready to fight for it against all who came to take it. Thus the settlement period opened in an atmosphere of attack and counterattack, defensive tactics and a general incorporation of guns and violence into daily life.

The Native Americans were subdued, and the fact of their having once been an outright and constant threat does not lessen the reality of their suffering in the wake of their defeat. They lost most of their land, their hunting grounds, their way of life, their autonomy, and experienced periods of severe deprivation even after they were nominally under the protection of the U.S. government; for the government was not able to fully control the embezzlement of food supplies meant for the Indians, or even prevent periodic attempts by settlers to encroach upon reservation lands. A metaphor for the fate of these people may perhaps be seen in the memory of early Lincoln resident Amelia Church, who in the 1880s was frequently startled to look up from kneading bread to see an unsmiling Indian staring at her through the window before moving silently away in stoic dignity.

Second it just happened that Hispanic settler groups began to enter southeastern New Mexico by way of the mountain valleys at about the same time that the first trickle of cattlemen and homesteaders began to cross the border from Texas into eastern New Mexico. Not only did the two groups have radically different cultures and traditions, but the misunderstanding of Hispanic culture that had long been a feature of Anglo-Texan culture was reinforced in New Mexico, as many additional settlers came directly from the Old South and brought with them an even harsher version of racism and cultural separatism. An odd sort of proof of the racist tendencies accompanying at least some of the emigrants with southern roots may be found by comparing the towns of Lincoln and Roswell in the early years.

In Lincoln during the 1870s and 1880s, many exsoldiers and officers, most of whom had fought with the Union Army during the Civil War, married Hispanic women. Among them was Major William Brady, several times sheriff of Lincoln County, who made his home a center for generally harmonious social interaction between Anglos and Hispanos. A look at Roswell during the same period, where Anglo women were in as short supply as at Lincoln but where the influence of ex-Confederate soldiers predominated, shows little if any intermarriage among Anglo and Hispanic families; they did not even occupy the same streets, as they did in Lincoln, where well-educated Hispanic community leaders such as Captain Saturnino Baca and Juan B. Patrón were elected to public office and ably represented the interests of the entire local population, both Anglo and Hispanic.

And a third important factor characterizing the southeastern New Mexico settlement period is that the region just happened to have one of the last great, open, largely unclaimed public domains during the 1870s and 1880s, when interest in the rapidly growing western beef-cattle industry was peaking among eastern capitalists and foreign investors, particularly from England and Scotland. Together with a few big cattle ranches owned by local interests, large outside-controlled companies monopolized the best range and virtually all of the surface-water sources in southeastern New Mexico.

The dominance of a handful of powerful interests was strengthened into the 1890s by political alliances formed between the companies and members of the Santa Fe Ring such as Tom Catron. The result of this

CHAPTER TEN

early development pattern was a two-tiered economy, with between ten and twelve giant cattle outfits on the top and small cattlemen, sheepmen, and farmers on the bottom in far larger numbers but holding only a small share of the best resources; having only a small per-capita share of the total hard currency in local circulation; and controlling even in combination far fewer head of cattle than were owned by the huge outfits.

Neither the impulse to quell Indians, nor a clash between two cultures, nor the economic and political influence of big money interests was unique to the Lincoln County frontier. Nevertheless these three prevalent features of the local scene in combination contributed to the particular configuration of the area's early history as a settler region. The ending of this frontier period was far from abrupt, and even the choice of the last decade of the nineteenth century as a time denoting the start of a postfrontier period is of limited value, for in a very real sense the twentieth century dawned for all of New Mexico, including its southeast quadrant, only with the granting of statehood in 1912. Even then southeastern New Mexico continued for some time to experience such aspects of frontier life as isolation, dependence upon emigration, and the lack of many amenities taken for granted elsewhere.

Even at the tail end of the frontier period, southeastern New Mexico was the focus of a settlement effort that poignantly illustrated the ongoing powerful hold of the frontier ideal for people seeking to better their lives. In 1901 the tiny settlement of Blackdom was founded sixteen miles south of Roswell by a college-educated descendent of black slaves who had walked all the way from Georgia to the Pecos Valley in 1896. His goal was to establish a self-sufficient farming community enabling blacks from the South to achieve economic independence through individual ownership of land, something most blacks found impossible in the southern states where they were sharecroppers.

Blackdom founder Francis Boyer worked on Pecos Valley ranches and farms for several years before saving enough money to homestead on dry land; he obtained a $4,000-loan to drill an artesian well and began farming. Advertisements placed by Boyer in southern newspapers eventually brought as many as twenty-five families, a total of about three hundred individuals, to join the community. But the new families were unable to afford artesian wells, and local bankers refused to lend them money. Most of the newcomers lacked even the $180 needed to drill shallow wells on their homestead sites. No settlers before them had succeeded at either ranching or farming without access to either surface or underground water.

But the residents of Blackdom were determined to survive; they engaged in dryland wheat farming, but more crops failed than survived. They hauled water for domestic use, vegetable gardens, apple trees, and a few cows from the water tanks of nearby ranchers. They constructed a community meeting house and used it as a church and to establish their own school, when local public schools refused to admit their children.

Boyer's wife, Ella, and their children had joined him in 1901. The Boyers provided temporary food and shelter at their home for every new family. Eventually Boyer was unable to meet payments on his loan, and the bank foreclosed on his farm. He and his family joined the other members of the Blackdom community on nonirrigated land. Soon afterward laws went into effect strictly limiting the drilling of new wells. In 1916 a worm infestation destroyed Blackdom's apple crop, and the prices received dropped from four dollars to fifty cents a box.

People began to leave Blackdom in despair, and even formal incorporation as a town in 1920 could not halt the community's disintegration. The Boyers, who had provided effective and dedicated leadership, left in 1921. Several families moved into Roswell. By the end of the 1920s, Blackdom no longer existed except as a memory.[1] Though but a footnote to the region's history, the Blackdom episode was a vivid reminder that the legacy of the nation's past was not left behind as the national frontiers moved westward.

While southeastern New Mexico's history certainly offers a microcosmic view of some dominant American themes, it also offers striking examples of the influence that singular individuals can have on their times. No better example can be found of the ripple effects sometimes set in motion by one person's actions and personality than that of George Curry, a political figure who emerged out of frontier Lincoln County and went on to play national roles.

Born in Louisiana in 1861, Curry arrived in New Mexico in 1879 after spending several years in the Texas panhandle. His early adventures in sprawling Lincoln County included an encounter with Billy the Kid while working as timekeeper for the huge Block Ranch and a later stint as clerk for James J. Dolan in the town of Lincoln. In 1888 Curry married Rebecca Hughes, daughter of a prosperous rancher, in the Catholic Church at Lincoln, where Curry was serving as county clerk. Ruddy-faced, plainspoken, and totally honest, the six-foot-tall Irish-American Curry was a born politician in the best sense of the word. Rising quickly in the Democratic party, he was elected sheriff in 1892 and in the same

CHAPTER TEN

year was a delegate to the national convention that nominated Grover Cleveland for his second term as president. He was elected to the twelve-seat Territorial Council in 1894 and reelected in 1896. An even-tempered, judicious man, Curry proved how innately moderate his political instincts were when he led the territorial Democratic Convention to an endorsement of the Cleveland administration despite his own personal commitment to the free-silver cause.

Rising star in Democratic politics though he was, Curry made a decision in 1898 that set his life on a new track and eventually affected New Mexico's drive for statehood. As a consequence of his decision to volunteer for the Spanish American war, Curry formed a lasting alliance with Theodore Roosevelt, the expansion-minded, activist young assistant secretary of the Navy who had been doing all he could to strengthen American naval resources to ready the nation for what he and his like-minded circle of influential colleagues saw as America's proper role as a world power.

The United States declared war on Spain on 25 April 1898, and President McKinley issued a call for two hundred thousand volunteers to augment the regular army of twenty-eight thousand men. Response to what Secretary of State John Hay called a "splendid little war" was enthusiastic in many parts of the country, including the Territory of New Mexico and especially its southeastern region. As Delegate to Congress Harvey B. Fergusson proudly noted, New Mexico met its quota for the Rough Riders Regiment, a special cavalry unit from the western territories, before a majority of the states had responded to the president's call.[2]

Curry was one of the first to enlist, and after being commissioned a first lieutenant he organized one of four companies from the territory. He named Charles Ballard of Roswell his second lieutenant, and the two arrived in Santa Fe with their men on 1 May 1898. Curry joined 350 other New Mexicans who embarked by train for San Antonio to the wild cheering of local citizens. Motivated by patriotic fervor tinged with a desire to avenge Spain's sinking of the battleship Maine, the volunteers gave little thought to the ways in which their action would strengthen respect for New Mexico and its people among national leaders and the general public.

In San Antonio Roosevelt joined the 1,000 members of the Rough Riders as second in command. Even before the regiment reached Florida, Curry drew favorable attention from Roosevelt by going outside normal channels to obtain urgently needed feed for the regiment's horses.

As some 30,000 troops prepared to invade Cuba, transport ships off the coast were in short supply, and some units had to be left on the mainland. Curry was placed in charge of supply logistics at one of the mainland camps. Although frustrated at not seeing combat as did the 271 New Mexicans who were at Colonel Roosevelt's side in the charge up Kettle Hill, Curry performed capably as a supply officer and was promoted to captain and commended by Roosevelt and General Leonard Wood.

Shortly after returning to New Mexico in September 1898, Curry joined the Republican party, as did many other Rough Rider officers.[3] He traveled to New York to campaign for Roosevelt in his successful bid to become state governor in 1898. Curry remained a loyal supporter of Roosevelt during his presidency and later followed him into the breakaway Bull Moose party.

In 1899 Governor Miguel Otero appointed Curry sheriff of the new Otero County. But when a call went out for volunteers against insurgents in the newly conquered Philippines in 1900, Curry recruited one hundred men and won a commission to serve as a combat officer, compensating for the disappointment he had felt during the battle for Cuba. After two years of fighting against Philippine guerrillas, Curry remained on the islands as civilian governor in four successive provinces. His administrative and personal qualities impressed William Howard Taft, governor general of the Philippines. Taft gave Curry the job of chief of police in the city of Manila and was well satisfied with Curry's effective restructuring of the police force. When President Roosevelt began talking about replacing New Mexico governor Herbert Hagerman in early 1907, Taft reminded the president of the capable, likable Curry, and the president quickly responded by asking Curry to come home and take on the territorial post.

Before accepting the governorship of the territory, Curry sought and won commitment from Roosevelt to support statehood for New Mexico in an unequivocal manner. Aided by a letter of support from Taft, Curry also obtained a pledge to support statehood from Senator Nelson Aldrich of Rhode Island, the most powerful man in the Senate. After his inauguration as governor in August 1907, Curry proved to be a healing force in territorial politics, managing by his even-handed policies and appointments to allay the suspicions of Hagerman supporters who believed the former governor had been unfairly hounded from office. Curry's standing in Washington was so high that he was able to convince the administration to name New Mexicans rather than outsiders to top federal posts in the territory.

CHAPTER TEN

When Taft succeeded Roosevelt as president in 1909, Roosevelt asked Curry to give Taft his full support. Curry agreed but asked Roosevelt to write a letter that he might carry to Taft, asking the new president to stand firmly behind the cause of New Mexico statehood. Roosevelt wrote the letter; Curry presented it to Taft; and for the first time a plank in the Republican party platform supported separate statehood for New Mexico and Arizona.[4]

President Taft signed an enabling act for New Mexico on 20 June 1910. A state constitution was ratified by voters in 1911, and on 6 January 1912 New Mexico became a state. Curry had played a small but significant part in the final push by using to the greatest possible advantage for New Mexico the alliances with national leaders that began when he and other territorial residents first responded to a president's call.

And certainly Curry must be seen as part of the process through which New Mexico, so long a Spanish colony, so long a U.S. territory, finally became an integral part of the United States. For New Mexico's frontier isolation was gradually lessened by the series of horizon-expanding events that included the coming of the railroad in the 1880s; the Spanish-American War of 1898; the granting of statehood in 1912; and the national mobilization entailed by America's participation in the First World War.

And yet for the sky-swept vastness of southeastern New Mexico, the changes that time brings can even now seem compressed under the weight of two ever-present realities. One is the land itself, which remains an open, wild, sweepingly free and somehow remote interior portion of the continent. And the other is a human community that evolved out of, and still reflects in startlingly direct ways, the legacy of a frontier past that saw ethnic groups, determined individuals, and disparate economic interests engage in a struggle for their place in the Western sun. Southeastern New Mexico blazed with activity from the late 1860s onward as its daunting, varied lands were sought for cattle and sheep range, gold and coal mining, cropland and townsites. The lingering effects of the social divisions that accompanied the boisterously optimistic American settlement are visible even today.

In the mid-1980s the Southwest Voter Registration Project joined forces with the Hispanic residents of several southeastern New Mexico communities and won civil suits that eliminated at-large city council elections, making it possible for Hispanos to elect their own political leaders to represent neighborhood-based districts. In the late 1980s the Mescalero Apache Tribe went to court seeking a larger share of the Hondo

River system's annual water allotment, precipitating a long and bitter legal battle with Hondo Valley residents already using the lion's share of existing water rights. Even old antagonisms generated by the Lincoln County War are not forgotten; in a fairly new book at the Roswell Public Library, some unsigned reader has scrawled in pencil at the end of a chapter on Pat Garrett that the real truth about the bad Sheriff Garrett who murdered the good Billy the Kid has never been told by any book. The frontier legacy is one of an eclectic, layered, evolving society, as well as one still learning to live with the inherent limits of a dry land in which water is a precious commodity affecting the region's economic and population-growth potential.

The human history that impressed itself upon this ancient land remains elusively yet palpably present in a landscape virtually unchanged from a century ago. The events that were pounded into the soil and the voices that resounded in the harmonies and disharmonies of human discourse can seem eerily alive in the very silence of the plains, river valleys, and mountains. On wild, windy spring days, when yellow and purple wildflowers bloom on the range and cottonwoods and aspens turn green along the mountain streams, and nothing visible is different from any other life-quickening springtime, it is easy to dip back in time to the second half of the nineteenth century, when history itself was quickening here, taking hold for the first time in all the millenniums of springtimes. The land is still tremulous with a timeless past. Never overwhelmed by urban populations, it is spaciously welcoming in all its vulnerability; the very dryness of the climate seems to preserve with a kind of brittle delicacy both the rarities of nature and the artifacts of humankind.

Just a short distance away from any of the region's scattered towns, all seems as it was when buffalo moved in shaggy herds to the banks of the silver-grey Pecos; or when possession-laden pioneer families, their hearts holding hope along with readiness to accept whatever would come, gazed steadily westward across the Llano Estacado shimmering before them in tones of tan and green. Because here the past is part of the present, because this is a place still in the process of being discovered, and because the land itself insistently fuses past and present, it may be the destiny of southeastern New Mexico to be forever frontier.

Notes

Chapter 1

1. Peter Farb, *Man's Rise to Civilization as Shown by the Indians of North America from Primeval Times to the Coming of the Industrial State* (New York: E. P. Dutton and Co., Inc., 1968), p. 235.
2. David E. Stuart, *Glimpses of the Ancient Southwest* (Santa Fe: Ancient City Press, 1985), p. 24.
3. Ibid., pp. 35–37.
4. Ibid., p. 45.
5. Ibid., pp. 52–53.
6. Ibid., p. 69.
7. Ibid., p. 70.
8. Warren A. Beck, *New Mexico: A History of Four Centuries* (Norman: University of Oklahoma Press, 1962), p. 33.
9. Farb, *Man's Rise to Civilization*, p. 125.

Chapter 2

1. Albert H. Schroeder and Dan S. Matson, *A Colony on the Move: Gaspar Castaño de Sosa's Journal, 1590–1591* (Santa Fe: School of American Research, 1965), pp. 3–9, 15, 65–67.
2. Marc Simmons, *New Mexico: A Bicentennial History* (Nashville: W. W. Norton and Co., Inc., New York, 1977), p. 36.
3. Ibid., p. 7.
4. Robert W. Larson, *New Mexico Populism: A Study of Radical Protest in a Western Territory* (Boulder: Colorado Associated University Press, 1974), p. 50.
5. David F. Myrick, *New Mexico's Railroads: An Historical Survey* (Golden: Colorado Railroad Historical Foundation, 1970), p. 8.

6. Beck, *New Mexico: A History,* p. 281.
7. Marc Simmons, "New Mexico's Smallpox Epidemic of 1780–1781," *New Mexico Historical Review,* vol. 41, (October 1966), p. 319.
8. Ibid.
9. Ibid., p. 320.
10. Calvin Horn, *New Mexico's Troubled Years: The Story of the Early Territorial Governors* (Albuquerque: Horn and Wallace, Publishers, 1963), p. 84.
11. Ibid., p. 121.
12. Paul Horgan, *Lamy of Santa Fe: His Life and Times* (New York: Farrar, Straus and Giroux, 1975), p. 431.
13. Lynn I. Perrigo, *Hispanos: Historic Leaders in New Mexico* (Santa Fe: Sunstone Press, 1985), p. 62.
14. Myra Ellen Jenkins and Albert H. Schroeder, *A Brief History of New Mexico* (Albuquerque: University of New Mexico Press, 1974), p. 23.
15. Ira G. Clark, *Water in New Mexico: A History of Its Management and Use* (Albuquerque: University of New Mexico Press, 1987), p. 9.
16. Ibid., p. 12.
17. Jenkins and Schroeder, *A Brief History of New Mexico,* p. 23.
18. Clark, *Water in New Mexico,* p. 15.
19. Ibid., p. 10.
20. Ibid., p. 25
21. Ibid.
22. Ibid., p. 10.
23. Ibid., p. 34.
24. Ibid., p. 36; G. Emlen Hall, "Tierra y Agua," *New Mexico Magazine* (September 1987), p. 63.
25. Clark, *Water in New Mexico,* p. 42.
26. Ibid., pp. 49–50.

Chapter 3

1. Sandra L. Myres, *Westering Women and the Frontier Experience 1800–1915* (Albuquerque: University of New Mexico Press, 1982), p. 57. Myres cites this figure from the 1979 book by John Unruh, *The Plains Across: The Overland Emigrants and the Trans-Mississippi West 1840–1860.*
2. Robert W. Larson, *New Mexico's Quest for Statehood 1846–1912* (Albuquerque: University of New Mexico Press, 1968), p. 4.
3. David J. Weber, ed. and trans., *Donaciano Vigil 1846: Arms, Indians and the Mismanagement of New Mexico* (El Paso: The University of Texas at El Paso, Texas Western Press, 1986), pp. ix–xx and 1–28.
4. Horn, *New Mexico's Troubled Years,* p. 29.
5. Ibid., p. 63.
6. Ibid., pp. 93–94.

7. Clifford E. Trafzer, *The Kit Carson Campaign: The Last Great Navajo War* (Norman: University of Oklahoma Press, 1982), p. 66.

8. Horn, *New Mexico's Troubled Years*, p. 105.

9. Trafzer, *The Kit Carson Campaign*, p. 54.

10. Ibid., pp. 63–64.

11. Ibid., p. 36.

12. Ibid., p. 38.

13. Ibid., p. 43.

14. James D. Shinkle, *Fort Sumner and the Bosque Redondo Indian Reservation* (Roswell: Hall-Poorbaugh Press, Inc., 1965), p. 56.

15. Eve Ball, with Nora Henn and Lynda Sanchez, *Indeh: An Apahce Odyssey* (Provo, Utah: Brigham Young University Press, 1980), p. 202.

16. Katherine Marie Osburn, "The Navajo at the Bosque Redondo: Cooperation, Resistance, and Initiative, 1864–1868," *New Mexico Historical Review* (October 1985), pp. 406–8.

17. Simmons, New Mexico, p. 152.

18. Shinkle, *Fort Sumner and the Bosque Redondo*, pp. 52, 66–67.

19. Trafzer, *The Kit Carson Campaign*, p. 243.

20. Edwin L. Sabin, *Kit Carson Days, 1809–1868* (Chicago: A. C. McClurg and Co., 1914), p. 497.

21. Ball, *Indeh*, pp. 216–17.

22. James D. Shinkle, *Missouri Plaza: First Settled Community in Chaves County* (Roswell: Hall-Poorbaugh Press, Inc., 1972), p. 11.

23. Ibid., pp. 26–27.

24. Patrick Dearen, *Castle Gap and the Pecos Frontier* (Fort Worth: Christian University Press, 1988), pp. 8–10.

25. Larson, *New Mexico Populism*, chapter 5.

26. James D. Shinkle, *Fifty Years of Roswell History 1867–1917* (Roswell: Hall-Poorbaugh Press, Inc., 1964), p. 59.

27. Larson, *New Mexico Populism*, p 51.

28. Morris B. Parker, *White Oaks: Life in a New Mexico Gold Camp 1880–1900* (Tucson: University of Arizona Press, 1976), p. 4.

29. Ibid., p. 85.

Chapter 4

1. Horn, *New Mexico's Troubled Years*, p. 45.

2. Myres, *Westering Women*, pp. 75–78. Also see Robert J. Rosenbaum, *Mexicano Resistance in the Southwest* (Austin: University of Texas Press, 1981), p. 5; "Mexican Americans came from a European-derived tradition. Yet the marked infusion of Indian culture and genes" led Anglos to regard them as inferior, an attitude similar to that displayed toward African-Americans and Indians.

3. James D. Shinkle, *Reminiscences of Roswell Pioneers* (Roswell: Hall-Poorbaugh Press, Inc., 1966), p. 124.

4. Ibid., p. 98.
5. Ibid.
6. Ibid., p. 92.
7. Shinkle, *Missouri Plaza*, p. 15.
8. Williams A. Keleher, *The Fabulous Frontier: Twelve New Mexico Items* (Albuquerque: University of New Mexico Press, 1982), p. 147.
9. Ibid.
10. Information concerning the origins of early Roswell-area residents was obtained from family records at the Chaves County Historical Museum Archives and from a survey of the biographical material contained in two books by James F. Shinkle, *Fifty Years of Roswell History, 1867–1917* and *Reminiscences of Roswell Pioneers,* published in 1964 and 1966, respectively, by Hall-Poorbaugh Press, Inc., Roswell. It is worthy of note that in *Reminiscences,* close to 75 percent of the early settlers represented make statements about their emigration to the Pecos Valley from a southern or border state.
11. Shinkle, *Reminiscences,* pp. 179–80.
12. Ibid., p. 20.
13. Larson, *New Mexico Populism,* chapter 12.
14. Williams A. Keleher, *Violence in Lincoln County: 1869–1881* (Albuquerque: University of New Mexico Press, 1982), p. 15.
15. Ibid., p. 17.
16. Ibid., p. 19.
17. Shinkle, *Reminiscences,* p. 180.
18. Larson, *New Mexico Populism,* p. 51.
19. Keleher, *Violence in Lincoln County,* p. 13.
20. Shinkle, *Reminiscences,* pp. 96–97.
21. Keleher, *Violence in Lincoln County,* pp. 13–15.
22. Maurice G. Fulton, *History of the Lincoln County War* (Tucson: University of Arizona Press, 1984), p. 23.
23. Shinkle, *Fifty Years of Roswell History,* p. 74.
24. Ibid., p. 189.
25. Ibid., pp. 53–54.
26. Larson, *New Mexico Populism,* p. 7.
27. Keleher, *The Fabulous Frontier,* p. 113.
28. Shinkle, *Reminiscences,* p. 60.
29. Jenkins and Schroeder, *A Brief History of New Mexico,* p. 61.
30. Ibid., pp. 57–61.
31. Clark, *Water in New Mexico,* p. 34.
32. Larson, *New Mexico Populism,* p. 89.
33. Ibid., p. 11.
34. *Historical Statistics of the United States,* vol. 1 (U.S. Department of Commerce, 1975), p. 32.
35. Larson, *New Mexico Populism,* p. 52.

36. Shinkle, *Reminiscences*, pp. 65–66.
37. Larson, *New Mexico Populism*, p. 52.
38. Ibid., p. 9.
39. Ibid., p. 10.
40. Fulton, *Lincoln County War*, p. 66.
41. Larson, *New Mexico Populism*, p. 99.
42. Ibid., p. 153.
43. Ibid., p. 177.

Chapter 5

1. Shinkle, *Reminiscences*, p. 50.
2. Harwood P. Hinton, Jr., "John Simpson Chisum, 1877–84," [part 1] *New Mexico Historical Review* (July 1956), pp. 184–85.
3. Elvis Fleming, "Book Provides Insight about Chisum's Children," *Roswell Daily Record* (10 April 1989). The information in this article comes from a book published in 1984 by Mary Clarke titled *John Chisum, Jinglebob King of the Pecos*, and a 1976 interview with Eugie Jones Thomas, who claimed to be a granddaughter of Chisum.
4. Hinton, "John Simpson Chisum," pp. 190–91.
5. Lily Klasner, *My Girlhood among Outlaws* (Tucson: University of Arizona Press, 1981), p. 223.
6. James Phelps White, "Recollections of Ranching Operations in New Mexico with George W. Littlefield," unpublished manuscript of interview conducted by J. Evetts Haley with White, Roswell, N.M., 2 March 1933, p. 1. Manuscript in possession of J. Phelps White III, of Roswell, N.M.
7. Robert M. Utley, *Four Fighters of Lincoln County* (Albuquerque: University of New Mexico Press, 1986), p. 4.
8. Fulton, *Lincoln County War*, p. 37.
9. Ibid., p. 43.
10. Ibid., p. 96.
11. John P. Wilson, *Merchants, Guns and Money* (Santa Fe: Museum of New Mexico Press, 1987), p. 58.
12. This account by Chisum may be misleading. Cattleman J. Phelps White, who knew Chisum well and had high respect for him, nonetheless firmly believed that Chisum did enter into a business partnership with the packers. White said in his 1933 "Recollections": "They got credit in New York, killed his cattle, and packed them. He quit the firm but never dissolved it according to law . . . The creditors went to court, got a judgment, and the only one solvent was Chisum. Tom Catron, the New Mexico lawyer, happened to be in New York, and he got the judgment and brought it back to Santa Fe, recorded it, and kept it alive."

13. Harwood P. Hinton, Jr., "John Simpson Chisum, 1877–84," [part 2] *New Mexico Historical Review* (October 1956), pp. 312–13. After a number of years, the case was decided in favor of Chisum's creditors, and the money judged to be due was paid from the estate of Chisum following his death.
14. Wilson, *Merchants, Guns and Money*, p. 84.
15 Hinton, "John Simpson Chisum," part 2, pp. 314–15.
16. Ibid., p. 327.
17. Klasner, *My Girlhood*, pp. 296–97.
18. Hinton, "John Simpson Chisum," part 2, pp. 331–32.
19. White, "Recollections," 1933, p. 22.
20. Klasner, *My Girlhood*, p. 298.
21. Harwood P. Hinton, "John Simpson Chisum, 1877–84," [part 3] *New Mexico Historical Review* (January 1957), p. 62.
22. Klasner, *My Girlhood*, p. 308.
23. Wilson, *Merchants, Guns and Money*, p. 29.
24. Ibid., pp. 29–30.
25. Utley, *Four Fighters*, p. 3.
26. Wilson, *Merchants, Guns and Money*, pp. 38–39.
27. Ibid., p. 40.
28. Ibid., pp. 56–57.
29. Fulton, *Lincoln County War*, p. 48.
30. Ibid., p. 105.
31. Utley, *Four Fighters*, p. 3.
32. Wilson, *Merchants, Guns and Money*, pp. 30–31.
33. Ibid., pp. 33–34.
34. Fulton, *Lincoln County War*, pp. 50–51.
35. Ibid., p. 51.
36. Philip J. Rasch, "The People of the Territory of New Mexico versus the Santa Fe Ring," *New Mexico Historical Review* (April 1972), pp. 85–86.
37. Fulton, *Lincoln County War*, p. 53.

Chapter 6

1. Irving McKee, *"Ben Hur" Wallace: The Life of General Lew Wallace* (Berkeley: University of California Press, 1947). Cited in Horn, *New Mexico's Troubled Years*, p. 200.
2. Keleher, *Violence in Lincoln County*, p. 55. A McSween descendent living on Prince Edward Island in the 1940s told Keleher that McSween, who emigrated from Scotland in the 1830s, had an adopted son known as "Aleck."
3. Fulton, *Lincoln County War*, pp. 56–57.
4. Frederick W. Nolan, *The Life and Death of John Henry Tunstall* (Albuquerque: University of New Mexico Press, 1965), pp. 152–54.
5. Ibid., p. 213.

6. Wilson, *Merchants, Guns and Money*, p. 71.
7. Fulton, *Lincoln County War*, p. 105.
8. Wilson, *Merchants, Guns and Money*, pp. 74–75.
9. Fulton, *Lincoln County War*, p. 110.
10. Ibid., pp. 113–14.
11. Ibid., pp. 117–18.
12. Wilson, *Merchants, Guns and Money*, p. 84.
13. Fulton, *Lincoln County War*, p. 137.
14. Wilson, *Merchants, Guns and Money*, p. 85.
15. Fulton, *Lincoln County War*, pp. 173–74.
16. It should be noted that at the time of McSween's death, and even when McSween's estate was settled, the Emil Fritz insurance proceeds remained unaccounted for, and there is no record that they were ever turned over to the brother and sister of Fritz. See Keleher, *Violence in Lincoln County*, p. 149.
17. Norman Cleaveland with George Fitzpatrick, *The Morleys* (Albuquerque: Calvin Horn Publisher, Inc., 1971), pp. 134–35.
18. Ibid., p. 145.
19. Rasch, "The People of the Territory versus the Ring," p. 185.
20. Fulton, *Lincoln County War*, p. 229.
21. Keleher, *Violence in Lincoln County*, pp. 140–41. Different historians have given different numbers of McSween fighters, Fulton stating that between fifty and sixty men made the final stand with McSween.
22. Fulton, *Lincoln County War*, p. 250.
23. Utley, *Four Fighters*, p. 46.
24. Fulton, *Lincoln County War*, pp. 258–59.
25. Robert M. Utley offers this assessment of the effect of Dudley's presence during the gunfight in *Four Fighters of Lincoln County* and *High Noon in Lincoln* (Albuquerque: University of New Mexico Press, 1987).
26. Fulton, *Lincoln County War*, p. 273.
27. Wilson, *Merchants, Guns and Money*, p. 129.
28. Cleaveland, *The Morleys*, p. 156.
29. Horn, *New Mexico's Troubled Years*, p. 194.
30. Cleaveland, *The Morleys*, p. 156.

Chapter 7

1. In lieu of actual money from Tunstall's father, she was given the small ranch property formerly belonging to Dick Brewer. With the six hundred dollars she received from the sale of this property, she entered the cattle business, and her financial situation eventually was stabilized when she received the proceeds from McSween's life-insurance policy. In later years she operated a successful cattle ranch at White Oaks, where she resided for many years. Her second marriage, in 1880, to Lincoln surveyor George B. Barber was dissolved by divorce in 1891.

2. Fulton, *Lincoln County War*, p. 324.

3. Utley, *Four Fighters*, p. 49. After being relieved of command, Dudley requested a military board of inquiry to clear his name. The request was granted, and by July 1879, following a lengthy hearing during which numerous participants in the Lincoln County War were witnesses, Dudley was cleared of charges of wrongful action, although the report recognized the impact the presence of troops had had on the course of the 19 July 1878 gunfight and fire. Several months later Dudley also won the civil suit brought against him by Mrs. McSween.

4. Fulton, *Lincoln County War*, p. 333.

5. Ibid., p. 336.

6. Evans and Campbell escaped from custody and were never recaptured. Dolan's attorney, Tom Catron, managed to have the Dolan case dismissed after trial was set to take place in Socorro. Dolan had admitted during a hearing at Mesilla that he had fired his gun during the attack on Chapman.

7. Robert M. Utley, *Billy the Kid: A Short and Violent Life* (Lincoln: University of Nebraska Press, 1989), p. 6.

8. Ibid., pp. 33–35.

9. Fulton, *Lincoln County War*, p. 346.

10. Pat F. Garrett, *The Authentic Life of Billy the Kid* (Norman: University of Oklahoma Press, 1954), pp. 83–85.

11. Ibid., pp. x–xii.

12. Hinton, "John Simpson Chisum," part 3, p. 54. Hinton, taking a view somewhat different from that of this writer, states that Billy the Kid had a "persecution complex."

13. Keleher, *Violence in Lincoln County*, p. 286. In actuality there was little basis for the newspaper's claim that an organized Billy the Kid gang existed, much less one of such size. But the report typified a sensationalizing of the Kid's activities during this period. The effect of such reports was to intensify public demand for the capture of the Kid.

14. Ibid., p. 293.

15. Ibid., p. 296.

16. Ibid., pp. 301–2.

17. Fulton, *Lincoln County War*, p. 390.

18. Garrett, *Authentic Life*, p. 133.

19. Utley, *Billy the Kid*, pp. 180–81.

20. Garrett, *Authentic Life*, p. 139.

21. Ibid., p. 141.

22. Ibid., pp. 145–47.

23. Ibid., p. 148.

24. Ibid., p. xxiv. Robert Utley, author of the most thoroughly researched study of Billy the Kid, agrees with this assessment of the number of killings that can be attributed to Bonney.

25. H. B. Hening, ed., *George Curry, 1861–1947: An Autobiography* (Albuquerque: University of New Mexico Press, 1958), p. 70.

26. Keleher, *The Fabulous Frontier*, p. 233.

27. Ibid., p. 271.

28. Jack DeMattos, *Garrett and Roosevelt* (College Station, Texas: Creative Publishing Co., 1988), p. 29.

29. Leon Metz, *Pat Garrett: The Story of a Western Lawman* (Norman: University of Oklahoma Press, 1973), p. 252.

30. DeMattos, *Garrett and Roosevelt*, p. 109.

31. Ibid., p. 112.

32. Metz, *Pat Garrett*, p. 277.

33. Keleher, *The Fabulous Frontier*, p. 87.

34. Metz, *Pat Garrett*, p. 277.

35. C. L. Sonnichsen, *Tularosa: Last of the Frontier West* (Albuquerque: University of New Mexico Press, 1980), p. 243.

Chapter 8

1. Elvis E. Fleming and Minor S. Huffman, eds., *Roundup on the Pecos* (Roswell: Chaves County Historical Society, 1978), pp. 279–80; and Elvis Fleming, "Wildy Brought Leas to Roswell," *Roswell Daily Record*, 30 July 1989.

2. Shinkle, *Fifty Years of Roswell History*, p. 14.

3. Fulton, *Lincoln County War*, p. 381.

4. Sophie A. Poe, *Buckboard Days* (Albuquerque: University of New Mexico Press, 1981), p. 21.

5. Shinkle, *Reminiscences*, pp. 109–11.

6. *Curry: An Autobiography*, p. 71.

7. Larson, *New Mexico Populism*, p. 7.

8. *Curry: An Autobiography*, p. 65.

9. Perrigo, *Hispanos*, pp. 52–54.

10. Fleming, *Roundup on the Pecos*, p. 282.

11. See "Title Abstract" for property in south Roswell, prepared by Harold Hurd, attorney, 1942. Document in Chaves County Historical Museum Archives, Roswell, N.M.

12. Larson, *New Mexico's Quest for Statehood*, p. 145.

13. Ibid., p. 168.

14. Fleming, *Roundup on the Pecos*, pp. 282–83.

15. Larry D. Ball, "Lawman in Disgrace: Sheriff Charles C. Perry of Chaves County, New Mexico," *New Mexico Historical Review* (April 1986), p. 134.

16. James D. Shinkle, *Martin V. Corn: Early Roswell Pioneer* (Roswell: Hall-Poorbaugh Press, Inc., 1972), pp. 9–11.

17. Ibid., pp. 19–22.

18. Ibid., p. 22.

19. Ibid., p. 49.
20. Interview by author with Clarence R. Corn, son of Martin Corn and Julia Corn, 16 January 1990, in Roswell, N.M. Clarence Corn was at this time the last surviving of Martin Corn's offspring. He was born in 1903 at Eden Valley Ranch north of Roswell.
21. Information taken from Corn family chronology and listing of Martin Corn descendents prepared by G. B. Redfield. This undated document, apparently written in the late 1960s, was made available to the author by Clarence Corn.
22. Shinkle, *Martin Corn*, pp. 26–27.
23. Ibid., p. 51.
24. Ibid., p. 59.
25. Poe, *Buckboard Days*, p. 30.
26. Ibid., p. 48.
27. Ibid., p. 65.
28. Ibid., pp. 84–85.
29. Ibid., p. 100.
30. Keleher, *Violence in Lincoln County*, p. 348.
31. Poe, *Buckboard Days*, p. 129.
32. Ibid., pp. 211–12.
33. Ibid., pp. 258–60.
34. Shinkle, *Martin Corn*, p. 28.
35. Poe, *Buckboard Days*, p. 267.
36. In 1933 Houghton Mifflin Company published this material as a book entitled *The Death of Billy the Kid*.
37. Poe, *Buckboard Days*, p. 193.

Chapter 9

1. Tom Sheridan, *The Bitter River: A Brief Historical Survey of the Middle Pecos River Basin* (Roswell, N.M.: Bureau of Land Management Roswell District Office, August 1975), pp. 70–71.
2. This source was made available to the author by historian Raymond Burrola of Roswell, former staff member of the Hispanic Studies Institute of the University of New Mexico.
3. J. Evetts Haley, *George W. Littlefield, Texas* (Norman: University of Oklahoma Press, 1943), pp. 5–7.
4. Ibid., p. 9.
5. Ibid., p. 16.
6. Ibid., p. 29.
7. Ibid., pp. 31–32.
8. White, "Recollections," 1933, p. 1.
9. Haley, *Littlefield*, p. 44.
10. White, "Recollections," 1933, p. 1.

11. Ibid., p. 2.
12. Ibid., pp. 3–4.
13. Ibid., p. 4.
14. Haley, *Littlefield*, p. 74.
15. White, "Recollections," 1933, p. 4.
16. Ibid., pp. 8–9.
17. Ibid., p. 16.
18. Ibid.
19. Ibid., pp. 17–18.
20. Ibid., p. 12.
21. Cecil Bonney, *Looking over My Shoulder: Seventy-Five Years in the Pecos Valley* (Roswell, N.M.: Hall-Poorbaugh Press, Inc., 1971), p. 136.
22. White, "Recollections," 1933, pp. 13–14.
23. Haley, *Littlefield*, p. 142.
24. White, "Recollections," 1933, p. 13.
25. Ibid., p. 19.
26. Haley, *Littlefield*, p. 146.
27. White, "Recollections," 1933, p. 13.
28. Ibid., p. 20.
29. Sheridan, *The Bitter River*, p. 50.
30. Ibid., p. 52.
31. White, "Recollections," 1933, p. 21.
32. May Price Mosley, *"Little Texas" Beginnings in Southeastern New Mexico* (Roswell, N.M.: Hall-Poorbaugh Press, Inc., 1973), p. 7.
33. Haley, *Littlefield*, p. 159.
34. Mosley, *Little Texas*, p. 13.
35. James Phelps White II, interviewed on 2 September 1983 by J. Phelps White III (Oral History Project, Chaves County Historical Museum, Roswell, N.M.), p. 2.
36. White, "Recollections," p. 21.
37. Sheridan, *The Bitter River*, p. 53.
38. Bonney, *Looking over My Shoulder*, p. 140.
39. Fleming, *Roundup on the Pecos*, p. 71.
40. Eugene H. Price, *Open Range Ranching on the South Plains in the 1890s* (Clarendon, Texas: Clarendon Press, 1967), p. 41.
41. Ibid., p. 45.
42. Ibid., pp. 50–51.
43. Ibid., p. 48.
44. J. P. White II, 1983 Interview, p. 3.
45. Bonney, *Looking over My Shoulder*, p. 137.
46. J. P. White II, 1983 interview, p. 3.
47. James Phelps White III, interview with author, 15 March 1990, in Roswell. Phelps White III, grandson of J. Phelps White, was born in 1932; his

grandfather died in 1934. He has been president of the family company, White Industries, since the death of his father, J. Phelps White II, in 1987.

48. J. P. White II, 1983 interview, p. 4.
49. Sheridan, *The Bitter River*, p. 72.
50. J. P. White II, 1983 interview, p. 3.
51. Ibid., p. 4.
52. J. J. Lipsey, *The Lives of James John Hagerman* (Denver: Golden Bell Press, 1968), pp. 3–7.
53. Ibid., p. 16.
54. Ibid., pp. 22–23.
55. Ibid., p. 16.
56. Ibid., p. 28.
57. Ibid., p. 27.
58. Ibid., p. 43.
59. Ibid., p. 30.
60. Ibid., p. 56.
61. Ibid., p. 60.
62. Ibid., p. 74.
63. Ibid., p. 81.
64. Ibid., p. 90.
65. Ibid., p. 252.
66. Sheridan, *The Bitter River*, pp. 57–58.
67. Lipsey, *Hagerman*, p. 224.
68. Ibid., p. 93.
69. Ibid., p. 118.
70. Ibid.
71. Shinkle, *Martin Corn*, p. 58.
72. Lipsey, *Hagerman*, p. 225.
73. Ibid., p. 152.
74. Ibid., p. 118.
75. Sheridan, *The Bitter River*, pp. 62–63.
76. Lipsey, *Hagerman*, p. 236.
77. Sheridan, *The Bitter River*, p. 63.
78. Lipsey, *Hagerman*, p. 210.
79. Ibid., p. 226.
80. Elvis Fleming, "Railroad Links Roswell to World," *Roswell Daily Record* (22 April 1990), p. 12.
81. *Curry: An Autobiography*, pp. 97–98.
82. Lipsey, *Hagerman*, p. 234.
83. Fleming, "Railroad Links Roswell," p. 12.
84. Sheridan, *The Bitter River*, p. 64.
85. Lipsey, *Hagerman*, p. 228.
86. Ibid., p. 245.

87. Robert Metzger, editor, *My Land is the Southwest: Peter Hurd Letters and Journals* (College Station: Texas A&M Press, 1983), p. xxviii.
88. Larson, *New Mexico's Quest for Statehood*, pp. 229–30.
89. Ibid., p. 248.
90. Ibid. p. 250.
91. Ibid., p. 254.
92. Ibid., p. 235.
93. Ibid., p. 256.
94. Ibid.
95. Ibid., p. 257.
96. Ibid.
97. Ibid.
98. Ibid.
99. Ibid., p. 258.
100. Lipsey, *Hagerman*, p. 151. Dated at Roswell June 1908, the memoir passed into the possession of Percy Hagerman, who made the manuscript available to Lipsey.

Chapter 10

1. Daniel Gibson, "Blackdom," *New Mexico Magazine* (February 1986), pp. 46–51.
2. Larson, *New Mexico Populism*, p. 161.
3. Richard Melzer and Phyllis Ann Mingus, "Wild to Fight: The New Mexico Rough Riders in the Spanish-American War," *New Mexico Historical Review* (April 1984), pp. 118–20.
4. *Curry: An Autobiography*, pp. 227–29.

Bibliography

Books

Adams, Clarence S. (ed.). *Little Town West of the Pecos*—1909. News stories taken from the Roswell Register Tribune. Roswell, N.M.: Pioneer Printing, Inc., 1983.

Ball, Eve, with Nora Henn and Lynda Sanchez. *Indeh: An Apache Odyssey*. Provo, Utah: Brigham Young University Press, 1980.

Beale, Howard K. *Theodore Roosevelt and the Rise of America to World Power*. New York: Collier Books, 1962. (First ed., Baltimore, Md.: Johns Hopkins Press, 1956.)

Beck, Warren. *New Mexico: A History of Four Centuries*. Norman: University of Oklahoma Press, 1962.

Bolton, Hubert Eugene. *Coronado: Knight of Pueblo and Plains*. New York: McGraw Hill Book Co., Inc., 1949.

Bonney, Cecil. *Looking over My Shoulder: Seventy-Five Years in the Pecos Valley*. Roswell, N.M.: Hall-Poorbaugh Press, Inc., 1971.

Briggs, Charles L., and John R. Van Ness, eds. *Land, Water, and Culture: New Perspectives on Hispanic Land Grants*. Albuquerque: University of New Mexico Press, 1987.

Calvin, Ross. *Sky Determines*. Albuquerque: University of New Mexico Press, 1948. (First ed. New York: Macmillan Company, 1934.)

Clark, Ira G. *Water in New Mexico: A History of Its Management and Use*. Albuquerque: University of New Mexico Press, 1987.

Cleaveland, Norman, with George Fitzpatrick. *The Morleys*. Albuquerque: Calvin Horn Publisher, Inc., 1971.

Coan, Charles F. *A History of New Mexico*. 3 vols. Chicago and New York: The American Historical Society, 1925.

Coe, Wilbur. *Ranch on the Ruidoso: The Story of a Pioneer Family in New Mexico, 1871–1966.* New York: Knopf, 1969.

Dearen, Patrick. *Castle Gap and the Pecos Frontier.* Fort Worth: Christian University Press, 1988.

DeMattos, Jack. *Garrett and Roosevelt.* College Station, Texas: Creative Publishing Co., 1988.

Dickerson, Patricia, Jerry Hoffer, and Jonathan Callender, eds. *Trans-Pecos Region: Southeastern New Mexico and West Texas.* New Mexico Geological Society, 1980.

Estergreen, M. Morgan. *Kit Carson: A Portrait in Courage.* Norman: University of Oklahoma Press, 1962.

Farb, Peter. *Man's Rise to Civilization as Shown by the Indians of North America from Primeval Times to the Coming of the Industrial State.* New York: E.P. Dutton and Co., Inc., 1968.

Fleming, Elvis E., and Minor S. Huffman, eds. *Roundup on the Pecos.* Roswell, N.M.: Chaves County Historical Society, 1978.

Fulton, Maurice G. *Roswell in Its Early Years.* Brochure reprint of article in Roswell Daily Record, 7 October 1937.

———. *Lincoln County War.* Tucson: The University of Arizona Press, 1984. (First ed. Tucson: University of Arizona Press, 1968).

Garrett, Pat F. *The Authentic Life of Billy the Kid.* Norman: University of Oklahoma Press, 1954. (First published in 1882.)

Gibbs, William E., and Keith E. Gibson, eds. *Treasures of History: Historic Buildings in Chaves County, 1870–1935.* Shawnee Mission, Kans.: Inter-Collegiate Press, 1985.

Haley, J. Evetts. *George W. Littlefield, Texan.* Norman: University of Oklahoma Press, 1943.

Hening, H.B., ed. *George Curry, 1861–1947: An Autobiography.* Albuquerque: University of New Mexico Press, 1958.

Hinkle, James F. *Early Days of a Cowboy on the Pecos.* (First printed privately in 35 copies in 1937. Reprinted in 1965 by Stagecoach Press of Santa Fe. Undated third printing by First National Bank of Roswell.)

Horgan, Paul. *Lamy of Santa Fe: His Life and Times.* New York: Farrar, Straus and Giroux, 1975.

Horn, Calvin. *New Mexico's Troubled Years: The Story of the Early Territorial Governors.* Albuquerque: Horn and Wallace, Publishers, 1963.

Jenkins, Myra Ellen, and Albert H. Schroeder. *A Brief History of New Mexico.* Albuquerque: University of New Mexico Press, 1974.

Keleher, William A. *The Fabulous Frontier: Twelve New Mexico Items.* Albuquerque: University of New Mexico Press, 1982. (First ed. Albuquerque: University of New Mexico Press, 1962.)

———*Violence in Lincoln County, 1869–1881.* Albuquerque: University of New Mexico Press, 1982. (First ed. Albuquerque: University of New Mexico Press, 1957.)

Klasner, Lily. *My Girlhood among Outlaws.* Tucson: University of Arizona Press, 1981. (First ed. Tucson: University of Arizona Press, 1972.)

Larson, Robert W. *New Mexico Populism: A Study of Radical Protest in a Western Territory.* Boulder: Colorado Associated University Press, 1974.

——— *New Mexico's Quest for Statehood, 1846–1912.* Albuquerque: University of New Mexico Press, 1968.

Lipsey, J.J. *The Lives of James John Hagerman.* Denver: Golden Bell Press, 1968.

Merrill, Horace Samuel. *Bourbon Leader: Grover Cleveland and the Democratic Party.* Boston, Toronto: Little, Brown and Company, 1957.

Metz, Leon. *Pat Garrett: The Story of a Western Lawman.* Norman: University of Oklahoma Press, 1973.

Miller, Darlis A. *The California Column.* Albuquerque: University of New Mexico Press, 1982.

Mosley, May Price. *'Little Texas' Beginnings in Southeastern New Mexico.* Roswell, N.M.: Hall-Poorbaugh Press, Inc., 1973.

Murrah, David J. *C.C. Slaughter: Rancher, Banker, Baptist.* Austin: University of Texas Press, 1981.

Myers, Leland C., ed. *Eddy County.* Artesia, N.M.: Valley Savings and Loan Association of Artesia, n.d.

Myres, Sandra L. *Westering Women and the Frontier Experience 1800–1915.* Albuquerque: University of New Mexico Press, 1982.

Myrick, David F. *New Mexico's Railroads: An Historical Survey.* Golden, Colo.: Colorado Railroad Historical Foundation, 1970. (Reprint, 1990: University of New Mexico Press.

Nolan, Frederick W. *The Life and Death of John Henry Tunstall.* Albuquerque: University of New Mexico Press, 1965.

Parker, Morris B. *White Oaks: Life in a New Mexico Gold Camp, 1880–1900.* Tucson: University of Arizona Press, 1976. (First ed. Tucson: University of Arizona, 1971.)

Perrigo, Lynn I. *Hispanos: Historic Leaders in New Mexico.* Santa Fe: Sunstone Press, 1985.

Poe, Sophie A. *Buckboard Days.* Albuquerque: University of New Mexico Press, 1981. (First ed. Caldwell, Idaho: Caxton Printers, 1936.)

Price, Eugene H. *Open Range Ranching on the South Plains in the 1890s.* Clarendon, Texas: Clarendon Press, 1967.

Rodriguez O., Jaime E. *The Emergence of Spanish America: Vicente Rocafuerte and Spanish Americanism 1808–1832.* Berkeley: University of California Press, 1975.

Rosenbaum, Robert J. *Mexicano Resistance in the Southwest.* Austin: University of Texas Press, 1981.

Sabin, Edwin L. *Kit Carson Days, 1809–1868.* Chicago: A. C. McClurg and Company, 1914.

Schroeder, Albert H., and Dan S. Matson. *A Colony on the Move: Gaspar Castaño de Sosa's Journal, 1590–1591.* Santa Fe, N.M.: School of American Research, 1965.

Sheridan, Tom. *The Bitter River: A Brief Historical Survey of the Middle Pecos River Basin*. Roswell, N.M.: Bureau of Land Management Roswell District Office, August 1975.

Shinkle, James D. *Fifty Years of Roswell History, 1867–1917*. Roswell, N.M.: Hall-Poorbaugh Press, Inc., 1964.

——— *Fort Sumner and the Bosque Redondo Indian Reservation*. Roswell, N.M.: Hall-Poorbaugh Press, Inc., 1965.

——— *Martin V. Corn: Early Roswell Pioneer*. Roswell, N.M.: Hall-Poorbaugh Press, Inc., 1972.

——— *Missouri Plaza: First Settled Community in Chaves County*. Roswell, N.M.: Hall-Poorbaugh Press, Inc., 1972.

——— *New Mexican Ciboleros of the Llano Estacado*. Roswell, N.M.: Hall Poorbaugh Press, Inc., 1970.

——— *Reminiscences of Roswell Pioneers*. Roswell, N.M.: Hall-Poorbaugh Press, 1966.

Simmons, Marc. *New Mexico: A Bicentennial History*. Nashville: W. W. Norton and Company, Inc., 1977.

Sonnichsen, C.L. *The Mescalero Apaches*. Norman: University of Oklahoma Press, 1958.

——— *Tularosa: Last of the Frontier West*. Albuquerque: University of New Mexico Press, 1960.

Stuart, David E. *Glimpses of the Ancient Southwest*. Santa Fe: Ancient City Press, 1985.

Trafzer, Clifford E. *The Kit Carson Campaign: The Last Great Navajo War*. Norman: University of Oklahoma Press, 1982.

Utley, Robert M. *Billy the Kid: A Short and Violent Life*. Lincoln: University of Nebraska Press, 1989.

——— *Four Fighters of Lincoln County*. Albuquerque: University of New Mexico Press, 1986.

——— *High Noon in Lincoln: Violence on the Western Frontier*. Albuquerque: University of New Mexico Press, 1987.

Weber, David J., ed. *Donaciano Vigil: Arms, Indians and the Mismanagement of New Mexico*. El Paso: University of Texas at El Paso Western Press, 1986.

Westphall, Victor. *The Public Domain in New Mexico, 1854–1891*. Albuquerque: University of New Mexico Press, 1965.

Wilson, John P. *Merchants, Guns and Money*. Santa Fe: Museum of New Mexico Press, 1987.

Periodical Articles

Ball, Larry D. "Lawman in Disgrace: Sheriff Charles C. Perry of Chaves County, New Mexico." *New Mexico Historical Review* 61 (April 1986).

Dippie, Brian W. "Of Documents and Myths: Richard Kern and Western Art." *New Mexico Historical Review* 61 (April 1986).

Gibson, Daniel. "Blackdom." *New Mexico Magazine* 64 (February 1986).
Greenleaf, Richard E. "Land and Water in Mexico and New Mexico." *New Mexico Historical Review* 47 (April 1972).
Hall, Em. "Tierra y Agua." *New Mexico Magazine* (September 1987).
Hinton, Harwood P., Jr. "John Simpson Chisum, 1877–84," part 1. *New Mexico Historical Review* 31 (July 1956).
———"John Simpson Chisum, 1877–84," part 2. *New Mexico Historical Review* 31 (October 1956).
———"John Simpson Chisum, 1877–84," part 3. *New Mexico Historical Review* 32 (January 1957).
Jones, Oakah L. "Lew Wallace: Hoosier Governor of Territorial New Mexico, 1878–81." *New Mexico Historical Review* 60 (April 1985).
Melzer, Richard, and Phyllis Ann Mingus. "Wild to Fight: The New Mexico Rough Riders in the Spanish-American War." *New Mexico Historical Review* 59 (April 1984).
Meyer, Michael C. "The Legal Relationship of Land to Water in Northern Mexico and the Hispanic Southwest." *New Mexico Historical Review* 69 (January 1985).
Osburn, Katherine Marie. "The Navajo at the Bosque Redondo: Cooperation, Resistance, and Initiative, 1864–1868." *New Mexico Historical Review* (October 1985).
Rasch, Philip J. "Exit Axtell: Enter Wallace." *New Mexico Historical Review* 32 (July 1957).
———"The People of the Territory of New Mexico versus the Santa Fe Ring." *New Mexico Historical Review* 47 (April 1972).
Seligmann, G.L., Jr. "The El Paso and Northeastern Railroad's Economic Impact on Central New Mexico." *New Mexico Historical Review* 61 (July 1986).
Simmons, Marc. "New Mexico's Smallpox Epidemic of 1780–1781." *New Mexico Historical Review* 41 (October 1966).
Spidle, Jake W., Jr. "An Army of Tubercular Invalids: New Mexico and the Birth of a Tuberculosis Industry." *New Mexico Historical Review* 61 (July 1986).
Utley, Robert M. "Billy the Kid and the Lincoln County War." *New Mexico Historical Review* 61 (April 1986).

Newspaper Articles

Fleming, Elvis. "Book Provides Insight about Chisum's Children." *Roswell Daily Record,* 10 April 1989.
———"Capt. Joseph Lea Was Truly 'Father of Roswell.'" *Roswell Daily Record,* 13 August 1989.
———"Leas Make Roswell Their Home." *Roswell Daily Record,* 6 August 1989.
———"Railroad Links Roswell to World." *Roswell Daily Record,* 22 April 1990.
———"Wildy Brought Leas to Roswell." *Roswell Daily Record,* 30 July 1989.

Unpublished Manuscripts

Haley, J. Evetts. "Beginning of the LIT Ranch," transcript of interview with J. Phelps White, Roswell, N.M., 15 January 1927. White family records, Roswell.

——— "Recollections of Ranching Operations in New Mexico with George W. Littlefield." Transcript of interview with J. Phelps White, Roswell, N.M., 2 March 1933. White family records, Roswell.

Larson, Carole. Transcript of interview with Clarence R. Corn, son of Martin Corn and Julia Corn, Roswell, N.M., 16 January 1990.

———Transcript of interview with J. Phelps White III, grandson of J. Phelps White, Roswell, N.M., 15 March 1990.

Perrigo, Lynn I. "Early Roswell: Pearl of the Pecos." Unpublished monograph, Roswell, N.M., 1988. Roswell Public Library.

Redfield, G.B. "Corn Family History." Compilation of genealogical and other data relating to the family of Martin Corn. Undated. Corn family records, Roswell.

White, J. Phelps III. "Interview with J.P. White, Jr." Transcript of interview conducted in Roswell, N.M., 2 September 1983, as part of Oral History Project, Chaves County Historical Museum.

Public Documents

"Second Supplemental Title Report to Lot 11, Block 7, South Roswell." A lengthy compilation of property records, abstracts and articles of incorporation, including those for Lea Cattle Company, prepared by Roswell attorney Harold Hurd. Report also includes copy of legislation creating Chaves and Eddy counties. Dated Roswell, 1942. Chaves County Historical Society Archives, Roswell.

Historical Statistics of the United States, vol. 1. Washington, D.C.: U.S. Department of Commerce, 1975.

Index

Adamson, Carl, 183
Alberding, Fred, 224
Aldrich, Nelson, 285
Alfalfa, 215–16, 228
American buffalo. *See* Buffalo
American National Bank of Roswell, 228
Anasazi, 9–11
Anderson Cattle Company, 241
Andrews, William "Bull", 272–74
Angel, Frank Warner, 126, 145; completion of investigative report by, 150
Antrim, Billy. *See* Billy the Kid
Antrim, William H., 158
Apache Indians, 13–14. *See also* Mescalero Apaches
Arroyo Acequia. *See* North Salt Creek
Atchison, Topeka and Santa Fe Railroad, 25, 27–28, 257, 269–270
Athabaskans, 7, 14
Avalon Dam: flooding of, 264–65; 270
Axtell, Samuel B., 118–19, 128; response to Tunstall killing of, 140, 143; removal from office of, 150

Baca, B. F., 170
Baca, Saturnino, 281
Bail, John D., 170
Baker, Frank, 117; death of, 140
Ballard, Charles L., 71, 284
Barnes, S. M., 150, 154
Battle of Glorieta Pass, 44. *See also* Civil War in New Mexico
Battle of Valverde, 43. *See also* Civil War in New Mexico
Baxter, John, 64
Bear, H. M. F., 82
Beckwith, H. M., 62, 114, 159
Bell, J. W., 170; death of, 172
Bering Straits, 6–7
Billy the Kid: character traits of, 102–3, 118, 120, 135, 139, 141; actions taken during July 1878 by, 148; secret meeting between Wallace and, 156–57; life story of, 157–63; 1880 capture of, 167–68; trial of, 169–70; escape of, 170–72; death of, 174–75, 222, 238
Bison, 8. *See also* Buffalo
Blackdom, 282–83
Blashek, G. F., 214
Blazer, Joseph C., 58–59

· 309 ·

INDEX

Blazer's Mill: gun battle at, 142
Bonney, C. D., 201, 214, 228
Bonney, William. *See* Billy the Kid
Bosque Grande, 107
Bosque Redondo, 48
Bowdre, Charles, 119, 139, 147; death of, 167
Boyer, Francis, 282–83
Brady, William, 75, 117, 128, 136; seizing of Tunstall and McSween property by, 138; Tunstall killing by posse of, 139; killing of, 141, 281
Brazel, Jessey Wayne, 183–84
Brent, Jim, 226
Brewer, Dick, 135, 139; death of, 142, 160–61
Bristol, Warren, 118, 169–70
Brown, Henry, 139
Bryan, William Jennings, 87–88
Buffalo, 8, 13–14, 24–25; commercial exploitation of, 220–21
Bull Moose party, 285
Bursum, Holm, 273–74
Burt, Billy, 172–73

Cahill, Francis, 159
Cahoon, E. A., 208–9, 228
Calfee, Ella, 239
Calhoun, James S., 41
Canadian River Cattlemen's Association, 222
Canby, Edward, 43–51
Capitan Mountains, 4
Carleton, James M., 44–48, 55–56
Carlisle, Jimmy, 171
Carnegie, Andrew, 252
Carper, James Oliver, 71
Carson, Josefa Jaramillo, 45–46, 57. *See also* Kit Carson
Carson, Kit, 43, 45–46, 54, 57–58
Casey, Lilly, 121
Casey, Robert, 60, 73, 135

Cass Cattle Company, 77
Catron, Thomas B., 79, 87–88, 113, 116, 126, 128, 140, 149–50, 180, 199, 206, 272–73
Cattle Association, 36
Cattle industry: development of, 27, 60–63; role of large cattle companies in, 76–78; ecological impact on public domain of, 77–78; impact of John Chisum on development of, 108–9; rustling impact on, 111; impact of Texas cattle drives on, 135–36; symbiotic relations between big and small operators in, 244–45; movement toward fenced ranching in, 245–46, 248
Chaco Canyon, 10–11
Chacon, Don Fernando, 31
Chamuscado, Francisco Sánchez, 19
Chapman, Huston J., 151, 154
Chaves County: creation of, 204–5
Chaves, Francis Xavier, 206
Chaves, J. Francisco, 50, 59, 80; life synopsis of, 204–7
Chaves, Juan, 72
Chaves, Manuel, 44
Chaves, Mariano, 206
Chihuahuita, 69–70
Chisum, Frank, 72, 114, 119–20
Chisum, James, 110, 116, 119–21
Chisum, John Simpson, 38, 61, 72, 78; character traits of, 102–3; early life of, 105–7; Civil War activities of, 107; entry into New Mexico of, 107–9; ranching and farming activities of, 110–12; Lincoln County War participation of, 112–19; last years of, 119–22, 136, 140, 200, 213–14, 224–25, 262
Chisum, Pitzer M., 108, 119–22
Chisum, Sallie, 110, 117, 119–20
Chisum, Walter, 110

· 310 ·

INDEX

Chisum, Will, 110
Chivington, John M., 44
Church, Amelia Bolton, 69–70, 280–81
Ciboleros, 22
Citizens' Bank of Roswell, 228
Citizens' National Bank of Roswell, 228
Civil War in New Mexico, 42–44
Cleveland, Grover, 83, 263–64, 284
Clovis Complex, 8
Coe, Frank, 85–86, 142, 160
Coe, George W., 85–86, 142, 160
Coe, Jasper N., 85–86
Coghlin, Pat, 111, 222
Colorado Midland Railway Company, 255–57
Comanche Indians, 13–14, 57
Connelly, Henry, 42–43, 45, 55–56
Constitution of 1889, 80, 208
Copeland, John, 118, 144
Corn: early development of, 8–9
Corn, Clarence, 214, 218
Corn, John R., 212
Corn, Julia Miller McVicker, 214–15
Corn, Martin Van Buren, 71; early life of, 212–13; emigration to New Mexico of, 213; second marriage of, 214–15; move to North Salt Creek of, 216–17; death of, 218
Corn, Mary Elizabeth, 213
Corn, Mary Elizabeth McMinn, 212
Corn, Mary Jane Nichols Hampton, 212, 214
Corn, Poe W., 215
Coronado, Francisco Vasquez de, 12, 19
Cortés, Hernán, 18
Cosgrove, William H., 228
Court of Private Land Claims, 34, 80
Cowden Brothers, 242
Crile, A. N., 249

Cripple Creek Strike of 1894, 265–67
Curry, George, 165, 180, 183, 203, 231, 275; career and influence of, 283–86

Day, Mabel Doss. *See* Mabel Doss Day Lea
Denver and Rio Grande Railroad Company, 255, 257
Dillon, Jerry, 73
Dills, Lucius, 71, 82, 202–3, 209
Dodd, Theodore, 54
Dodge, Henry Lafayette, 50
Dolan, James J., 113, 115, 118; biographical information about, 124–25, 145; post-Lincoln County War career of, 149, 161
Dowlin, 73
Dudley, Nathan A. M., 142, 154–55; role in Lincoln County War five-day gunfight of, 246–48

Ealy, Rev. Taylor, 148
Eddy and Bissell Live Stock Company, 241, 258
Eddy, Charles B., 77, 104, 176–77, 204, 258–60, 263, 265, 268–69
El Berrendo, 69
Elkins, Stephen B., 144
Ellis, Isaac, 170, 225
El Torreon, 69
Espejo, Antonio de, 19
Evans, Jesse: role in Tunstall killing of, 139, 154, 159, 161

Fall, Albert Bacon, 179–81
Farmers' Alliance and Industrial Union. *See* Southern Alliance
Fergusson Act, 31, 207
Fergusson, Harvey B., 88, 180, 231, 284
First National Bank of Roswell, 228
Folsom Complex, 8

· 311 ·

INDEX

Fort Stanton, 41, 58, 70
Fort Sumner: establishment of, 48
Fountain, A. J., 170, 178–79
Fowler, Stephen, 106
Frémont, John Charles, 46
Fritz, Caroline, 149
Fritz, Charles, 149
Fritz, Emil, 115, 124, 137
Frost, Max, 273
Fruit production in Pecos Valley, 216

Gaither, George, 182
Garfield, James A., 169
Garner, John Nance, 178, 181
Garrett, Apolinaria, 177
Garrett, Elizabeth, 177–78
Garrett, Patrick F., 78; early career of, 164–66; confrontations between Billy the Kid and, 166–75; later career of, 175–85, 204, 215, 222–23, 260
Gaullieur, Henri, 261
Gauss, Godfrey, 161, 172
Geronimo, 39
Giddings, Marsh, 25–26, 75
Gilliland, Jim, 180
Godfroy, Frederick, 142–43
Goodnight, Charles, 61
Goodnight-Loving Trail, 61–62
Goss Military Academy, 32, 209. *See also* New Mexico Military Institute
Goss, Robert H., 209
Greene, Charles, 177
Guadalupe Mountains, 3–4

Hagerman, Anna Osborne, 251–52, 259, 271
Hagerman, Herbert, 252, 272–75
Hagerman, James J., 177, 209, 215–16, 228; early life of, 250–52; role in U.S. steel industry played by, 252–53; move to Colorado of, 253; character of, 253–54; investment activities of, 254–55; railroad building by, 255–57; New Mexico investments made by, 258–63; crises confronted by, 263–70; Pecos Valley residency of, 270–77
Hagerman, James Parrott, 250–51
Hagerman, Margaret Crawford, 250–51
Hagerman, Percy, 252, 260–61, 265
Hale, William, 82
Hanna, Mark, 253, 272
Harold, Whitefield, 249
Hartman, G. W., 199
Hatch, Edward, 154
Hayes, Rutherford B., 150, 153–54
Hindman, George, 117; killing of, 141
Hinkle, James F., 63, 209, 249, 275
Hinkle, Lillie Roberts, 71
Holliman, William, 213
Homer, Susan E. *See* Susan McSween
Homesteading: ecological conditions as factor in, 78–79
Hondo Reservoir, 232
Hopewell, W. S., 274–75
Horrell brothers, 74–75
Horsehead Crossing, 61
Hough, Emerson, 182
Hunter, Evans and Company, 109
Hoyt, Henry E., 238
Hudson, Dan, 219
Hurd, Harold, 271
Hurd, Peter, 271

Ice Ages, 4
Ilfeld, Charles, 215

Jacobs, John, 220–21
Jaffa, Nathan, 82
Johnson, Andrew, 56
Jones, Heiskell, 70, 159–60

INDEX

Joseph, Antonio, 87
Joyce, John R., 71

Kearny, Stephen Watts, 23, 38, 206
Kellahin, Lily James, 71
Kimball, George, 151, 165
Kinney, John, 151

Lamy, Archbishop Jean Baptiste, 23, 30, 55
Land grants, 32–35, 79–80
Lane, William Carr, 25
Lea, Alfred E., 202
Lea Cattle Company, 203, 209–10
Lea, Ella, 201–2, 207
Lea, Frank H., 202
Lea, Gertrude, 203
Lea, Harry Wildy, 199, 202, 207
Lea, Joseph C., 71, 75, 119; early life of, 197–98; emigration to southeast New Mexico frontier of, 199–200; emergence as cattleman of, 203; political leadership of, 203–4; initiatives in education arena of, 208–9; last years of, 210–11, 223, 225
Lea, J. Smith, 203, 225–28
Lea, Joseph D., 82, 202
Lea, Lucinda Callaway, 197–98
Lea, Mabel Doss Day, 207
Lea, Pleasant J. G., 197–98
Lea, Sally Wildy, 198–202
Lea, Stephen A., 224
Lea, Willie Day, 207
Lee, Oliver M., 179–81
Leonard, Ira, 169
Lesnet, Frank, 82
Leverson, Montague, R., 144
Lincoln County: creation of, 24; enlargement of, 204; dividing of, 105
Lincoln County Alliance, 85–87
Lincoln County Rifles, 155

Lincoln County War: ethnic hostilities as an element in, 76; economic causes of, 112; factors precipitating, 129
Littlefield, Fleming, 233–34
Littlefield, George W., 111, 222; biographical information about, 233–40, 243, 248–50
Littlefield, Mildred Satterwhite White, 233
Llano Estacado, 3
Llewelyn, William H. H., 204, 273, 275
Long, John, 141
Louisiana Territory, 21
Loving, Oliver, 61
Lund, Sara, 214

McCarty, Catherine, 158
McCarty, Henry. *See* Billy the Kid
McDonald, William C., 231
Macho Draw. *See* North Salt Creek
McKinley Tariff Act, 83
McKinley, William, 88, 272, 284
McKinney, Thomas, 173–74
McKittrick, Felix, 110
MacMillan Dam, 262
McNabb, Frank, 111–12, 139
McSween, Alexander, 74, 112–14; biographical information about, 133–34; death of, 148
McSween, Susan, 134; actions during five-day gunfight of, 147–48, 151, 153–54
Maize. *See* Corn
Manuelito (Navajo chief), 51, 54, 56
Martínez, Padre Antonio José, 46, 58
Mathews, Jack B. "Billy", 71, 126; Brady posse actions by, 138, 141, 170
Maxwell, Jack, 180
Maxwell Land Grant, 143
Maxwell, Pete, 77, 173–74

· 313 ·

INDEX

Meadows, John, 171
Meriwether, David, 41
Mescalero Apaches, 14, 41–42, 44, 48–49, 55–56, 59
Mexican War, 23
Middleton, John, 135, 139, 147
Military forts: location of, 39; economic impact of, 58–61
Miller, James M., 64, 71, 78, 84, 215
Miller, Jim, 184
Mills, T. B., 87
Missouri Plaza, 59–60
Mitchell, Robert B., 31, 55
Mogollon culture, 9–11
Mollie Gibson Mine, 262
Montaño, José, 75, 146, 154
Morley, William Raymond, 144
Morton, William, 117; role in Tunstall death of, 139; death of, 140
Murphy, Lawrence G., 50, 75, 112–13; biographical information about, 124; death of, 149

National Farmers' Alliance. *See* Northern Alliance
Navajos, 38, 41–42, 45, 48; Carson campaign against, 50–53; internment at Bosque Redondo of, 53–56; return to northwest New Mexico of, 56
New Mexico: origin of name of, 18
New Mexico Military Institute, 32, 208–9
Nichols, J. L., 213
Niza, Fray Marcos de, 19
Nogal Nugget, 85
Northern Alliance, 85
North Salt Creek, 217

O'Folliard, Tom, 167
Olinger, Robert, 170–72
Oñate, Juan de, 20–21, 61

Otero, Miguel S., 180, 210, 272, 285
Otis, Charles A., 256, 267, 270

Paleo Indians: origins of, 6–7; food sources of, 9; Pecos Basin settlements of, 12–14
Patron, Juan B., 75, 148, 155, 281
Patterson, James, 107–8
Pecos River and Valley, 3, 5
Pecos Valley Company, 263
Pecos Valley Irrigation Company, 177, 260
Pecos Valley Irrigation and Improvement Company, 260–62
Pecos Valley and Northeastern Railway Company, 269–71
Pecos Valley Railroad Company, 28, 260, 267–69
Pecos Valley Register, 82
Pecos Valley Town Company, 261
Pennsylvania Development Company, 274–75
People's party. *See* Populists
Peppin, George, 118–19, 141, 144–45; resignation as sheriff of, 151
Peralta, Pedro de, 21
Perea, Pedro, 42
Perry, Charles C., 82, 210
Pike, Zebulon, 21
Pile, William S., 25–26
Pleistocene epoch, 4
Poe, John, 78, 119–20, 173–74, 176, 215; early life of, 219–20; Texas adventures of, 219–22; entry into New Mexico of, 222–23; marriage of, 225; South American travels of, 226–27; business career of, 227–29; 262
Poe, Sophie Alberding, 202, 223–26, 229
Polk, James K., 23
Populists, 87–88
Portales, 222

INDEX

Powers, Tom, 182
Prince, L. Bradford, 62, 206, 209
Pueblo peoples of Rio Grande Valley, 11–12; 1680 revolt of, 15

Rapp, I. H. and William, 209
Redfield, Georgia B., 71
Regulators, 117; formation of, 139; role in Brady killing of, 141, 151; role of Billy the Kid in, 162
Rencher, Abraham, 51
Reymond, Numa, 178
Richardson, Granville A., 71, 82
Riley, John H.: biographical information about, 125–26; post-Lincoln County War career of, 149–50
Rio Feliz, 4
Rio Hondo (the place), 69. *See also* Chihuahuita
Rio Hondo (the river), 4
Rio Peñasco, 4
Robert, Sallie Chisum. *See* Sallie Chisum
Robert, William, 120–21
Roberts, Andrew "Buckshot", 142
Rodrigues, Fray Augustín, 19
Rodey, Bernard S., 181, 272
Rogers, A. C., 239
Rogers, Asbury, 214
Roosevelt, Theodore, 181–82, 272, 274–75, 284–86
Rosenthal, William, 115, 125, 149
Ross, Edmund G., 205
Roswell Daily Record, 82
Roswell Record, 82
Rough Riders Regiment, 284–86
Rynerson, W. L., 115, 128, 137, 149, 157, 162–63

Sacramento Mountains, 4
Sandia Man, 7
San Patricio, 145

Santa Fe Ring: origins of, 128, 143
Scholand, Emilie Fritz, 137
Schurz, Carl, 144, 150
Scurlock, Doc, 139, 147
Sedillo, Cosme, 72
Selman, John, 151
Sharpe, A. L., 182
Shaw, G. B., 177
Sheldon, Lionel A., 169
Sherman Antitrust Act, 83
Sherman Silver Purchase Act, 84
Sherman, William T., 56
Shield, David, 141
Sibley, Henry Hopkins, 43–44
Siringo, Charles, 176
Slaughter, C. C., 241
Sligh, J. E., 85
Smith, Sam, 139
Smith, Van C., 79, 199
Sosa, Gaspar Castaño de, 19–20
Southern Alliance: Lincoln County chapter of, 85–88
South Spring River, 108
Spanish American War, 284–86
Spanish land grants. *See* Land grants
Springer Omnibus Bill, 208
Stanton, Henry W., 41
Steck, Michael, 41, 48
Stewart, Frank, 167
Stone, Edmund T., 64, 78, 225
Sumner, Edwin Vose, 48, 51

Taft, William Howard, 285–86
Tansill, Robert Weems, 177, 258–59
Taylor, Zachary, 23
Thornton, William T., 77, 79, 115, 210, 267
Thurber, Horace, 202–3, 210
Tomlinson, David, 244, 247
Treaty of Guadalupe Hidalgo, 23
Trujillo, Andricus, 69
Tularosa Basin, 27

INDEX

Tunstall, John, 112, 116; biographical information about, 134–35; killing of, 138–39, 141
Turner, Marion, 119, 145, 199
Tyler, John, 26

U.S. Reclamation Service, 232, 270
Upson, Ash, 166, 175, 177, 201

Vaca, Alvar Núñez Cabeza de, 18
Van Buren, Martin, 26
Van Dyke, John H., 256
Vargas, Diego de, 15
Vigil, Donaciano, 40

Waite, Davis H., 267
Waite, Fred, 135, 139, 161, 238
Wallace, Lew, 25, 119; gubernatorial appointment of, 150–52, 153–57, 166; departure from New Mexico of, 169, 173, 181
Walz, Edgar, 149
Water: Spanish law pertaining to, 32–34; Anglo law pertaining to, 34–35; artesian well drilling for, 82; impact upon Pecos Valley agriculture of, 227; problems encountered in creating reservoirs of, 232; impact of flooding on reservoirs of, 264–65; local conditions as factor in agricultural use of, 269
Wheeler, J. B., 262, 276

White, J. M., 38
White, George Littlefield, 247
White, James Phelps, 111, 121; early life of, 233–36; entry into cattle ranching of, 236–38; entry into New Mexico of, 239–40; response to 1886–87; drought of, 241–43; first windmills in New Mexico installed by, 242–43; business diversification of, 248–49; death of, 250
White, James Phelps Jr., 247
White, Lou Tomlinson, 244
White Mountains, 4
White, Thomas Jefferson, 233, 248
White, Tom David, 247
White, Tom, 235, 239–40, 245–46, 248
White, Zoa Elizabeth, 247
Whitlock, Maria Eva, 149
Widenmann, John, 139
Wildy, William W., 198–200
Willburn, Aaron, 75, 199
Willburn, Frank, 75
Wilson, John B., 139–40, 146
Wilson, William, 73
Wood, Leonard, 285
Wortley Hotel, 146, 172
Wroe, H. A., 249

Yellow House Ranch, 243–44, 248–49
Yunque-Yunque Pueblo, 20